CRE▲TIVE
HOMEOWNER®

WIRING

BASIC AND ADVANCED PROJECTS

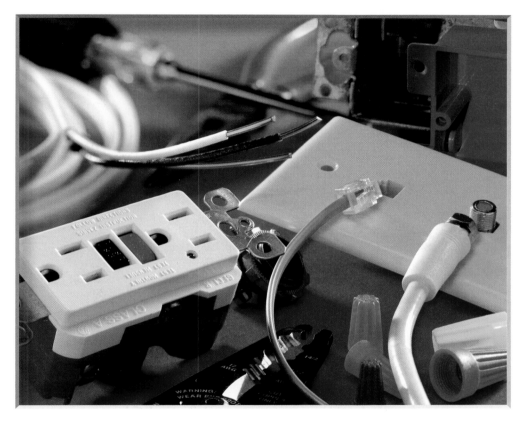

By the Editors of Creative Homeowner

CREATIVE HOMEOWNER®, Upper Saddle River, New Jersey

Editorial Director: Timothy O. Bakke
Art Director: W. David Houser
Creative Director: Clarke Barre
Production Manager: Stan Podufalski

Editor: Joseph Fucci, R.A.
Contributing Writer: Rex Cauldwell
Copy Editor: Ellie Sweeney
Editorial Assistants: Stanley Sudol, Dan Lane
Photo Research: Amla Sanghvi
Technical Advisors: Charles L. Rogers, Certified Instructor, National Center for Construction and Research; Joseph A. Ross, Ross Electrical Assessments; David Shapiro

Design and Layout: David Geer
Cover Design: Clarke Barre
Illustrations: Clarke Barre (various, including chapter openers), Robert Strauch, Charles Van Vooren, Ian Warpole

Manufactured in the United States of America

Current Printing (last digit)
10 9 8 7 6 5 4

Wiring: Basic and Advanced Projects
Library of Congress Catalog Card Number: 00-105442
ISBN: 1-58011-062-2

CREATIVE HOMEOWNER®
A Division of Federal Marketing Corp.
24 Park Way, Upper Saddle River, NJ 07458
Web site: **www.creativehomeowner.com**

Photo Credits

Cover and Interior Photography: Brian C. Nieves
Supplemental Studio Photography: Hal Charms
Photography Studio Manager: Christine Elasigue
Photography Studio Intern: James Umstead

Additional Photos
Directionals: T-top, B-bottom, R-right, L-left

p. 3: Comstock, Inc.
p. 14TL: Andy Pernick/Bureau of Reclamation
p. 135TR: Mark Samu; designer, Montlor Box, AIA
p. 136B: davidduncanlivingston.com
p. 138L: Jessie Walker R: courtesy Lindal Cedar Homes; designer, Feroe
p. 139T: Mark Samu, reprinted with permission from *House Beautiful Kitchens/Baths*, 1998/The Hearst Corporation; stylist, Margaret McNicholas BL: Jessie Walker; designers, Kay McCarthy and Alfie McAdams BR: davidduncanlivingston.com
p. 140TL: courtesy Lindal Cedar Homes TR: Brian Vanden Brink; designer, Jack Silverio BL: Mark Samu, reprinted with permission from *House Beautiful Kitchens/Baths*, 1998/The Hearst Corporation; stylist, Margaret MacNicholas BR: Jessie Walker; designer, Linda Brown/LaRue Creatives
p. 141: Melabee M Miller; designer, Ellen Brounstein
p. 142T: Holly Stickley
p. 161T: Tria Giovan
p. 192TL: Stefan Lawrence/International Stock TR: courtesy Malibu Lighting/Intermatic Inc. B: courtesy California Redwood Association
p. 193T: courtesy Malibu Lighting/Intermatic Inc. B: Crandall & Crandall
p. 204 all: courtesy Malibu Lighting/Intermatic Inc.
p. 208T: Scott Campbell/International Stock B: J. Shive/H. Armstrong Roberts
p. 209T: K. Rice/H. Armstrong Roberts BL: Crandall & Crandall BR: Henry Mills/International Stock
p. 211: Kent Wood/Peter Arnold.

Acknowledgments

Special thanks to the following: DirecTV, US Electronics, Rainbird, Dave Houser for pool sequence shots, Automatic Lightning Protection, Gen/Tran, Umberto Ciliberti for backup generator shots, Makita Tools, Ryobi Tools, Triple S, Home Intelligence, X-10. Their cooperation was key to the completion of this book.

Electrical Safety

Though all methods in this book have been reviewed for safety, the importance of following safe procedures cannot be overstated. What follows are reminders—some do's and don'ts of basic electrical work. They do not substitute for common sense.

○ Always use caution, care, and good judgment when following the procedures described in this book.

○ Always be sure that the electrical setup is safe; be sure that no circuit is overloaded, and that all power tools and electrical outlets are properly grounded. Do not use power tools in wet locations.

○ Never modify a plug by bending or removing prongs. When prongs are bent, loose or missing, replace the entire device.

○ Don't use 3-prong-to-2-prong cord adapters to overcome ground connections.

○ Be sure all receptacles and electrical conductors are properly grounded.

○ If a plug prong breaks off in a receptacle, do not attempt to remove it. Turn off the circuit, and call a licensed electrician.

○ Be sure receptacles are mounted securely in their boxes and do not move when the plug is inserted. A loose receptacle can cause a short circuit.

○ Do not use loose receptacles or other faulty electrical equipment until it is repaired or replaced and inspected by a licensed electrician.

○ Replace all damaged electrical enclosures such as receptacle, switch, and junction boxes.

○ Use extension cords only when necessary, on a short-term basis; never use extension cords in place of permanent wiring.

○ Be sure all extension cords are properly sized and rated for the use intended.

○ Keep electrical cords away from areas where they may be stepped on, pinched between door jambs, or otherwise damaged.

○ Don't use appliance or extension cords that show signs of wear, such as frayed or dried sheathing or exposed wires.

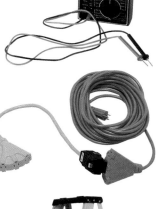

○ Visually inspect all electrical equipment and appliances before use.

○ Never staple, nail, or otherwise attach an extension cord to any surface.

○ Always turn off tools and appliances before unplugging them.

○ Never unplug a tool or appliance by yanking on the cord; always remove the cord by the plug.

○ Always keep the area in front of your main panel clear and dry. Work on a rubber mat or dry board and maintain an unobstructed area of at least 3 feet in front of the panel. The panel must be easily accessed.

○ Keep dust, lint, and other combustible materials away from electrical panels, receptacles, and apppliances.

○ Keep electrical panel doors closed and latched when not in use.

○ Keep all electrical equipment away from any source of water unless it is rated for use in wet areas, such as a wet-dry shop vacuum.

○ Use ground-fault circuit interrupters (GFCIs) wherever possible. GFCIs are required in all wet, damp, or moist areas.

○ Limit use of receptacles to one appliance. If more than one appliance will be on a circuit, use an approved plug strip with a built-in circuit breaker.

○ Use proper lighting in areas where the risk of an electrical hazard is present and keep emergency backup lighting readily available.

○ Keep all energized parts of electrical circuits and equipment enclosed in approved cabinets and enclosures.

○ Use only tools that have double insulated casings.

○ Always be aware of the potential hazards when doing electrical work of any kind.

○ Be sure to use appropriate protective equipment when doing electrical work (safety glasses, insulated gloves, rubber mats, etc.).

Contents

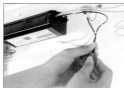

About this Book

Working efficiently and safely with electricity requires an adequate knowledge of how electricity works. This knowledge often seems beyond the reach of the average homeowner, obscured by a veil of confusing codes, complicated formulas, and hieroglyphic symbols. To make matters worse, many supposedly basic books assume that you already have a working knowledge of electricity and electrical codes. Some go too far in the other direction, quoting code requirements without explaining how or why they affect the actual work you want to do. *Wiring: Basic and Advanced Projects* is designed to provide you with a basic understanding of how electricity works, how it is supplied to your home, and how you can work with it safely. It explains which wires to use, where they go, and what they do, as well as which tools and materials you will need to perform the work at hand. Written in easy-to-understand language, this book delves thoroughly into different wiring methods; low-voltage and high-voltage wiring; outdoor wiring; and emergency power equipment. It even introduces you to home automation.

Wiring: Basic and Advanced Projects will teach you to approach your home wiring projects with the confidence that comes from knowledge. You will see that there is really nothing mystical about installing a dimmer switch or changing a receptacle. Like changing a lightbulb, the work can be simple once you know how to do it, and to do it safely.

As a teaching tool, *Wiring: Basic and Advanced Projects* tries to use clear instruction, ease of use, and an entertaining presentation as its main atributes. Following are some of the features that help the book meet those criteria:

- **Step-by-step photographs** illustrate how to wire electrical boxes, switches, receptacles, and even specific appliances. Great effort has been made to include photos that will help you to understand how circuits work, show you real components and wiring, and take you step-by-step through projects. Projects include difficulty ratings (box at right), tools, and materials.

- **Informative art,** including cutaway drawings, clarify concepts not easily demonstrated in photographs.

- **Charts and tables** provide information such as the correct size and type of wire for a particular project.

Informative Art

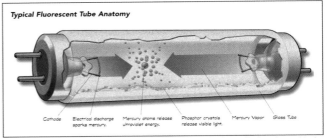

Typical Fluorescent Tube Anatomy

Cathode   Electrical discharge sparks mercury.   Mercury atoms release ultraviolet energy.   Phosphor crystals release visible light.   Mercury Vapor   Glass Tube

In a fluorescent tube, mercury and argon gases emit ultraviolet (UV) light. A phosphor powder glows when struck by the UV light, making the light visible.

Step-by-Step Photographs

HOW TO: Wire a Split-Circuit Receptacle

Difficulty Level: ✎

Tools and Materials ⎯⎯⎯⎯⎯⎯⎯⎯
For metal boxes

- Insulated screwdriver
- Receptacle box
- Green wire connector
- Multipurpose tool (optional)
- Wire stripper
- Cable clamps*
- Duplex receptacle
- Cable ripper
- 12/3G NM cable
- Diagonal-cutting pliers
- Long-nose pliers
- Grounding pigtail and screw*

Wire the Split Circuit. Install the receptacle box, secure and rip the cable, and strip the wires. Then remove the tab connector on the receptacle and connect the wiring. The cable contains three wires and a ground. Connect the hot black and red wires to separate brass screw terminals and the white neutral wire to a silver screw terminal. **(Photo 1)**

Ground the Split Circuit. Using a green wire connector, pigtail the grounding wire to the grounding screw terminal on the receptacle and to the grounding screw in the receptacle box if the box is metal. **(Photo 2)**

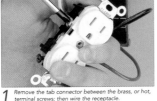

1   Remove the tab connector between the brass, or hot, terminal screws; then wire the receptacle.

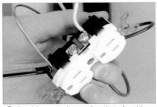

2   Pigtail the receptacle grounding wire to the cable grounding wire and the grounding screw in the box.

Charts

American Wire Gauges

Wire Diameter (Gauge)		Ampacity (Current Capacity)	Volts (Power Capacity)	Typical Usage
	18	7 Amps	24 Volts (134 Watts) Continuous load	Low-Voltage Wiring Bells, chimes, timers, thermostats, etc.
	16	10 Amps	24 Volts (192 Watts) Continuous load	Light-Duty Wiring Low-voltage lighting, etc.
	14	15 Amps	120 Volts (1,440 Watts) Continuous load	Common House Wiring Receptacles, lights, some A/Cs
	12	20 Amps	120 Volts (1,920 Watts) 240 Volts (3,840 Watts) Continuous load	Common House Wiring Receptacles, lights, small appliances
	10	30 Amps	120 Volts (2,880 Watts) 240 Volts (5,760 Watts) Continuous load	Large Appliances Clothes dryers, room A/Cs
	8	40 Amps	240 Volts (7,680 Watts) Continuous load	Large Appliances Central A/Cs, electric ranges
	6	60 Amps	240 Volts (9,600 Watts) Continuous load	Large Appliances Central A/Cs, electric ranges, furnaces

The NEC requires that all conductors and cables be marked, to indicate their AWG size, at intervals not to exceed 24 inches (Section 310-11). Each wire size can carry a limited amount of current under continuous load (80% of its maximum), which is defined as operating for 3 hours or more. The measure of how much current a wire can safely conduct is called its ampacity.

○ **Detailed how-to wiring diagrams** reinforce the step-by-step procedures and often add variations and alternative approaches.

○ **Smart Tips**® provide tidbits of interesting and insightful information about various subjects, often related to your project.

○ **Sidebars** accompanying the how-to steps frequently discuss related topics that don't require a tremendous amount of detail.

Of course, mastering this book will not qualify you to become a licensed electrician, but it should provide you with enough knowledge of electrical work to realize when someone else is doing it wrong. Inevitably, either for reasons of safety or simply because it is required by your local or state electrical code, you may need the services of a licensed electrician, especially for work on your service entrance or within your main electrical panel. In those cases, you should know not only what an electrician must do but also how he or she must do it. *Wiring: Basic and Advanced Projects* will help you to do just that.

Wiring: Basic and Advanced Projects conforms to the 1999 National Electrical Code (NEC). However, electrical codes are not design manuals. Codes are written to establish *minimal* standards. It is always better to exceed code requirements. Also, be aware of local code restrictions that may be more stringent than the NEC. If you are ever uncertain about an electrical requirement, don't take unnecessary risks! When in doubt, call a licensed electrician or question your local electrical inspector.

Each step-by-step project begins with a level-of-difficulty rating for the work to be done, signified by one, two, or three hammers:

🔨 Easy, even for beginners.

🔨🔨 Moderately difficult. Can be done by beginners who have the patience and willingness to learn.

🔨🔨🔨 Difficult. Can be done by the do-it-yourselfer but requires a serious investment of time and patience as well as money for specialty tools. Consider consulting a specialist.

These difficulty ratings help you decide whether or not to tackle a particular project; you'll never find yourself too far into a project before realizing you're in over your head. Following each difficulty rating is a list of tools and materials required for the project. Step-by-step instructions explain how to complete the work, reinforced by photographs of the work as it's being done.

Detailed How-To Wiring Diagrams

Single-Location GFCI Receptacle Circuit

All kitchen countertop and bathroom receptacles—and receptacles within 6 ft. of a wet-bar sink—must be GFCI protected. To protect a single location using a GFCI receptacle, connect the feed cable to the LINE terminals. Receptacles downstream will remain unprotected.

Multiple GFCI Receptacle Circuit

In some locations the electrical code may require more than one protected receptacle where multiple receptacles must be GFCI protected, such as over kitchen counters. They should be wired for single-location protection. This will require both two- and three-wire cables.

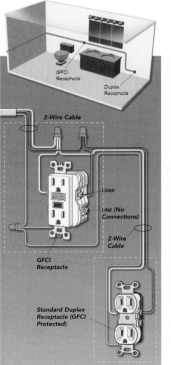

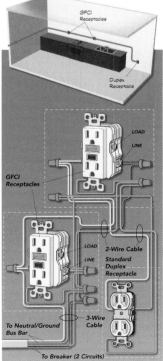

Smart Tips®

CREATIVE HOMEOWNER® **SMART TIP**

Avoid Push-In Terminals

Some receptacles have wire holes instead of screw terminals. On this type of receptacle, the end of each stripped wire (14-gauge copper only) is pushed into the appropriate hole to complete the connection. Although simple to use, these kinds of connections can be problematic and are not recommended.

Some types of receptacles have push-in terminals—you simply insert the end of each wire into an appropriate hole to complete the connection.

Sidebars

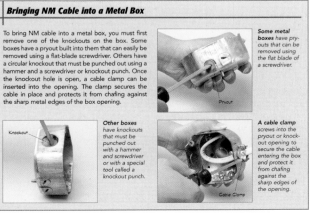

Bringing NM Cable into a Metal Box

To bring NM cable into a metal box, you must first remove one of the knockouts on the box. Some boxes have a pryout built into them that can easily be removed using a flat-blade screwdriver. Others have a circular knockout that must be punched out using a hammer and a screwdriver or knockout punch. Once the knockout hole is open, a cable clamp can be inserted into the opening. The clamp secures the cable in place and protects it from chafing against the sharp metal edges of the box opening.

Some metal boxes have pryouts that can be removed using the flat blade of a screwdriver.

Other boxes have knockouts that must be punched out with a hammer and screwdriver or with a special tool called a knockout punch.

A cable clamp screws into the pryout or knockout opening to secure the cable entering the box and protect it from chafing against the sharp edges of the opening.

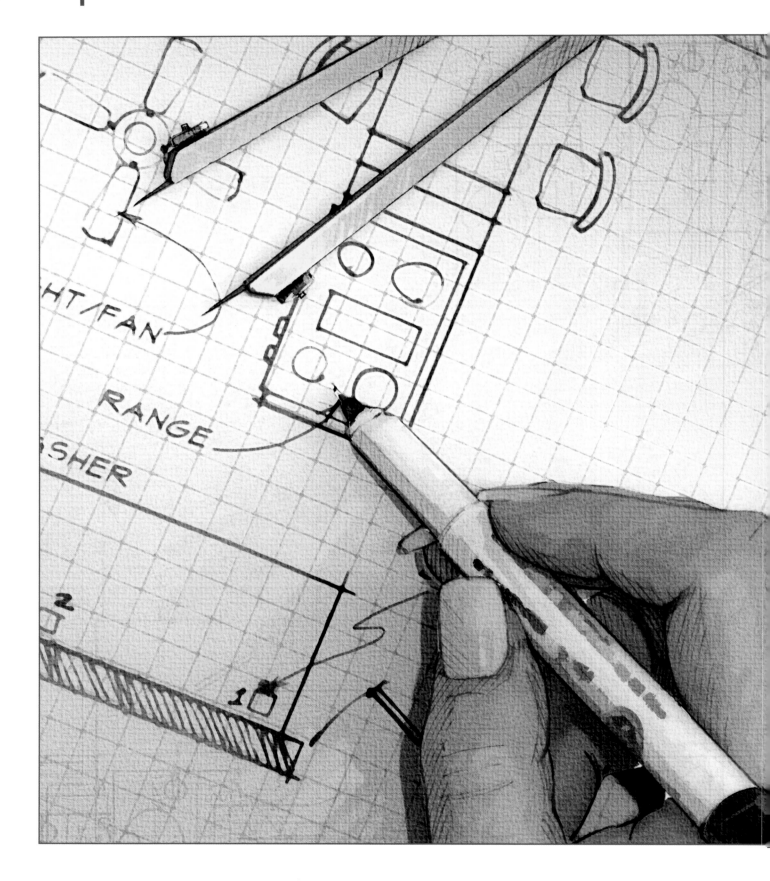

CHAPTER 1

Understanding Electricity

Possessing a basic knowledge of electricity may not seem essential to doing electrical work, especially if you are using a "how-to" book with simple step-by-step instructions. However, nothing could be farther from the truth. Not every step in a process may be obvious, and very often knowing the basic theory behind a practice may enable you to figure out how to do something you have never done before. The purpose of this chapter is to give you a basic understanding of electricity—what it is, how it is provided, how it works, and how you can work with it safely.

Fundamentals of Electricity

Electricity Defined

Electricity is nothing more than an organized flow of electrons and protons behaving in response to the attraction of oppositely charged particles and the repulsion of like-charged particles. If you can get enough electrons to break free of their orbits and start flowing in one direction or another, you have a flow of current. This current, or power, is defined as electricity. The device that frees the electrons from their orbit is called a power generator. To create vast amounts of electrical power, large generators must be turned on a massive scale. (See "How Electricity is Provided," page 12.)

Terminology of Electricity

As with most subjects, electricity has its own vocabulary. For this book, however, it is important to know the meaning of only four key terms: ampere (amperage), volt (voltage), watt (wattage), and ohms (resistance). By mastering these terms, you will better-understand electricity.

Ampere: An *ampere*, or *amp*, measures the rate, or strength, of electrical flow. A typical contemporary home, for example, might have an electrical system of 150 to 200 amps. *Amperage*, in contrast, is the actual measure of current flowing in a circuit to an appliance. Although this can be measured only when the circuit is turned on, the rating of an electric appliance, in volts and amperes, or volts and watts, is required by the National Electrical Code (Section 422-60) to be marked on the identifying nameplate of the appliance. Amperes are designated by the letter A.

Ampacity is the measure of how much current in amperes a wire can safely conduct. Determining the correct ampacity of a wire is important because using an incorrect-size wire can create a fire hazard. Each wire carries a limited amount of current before it will heat to the point of damaging its insulation. For example, a 14-gauge wire can take a maximum current of 15 amps, a 12-gauge wire 20 amps, and so on. If a wire is too small for a job, generated heat can destroy its insulation, causing a fire. Amperage ratings are also important when you buy fuses or circuit breakers. Amperage of fuses or breakers, circuits, and appliances must match. Too little fuse or circuit-breaker amperage will cause these protection devices to blow or trip. Too much will permit a dangerous amount of overcurrent, or flow, which occurs when too many appliances are used on the same circuit or during a power surge. The result is overheating of the circuit, which will create a potential for fire.

American Wire Gauges

Wire Diameter (Gauge)		Ampacity (Current Capacity)	Volts (Power Capacity)	Typical Usage
	18	7 Amps	24 Volts (134 Watts) Continuous load	**Low-Voltage Wiring** Bells, chimes, timers, thermostats, etc.
	16	10 Amps	24 Volts (192 Watts) Continuous load	**Light-Duty Wiring** Low-voltage lighting, etc.
	14	15 Amps	120 Volts (1,440 Watts) Continuous load	**Common House Wiring** Receptacles, lights, some A/Cs
	12	20 Amps	120 Volts (1,920 Watts) 240 Volts (3,840 Watts) Continuous load	**Common House Wiring** Receptacles, lights, small appliances
	10	30 Amps	120 Volts (2,880 Watts) 240 Volts (5,760 Watts) Continuous load	**Large Appliances** Clothes dryers, room A/Cs
	8	40 Amps	240 Volts (7,680 Watts) Continuous load	**Large Appliances** Central A/Cs, electric ranges
	6	60 Amps	240 Volts (9,600 Watts) Continuous load	**Large Appliances** Central A/Cs, electric ranges, furnaces

The NEC requires that all conductors and cables be marked, to indicate their AWG size, at intervals not to exceed 24 inches (Section 310-11). Each wire size can carry a limited amount of current under continuous load (80% of its maximum), which is defined as operating for 3 hours or more. The measure of how much current a wire can safely conduct is called its ampacity.

Volt: A *volt* measures the pressure exerted by electrical power. *Voltage* is the moving (electromotive) force that causes current to flow in an electrical circuit. A generator creates the pressure that keeps the electrical current flowing through conductors, known as *wires*.

Voltage, designated by the letter V, pushes a current that alternates between positive and negative values. This is known as an *alternating current* (AC). It periodically reverses, or alternates, direction in cycles, called *Hertz*. One cycle takes ¹⁄₆₀ second to complete. This is usually expressed as a rate of 60 cycles per second. The average voltage on this cycle is measured at 120 volts on the return, or neutral, wire and 240 volts across both of the two hot utility wires entering a home.

Contemporary three-wire residential wiring carries both 120- and 240-volt power. Large appliances like air conditioners, electric ranges, and clothes dryers typically use 240-volt wiring. Electrical devices must be labeled with their voltage capacity. This means that the product has been designed to operate at the listed voltage only. Do not, for example, hook up an electrical device rated at 125 volts to a circuit that supplies 220 to 240 volts. You'll burn it out.

Watt, Wattage: In practical terms, *wattage* is the amount of energy used to run a particular appliance. The wattage rating of a circuit is the amount of power the circuit can deliver safely, which is determined by the current-carrying capacity of the wires or cables. Wattage also indicates the amount of power a fixture or appliance needs to work properly.

To calculate the wattage, or *power*, available in a circuit, first determine its amperage (amp rating). It will be marked on the circuit breaker or fuse for that circuit in the service-entrance, or main, panel—15 or 20 amps for most room circuits, 30 to 50 amps for most heavy-duty circuits. Then, Watts = Volts × Amps. A 15-amp circuit with 120 volts carries 1,800 watts (15×120); a 20-amp circuit carries 2,400 watts (but not under continuous load).

Resistance: *Electrical resistance*, measured in *ohms*, restricts the flow of current. The higher the resistance, the lower the current. This resistance causes a change of electrical energy into some other form of energy, usually heat. It is this heat, for example, that is used to warm the water in your water heater.

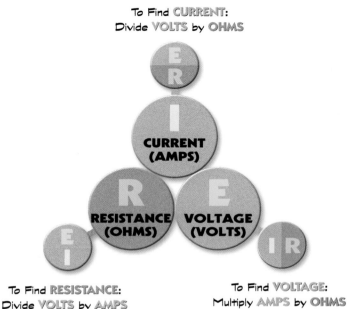

To Find **CURRENT**:
Divide **VOLTS** by **OHMS**

CURRENT (AMPS)

RESISTANCE (OHMS)   VOLTAGE (VOLTS)

To Find **RESISTANCE**:
Divide **VOLTS** by **AMPS**

To Find **VOLTAGE**:
Multiply **AMPS** by **OHMS**

Ohm's Law formally states that the current in an electrical circuit is directly proportional to the voltage and inversely proportional to the resistance. From this we can derive equations to solve for all three; current, voltage, and resistance.

CREATIVE HOMEOWNER®   SMART TIP

Calculating Current

A quick way of calculating 240-volt current is to figure 4 amps per 1,000 watts of power (8 amps for 120-volt). In the water-heater example given below, you would divide 4,500 watts by 1,000, getting 4.5. Multiplying this by 4 amps yields 18 amps; which is close to the formula answer.

Calculating Capacity of an Electric Water Heater

If you want to install a new electric water heater in your home, you must first determine its capacity. Let's assume that you have a family of four in a home with two tubs/showers, one dishwasher, and one clothes washer. Referring to the table below, "Usage Points," this gives you a total of 8 points. An adequately sized water heater for your home would have a 65-gallon capacity. A standard 65-gallon water heater has heating elements rated at 4,500 watts and 240-volt AC wiring. From this information, you can calculate how much current the water heater will use so that you can determine the correct-size wire to use when you install the heater. Because power (wattage) equals voltage (volts) multiplied by current (amps), and you know power and voltage, you can calculate the current:

4,500 watts divided by 240 volts equals 18.75 amps

The wire-gauge table on page 10 indicates that a 12-gauge wire would be adequate to carry 20 amps. However, always be aware of maximum wattage capacity. This example uses a water heater having a 4,500-watt rating. The wire-gauge table shows that the maximum continuous safe carrying capacity for a 12-gauge wire at 240 volts is 3,840 watts. The water heater exceeds this, so you must use the next-larger-size wire, which is a 10-gauge wire having an ampacity of 30 amps.

Usage Points

If your usage points equal	Then you need a
4 or less	40-gal. water heater
5 or 6	50-gal. water heater
7 or 8	65-gal. water heater
9 or more	80-gal. water heater

To select the proper size electric water heater for your home, calculate one usage point for each person, bathtub/shower, dishwasher, and clothes dryer in your household, and consult the table to determine the capacity water heater that you need.

Understanding Electricity

How Electricity Is Provided

Generation

Utility companies generate electricity in a variety of ways. One of the most common methods uses the energy of running water to power a generator. Electrical power created in this way is termed hydroelectricity. To harness the energy of flowing water on a scale this enormous, a dam may be built across a narrow gorge in a river or at the head of a man-made lake. Water backed up behind this dam, in what is called the forebay, is then allowed to flow through a submerged passage, or penstock, in a controlled release. The massive force of this elevated water spins the generator's giant turbines as it falls, producing electricity. Electrical power produced in this way is called AC power, or alternating current.

Transmission

Once a utility company produces electricity, it must then transmit it through a distribution system for use by its customers. For ease of transmission, the electrical power is raised to many thousands of volts and conducted over high-voltage transmission lines to the utility company's regional switching stations, where it is then stepped down to a lower voltage for transmission to local substations. A typical transmission starts at 230,000 volts, is stepped down to 69,000 volts at a switching station, then is stepped down further at a substation to 13,800 volts for direct distribution to a local area. Once at your home, this is again reduced, to 240 volts.

Point of Use

To be stepped down, the electricity that arrives at your home must first pass through a utility transformer. It then leaves this transformer via three terminals, mounted on its side, which are connected to three wires. These wires constitute the service drop that leads to your house service entrance. They include two insulated hot wires, or legs, and a grounded neutral. The two hot wires can each carry 120 volts to the neutral conductor (usually bare on overhead and insulated on underground service laterals) or combine to supply 240 volts or power.

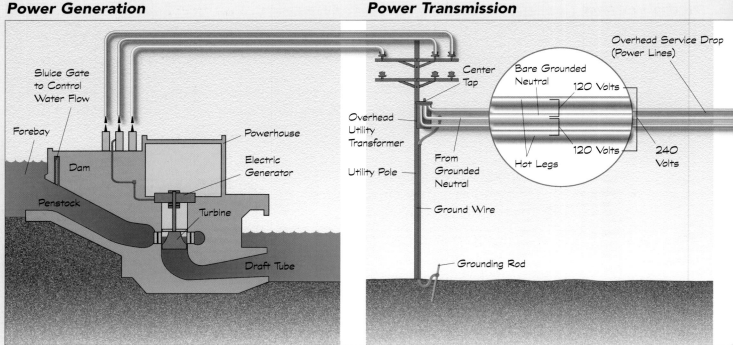

Power Generation

Power Transmission

At a hydroelectric plant, *the massive kinetic force of elevated water that drops down through a dam penstock in a controlled release turns giant turbines that generate electricity. Electrical current travels over high-voltage power lines to a step-down utility transformer near your house.*

The current then leaves the transformer, enters your home as available voltage for use (120-volt and 240-volt), and then returns to the transformer. It is transmitted to your main service-entrance panel (SEP) by means of two insulated hot conductors and a bare grounded neutral wire.

A glass-domed meter is connected to the two hot wires leading from the utility transformer. This meter, generally mounted on the outside of your house, is provided by your utility company to measure the amount of electrical energy in kilowatt hours consumed by your household. This is the rate of energy consumption in kilowatts multiplied by usage in hours. Directly from the utility meter, the two hot wires and the grounded wire continue on to a service-entrance panel (SEP), which distributes power throughout your house. The service panel also contains circuit breakers or fuses that will open if a short circuit or overload occurs in the system.

Service-Entrance Panel

It is the service-entrance, or main, panel that controls the flow of power to individual circuits within your home. These circuits may be 120-volt, 240-volt, or both (120/240-volt). All 240-volt devices pull current from both of the hot insulated legs. At any given moment, electricity is exiting from one terminal on the utility transformer and returning by the other. Current flows from one terminal, travels through the service

drop to the house, and then down the service-entrance conduit or cable into the meter base. From here it flows through the meter into the main panel and is then distributed to each of the circuits within your home, flowing through the main panel via one (or two) insulated hot leg(s), or wire(s), and returning to the panel via another insulated wire—directly through the utility meter and back to the transformer. The final result is that you never actually "consume" electricity—you just borrow it (although you transform much of its energy, which is what you pay for).

All 120-volt devices draw from one of the two hot insulated wires going to the device and use the grounded wire as the return. The grounded conductor is connected to ground (via a ground electrode) at both the transformer and at the main service-entrance panel. All 120/240-volt appliances draw from both of the hot insulated wires as well as using the grounded conductor as the return. An electric clothes dryer, for example, uses 240 volts to heat the element but also uses 120 volts for the timer, motor, and alarm circuits. Such circuits carry current on all three wires at the same time.

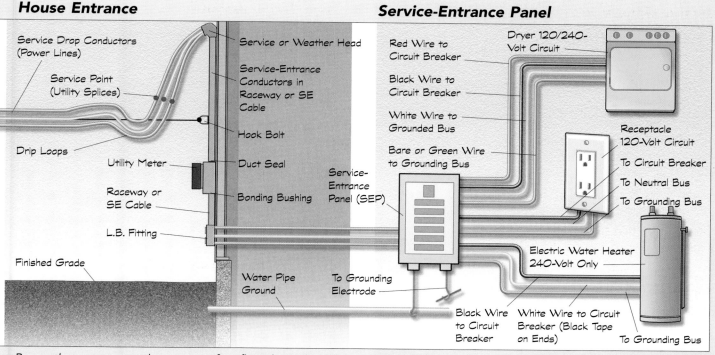

House Entrance

Service Drop Conductors (Power Lines)
Service Point (Utility Splices)
Drip Loops
Utility Meter
Raceway or SE Cable
L.B. Fitting
Finished Grade

Service or Weather Head
Service-Entrance Conductors in Raceway or SE Cable
Hook Bolt
Duct Seal
Bonding Bushing
Water Pipe Ground
To Grounding Electrode

Service-Entrance Panel

Red Wire to Circuit Breaker
Black Wire to Circuit Breaker
White Wire to Grounded Bus
Bare or Green Wire to Grounding Bus
Service-Entrance Panel (SEP)

Dryer 120/240-Volt Circuit
Receptacle 120-Volt Circuit
To Circuit Breaker
To Neutral Bus
To Grounding Bus
Electric Water Heater 240-Volt Only
Black Wire to Circuit Breaker
White Wire to Circuit Breaker (Black Tape on Ends)
To Grounding Bus

Power that enters your home must first flow through the utility company's electric meter to be measured. The electricity then goes to your service panel, where it is distributed to the various electrical circuits in your home. A 120/240-volt appliance, like a clothes dryer, needs two insulated hot wires, one insulated grounded wire, and one grounding conductor. A 120-volt duplex outlet needs an insulated hot wire, an insulated grounded wire, and a bare or green grounding wire. A 240-volt-only appliance needs just two insulated hot wires and a grounding wire.

▲ **Hydroelectric dams** take advantage of the kinetic energy in falling water to drive immense turbines that in turn generate usable electrical energy.

Step-down utility transformers can be either overhead on a utility pole (above) or pad-mounted on the ground (below). Before electricity can enter your home, a transformer must lower the voltage from several thousand volts to a level appropriate for residential use.

◄ **Electric utility meters,** mounted on the side of your home, measure the amount of electricity that flows through your service-entrance panel, allowing the utility company to bill you for power consumption.

Circuit Anatomy

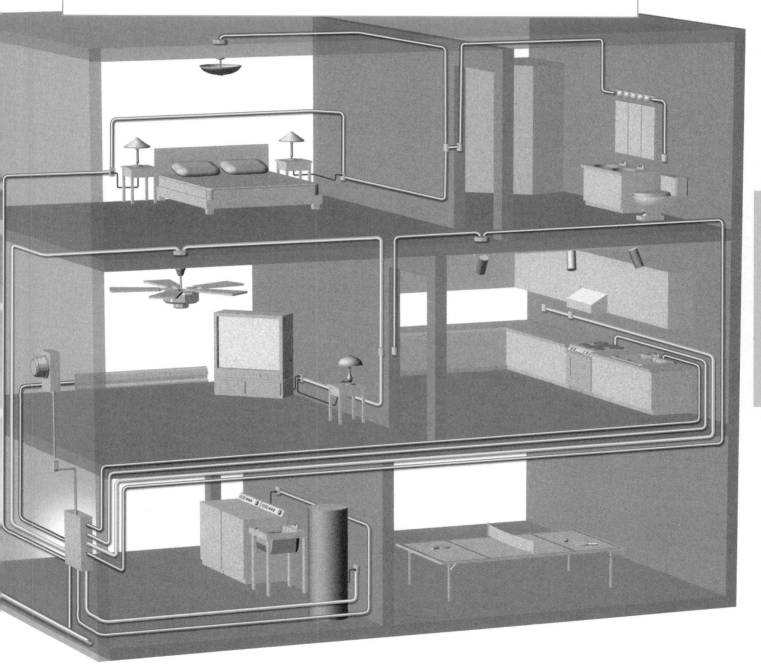

- 120 volts, 20 amps – disposal
- 120/240 volts, 60 amps – range
- 120 volts, 20 amps – small appliances
- 120 volts, 15 amps – lights
- 240 volts, 20 amps – baseboard heater
- 120/240 volts, 30 amps – dryer
- 240 volts, 30 amps – water heater
- ground

This simplification of a house wiring system shows power split into 120- and 240-volt circuits at the service-entrance panel (SEP). Black or red wires in the branch-circuit cables are always hot (power present). White wires are neutral (no power present) when no current is flowing; they are hot whenever the circuit is turned on. Circuit breakers or fuses in the panel protect the branch circuits from overload. The grounding system (not shown) for metal switch and outlet boxes uses bare or green wires, or metal raceway. The system ground connects to the grounding electrode.

Service-Entrance Panel

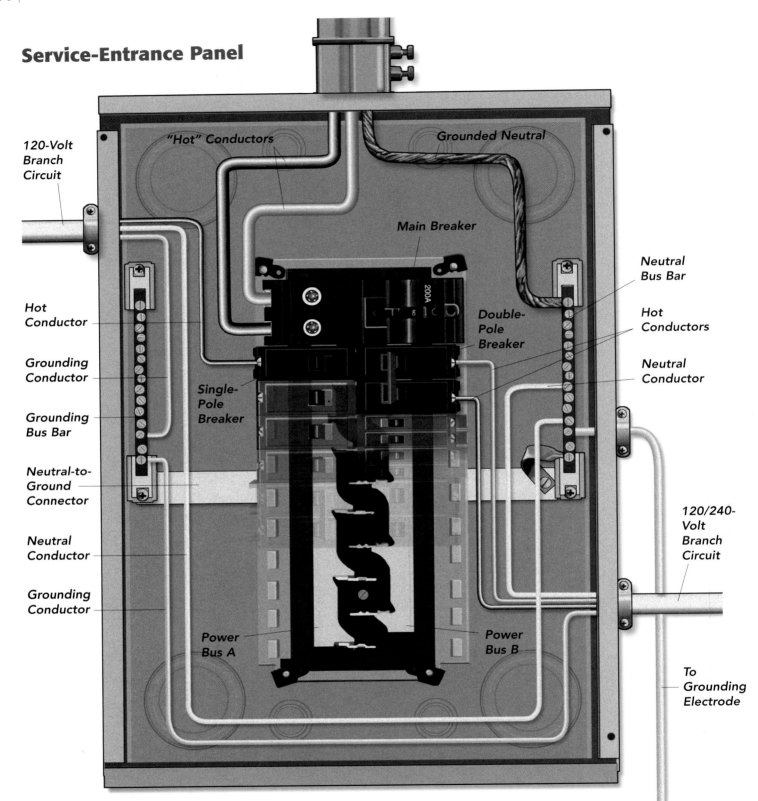

120-Volt Branch Circuit

"Hot" Conductors

Grounded Neutral

Main Breaker

200A

Double-Pole Breaker

Single-Pole Breaker

Neutral Bus Bar

Hot Conductors

Neutral Conductor

Hot Conductor

Grounding Conductor

Grounding Bus Bar

Neutral-to-Ground Connector

Neutral Conductor

Grounding Conductor

Power Bus A

Power Bus B

120/240-Volt Branch Circuit

To Grounding Electrode

Also called the circuit-breaker panel, the main service-entrance panel (SEP) is the distribution center for the electricity you use in your home. Incoming red and black hot wires connect to the main breaker and energize the other circuit breakers that are snapped into place. Hot (black or red) wires connected to the various circuit breakers carry electricity to appliances, fixtures, and receptacles throughout the house. White and bare-copper wires connect to the neutral and grounding bus bars, respectively. (Representative 120-volt and 120/240-volt circuits are shown.)

CREATIVE HOMEOWNER®

SMART TIP

Appliance Ratings

Today, major appliances like freezers, refrigerators, water heaters, dishwashers, clothes washers, furnaces, and air conditioners are energy-rated for the amount of power (wattage) they use. This information appears on a large yellow "Energy Guide Label" affixed to each device. Smaller appliances may not be so labeled, but their wattage rating should be listed on their packaging. The wattage rating can be used to calculate the actual operating cost of the appliance. The higher the wattage rating of the appliance, the more you will have to pay to operate it. For example, if a 4-foot long baseboard heater uses 250 watts per foot, it will require 1,000 watts to run. An 8-foot long baseboard heater would need 2,000 watts to operate. At 10¢ per kilowatt-hour (1,000 watts used by an appliance in one hour), it will cost 10¢ per hour to run the 4-foot baseboard and 20¢ per hour to operate the 8-foot baseboard. Clearly, it will cost twice as much to operate the longer unit. If the wattage of an appliance is not listed on the appliance or the packaging, then look for the voltage and current. To obtain wattage, simply multiply the two terms together. Voltage times current equals power (wattage). (See "Terminology of Electricity," pages 9–10.)

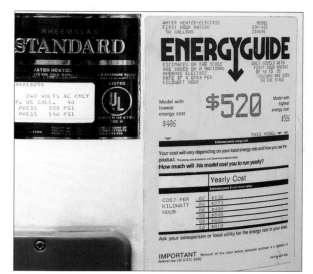

The energy-rating sticker on the side of this 4,500-watt water heater tells the prospective buyer approximately what he or she will be paying per year for the use of the appliance. Running a 4,500-watt water heater for one hour, at 10¢ per kilowatt-hour, would cost 4.5 x 10¢, or 45¢ per hour.

Appliance Wattage

Appliance	Average Wattage
Attic fan	400
Blender	400–1,000
Broiler	1,400–1,500
Can opener	150
Central air conditioner	2,500–6,000
Clock	2–3
Clothers dryer	4,000–5,600
Clothes washer	500–1,000
Computer with monitor	565
Coffee maker	600–1,500
Crock pot	100
Deep fat fryer	1,200–1,600
Dehumidifier	500
Dishwasher	1,000–1,500
Electric blanket	150–500
Electric water heater	2,000–5,500
Exhaust fan	75–200
Floor polisher	300
Food freezer	300–600
Food mixer	150–250
Frost-free refrigerator	400–600
Frying pan	1,000–1,200
Gas furnace	800
Garbage disposal	500–900
Hair dryer	400–1,500
Hot plate	600–1,000
Iron	600–1,200
Laser printer	1,000
Microwave oven	1,000–1,500
Oil furnace	600–1,200
Portable heater	1,000–1,500
Radio	40–150
Range	4,000–8,000
Range oven	3,500–5,000
Refrigerator	150–300
Roaster	1,200–1,650
Room air conditioner	800–2,500
Sewing machine	60–90
Stereo/CD player	50–140
Television	50–450
Toaster oven	500–1,450
Waffle iron	600–1,200

Today, appliances are typically rated for how much power (wattage) that they draw. Because your utility bill states how much you pay per kilowatt-hour of electricity, this information can be used to calculate the actual operating cost of any appliance.

How Electricity Works

Electric Current Flow

Electric current flow can be defined as the flow of electrons through a conductor (wire) or circuit. This passage of electrons is often described as being analogous to the flow of water in a pipe or hose. For example, water flows through a pipe or hose because it is under pressure. Similarly, electric current surges through a wire because it is under pressure. Earlier, voltage was defined as the pressure, or moving (electromotive) force, that causes current (electrons) to flow in an electrical circuit. (See "Terminology of Electricity," pages 9–11.) Furthermore, just as the size of a hose or pipe can affect the degree of water pressure, the size of an electrical wire can affect the flow of current passing through it. The maximum current-carrying capacity of a particular-size wire is called its ampacity. (See page 9.)

As electric current passes through your electrical system, it reaches your receptacles and switches where, again like water, it becomes available for use—provided that you flip the switch on your wall or appliance just as you would turn the faucet on at your sink. And, like the water, once the electric current is used, it exits the system. Instead of exiting through a drainpipe, the current exits (or returns to the utility) by means of a grounded conductor.

Flow Resistance

The passage of electric current through a wire is not only restricted by the size of the wire and the amount of voltage pressure but also by the material of which it is made. Some materials resist the flow of electricity more than others because of their chemical composition. Imagine water trying to flow along an incline; if the incline is downward, the flow will be unrestricted; if the incline is upward, the flow will be resisted. Whether the incline is sharp or shallow will affect the speed of the water flow, and if the pressure is not sufficient or the upward incline is too great, then the flow may be stopped altogether. Further, if the incline is strewn with obstacles, like the bed of a stream is strewn with boulders and stones, then the flow will be slowed in comparison with that on a smooth incline. It is the chemical composition of a given material that determines whether it is "rock strewn" or "smooth."

Materials that allow electric current to pass through them fairly easily are electrical conductors, while materials that prevent the passage of electric current are insulators. Common conductors include copper and aluminum, which are used in the manufacture of electrical wiring. Most metals are good electrical conductors, yet even these offer some resistance to the flow of electric current. This property can be measured in units of resistance called ohms. (See "Terminology of Electricity," pages 9–11.) Materials commonly used as insulators include glass, various plastics, and rubber.

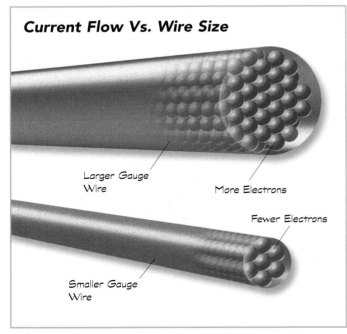

Current Flow Vs. Wire Size

Larger Gauge Wire

More Electrons

Fewer Electrons

Smaller Gauge Wire

A larger wire gauge permits more electricity to flow through it than a smaller gauge wire.

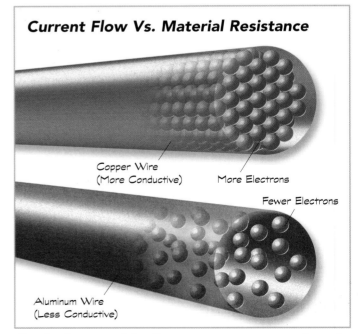

Current Flow Vs. Material Resistance

Copper Wire (More Conductive)

More Electrons

Fewer Electrons

Aluminum Wire (Less Conductive)

Conductive materials allow more current to pass through them than less conductive materials of the same size.

Working Safely with Electricity

Basic Rules of Safety

Safety is, without question, the most important aspect of any electrical work. One split-second mistake can result in serious injury or even death. Many errors are made because of impatience, ignorance, or unnecessary risk-taking. If you consider the potential cost of not following simple, common-sense rules of safety when you are working with electricity, then you will certainly realize the importance of avoiding such mistakes.

The first rule of working with electricity is to shut off the power at your main service-entrance panel before working on a circuit. Always keep a well-maintained flashlight near the panel so that when power is cut off you will not be left standing in the dark. Also, be sure to stand on a rubber mat or dry boards, especially if your utility room is damp, and use only one hand to remove or replace a fuse or flip a circuit-breaker switch. After

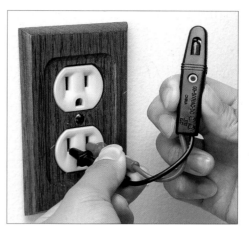

Before working on any circuit, test it to be sure that the power has been turned off. Test both receptacles on an outlet. It may be a split circuit.

shutting off the power, secure the panel so that no one else will accidentally turn the circuit back on while you are working on it. All circuits should be clearly marked to avoid confusion as to which circuit to shut off. Nevertheless, whenever you do work on a circuit, be doubly sure that it is not hot by testing it, using a circuit tester.

Second, be absolutely positive that you have carefully planned your work, that you know every step you'll take, and that you are not in over your head. For this reason, it is probably best to limit yourself to doing work outside your electrical panel. Leave adding circuits and making panel repairs to a licensed electrician.

Third, when doing actual wiring and electrical repairs, take precautions to use the correct tools, equipment, and techniques. For example, use a wooden or fiberglass

Keep a well-maintained flashlight *near your service-entrance panel, and always stand on a rubber mat or dry boards when working on the panel.*

To prevent a ladder *from slipping out from under you when working outside, swivel the feet into a vertical position; then dig them into the ground.*

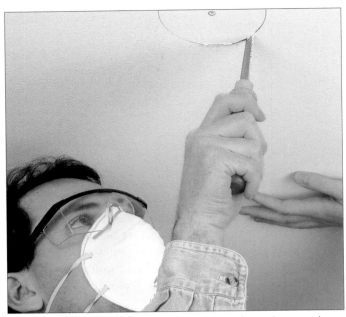

Always wear comfortable, adjustable safety glasses when doing electrical work, to protect yourself from flying debris or sparking wires.

ladder, never one that is made of metal; always wear safety glasses to protect yourself against sparks and flying debris; and make sure that all of your tools are properly insulated for electrical work. Be conscious of details, like properly wrapping wire terminals with electrical tape and using the correct-size electrical boxes for the work you are doing. And, especially if you are working

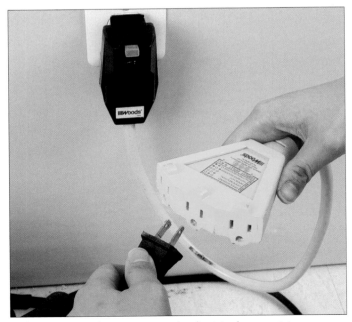

AC power tools carry enough electrical current to cause electrocution. To be safe, use a heavy-duty extension cord that has a GFCI built directly into it.

with power equipment outside, be certain that the electrical circuit is thoroughly protected by a ground-fault circuit interrupter (GFCI), or use a GFCI extension cord. (See page 21.) If a tool malfunctions and has a fault to ground, this type of protection can save your life. For portable power tools, be sure to use heavy-duty 12-gauge extension cords. Under-gauged cords are a potential fire hazard. In addition, all electrical supplies should be UL-listed—which means that they carry the symbol of the Underwriters Laboratories, your assurance that the product meets the minimum safety standards set by this and other governing agencies.

Lastly, observe the rules and regulations established by your local, state or regional safety, building, electrical, and fire codes. These codes are written for your protection as well as the health, safety, and welfare of the general public. Some codes may, in fact, prohibit you from doing certain types of electrical work or using a particular type of electrical cable. Most requirements are based on the National Electrical Code, which explains safe electrical procedures.

Short Circuits

When an accidental connection is made between two hot wires or one hot wire and a grounded wire, and excess current flows across the connection, this is known as a short circuit. A short-circuited device can be life-threatening if you come into physical contact with it. Because electrical current travels along the path of least resistance, you can literally become part of the electric circuit—the part through which the current attempts to flow back to its original source. Normally, this is done through a neutral wire in the circuit. However, for safety's sake, an alternative route is usually provided by a grounding wire, or circuit, leading to the earth, where the misdirected current is harmlessly dissipated.

Grounding

The grounding circuit typically connects all of the electrical devices, including fixtures, switches, receptacles, electrical boxes, and so on, to a terminal, or bus bar, in the main panel. The bus bar is in turn connected to a metal cold-water pipe and a grounding rod driven into the earth "such that at least 8 feet of length is in contact with the soil" [NEC Section 250-52(c)]. (See illustration, "Grounding Rods," page 22.) Individual appliances or tools that are metal-clad are connected to this grounding system through the third prong on a three-prong plug. (For further information, see "Grounding Systems," page 21.)

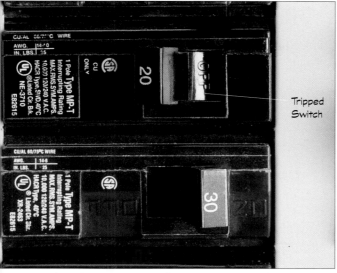

*A **circuit breaker** switches off (trips) when the flow of current exceeds the breaker's capacity.*

Overload Protection

The excessive current that is created by a short circuit, or by too large a power connection, can easily cause irreparable damage to electrical equipment. An electrical system must, therefore, have some type of overload protection. This type of protection is provided by fuses and circuit breakers. (See "Service Panels," Chapter 3, page 48.) A fuse guards against overload by melting when too much heat is caused by excessive current in the line. Once the metal wire in the fuse melts, the circuit is effectively broken. A circuit breaker, on the other hand, is an automatic switch designed to cut off the flow of electric current in a circuit that exceeds its rated capacity. Unlike a fuse, it doesn't have to be replaced; the switch, once "tripped," simply needs to be reset.

Ground-Fault Circuit Interrupters (GFCI)

Although a powerful current surging through a grounding system will melt (blow) a fuse or switch off (trip) a circuit breaker, a less powerful current may not be sufficient to do this. Nonetheless, such a current may be forceful enough to cause serious injury, or worse. The risk of this happening is especially great in moisture-prone locations, such as outdoors or in bathrooms. A way to protect against the danger of this type of electric shock is by using what is called a ground-fault circuit interrupter, or GFCI. This device can detect minute amounts of current leakage in a circuit. If the amperage flowing through the black and white wires is equal, then the circuit is operating properly. But if the GFCI detects as little as a 0.005-amp difference between the two wires, then leakage is presumed and device breaks the circuit—rapidly enough to prevent a hazardous shock.

Grounding Systems
Main Panel Ground

As noted above, a grounding system is absolutely indispensable for electrical safety; it provides the fundamental means by which an irregular electric current can be safely brought to ground, or zero voltage. It is also a requirement of the NEC for all 120- and 240-volt circuits (Article 250).

The main service-entrance ground is the principal ground in a home. It is an easily seen copper grounding wire, known as the grounding electrode conductor, attached to a bus bar in the main service panel. Two such wires are visible if your water pipes are metal. One service ground runs from the terminal bus bar to the grounding-rod system, while the other goes to the main metal plumbing pipe. (Be aware that the metal plumbing pipes beyond the first 5 feet of entrance are not part of the grounding system but are, rather, grounded to the system by the grounding rod.) Minimum size requirements for grounding electrode conductors are specified by the NEC (Section 250-66).

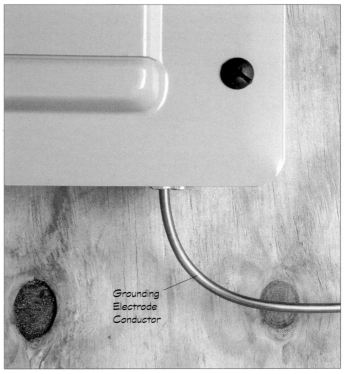

*The **main service-entrance ground,** known as the grounding electrode conductor, is a copper grounding wire attached to a bus bar in the main service panel. If your water pipes are metal, there will be two wires—one running from the terminal bus bar to the grounding rod, and another running to the main metal cold-water pipe.*

Grounding Rods

Grounding rods are usually composed of galvanized or copper-clad metal ⅝ inch in diameter and typically 8 feet long or longer. A good grounding system may include several grounding rods. A single grounding electrode composed of a rod or pipe must have a resistance to ground not to exceed 25 ohms (NEC Section 250-56), otherwise one or more additional grounding rods must be used. Multiple rods or pipes must be placed at least 6 feet apart and be connected to the neutral bus bar with a continuous copper conductor. Never overlook these code requirements. Note, for example, that effective grounding is essential for the proper functioning of a surge arrester. Unless low ground resistance is available, a surge arrester will not be able to draw the spikes, or massive intermittent increases in voltage or amperage, coming into a circuit during a power surge.

▶ *Because of their length and awkwardness,* it is best to drive grounding rods using a borrowed or rented rotary hammer. This tool enables the rods to vibrate through soil and past small rocks with little or no difficulty.

Grounding Rods

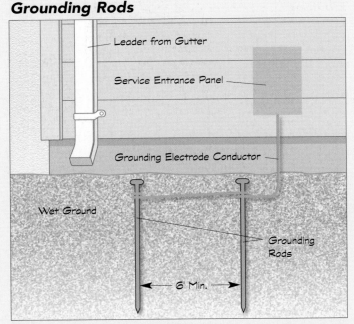

Leader from Gutter

Service Entrance Panel

Grounding Electrode Conductor

Wet Ground

Grounding Rods

6' Min.

Typical Grounding-Rod System. *Grounding rods conduct electricity from the grounding electrode conductors directly into the earth, where it is harmlessly dissipated. Some grounding systems may require more than one rod, in which case they must be spaced at least 6 feet apart. Rainwater directed near grounding rods helps to lower the ground resistance.*

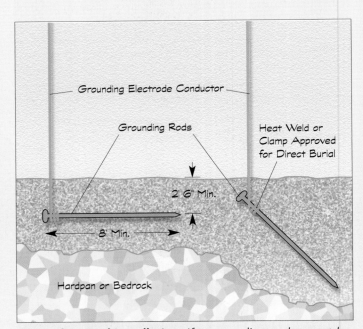

Grounding Electrode Conductor

Grounding Rods

Heat Weld or Clamp Approved for Direct Burial

2' 6" Min.

8' Min.

Hardpan or Bedrock

Grounding-Rod Installation. *If a grounding rod cannot be driven directly into the earth because of boulders or bedrock, the NEC requires (Section 250-52) that it still must have at least 8 feet of length in contact with the soil. To accomplish this, a rod may either be driven at an angle not less than 45 deg. or placed horizontally in a trench at least 2½ feet deep.*

◄ *A surge arrester can be installed directly into a service panel, just like a standard circuit breaker. How well it functions, however, depends on the effectiveness of your grounding system.*

Equipment Grounding

Equipment that is capable of becoming electrically powered, such as an appliance, fixture, or other device, is also required by the NEC to be connected to a grounding system (Sections 250-110–116). Such devices use equipment grounding conductors. These bare wires, included in the nonmetallic (NM) cable typically found in modern homes, connect to the grounding (green) terminals of receptacles. They run back to the neutral/grounding bus bar in the main service-entrance panel and serve as the grounding wires that bring an electrical appliance to zero voltage. An equipment grounding conductor can either end (terminate) at a receptacle grounding screw and con-

Ground Faults on Appliances

A ground fault can occur in an appliance any time that excess or misdirected current (a short circuit) causes the appliance to become electrically energized. A grounding system, including an equipment grounding conductor, is intended to direct current back to its source to prevent an electric shock or possible electrocution.

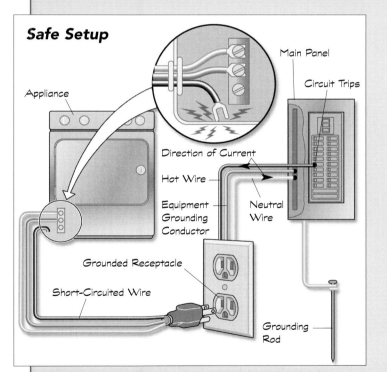

Safe Setup

Main Panel
Circuit Trips
Appliance
Direction of Current
Hot Wire
Equipment Grounding Conductor
Neutral Wire
Grounded Receptacle
Short-Circuited Wire
Grounding Rod

Grounded Appliance. *If the metal framework of a grounded appliance becomes electrically energized, the ground-fault current will return to the service-entrance panel through the equipment grounding conductor. In this system, the current remains within the wiring system and trips the affected circuit breaker at the panel, rather than being directed to a grounding rod.*

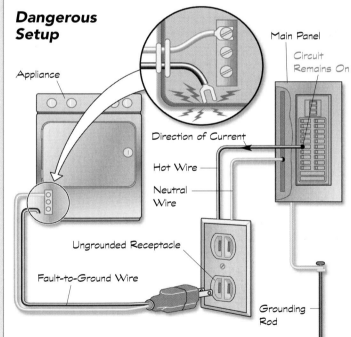

Dangerous Setup

Main Panel
Circuit Remains On
Appliance
Direction of Current
Hot Wire
Neutral Wire
Ungrounded Receptacle
Fault-to-Ground Wire
Grounding Rod

Ungrounded Appliance. *If the metal framework of an ungrounded appliance becomes energized, then the ground-fault current will not be sufficient to trip the affected circuit breaker at the panel. As a result, the appliance frame will remain electrically powered, and anyone touching it and a grounded surface may be electrocuted.*

Understanding Electricity

nect to the appliance by means of a plug and cord connector, or it can connect directly to the appliance. Take precautions when working with bare copper and green wires such as these because you can never be sure whether or not the installation was done properly.

Testing

If you wish to check whether or not your home is properly grounded, begin by testing the receptacles. Check whether they have two or three wires. If a receptacle is missing a grounding terminal, clearly it is not grounded. If a two- or three-wire plug adapter is employed, unless the house has armored cable and metal boxes, the appliance is probably still not grounded. In this case, the receptacle won't be grounded unless it is an automatic grounding receptacle, which has a spring clip on one of its attachment screws. This clip grounds the receptacle to any grounded metal electrical box. Standard receptacles are not approved for such automatic grounding. However, if the electrical box is grounded back to the main panel by means of armored cable, then you can install a standard three-pronged receptacle and connect its grounding terminal to the metal box.

To test whether an existing three-pronged terminal is grounded, use a plug-in circuit tester. Never assume that a three-pronged receptacle is grounded. If the ground is missing, the light sequence on the tester will indicate as much. The ground may even be properly connected at the receptacle but disconnected farther down the line.

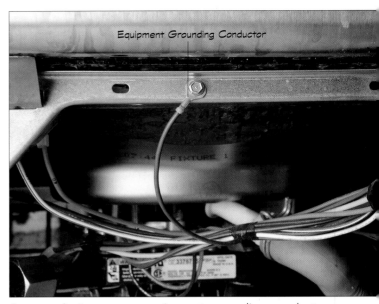

In many instances, an equipment grounding conductor may be directly connected to an appliance.

A two- or three-wire plug adapter cannot ground an appliance if there is no grounding path back to the main panel; it merely permits the appliance to be plugged in. A short to the appliance may still cause a severe shock or electrocution.

The inside of this ungrounded receptacle box reveals the lack of a grounding wire to connect the grounding circuit back to the main panel.

Higher-quality receptacles feature an automatic grounding clip on one of their attachment screws, which provides a grounding path through any grounded metal electrical box.

Common grounding problems that occur at or near the main electrical panel include grounding connections made to rusted rebar or pipe, cut or loose grounding wires, or improper connectors on a grounding rod. Be sure that the clamp used on your rod is a listed (approved) connector, which must be cast bronze, brass, or plain or malleable iron. A heat-welded connection is also acceptable (NEC Section 250-70). The grounding rod itself, if iron or steel, must be at least ⅝ inch in diameter. Stainless-steel and nonferrous metal rods

must be at least ½ inch in diameter [Section 250-52(c)]. The use of improper materials may lead to corrosion and result in a high-resistance connection.

Bonding Jumper

Homeowners frequently make the mistake of thinking that they can ground an electrical system or appliance by connecting it to metal plumbing pipes. Nothing could be further from the truth! All metal pipes must themselves be connected to the grounding system. If the water pipes are connected to the grounding system by means of a clamp and bonding wire to the service panel grounding/neutral bus bar, then the circuit breaker will trip off whenever a bare wire touches the metal pipes. Where there's a break in pipe continuity, such as when a water heater is not made of metal, for instance, a bypass, or bonding jumper, must be made to connect the incoming and outgoing pipes. Such bonding jumpers are required wherever necessary to ensure electrical continuity and the ability of the grounding system to safely direct any ground fault likely to be imposed upon it (NEC Section 250-90). The main service panel itself must be bonded by a connection from the neutral bus bar to a bonding screw on the metal frame of the panel, and the panel in turn connected to the grounding (electrode) rod.

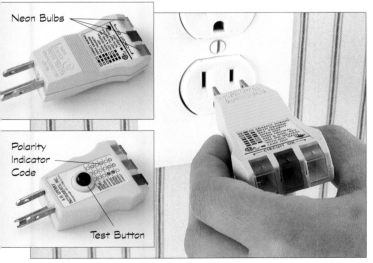

A plug-in receptacle analyzer checks grounded outlets for correct/incorrect wiring. Three neon bulbs light up in various combinations to indicate correct wiring, open ground, open neutral, open/hot, hot/ground reversed, or hot/neutral reversed.

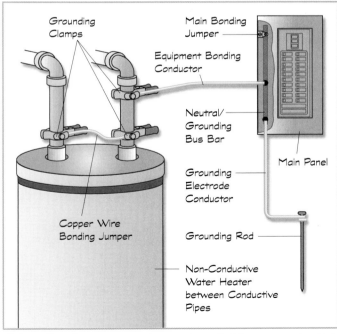

A bonding jumper must be made to bridge any potential break in a ground circuit. Bonding jumpers are required to ensure electrical continuity, as well as the ability of a grounding system to safely direct any ground fault that might be imposed on it.

Understanding Electricity

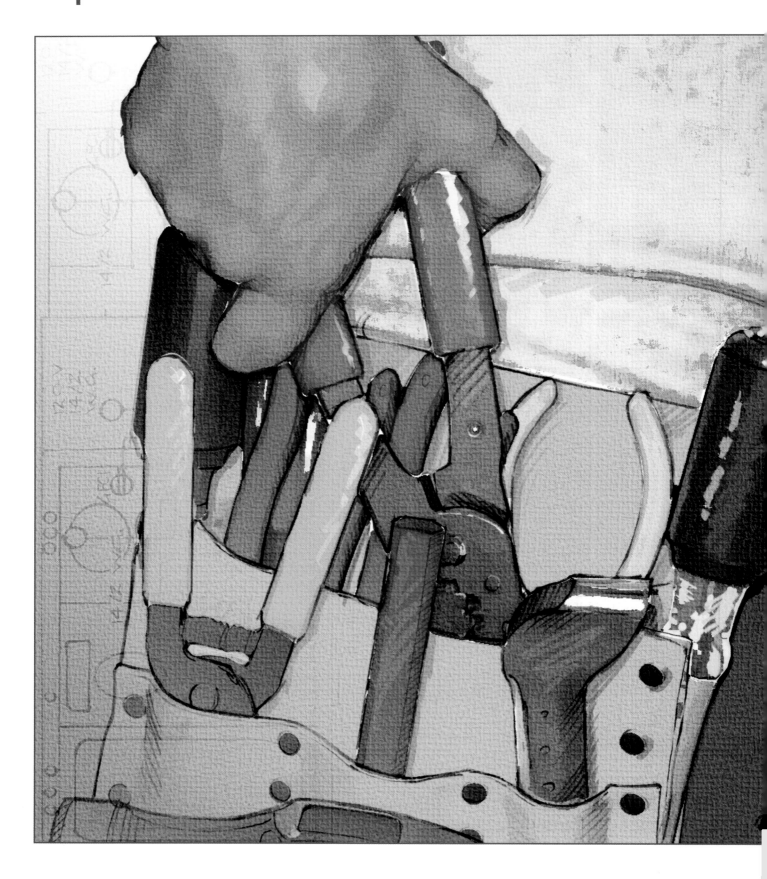

CHAPTER 2

Tools and Their Uses

Some electrical work can be done using standard tools, many of which you may already have in your tool kit or workshop. Most tools used in electrical work, however, are specifically designed to perform a given task. These tools make work easier and safer. More importantly, even if you already own common tools—like hammers, chisels, utility knives, measuring tapes, screwdrivers, etc.—not all of these can be used safely. For example, screwdrivers and hammers, as well as other metal tools, must be insulated to prevent current from flowing into the user's hand, causing a shock. As for specialized work, the right tool is necessary to do the job properly, whether it's cutting and stripping wire or measuring current and voltage in a line.

While safe electrical work requires the use of specific tools, it depends even more on the use of high-quality tools. Such tools are best purchased from a reputable home center or distributor of electrical supplies and equipment, rather than from a discount store. In the long run, a bargain is seldom a bargain if it endangers your life or property. Besides, well-maintained, high-quality tools will add to the versatility and reliability of your tool collection, and they can last a lifetime.

Pulling Wires and Fuses

Fish Tape. Also known as fish wire, fish tape is a flexible wire used by electricians to snake electrical cable through walls, ceilings, and other inaccessible spaces. Various wire "fishing" techniques use either one or two fish tapes to hook and pull wire. (See "Fishing Cable," page 80.) Fish tapes come in lengths from 25 to 250 feet and widths of ⅛ to ¼ inch. Usually, the tape, or wire, is wound inside a self-tensioning winder case with a handle grip for better control and ease of use. The tape is made either of steel, flexible steel, nylon, or fiberglass. Some flexible steel tapes, rather than consisting of a solid strand of steel wire, consist of multiple strands, while others are constructed of a solid spring-like steel. The drawback to steel tape is, of course, that it is conductive. Nylon tape is nonconductive and somewhat safer to use except for the tip and leader, which are made of steel. Fiberglass tape, though expensive, is superior because it is nonconductive and has a low-friction coating that makes it the fastest fish tape available. Friction-reducing lubricants can be purchased separately, however, and applied to any fish tape.

Fish Tape and Lubricant

Fuse Puller. A fuse puller is specially designed for the removal of cartridge type fuses. (See "Fuses and Circuit Breakers," page 52.) The grips on one end of the puller enable you to remove cartridge fuses up to 60 amps in size, while those on the other end can pull fuses of greater capacity. You clamp the puller tightly around the center of a blown cartridge fuse, and then wrench the cylinder firmly out of its fuse box. The fuse puller is also used to insert the new or replacement fuse between the fuse box spring clips. This tool must be made of a nonconductive material, such as plastic, because the spring clips that hold the cartridge fuses are metal and can carry deadly current. Always be sure that the fuse box has been switched off before you pull a fuse, and take care never to touch the spring clips with steel pliers or any other metal tools.

Fuse Puller

To remove a cartridge fuse, *grasp it firmly with a fuse puller, and pull it straight out.*

Cutting and Twisting Wires

Lineman's Pliers

Lineman's Pliers. You'll use heavy-duty lineman's pliers to shape, bend, and twist wires, as well as to pull cable into electrical boxes. In a pinch, use it in place of a punch to remove knockout plates from electrical boxes. Although hardware stores rarely carry high-quality lineman's pliers, you can easily obtain a pair at any electrical supply shop.

Long-Nose Pliers. Long-nose, or needle-nose, pliers are well suited for getting into tight spaces and twisting wire ends into loops for hooking under screw terminals. They are also good for pulling out wire staples, and they have a cutting edge for snipping wires.

Long-Nose Pliers

Diagonal-Cutting Pliers. These pliers are used for getting into tight spaces like receptacle and switch boxes to snip small wires. The angled and tapered blades enable you to reach and cut wires not accessible to conventional wire cutters. It is more sensible, as well as cost-effective, to buy a multipurpose or combination tool that can also notch, strip, and crimp wires of various types and sizes.

Diagonal-Cutting Pliers

Stripping and Crimping Wires

Wire Stripper. This is an absolute necessity when removing insulation from wire ends, although a utility knife can be used to cut the sheathing away from larger cable wires. A wire stripper is designed with precision blades to both cut and strip wires . They have depth-of-cut gauges for stripping just the right amount of insulation from a wire of a given size without cutting into the wire. Different models are sold for stripping solid wire, stranded wire, or small-gauge wire.

Automatic Wire Stripper. An automatic wire stripper is designed to simultaneously cut and strip both solid and stranded wire insulation. One pair of jaws holds the wire while the other cuts and removes the insulation, exposing the bare wire inside.

Crimper. Crimpers are used with special connectors that are designed to connect wires together. Some examples include spade connectors, ring connectors, and splices, sometimes called crimping ferrules. (See "Using Crimping Ferrules," page 32.) After you've twisted the wires using a pair of pliers, you crimp them together inside the ferrule by squeezing the jaws on the crimper together. This clinches the wires and ferrule into a permanent connection. Note that aluminum wires are rarely spliced this way.

Multipurpose (or Combination) Tool. A multipurpose tool, as its name implies, can be used for many different purposes: it can crimp; cut and strip wire; and in some cases even cut and rethread bolts. Like a conventional wire stripper, it has a depth-of-cut gauge for stripping wire. A multipurpose tool usually handles 22- to 10-gauge wires.

Cable Ripper. When multiple wires are cabled together in a protective nonmetallic sheathing, it becomes necessary to expose the wire ends so that you can splice them to other wires or connect them to wire terminals. It is important that you be able to cut back the protective plastic sheathing without damaging the insulation on the individual wires inside the cable. You can easily do this using a cable ripper, which has an internal tooth that bites into the sheathing when the tool is clamped over the cable and squeezed. Once the sheathing is punctured by this tooth, you pull the cable ripper toward the end of the cable, ripping the sheathing open along the length of the pull. You can then draw back the split sheathing to expose the wires inside—wires that can now be stripped individually, using a wire stripper or multipurpose tool.

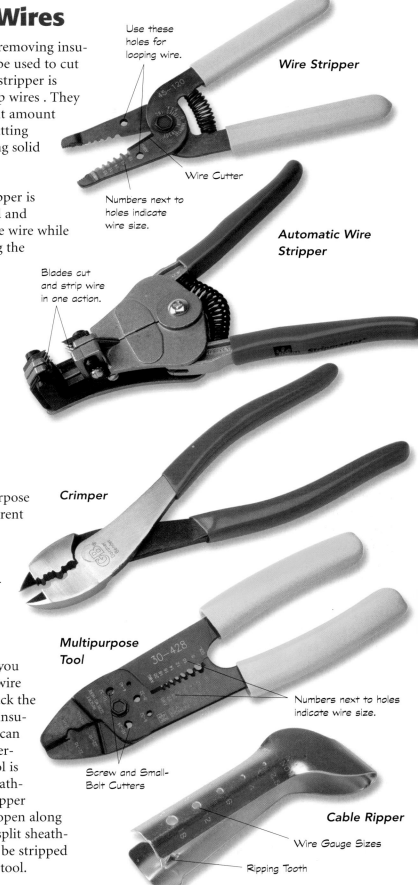

Use these holes for looping wire.

Wire Stripper

Wire Cutter

Numbers next to holes indicate wire size.

Automatic Wire Stripper

Blades cut and strip wire in one action.

Crimper

Multipurpose Tool

Numbers next to holes indicate wire size.

Screw and Small-Bolt Cutters

Cable Ripper

Wire Gauge Sizes

Ripping Tooth

Tools and their Uses

Aviation Snips. Though not a specialized electrical tool, aviation snips often come in handy. After you've split and drawn back the protective sheathing around the cable, for example, you can use aviation snips (or diagonal-cutting pliers) to cut away the excess sheathing. They are also good for cutting metal lath, when trying to establish access for wiring in plaster and lath walls, and for cutting through other metal materials you may encounter or use, such as electrical boxes or fixtures.

Aviation Snips

Connecting, Supporting, and Protecting Wires

Insulated Screwdrivers and Nut Drivers. Screwdrivers are needed to do many things, from installing receptacle covers to tightening terminal screws. Needless to say, a screwdriver handle must be insulated to protect you against electric shock in case the blade accidentally comes in contact with a live wire or circuit. Screwdrivers come in several types, including flat blade, Phillips (cross-blade), and Robertson (square-blade). Some screwdrivers have offset shafts and handles that allow you to get into tight or difficult-to-reach spaces to loosen or fasten screws. For hex-head screws commonly encountered on metal fixtures and appliances, you will need a nut driver, which is really nothing more than a socket wrench with a screwdriver handle.

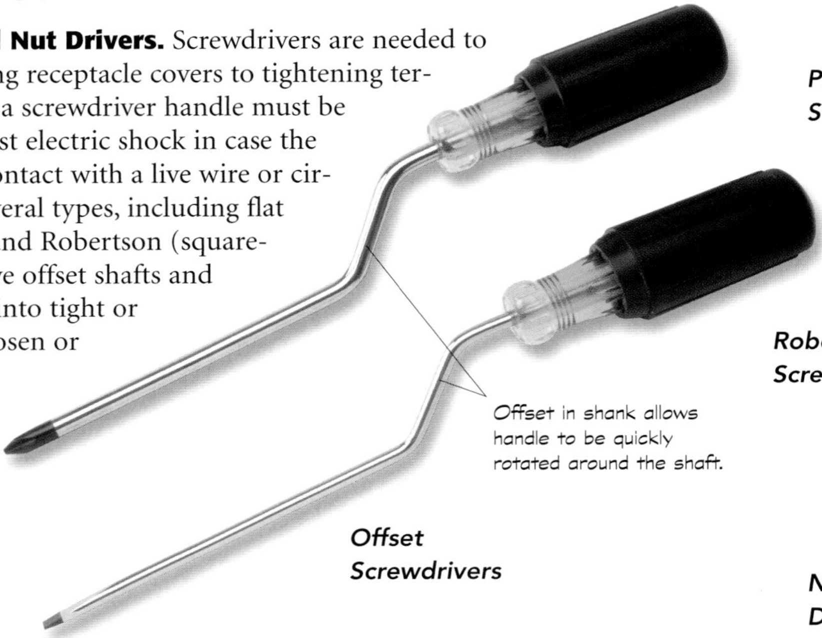

Flat-Blade Screwdriver

Phillips Screwdriver

Robertson Screwdrivers

Nut Drivers

Offset in shank allows handle to be quickly rotated around the shaft.

Offset Screwdrivers

Cable Staples. You'll need cable staples to secure wires safely to framing members inside walls, floors, ceilings, and other concealed spaces. Various types of staples are made in metal with plastic coatings for different sizes and numbers of wires. The NEC (Section 336-18) requires that nonmetallic sheathed cable be supported at intervals not to exceed 4½ feet and must be fastened within 1 foot of any electrical box or fitting.

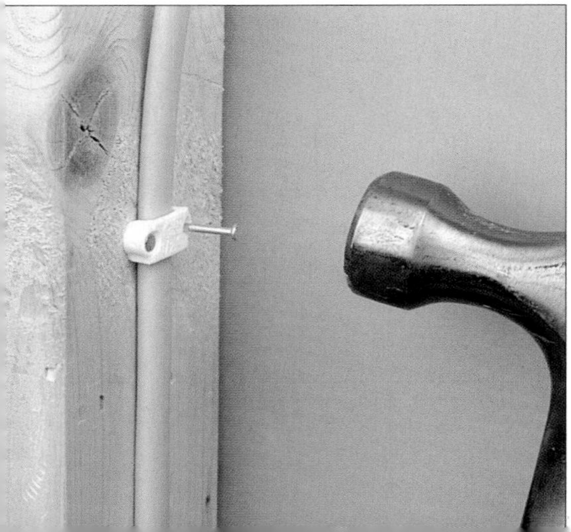

Cable Staples

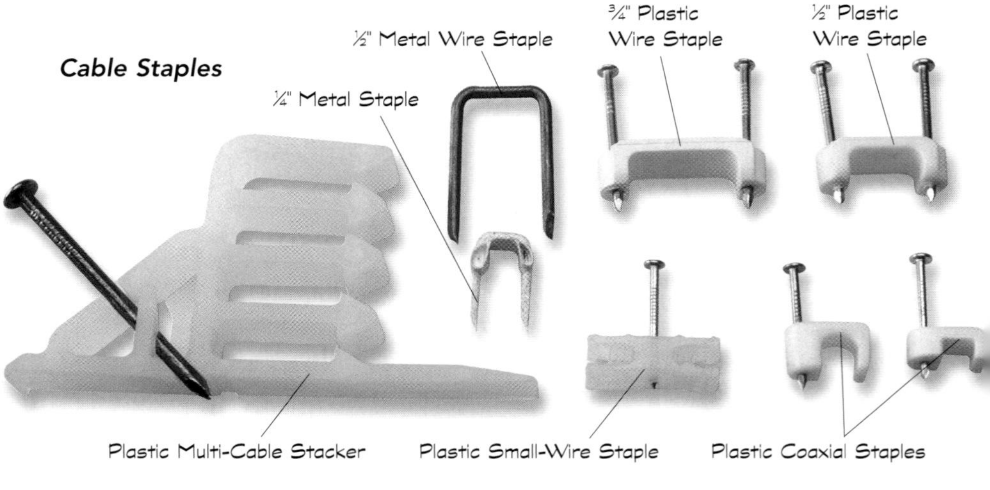

¼" Metal Staple

½" Metal Wire Staple

¾" Plastic Wire Staple

½" Plastic Wire Staple

Plastic Multi-Cable Stacker

Plastic Small-Wire Staple

Plastic Coaxial Staples

Straps. Conduit straps, which are screwed into place, are used to support metal conduit where wiring is exposed, such as in a basement. Metal conduit must be supported at intervals not to exceed 10 feet and must be fastened within 3 feet of any electrical box or other conduit termination (NEC Sections 345-12, 346-12, and 348-13).

Clamps. Grounding and acorn clamps connect ground wires to ground rods; split-bolt connectors splice together larger wire sizes, and cable connectors with locknuts are used to secure insulated wire cable to electrical boxes. This way the unsheathed wires from the cable are protected from fraying against the metal box.

Wire Connectors. Whenever two or more wires are stripped to be spliced together, bare wires become exposed. They must be protected and prevented from coming into contact with other wires, connections, and metal surfaces that may cause a dangerous fault or short circuit. This is typically done using wire connectors or crimping ferrules.

When connecting wires using twist-on wire connectors, be aware of several things. Although the color schemes may vary from one manufacturer to the next, wire connectors are color-coded by size according to the minimum and maximum number of wires they can safely connect. Wire connectors should not be used to connect wires of dissimilar materials, unless so rated, and must completely encase the

Although they vary from manufacturer to manufacturer, wire connectors are generally color-coded according to the minimum and maximum number of wires they connect. All wire connectors can be used for either conducting or grounding wires, but green wire connectors should only be used for grounding wires.

Conduit Straps

Split-Bolt Connector

Acorn Clamp

Nonmetallic-Sheathed Cable Connector

Grounding Clamp

Wire Connector Ratings

Wire Connector	Color	Minimum		Maximum	
		Gauge	No. Wires	Gauge	No. Wires
	Orange	18	2	14	2
	Yellow	16	2	14	4
	Red	14	2	12	4
				10	3
	Green	Green wire connectors are used for grounding wires only.			

Tools and their Uses

Splicing with Wire Connectors

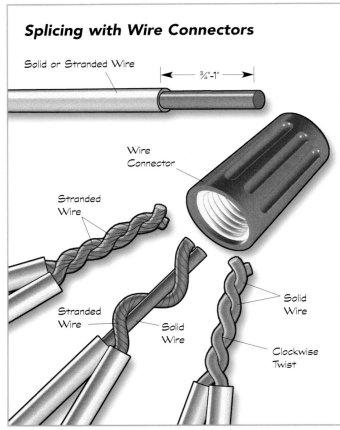

Use a wire connector to splice two or more wires securely together, adhering to the minimum and maximum wire capacity rating for the connector you are using. Hold the wires tightly, slip the connector over the stripped ends, and turn the connector clockwise to secure the wires together.

bare ends of the wires joined within the connector. Green wire connectors should always and only be used for connecting grounding wires.

Crimping Ferrules. Wires can loosen from twist-on wire connectors. Crimping ferrules make a more permanent connection, especially when splicing together bare grounding wires. After twisting the wires together, you slide the crimping ferrule, or compression ring, over the wires and crimp them together using a crimping tool. (See below.) For insulated wire, the ferrule must be covered with a special wire cap.

Crimping Ferrules

Punch-Down Tool. A punch-down, or impact, tool is used to push unstripped telephone or data communications wire down into a connecting block. A terminal post or clip pierces the insulation to complete the connection between the post and the wire. Blade tips can be obtained for either 66 or 110 punch-down wire connecting blocks. Never use ordinary pliers or other tools in place of a punch-down tool because they may cause severe damage to the connectors.

Punch-Down Tool

CRE▲TIVE
HOMEOWNER® | **SMART TIP**

Using Crimping Ferrules

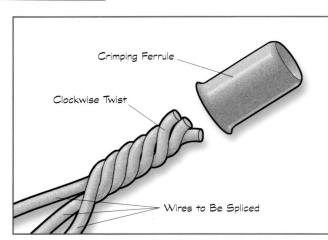

Twist the wires to be spliced together in a clockwise direction; then cut them evenly at the ends.

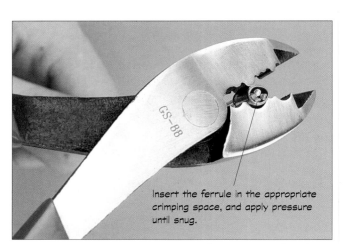

Insert the ferrule in the appropriate crimping space, and apply pressure until snug.

Use a wire crimper to compress the crimping ferrule around the twisted wires.

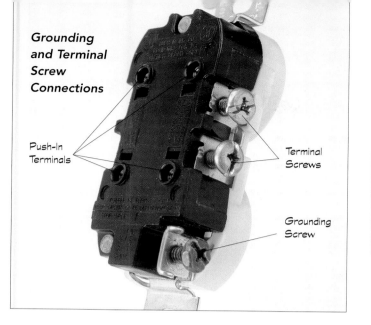

Grounding and Terminal Screw Connections

Push-In Terminals

Terminal Screws

Grounding Screw

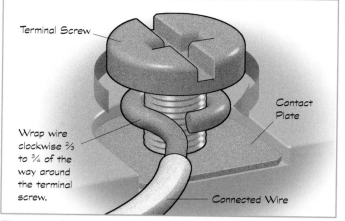

Terminal Screw

Wrap wire clockwise ⅔ to ¾ of the way around the terminal screw.

Contact Plate

Connected Wire

To properly connect a wire, first strip the wire; then wrap it clockwise two-thirds of the way around the terminal screw. Tighten the screw until the wire is firmly and fully in contact with the contact plate.

Grounding and Terminal Screws. Grounding and terminal screws can be thought of as tools for safely securing grounding and circuit wires. Grounding wires must be pigtailed to the grounding screw in an electrical box that is grounded, for example, in order to connect the circuit to the grounding system.

Terminal screws connect wires to receptacles, switches, and other electrical equipment. They are generally coded by color or material to reduce the chance of mismatching wires. Brass-color screws indicate hot terminals; white or silver, neutral; and the grounding screw, green. In a three-way switch, for example, a dark-color screw designates the common screw terminal connecting paired switches; the connecting wire should not be moved to either of the other two lighter-color terminal screws. Make all connections in accordance with NEC guidelines.

Some devices have terminal connections that allow you to simply push a wire into a hole rather than wrapping it around a screw. In this type of connection the bare wire must be totally pushed into the opening—no bare wire may be exposed. This type of screwless pressure connection can only be made with 14-gauge copper wire (NEC Section 110-14). These connections can be problematic and are not recommended. Use screw terminals wherever possible.

Wire Shields. Even after a job is finished, wiring still can be subject to unintentional damage. It is difficult to know the exact location of wires inside the wall. Someone nailing into a wall stud could inadvertently hit a hot wire and receive a deadly shock. For this reason, when wires are run through framing members and are subject to penetration by nails or screws, you must place wire shields on the edges of the studs along the path of the wire (NEC Section 300-4). (See illustration, page 75.) If a nail hits this metal shield, the impact will be apparent and the nail or screw will be deflected from the path of the wiring run.

Wire Brush and Antioxidant Paste. You can use a wire brush to remove corrosion from wires or simply to clean wires. Aluminum wires should be treated with an antioxidant paste to prevent corrosion from recurring.

Electrical Tape. Use tape for temporary emergency wire splices; color-coding circuit wires; and attaching cables to fish tape for secure wire-pulling. It is also a good idea to tape the side terminals when pushing a receptacle into a metal outlet box.

Wire Brush and Antioxidant Paste

Wire Shields

To Clean Outer Surfaces of Wire and Conduit

Electrical Tape

Conduit and Accessories.

Metal conduit, or tubing, is typically used to protect wires from damage and moisture in an exposed location such as a basement or outdoors. If exposed to harsh atmospheric conditions, however, it must be corrosion-resistant. There are five basic types of metal conduit: EMT (electrical metallic tubing), and the similar IMC (intermediate metallic conduit) *not shown*, rigid metal conduit, flexible metal conduit in a nonmetallic PVC cover (liquid-tight) *not shown*, and flexible metal conduit (helically wound). There are also two types of nonmetallic conduit generally used in residential work—electrical nonmetallic tubing (ENT) and rigid nonmetallic conduit (Schedule 40). These are made of polyvinyl chloride (PVC). Conduit sizes permitted by the NEC range from a minimum of ½ inch to a maximum of 6 inches in diameter, depending on the type and use of the conduit. Various accessories are used to connect conduit, just as with water pipes, including bends, couplings, compression and screw connectors, conduit bodies, and pipe supports. Check your local code and the NEC carefully before doing electrical work involving conduit. Note, for example, that no wire splices are permitted within conduit itself but only in electrical boxes or wherever wires remain accessible. There's also a limit on the size and number of wires permitted in conduit. The table at right, for example, indicates the maximum number of conductors allowed in electrical metallic tubing.

Conduit is used to safeguard wire cable where it is exposed to potential damage, such as in a basement workroom or outdoors. Shown here are some of the accessories used to extend and fasten conduit and protect cables wherever conduit changes direction.

Wire Capacities of Electrical Metallic Tubing (EMT)

Wire Type	Gauge	Maximum No. of Wires Permitted in EMT				
		½ Inch	¾ Inch	1 Inch	1¼ Inch	1½ Inch
TW	14	8	15	25	43	58
	12	6	11	19	33	45
	10	5	8	14	24	33
	8	2	5	8	13	18
THW	14	6	10	16	28	39
	12	4	8	13	23	31
	10	3	6	10	18	24
	8	1	4	6	10	14
THHN THWN	6	2	4	7	12	16
	4	1	2	4	7	10
	3	1	1	3	6	8
	2	1	1	3	5	7
	1	1	1	1	4	5

The NEC limits the total number of individual wires of the same gauge in a conduit. (See NEC 1999, Chapter 9, Tables.)

Locating, Measuring, and Marking

Electronic Stud Finder. When you want to locate wood framing inside a wall, you should use an electronic stud finder. Locating concealed framing makes it easier to plan wire runs and to be sure that fasteners applied to the wall will be secured to the framing—not just the drywall. Knowing where framing is located will allow you to avoid drilling and cutting holes in the wrong place or locating electrical boxes where framing will interfere with installation. You can also use a stud finder to determine the location of hidden pipes and existing wiring runs.

Measuring Tape. A heavy-duty 30-foot measuring tape is adequate for most indoor work, whether you are measuring the length of a wire run or the dimensions of a room.

Range Finder. If you want to take a high-tech approach, use an electronic range finder to soni-cally measure the distance between walls. Then you can use the dimensions to calculate power usage requirements.

Pencils/Felt-Tip Marker. A graphite-lead No. 2 or carpenter's pencil is useful for marking accurate measurements of any kind, whether on framing members, drywall, or any other surface on which you can write. A medium-weight black or blue felt-tip marker or grease pencil may do for surfaces that are hard to mark with a lead pencil. Markers are especially handy for label-ing wires and circuits to prevent hazardous mistakes. It is impor-tant that you switch off the appropriate circuit breaker and connect the right wires whenever you are doing electrical work.

Electronic Stud Finder

Indicator Light

Digital Display

Range Finder

Measuring Tape

Carpenter's Pencil

Marker

Mechanical Carpenter's Pencil

Grease Pencil

Pencils and Marker

Hole-Making, Cutting, and Striking

Wood and Masonry Chisels. A wood chisel can be used to notch through the outer edge of a top plate or across the face of a stud in a wood-framed wall to make a pathway for fishing wires between a ceiling and a wall or across a wall. A cold chisel is helpful when you must notch, chip, and punch holes in masonry, though a star drill may be more useful for hole-making. A star drill is a hardened-steel chisel with a star-shaped tip. It is an impact tool that can be easily used with a handheld sledgehammer to punch holes through con-crete block or other masonry.

Wood Chisels

Cold Chisel

Star Drill

Cordless Drill. It's essential that you have a drill with enough torque and power to drill holes for running wires through wood framing. Even a simple task such as installing a screw into wood can be made easier by predrilling the screw holes. If you have a standard corded electric drill, using it safely requires that you must always power it through a ground-fault protection device. A cordless drill is safer and more convenient. Today's better battery-operated drills are powerful enough to handle almost any situation you'll face in a wiring project, and they reduce the potential risk of electric shock from tool wires being dragged through moist areas. They are also handy when working on a ladder. It is difficult and dangerous to haul an electric drill with a long extension cord up a tall ladder. The cord may get in your way, trip you, or catch on something. The plug-in connection may come apart. Maintaining enough balance to drill a hole while holding onto a ladder, a cord, and a drill at the same time can be extremely difficult, if not impossible. Get a drill with a lanyard attached to the handle, and fashion a hook onto your ladder to hold it. This will free up both of your hands for doing work.

Purchasing a battery-operated drill of 12 volts or more with a charger and second battery will make your work much easier. These drills come in two different chuck sizes—⅜ inch and ½ inch. The ½-inch chuck is a better choice, especially if you will need to make larger-diameter holes, because it will take both small and large bits.

Drill Bits. Whether you use a conventional or a cordless drill, a variety of drill bits will come in handy. A masonry bit is a necessity when you need to drill a hole for conduit through poured-concrete or block walls. (You may have to rent a hammer drill.) Likewise, Forstner and spade bits are convenient for drilling holes through wood studs when you need to fish wires through a framed wall. For difficult-to-reach places inside a wall cavity, a special flexible drill extension is available.

Hole Saws. A good set of hole saws (hole-cutter attachments) for your drill will make easy work of cutting holes to run wire or conduit. Hole saws are also available with carbide tips, which stay sharp under extreme use.

Cordless Drill

Forstner Bit

Masonry Bit

High-Speed Steel Bit

Spade Bit

Flexbits

Hole Saws

Bit and mandrel section is unbolted for use with other cutter heads.

Battery Chargers

Battery-operated tools are safer and a lot more convenient to use than standard electric tools. The new cordless tools have plenty of torque and power to perform almost any task. It is no longer necessary for you to hunt for an outlet or extension cord or to worry about the gauge of the extension cord.

Specialty battery-operated tools are increasingly popular and available, from battery-operated screwdrivers and circular saws to reciprocating saws and drills. Of course, to keep these new tools powered, you need to have a high-quality battery charger as a permanent part of your tool collection.

Battery and Charger

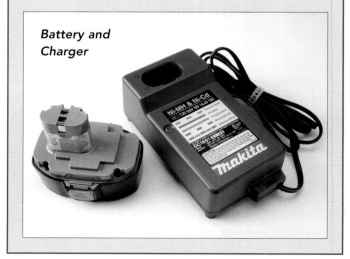

Cordless Reciprocating Saw. You can quickly rough-cut through virtually any material, from wood to metal, using a reciprocating saw. Battery-operated models are perfect for doing electrical work safely without having to drag around tool wires. Be sure to have on hand appropriate blades for cutting through different materials.

Electrician's Hammer. An electrician's hammer differs from a conventional curved-claw hammer in four important ways. First, the shaft is constructed of fiberglass to insulate against electric shock; second, the head is narrower and longer for better reach; third, the claw is flatter and longer, like that of a straight-claw or ripping hammer; and fourth, the head is designed to be non-sparking.

Knockout Punch. For twisting the slugs off of electrical boxes, a lineman's pliers will do in a pinch, but a standard round knockout punch will do a better, cleaner job of slug-splitting and removal. A heavy-duty model will also enable you to punch holes in thick sheet metal, stainless steel, plastic, fiberglass, and other similar materials.

Utility Saw and Utility Knife. Utility saws and utility knives are ideally suited for cutting into or through drywall. You'll find a utility knife especially useful for slicing through drywall to reach stud framing that must be notched for wire-pulling behind a wall.

Electrician's Hammer

Insulated Handle

Extended Non-sparking Head

Sharpened edge cuts a new hole.

Knockout Punch

Utility Saw and Utility Knife

Working with Conduit

Manual Conduit Bender. A manual pipe or conduit bender is used for bending metal conduit smoothly and efficiently. You can operate a pipe bender by hand or by using foot pressure to bend conduit to a 10-, 22½-, 30-, 45-, 60-, or 90-degree angle as marked on the conduit bender. This tool is essential for making accurate saddle bends, stub-ups, and back-to-back bends, as well as simple up and down bends, without crimping the pipe.

Manual Conduit Bender

Hacksaw. You'll need a hacksaw to cut through metal pipe or conduit or metal-sheathed cable. The number of teeth in the blade determines the thickness of metal that can be cut. In general, thicker metals require coarser-toothed blades. A wing nut on the hacksaw handle allows you to remove the blade or adjust its cutting angle and tightness.

Hacksaw

Tools and their Uses

Wrenches and Pliers

Combination Wrench

Open-End Wrench

Groove-Joint Pliers

Adjustable Wrench

Locking Pliers

Conduit Connectors. Special types of connectors are needed to secure conduit at junctions and connection points.

Below are examples of straight conduit connectors for rigid and intermediate metallic conduit. **A** straight compression; **B** concrete-tight straight compression; **C** straight compression with insulated throat; **D** concrete-tight setscrew; and **E** setscrew with insulated throat.

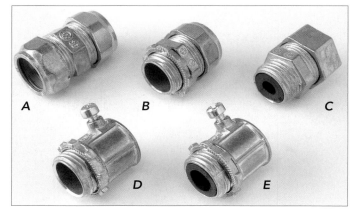

A   B   C

D   E

Wrenches and Pliers. Many conduit connections, as with conventional plumbing pipes, consist of compression fittings. You will need pliers and sized or adjustable wrenches to properly secure these connections.

Testing Circuits

Neon Circuit Tester. Use the two probes on a circuit tester to check for live voltage in a circuit. The neon bulb will light if the circuit is live. You can also use the tester to verify that the power to a circuit has been turned off before you work on it.

Receptacle Analyzer. Use a receptacle analyzer to identify faults in receptacle wiring: simply plug the device into the outlet being tested; then read the lighting pattern made by the three bulbs on the analyzer. Different combinations of lighted and unlighted bulbs indicate specific problems with the wiring, such as hot and neutral wires connected in reverse.

Multi-tester. An analog or digital multi-tester, or multimeter, is required to measure voltage and current, as well as to make continuity and resistance checks in switches, fixtures, low-voltage transformers, and other electrical devices.

Continuity Tester. A continuity tester is powered by its own battery, which is used to generate an electrical current through an attached wire and clamp. It must only be used when the power to a circuit is

Indicator Light

Combination of lights indicates wiring sequence.

Neon Circuit Tester

Receptacle Analyzer

Red Test Lead

Black Test Lead

Multi-Tester

Range Selector Switch

turned off. The tester is especially useful for determining whether or not a cartridge fuse has blown. You can test this type of fuse by touching the tester clamp and probe to the opposite end caps of the fuse. A lighted bulb indicates a working fuse, an unlighted bulb means that the fuse has blown and is in need of replacement. The tester can also be used to detect faults and current interruptions in switches and other types of electrical equipment.

Do not attach to live circuits.

Reverse this clip to use as a test prod.

Low-Voltage Circuit Tester

Low-Voltage Circuit Tester. A low-voltage circuit tester looks similar to a neon circuit tester, but it is strictly limited to testing circuits less than 50 volts such as doorbells, transformers, low-voltage lamps, and outlets, etc.

Telephone Line Tester. Use a telephone line tester to resolve problems with standard telephone wiring. A telephone line tester has a phone-jack plug on one end and an LED on the other. Some testers come with a splitter that enables you to strip as well as test telephone wires. Plugging the tester into a modular jack allows you to test whether any of the circuit wires have been reversed or are loose or disconnected. You can also use a telephone line tester used to check the telephone itself for dial-tone and wiring function.

Telephone Line Tester

Telephone Line Tester
GC ELECTRONICS 30 - 9451
Green means correct wiring
Red means reversed polarity
No light means not operational

Indicator Lights

Safety

Electrician's Gloves. For electrical work you should use a pair of insulated electrician's gloves, rather than using ordinary work gloves. Some high-voltage gloves can protect you up to 20,000 volts, while low-voltage gloves are sufficient for up to 1,000 volts.

Safety Glasses. When doing electrical work of any kind, you should always wear safety glasses or goggles. A sudden spark or a bit of clipped wire could shoot out and burn or scratch your eye. When drilling overhead it is important to wear safety goggles to keep debris from falling into your eyes as you work. Be sure that the glasses you buy have extendable arms to fit properly around your ears.

Extension Cords. Because you should never plug a power tool into an electrical circuit unless it is ground-fault protected, a GFCI extension cord can literally be a lifesaver. This device can save your life if a tool malfunctions and short-circuits to the housing while you are using it. You can never assume that the receptacle from which you are working has GFCI protection. A 3-foot extension cord with GFCI protection built in is ideal because of its portability. It is sold at most electrical wholesalers and retailers. Use, at minimum, a 12-gauge heavy-duty extension cord to allow your high-voltage tools to obtain maximum voltage, which prolongs their life. Under-gauged extension cords can be a fire hazard.

CRE▲TIVE HOMEOWNER®

SMART TIP

Using Ladders

Always use nonconductive ladders—wood or fiberglass. Aluminum ladders can be an electrician's nightmare. Should you accidentally cut into a hot wire, you must be insulated from ground—not connected to it. Always wear rubber-soled shoes and electrician's gloves to serve as additional insulators. If you are in doubt about the security of the ladder base, hammer stakes into the ground to brace it. It is also important to maintain good balance while working on a ladder. Never lean too far right or left or do work from an awkward angle.

Safety Glasses

GFCI Extension Cord

Woods

Tools and their Uses

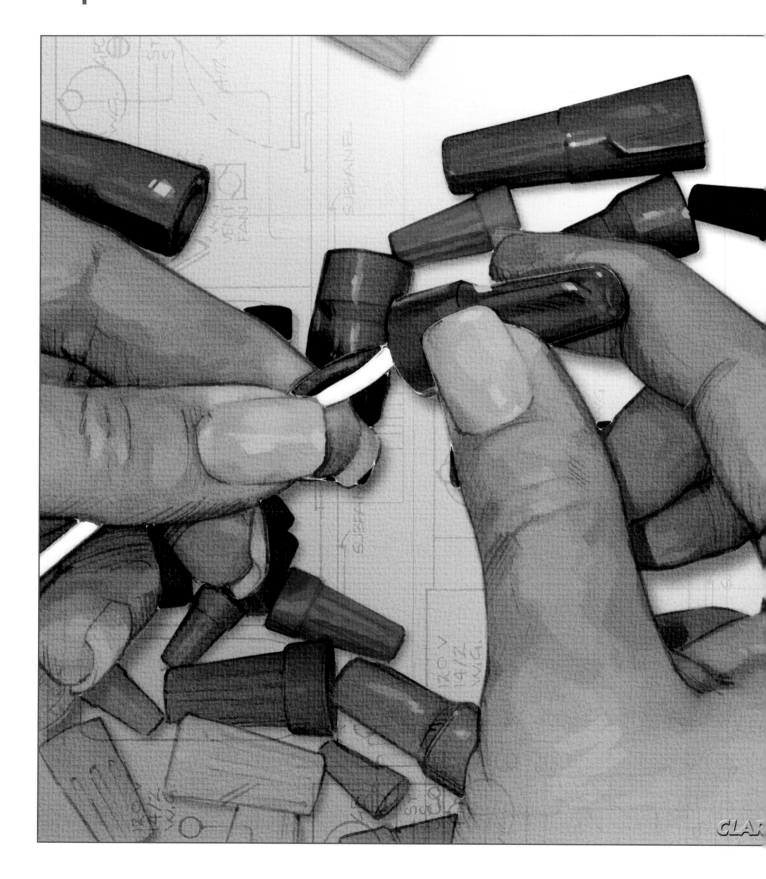

CHAPTER 3

Materials and Equipment

Even if you have the proper tools to do your own electrical work, you are only half-prepared for the task. You must also have the right materials and equipment. Every code requirement must be carefully considered before you purchase a single item. Plan your electrical work on paper first so that you will know exactly what to purchase—from the service panel and electrical boxes to the receptacles, switches, and fixtures. First, you must determine what you're installing and how much power it requires. Then you can decide what categories and quantities of wire to buy; how many circuit breakers and at what amperage; whether or not conduit or cable will be used, and what type; and the accessories needed to connect and fasten wires, conduit, cable, and other materials. Carefully identifying everything you need in advance saves you time and money as well as effort.

Wires and Cables

Types and Designations

Technically, the metallic material through which electric current flows is called a conductor. In practical terms, most people call it wire. Wire is designated as bare or insulated, stranded or solid, single or multiple, sheathed in cable or encased in insulated cord. In residential work, most wires made of a solid conductive material, such as copper, are encased and protected in plastic insulation. You can buy this type of wire in custom lengths cut from a roll or precut and packaged in standard lengths. Cables usually consist of two or more insulated wires wrapped together in a second protective layer of plastic sheathing. If the cable includes a grounding wire, it can be insulated or bare copper wire. Cable is commonly sold boxed in precut lengths. Stranded wires are typically enclosed in an insulating jacket, called a cord. Flexible cord is sometimes precut and packaged but is usually sold off the roll. Whether on a roll or precut, conductors are always sold by the linear foot.

Aluminum and copper-clad aluminum wires have also been used in the past, in addition to copper, as conductive materials. For any electrical work you do, you should use only the kind of wire that is already installed in your home. To find out which kind of wire you have, check the cable type at the main service panel by reading the designation printed on the plastic sheathing. For this, you need to have an accurate circuit map to identify the circuit you are planning to check. An abbreviated coding system reveals the voltage, the wire or cable type, and the American Wire Gauge (AWG) wire size. (See table "American Wire Gauges," page 10.)

Bare Wire

Insulated Solid Wire

Insulated Stranded Wire

Nonmetallic Cable (NM) Sheathed Wire

Armored Cable (AC) Sheathed Wire

Wire comes in many types: bare or insulated; solid or stranded; single or multiple; sheathed in plastic or metal. Each type serves a different purpose.

Gauge — Number of Wires — Grounding Label — Type — Voltage Rating — UL Listing

Markings on a cable jacket *indicate the gauge and number of wires in the cable, the UL-listing, voltage rating, and whether a grounding wire is included.*

For example, consider the following designation: 14/3 WITH GROUND, TYPE NM-B, 600 Volts (UL). The first number shows that the insulated wires inside the cable are 14 gauge (AWG). The second number indicates that the cable contains three wires. "With ground" signifies that a fourth bare copper or green insulated grounding wire is incorporated within the cable. This may simply be designated with the letter G following the number of wires in the cable. "Type NM-B" denotes that the wire is rated at 90 degrees Centigrade (194 degrees Fahrenheit) and is encased in a nonmetallic (plastic) sheathing. Next, the maximum voltage safely carried by the cable is specified as 600 volts. And, finally, the UL notation ensures that the cable is rated as safe for its designated use.

Wire Sizes. You will be concerned mostly with solid-copper wires of 14, 12, and 10 gauge because these are most commonly used for house wiring. Again, the term wire refers to a single conductor. In a cable containing two or more wires, they will all be the same gauge. The AWG system codes the wire diameter as a whole number. The smaller the number, the greater the diameter and current-carrying capacity of the wire. Because wire size recommendations are for copper wires, you must readjust the designation to the next larger size whenever you use aluminum or copper-clad aluminum wire. (12- and 10-gauge aluminum and copper-clad aluminum are no longer manufactured and are not available.)

Aluminum Concerns. Be extremely cautious if you use aluminum wire. Though commonly used for heavy appliance circuits, aluminum wire requires special attention in switches and receptacles. Don't use aluminum wire where copper wire is designated. If aluminum wire is used in a device designed for copper wire, the wire will expand and contract as it heats and cools, eventually working loose from the terminal screws. This will create a dangerous situation and may result in an electrical fire. If your home contains copper-clad aluminum wiring, do not add aluminum wiring to it. Instead, use copper wires. If your home has aluminum wire, check whether the switches and receptacles are marked CO/ALR (rated to be connected to aluminum). If the

switches and receptacles do not bear this marking, replace them with those that do. Be careful, too, when working with single-strand aluminum wire because it breaks easily. Also, never connect aluminum wire to a back-wired switch or receptacle that uses push-in terminals. Aluminum wire must always be connected to terminal screws (NEC Section 110-14). Note, too, that you can buy UL-listed crimp and twist-on connectors that are specifically made to connect aluminum to copper wire pigtails. These devices are recommended by the Consumer Product Safety Commission.

Aluminum cable is sometimes used for service-entrance cable and large appliances such as electric ranges and electric furnaces. If large diameter, multistranded aluminum cable is used, the ends must be coated with a noncorrosive compound. (NEC Section 110-14)

Connection Rating

Connect aluminum wire *only to receptacles or switches approved for it and clearly marked with the letters CO/ALR.*

Color-Coding

In addition to the markings on plastic wire insulation, wires are coded by color. Black wires are always hot, as are the red, blue, and yellow wires. White or gray wires are generally (grounded) neutral, with the exception noted below. Green wires are used for grounding only. In addition to having green insulation, grounding wires may also be bare copper. An exception: when a white wire is combined with a black wire in a two-wire cable, the white wire may be used as a hot wire in a switch loop or in a single 240-volt appliance receptacle. In these cases, the white wire must be wrapped with black electrical tape at

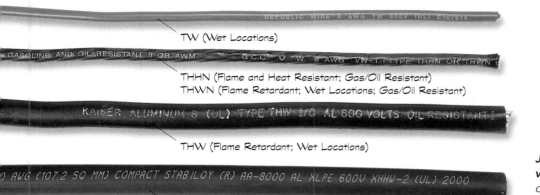

TW (Wet Locations)

THHN (Flame and Heat Resistant; Gas/Oil Resistant)
THWN (Flame Retardant; Wet Locations; Gas/Oil Resistant)

THW (Flame Retardant; Wet Locations)

XHHW (Service Entrance; Flame and Heat Resistant; Wet Locations)

Just as there are many types of wires, wire insulation comes in categories, each having a maximum operating temperature and ampacity rating.

visible points to identify it as a hot wire. Two-wire cable has a black and white wire; three-wire cable, white, black, and red; four-wire cable, black white, red, and blue; and five-wire cable, white, black, red, blue, and yellow.

Wire terminal screws are also coded by color. Neutral wires are typically connected to silver or white; grounding or bonding (ensuring a continuously conductive path) wires to green; and hot wires to brass or copper. In a three-way switch, the common (COM) wire is usually connected to a screw with a dark finish.

Insulation Categories

Wire comes in a variety of insulation types. Be sure that you select the appropriate type for the use and location you have in mind. Always check local code before doing any work to be sure that your materials meet code requirements. The most common insulation categories used in residential wiring are THHN, THW, and THWN. The T stands for ordinary thermoplastic insulated cable. You will probably use more of this than any other type of cable in residential wiring projects. The letter H specifies wire that is heat resistant. A double H indicates wire that can operate at a higher temperature (up to 194 degrees Fahrenheit) than wire designated with a single letter H. The W denotes wire that can be used in dry, damp, or wet locations. The letter N (nylon) specifies that the wire also resists gasoline and/or oil.

Wire Types. THHN wire has flame-retardant, heat-resistant insulation specified for both dry and damp locations. The absence of a W, however, means that the wire is not approved for wet locations. Because nylon insulation is thinner than other kinds of plastic insulation, THHN wire is often used to fit more wires into a conduit. THW wire is flame retardant, and heat and moisture resistant. THWN wire also resists gasoline and oil. Both THW and THWN can be used in dry, damp, or wet locations. They are commonly used in place of THHN in conduit. Another type of wire, XHHW, is

often used for service entrance (SE) cable in wet areas instead of THWN. The X indicates that the wire insulation is a flame-retardant, synthetic polymer. It is specified for use in dry, damp, and wet locations.

Cable Sheathing Insulation. Indoor house circuits are usually wired using nonmetallic (NM) cable, which is wire contained in a plastic sheathing that's labeled with its specific use. This flexible cable is sometimes known by its trade name, Romex. NM cable contains insulated neutral and power wires and a bare grounding wire. It is used in dry locations only. Each wire is individually wrapped in plastic insulation that is color-coded according to the type of wire inside. Again, hot wires are typically wrapped in black and neutral wires in white. Where the grounding wire is insulated, it is wrapped in green. If it is bare, it will be wrapped in paper.

The wires in NM cable for common receptacle, light, and small appliance circuits are usually 12/2G or 14/2G. Wire a 20-amp circuit with 12/2G cable. Larger appliance circuits require larger wire sizes. A 30-amp clothes dryer requires 10/3G cable, while a 60-amp range requires 6/3G cable. See the table, "Representative Loads and Circuits for Residential Equipment," page 44, for other common residential appliance and power needs.

If a cable is designated type UF (underground feeder and branch-circuit cable), this means that it is suitable for use in wet locations, including direct burial underground. UF cable can be used in place of wire in conduit in some areas and is permitted for interior wiring in place of Type NM cable [NEC Section 339-3(a)]. Check local code requirements. The distinguishing characteristic of this type of cable is that the individually insulated wires are embedded in solid, water-resistant plastic.

Cord Insulation. Wire designated as cord differs from cable. The type of wires sheathed in cord are stranded wires The sheathing usually consists of some type of

Representative Loads and Circuits for Residential Electrical Equipment

Appliance	Volt/Amperes	Volts	Gauge/No. of Wires	Circuit Breaker or Fuse in Amps
Range	12,000	115/230	6/3	60
Built-in oven	4,500	115/230	10/3	30
Range top	6,000	115/230	10/3	30
Dishwasher	1,200	115	12/2	20
Waste-disposal unit	300	115	14 or 12/2	15 or 20
Broiler	1,500	115	12/2	20
Refrigerator	300	115	14 or 12/2	15 or 20
Freezer	350	115	14 or 12/2	15 or 20
Washing machine	1,200	115	12/2	20
Clothes dryer	5,000	115/230	10/3	30
Iron	1,650	115	14 or 12/2	15 or 20
Workbench	1,500	115	12/2	20
Portable heater	1,300	115	12/2	20
Television	300	115	14 or 12/2	15 or 20
Fixed lighting	1,200	115	14 or 12/2	15 or 20
Room air conditioner	1,200	115	14 or 12/2	15 or20
Central air conditioner	5,000	115/230	10/3	30
Sump pump	300	115	14 or 12/2	15 or 20
Forced-air furnace	600	115	14 or 12/2	15 or 20
Attic fan	300	115	12/2	20

Wherever the information is available, use actual equipment ratings. A heavy-duty, fixed-location appliance should generally be on its own circuit. Check the manufacturer's literature to determine circuit and direct connections for any appliance before installing and connecting it to your electrical system.

plastic, rubber, or cloth insulation. Zip cord, for example, contains two wires, usually 18 gauge, encased in a neoprene, synthetic, or other rubberlike insulation. A thin strip of this insulation between the wires is all that holds them together. You can easily separate the wires by pulling, or zipping, them apart. Cord is used primarily for lamps, small appliances, and other wires that have plugs or receptacles attached to one or both ends of the cord. Because flexible cords contain smaller gauge wires, never use them for fixed appliances.

Wire Ampacity

When selecting wire, you must also consider its ampacity. This is the amount of current in amperes that a wire can carry safely and continuously under normal conditions of use, without exceeding its temperature rating. For example, 10-gauge copper wire is rated to carry up to 30 amps;

CREATIVE HOMEOWNER® **SMART TIP**

Estimating Wire

To estimate the amount of wire or cable you will need for a project, measure the distance between the new switch, receptacle, or fixture box and the main panel. Because you will probably not be going in a straight line, remember to allow for curves and offsets. Add 1 foot for every junction you will make; then provide a margin of error by adding 20 percent to the total calculated distance. If, for example, you measure 13 feet from an existing receptacle to a new receptacle, add 1 foot for each electrical box, bringing the total to 15 feet. Add 20 percent, or 3 feet, to this distance for a total length of 18 feet that you should have on hand.

Splicing Wires

According to the NEC, all wire splices must be enclosed in a switch, receptacle, fixture, or junction box. To make a wire splice, you must first strip insulation from the end of the wires. Although it may be used for this, a utility knife will most likely nick the wire. Instead, use an electrician's wire stripper or multipurpose tool. A wire stripper is operated either manually or automatically. (See "Stripping and Crimping Wires," page 29.) A manual wire stripper requires that you cut the insulation, without cutting the wire, and then pull the cut insulation from the end of the wire. Automatic wire strippers cut and strip the insulation in one motion.

To splice solid wire to solid wire, strip approximately ½ inch of insulation from the end of each wire. Then, using pliers, spirally twist one piece of wire around the other in a clockwise direction. Make the twist tight but not so tight it will cause the wire to break. Cap the splice with a wire connector. (You can also cap the wires without twisting first.) Some people tape around the connector as an added precaution to ensure that the wires will not come out. Splice stranded wires in the same way, but do not strip either type of wire by circling the insulation with cutting pliers and then pulling off the insulation. This will cut into the conductors and cause them to break if they are bent.

To splice a stranded wire to a solid wire, strip the same ½ inch of insulation off the solid wire, but an inch from the stranded wire. Spirally twist the stranded wire clockwise around the solid wire. Cap the splice with a wire connector.

To splice solid wire to solid wire, *spirally twist one wire around the other in a clockwise direction. Cap the splice using a wire connector.*

Splice a stranded wire to a stranded wire *in the same way as a solid wire to a solid wire, but be careful not to cut or break the individual wire strands. Strip stranded wires to expose 1" of bare wire before splicing.*

To splice a stranded wire to a solid wire, *spirally twist the stranded wire around the solid wire, and cap the splice using an appropriate-size wire connector. Before splicing, solid wire needs to be stripped to ½".*

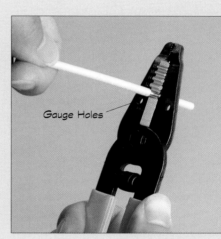

Gauge Holes

To use a manual wire stripper, *insert the wire into the matching gauge hole, close the stripper to cut the insulation, and pull it toward the end of the wire.*

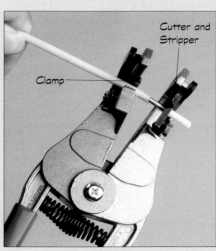

Cutter and Stripper

Clamp

Though more expensive, *an automatic wire stripper combines both steps, cutting and stripping the wire insulation, in one motion.*

Amperage Ratings for Residential Cable

AWG Size	Insulation Type	Copper		Aluminum/Copper-Clad Aluminum	
		Ordinary Use	Service Entrance	Ordinary Use	Service Entrance
4/0	THW, THWN	230	250	180	200
2/0	THW, THWN	175	200	135	150
1/0	THW, THWN	150	175	120	125
1/0	TW	125	NA	100	NA
1	THW, THWN	130	150	100	110
2	THW, THWN	115	125	90	100
2	TW	95	NA	75	NA
4	THW, THWN	85	100	65	NA
4	TW	70	NA	55	NA
6	THW, THWN	65	NA	50	NA
6	TW	55	NA	40	NA
8	THW, THWN	50	NA	40	NA
8	TW	40	NA	30	NA
10	THW, THWN	35	NA	30	NA
10	TW	30	NA	25	NA
12	THW, THWN	25	NA	20	NA
14	THW, THWN	20	NA	NA	NA

Wires sheathed in thermoplastic insulation (cable) have maximum amperage capacities (ampacities) for which they are rated. The ratings above are for typical residential wires. (NEC Table 310-16)

12-gauge wire, 20 amps; and 14-gauge wire, 15 amps. If a wire is too small for the current it carries, it will present a greater-than-normal resistance to the current flowing around it. This will generate enough heat to destroy the wire insulation, possibly causing a fire.

Armored Cable

Wire enclosed in metal sheathing is called armored cable (AC). It is sometimes called by its trade name, BX. Inside the flexible metal sheathing are insulated hot and neutral (grounded) wires and a bare bonding wire. BX is restricted to use indoors in dry locations. It is rarely used in new construction (except in high-rise buildings) because it is expensive and difficult to install. Nevertheless, it is often found in older homes. Metal-clad cable (MC) is a more common type of armored cable. The two cables look alike but are easy to tell apart if you know what to look for. MC cable includes a green grounding wire while AC cable does not. The metal covering on MC cable is not permitted to be the grounding conductor. The wires in MC cable are wrapped in a

Armored cable (AC) is sometimes called by its trade name, BX. It consists of hot, neutral, and grounding wires in a protective metal (armor) sheathing.

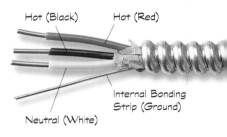

Metal-clad (MC) cable is similar to AC cable, but the wires are wrapped in plastic tape instead of paper.

All types of armored cable require a plastic sleeve placed between the sharp metal edges of the cut cable and the emerging wires.

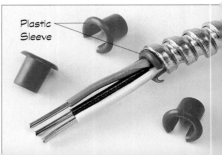

plastic tape to protect them from chafing against the armored sheathing. Be sure to insert a plastic sleeve between the wires and the armor wherever wires emerge from the armored cable.

For BX, different fittings are used to attach the cable to electrical boxes. All BX fittings work the same way—the cable goes through center of the fitting. The armor itself is connected within the fitting and is held in place by one or two clamps or a twist-on mechanism. As stated, BX is not easy to work with. To splice one BX cable into another requires cutting the armor sheathing without harming the wires inside. This can only be done using a hacksaw or a specialized tool that cuts any type of armored cable. The tool just barely cuts through the armor, which is then twisted to break cleanly, exposing the wires inside. Another drawback to BX is that it cannot turn a tight radius because of the metal sheathing. Too tight a turn will kink the armor, creating a sharp edge. Sharp edges are also created wherever armored cable is cut. This is why it is so important to always install a protective sleeve on the cut ends of the cable to protect the wires inside.

Nonmetallic Cable

Nonmetallic (NM) cable is the most common type of cable used in residential work. Again, NM cable consists of wires encased in a thermoplastic sheathing. The wires include one or more hot wires, a neutral wire, and a grounding wire. The most common type is two wires with a ground—one hot wire in black insulation, one neutral in white, and a bare copper grounding wire. Three-wire cable is commonly used for house circuits to wire three-way switching or where an extra hot wire is needed, such as for wiring a switch-operated outlet. The third wire is typically encased in red insulation. In some cases, the grounding wire in NM cable may not be included. This is particularly true of older-style NM cable (prior to 1960).

When you work with NM cable, be sure to avoid two common errors: first, putting a kink in the wires by bending the cable too sharply and, second, damaging the cable sheathing by pulling it through too small an opening. A kink may damage the copper wire inside the cable and can cause it to overheat and create a fire hazard. This also applies to working with the individual wires—never bend them at a right angle but rather bend them gradually. As for sheathing, if it is torn by pulling it through a tight opening, around a sharp turn, or getting it caught on something, the cable may be taped as long as the insulation on the individual wire within the cable is not damaged. Otherwise it must be replaced.

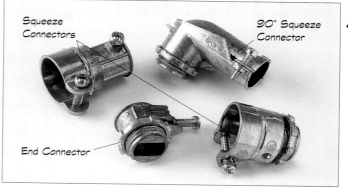

To comply with code requirements, use the correct type of connector to properly connect BX armored cable to an electrical box.

To cut armored cable easily, use a specialized cutting tool. Insert the cable in the tool, and turn the knob clockwise to tighten down on and cut the armor.

A standard NM cable contains two insulated wires and one bare copper grounding wire. The hot wire is encased in black insulation and the neutral in white. In a three-conductor NM cable, the additional hot wire is encased in red insulation.

To prevent damage to wires, never bend individual wires or NM cable at a sharp angle. Always make gentle bends and turns. Because of its fragility, even the sheathing on NM cable will easily rip if it is caught on or scraped against something sharp.

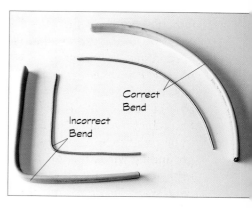

SMART TIP

Removing NM Cable Sheathing

To remove the sheathing on NM cable, insert the cable into a cable ripper, and squeeze the cutting point into the flat side of the cable 8 to 10 inches from the end. Pull lengthwise down the center of the cable. Because the center wire is the bare grounding wire, if you accidentally cut too far into the cable you will not be likely to cut into the insulation on the conductor wires. Peel back the thermoplastic sheathing and the paper wrapping; then cut them off using diagonal-cutting pliers or aviation snips.

Use a cable ripper to slice open the center of the sheathing on NM cable. This will protect the insulated wires from being cut.

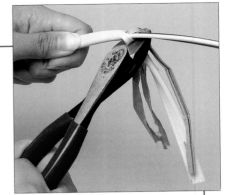

Pull back 8 to 10 in. of the sheathing; then cut away the paper wrapping and excess sheathing, using diagonal-cutting pliers or aviation snips.

UF Label   Resistance Label

***Underground feeder and branch-circuit cable** is marked with the letters UF. The label also indicates whether the cable is corrosion- and/or sunlight-resistant.*

Underground Cable

Underground feeder and branch-circuit cable, or UF cable, can be used for interior wiring wherever NM cable is permitted. However, it is primarily approved for wet locations such as direct burial underground. This kind of cable is used to wire an outside light or outbuilding where type NM is not approved for this use. It must be buried 1 foot underground if it is a 120-volt circuit and is GFCI-protected to keep it from damage. If it is not protected by a GFCI or the circuit exceeds 20 amps, bury it at least 2 feet underground. Check local code regarding direct-burial cable before you do any work.

The outer sheathing on UF cable is solid thermoplastic, encasing the inner wires completely. This makes it more difficult to separate the wires from the sheathing, as compared with the wires in standard NM cable. The wires inside UF cable are solid and can be spliced in the same way as standard NM wire, but all splices must be made within an approved watertight box where used outdoors.

▶ ***The service-entrance, or main, panel** is both the entry and distribution point for all the circuits in your home. If the panel cover, breakers, and wires were removed, you would see the two power buses into which all of the circuit breakers are plugged.*

Service Panels

Types and How They Work

The service-entrance panel (SEP) is the main house panel. It serves two primary purposes. First, the main panel is the only location in or outside the house where all electrical power can be cut off at once. Every adult member of your household should know the location of this panel and how to cut the power in case of an emergency. Second, the main panel is the distribution point and protection center for all of the circuits. All the branch circuits, ones that go to the receptacles, switches, and appliances throughout your house, originate here.

Power
Buses

The main breaker controls power entering the hot buses. Turn off the power by moving the handle to the OFF position on the main disconnect. It trips automatically if the circuit shorts or is overloaded.

To install an individual breaker, first turn off the main power; then hook the notched end onto the hot bus tab, and snap it firmly in place.

Under the panel cover, circuit breakers, and wires are two copper or aluminum strips. These are the power buses, called hot buses. Each bus is connected to a hot incoming main cable. The circuit breakers are all plugged into these two buses, which provide the breakers with power. Neutral and grounding wires from each circuit are connected to the aluminum neutral/grounding buses on each side of the hot buses. Dead center in the upper part of the panel is a very large breaker, called the main breaker. This breaker controls all of the house power. Its purpose is to monitor the current being drawn, opening the circuit when there is a short or an overload. It also provides manual control over the house power. When the handle is in the ON position, power is on. If you want power off, simply push the handle to the OFF position. Never forget that the power buses remain hot whenever the handle is in the ON position.

Panel Sizes. A typical house panel may provide 100, 150, or 200 amps. Today, 200 amps is most common, although larger all-electric-power homes may use up to 400 amps. These houses usually have two 200-amp panels. Though the most common service panel for today's homes is 200 amps, it is possible that your home has a smaller panel. The smallest panel permitted by code is 100 amps. Your house's power capacity is noted either on the panel or on the main breaker.

Panels rated for the same maximum current capacity, such as 200 amps, are subdivided by the number of breakers they can hold. The maximum number of breakers a residential panel can hold is 40 breakers plus the main breaker. This type of panel is called a 40/40 panel. It is the proper size panel for 200-ampere residential service. The first number refers to the number of full-size breakers the

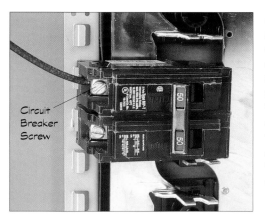

Circuit Breaker Screw

A circuit's hot wire is secured beneath a circuit breaker screw. Insert the bare wire end in the terminal hole, and tighten the screw over the wire.

panel can hold, and the second number refers to the maximum number of breakers the panel can hold regardless of breaker type. The next panel size below a 40/40 is a 30/40 panel. It can hold only 30 full-size breakers. To increase the panel to 40 breakers, half-size breakers must be used. It is preferable to use full-size breakers for safety reasons. The smallest panel size that can fit 40 breakers is a 20/40 panel. Smaller panels may hold a maximum of 20 or 30 breakers. Avoid these panels because they may not have sufficient breaker space to serve the house and aren't likely to provide for future expansion.

Circuit-Breaker Sizes. The individual breakers within the main panel distribute power from the hot buses to individual circuits. Each breaker snaps over an angled tab on one of the hot buses. Once pushed onto the tab (the main panel turned on), the breaker provides power through the wire that is connected to its terminal screw. A standard-tab hot bus will accept only standard full-size breakers; a split-tab hot bus can accept either twin (dual) or half-size breakers. A twin breaker consists of two breakers installed within the space usually occupied by a single breaker.

Twin breakers are used when you don't have enough room in a panel for all the breakers you need. New panels physically limit the number of twin breakers that may be used.

Hot Buses

When the main breaker is turned on, electricity flows through the two hot buses, or legs. These two vertical metal strips, normally aluminum or copper, extend below the main breaker to the bottom of the panel. They are electrically isolated (separated) from the panel frame. The voltage between one of the buses and the grounded bar equals 120 volts. The voltage from bus to bus equals 240 volts. This is the same voltage level that comes from the utility transformer. The main breaker acts like an on-off switch. When the breaker is on, power is carried through the circuit breaker that serves the fixture, appliance, etc. If it is a 120-volt light fixture, the current will leave the breaker and go through the black hot wire to the light. It returns through a white wire from the light, directly to the neutral bus. If an appliance requires 240 volts, such as a baseboard heater, then current flows through one side of the double-pole breaker, goes through the heating element, and returns through the other hot wire to the second pole on the breaker. No neutral is required. In either case, if the wire is carrying more current than is safe, the circuit breaker will automatically trip.

A standard hot-bus tab will only accommodate a full-size breaker.

A split tab can accommodate a twin breaker or a full-size breaker. Do not attempt to fit a twin breaker in a standard hot-bus tab.

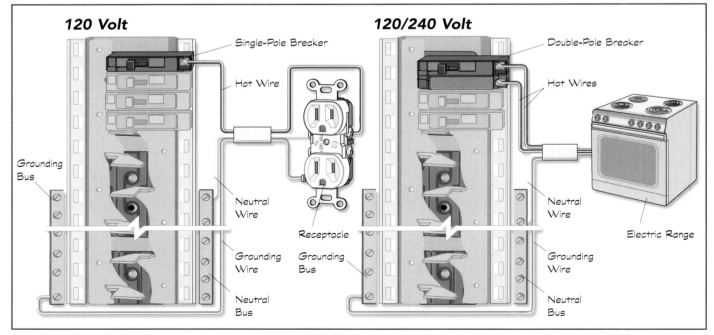

120 Volt

Single-Pole Breaker

Hot Wire

Grounding Bus

Neutral Wire

Receptacle

Grounding Wire

Grounding Bus

Neutral Bus

120/240 Volt

Double-Pole Breaker

Hot Wires

Neutral Wire

Electric Range

Grounding Wire

Neutral Bus

Power rated at 120 volts travels from a black wire on a single-pole circuit breaker to the device. It returns through a white wire from the device to the neutral bus. In a 120/240 volt circuit, 240-volt power flows from one pole of a double-pole circuit breaker to the appliance and back to the second pole on the breaker. Additionally, 120-volt power that runs the lights, clock, and timer travels through a hot wire and back on a neutral white wire.

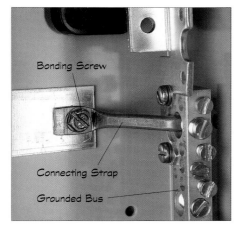

A panel frame is usually bonded (connected) to a grounded bus by a short metal strap running between the green bonding screw on the panel and a terminal on the bus.

Bonding Screw

Connecting Strap

Grounded Bus

A large lug on the neutral bus connects the neutral cable from the utility line to the main panel.

Oversize Wire Lug

Use other large lugs to connect any neutral wire that is too big to fit into a standard screw terminal.

Neutral and Grounding Buses

As mentioned earlier, the two aluminum bus bars running parallel to the hot buses are known as the neutral and grounding buses. All white insulated neutral wires connect to the neutral bus, while all bare or green grounding wires connect to the grounding bus. In the main panel, the NEC also requires that the metal panel frame be connected to the neutral and grounding buses. This is commonly done using a bonding (connecting) screw and strap supplied with the panel box. The strap grounds the panel frame; if a bare hot wire touches it, the breaker will trip, preventing electrocution.

On all 120-volt circuits, when power returns from the device or appliance, it reenters the main panel through a white neutral wire. The white neutral wire is connected to the grounded neutral bus, which is connected to the grounded neutral conductor in the service entrance cable. From here the current returns through the meter to the utility transformer.

The neutral bus contains two large lugs, in addition to the many smaller screw terminals. The neutral service conductor that comes from the meter is connected to the larger lug. The other lug provides a terminal for any neutral conductor that is too large to fit under one of the smaller screws on the bus.

Installation

In new installations, a main panel is mounted back-to-back with the utility meter. This saves the expense of running cable and having to install a second cutoff panel near the meter base, as required by most local codes. Maintain clearances at front of the panel at least 3 feet deep by 2 feet 6 inches wide by 6 feet 6 inches high. The panel must be readily accessible in an emergency.

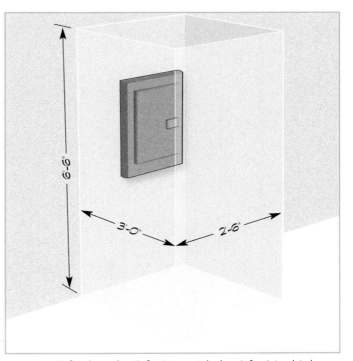

6'-6"

3'-0"

2'-6"

An area 3 ft. deep by 2 ft. 6 in. wide by 6 ft. 6 in. high must be kept clear in front of a service panel so that the panel will be readily accessible in an emergency.

Fuses and Circuit Breakers

Fuses

The fuse was the most common type of circuit protection in homes prior to World War II. Fuses are still used in many older homes. The two most common types of fuses are the plug, or glass fuse, and the cartridge fuse. Plug fuses control 120-volt circuits and are commonly available in sizes ranging from 15 to 30 amps. Inside a plug fuse is a metal strip that extends from the fuse's center contact to the threaded base. The narrow portion of the strip is called the element. If the circuit is overloaded, the element will burn, disconnecting the circuit and blowing the fuse. Cartridge fuses for residential use control 240-volt circuits and typically range in size from 30 to 100 amps. The element in a cartridge fuse runs down the center of the cartridge and is surrounded by a fireproof material that resembles sand.

Most fuse panels in use today are probably quite old. It is rather common for fuse boxes like these to require troubleshooting. Loose connections in an old fuse holder may produce enough heat to instantaneously vaporize a fuse element. If a fuse or fuse holder is dis-

An obsolete fuse box, such as the one shown here, is commonly found in older homes. Such boxes are frequently in need of troubleshooting or replacement.

Fuse Types

Glass Fuses

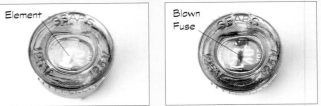

Glass, or plug, fuses are commonly found in older homes. Never replace a fuse with one of larger capacity. It's a fire hazard because the fuse will allow enough current through the wire to damage the wire insulation. A metal element inside the fuse will burn and blow out a correctly sized fuse (right), indicating an overload or short circuit if the current exceeds capacity.

Cartridge Fuses

A 60-amp cartridge fuse may be used as the main fuse in an older home. Cartridge fuses range from 30 to 100 amps. A cartridge fuse contains an element not unlike that in a glass fuse, except that it is embedded in nonflammable material (right).

Type S Fuses

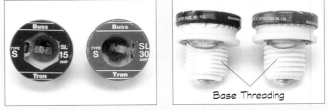

The Type S fuse was designed to replace the standard glass fuse. Each Type S fuse size has a different base-threading configuration (right) to prevent a homeowner from installing a high-amp fuse in a low-amp fuse socket.

Time-Delay Fuses

Some glass fuses are designed to withstand a temporary surge in power without blowing. This type of fuse should be marked "time-delay" on the edge.

colored (brown or black) or if burn or melt spots are obvious, it is recommended that you replace the entire fuse panel with a circuit-breaker panel.

Replacing a fuse with another one that has a higher amperage rating can allow excessive current on a circuit wire, damaging the wire insulation and possibly causing a fire. Type S fuses were developed to solve this problem. Because each fuse size has a different base threading design, only one size can be installed in a particular circuit.

Sometimes a fuse may blow because of a momentary surge of power coming into the electrical system. Another type of fuse, called a time-delay fuse, can withstand this kind of power surge without blowing.

Fuse Overload. When a circuit is overloaded and the fuse element melts, disconnecting, or opening, the circuit, the damage to the element can be seen easily by looking through the fuse glass.

An overload occurs whenever the amount of current drawn by one or more fixtures or appliances exceeds the fuse rating. You determine a fuse rating by the gauge of wire that the fuse protects. In the absence of a fuse (or other circuit protection), when devices use too much current, the wire becomes overheated, damaging the insulation, possibly causing a fire. Some fuses can be reset rather than replaced (not recommended). Be careful that this type of fuse fits properly into your panel and does not interfere with door closure.

Short Circuits and Ground Faults. A short circuit occurs when a hot wire touches a neutral wire. This sometimes happens by accident when wires are improperly connected. It may also happen when an appliance malfunctions or a circuit is improperly wired. In any case, a short circuit will result in a massive current flow through the fuse, causing the element to destruct and open the circuit. When this happens, the view through the glass on a plug fuse will be obscured by a black/silver discoloration. If this happens to a cartridge fuse, however, it will reveal no visible sign that it has been blown. You must test the fuse using a multitester. (See "Testing Fuses," page 54.)

A ground fault occurs when a hot wire touches a grounding wire or any grounded surface. As in a short circuit, massive current flow will cause the fuse to blow. Unfortunately, you cannot tell a short circuit from a ground fault by looking at the blown fuse.

When a black hot wire comes into contact with a white neutral wire, a short circuit results. This often occurs when wires are poorly connected.

When a short circuit or ground fault occurs, a massive amount of current will surge through a glass fuse, causing the element to be instantaneously vaporized.

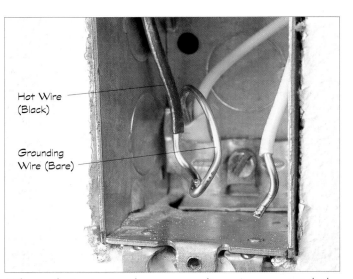

When a hot wire touches a grounding wire or grounded metal appliance frame, a ground fault will occur.

Testing. A plug fuse will sometimes look perfectly functional through the glass but actually be inoperable. The element may have separated in a way that is not visible, or it may have become detached from the screw shell or center contact. To test a plug fuse, use a continuity tester or multi-tester to check the continuity between the center contact and the screw shell. Always test a cartridge fuse before installing it to determine its condition unless it is apparent that it is badly burned or disintegrating.

SMART TIP

Testing Fuses

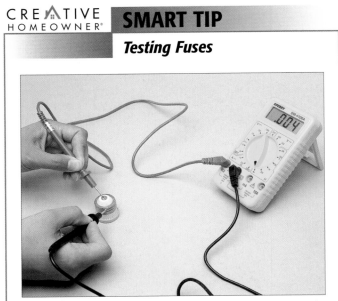

To perform a continuity test on a glass fuse, touch one probe of a multi-tester to the center contact and the other to the screw shell. A zero reading means the fuse is working properly.

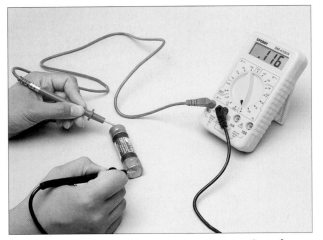

Test a cartridge fuse by touching one probe of a multi-tester to each end terminal on the fuse. The knob setting shown will give an audible signal as well as a meter reading.

Circuit Breakers

Circuit breakers have replaced fuses as the preferred type of circuit protection. Technically, they are called molded-case circuit breakers, or MCCBs. Circuit breakers use a two-part system for protecting circuit wiring. When a small overload is on the circuit, a thermal strip will heat up and open, or trip, the circuit. When a massive amount of current comes through very quickly, as in a ground fault or short circuit, an electromagnet gives the thermal strip a boost. The greater the amount of trip current, the faster the breaker will trip.

The most important advantage circuit breakers have over fuses is that they can be easily reset; you don't have to buy a new one every time an appliance draws excessive current. When a breaker is tripped, it won't work unless you throw it all the way to the off position before you turn it back on again. Another characteristic of circuit breakers is that they are air-ambient-compensated—the hotter the air around them gets, they sooner they will trip. For example, if all the circuit breakers around a specific 20-amp breaker are running hot, because of an excessive flow of current, the 20-amp breaker may trip at only 18 amps.

Residential circuit breakers typically range in size from 15 to 60 amps, increasing at intervals of 5 amps. Single-pole breakers rated for 15 to 20 amps control most 120-volt general-purpose circuits. Double-pole breakers rated for 20 to 60 amps control 240-volt circuits.

Standard circuit breakers are universal and have clips on the bottom that snap onto the hot-bus tabs in the panel box. Contact with the hot bus brings power into the breaker. Be aware, however, that some manufacturers

Two contacts, or pressure clips, on the underside of a circuit breaker snap over a hot-bus tab in the main panel. These contacts bring power into the breaker.

make breakers with wire clips that mount on the side. These clips slide over the tab on the hot bus, requiring you to remove one or more of the other breakers to get at the one you want.

Common Breaker Types. In addition to single- and double-pole breakers, quad breakers, GFCI breakers, and surge-protection devices are also available. Single-pole breakers supply power to 120-volt loads such as receptacle and light circuits. A hot black or red wire is usually connected to the breaker. Single-pole breakers come full size or in a two-in-one configuration (twin). The latter type will only fit into a panel having a split-tab hot bus.

Double-pole breakers provide power to 240-volt appliances such as electric water heaters and dryers. If a standard NM cable is used as the conductors, both the black and the white wire are connected to the breaker. The white wire must be marked with black tape at both ends. Larger double-pole circuits have two black conductors in the circuit.

Specialty Breakers. A quad breaker falls within the half-size breaker family and can contain several configurations within one unit. It may, for example, contain two double-pole circuits, such as a double-pole 30-amp and a double-pole 20-amp circuit; it may have two single-pole circuits and one double pole; or it may provide power to some other combination of circuits. The advantage of a quad breaker is that it takes up half the space of a standard breaker. The panel, though, must be specially designed to accept quad breakers. Furthermore, if the panel is too small, it may end up resembling a tightly interwoven nest of wires.

A GFCI circuit breaker fits into the main panel just like a standard circuit breaker. On its face is a test button but no reset. If properly installed, pressing the test button places a deliberate, preset current imbalance (6 milliamperes) on the line to verify that the breaker will trip when there is an unintended imbalance. When tripped, the breaker arm will go to a halfway off position, cutting power to the circuit. The circuit cannot be reset unless someone first turns the breaker arm completely off.

At first glance, a surge-protection device can be confusing. You will see a device that looks like a double-pole body. This type of device also has two lights that glow when power is applied to the panel. Nevertheless, a surge-protection device connects to the buses in the same as any other circuit breaker.

Breaker Types

A single-pole breaker is the most prevalent type of circuit breaker found in residential use. It will power anything that requires 120-volt current.

A double-pole breaker is used with a 240-volt appliance, such as a 20-amp base-board heater or a 30-amp clothes dryer.

Use a quad breaker to serve two double-pole circuits in the same space as one standard double-pole breaker.

A GFCI circuit breaker will cut power to a circuit when it is tripped by an imbalance in current flow through the wires.

A surge-protection device provides protection for an entire service panel and simply installs in place of two single-pole breakers.

Limits. Circuit breakers are limited in protecting wires, and therefore life and property. Breakers other than GFCI cannot prevent electric shock, for instance. Although breakers trip at 15 amps and above, it only takes about 0.06 amp to electrocute someone. Circuit breakers cannot prevent overheating of a fixture or appliance or other device, and they can't prevent low-level faults. For a breaker to trip, a fault must occur when enough current is being demanded to exceed the trip current of the breaker. Breakers cannot trip fast enough to completely block lightning surges from entering the house circuits. They cannot prevent fires within appliances. Circuit breakers are meant to save the wiring to the appliance—not the appliance itself.

Electrical Boxes

Types and Capacities

Electrical boxes are used for a variety of purposes, such as holding receptacles and switches, housing wire junctions, and supporting ceiling fans and lights. Many types of boxes are made for different purposes, and they can be metal or nonmetallic (plastic or fiberglass). Today, plastic boxes are the type most commonly used. However, metal boxes are still found in many homes. Check code requirements before installing electrical boxes. Plastic boxes have the advantages of low cost and simplicity of installation.

Electrical boxes come in standard shapes for each type of use. For example, they may be shallow for furred walls, wider for ganged arrangements, or waterproof for outdoor applications. Be sure to use the right box. No matter what the purpose, though, every box must be covered and accessible. It is also important not to use a box that is too small for the size and number of wires it will house. An electrical box can hold only a limited number of wires. Determining how many wires a box can safely hold can be complicated. Requirements change as the code changes.

Although plastic boxes are labeled according to the number of wires they can house, and/or their size in cubic inches, metal boxes are not. Cubic-inch capacities for a variety of metal boxes are listed in NEC Table 370-16(a). The safest way to overcome this problem is by purchasing the deepest box that will fit into your stud wall—one that is 3¼ to 3½ inches deep. For a single-gang box, this will provide 20.3 cubic inches of wiring space. Use common sense, and don't overcrowd any box. (See "Maximum Wires in a Box," page 73.)

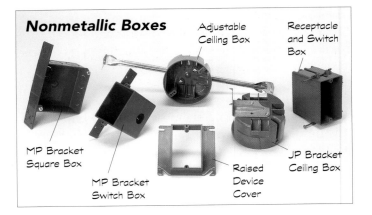

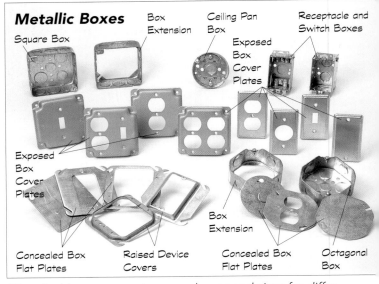

Electrical boxes come in many shapes and sizes for different purposes and are made of metal, plastic, or fiberglass. Though use of plastic boxes is widespread today, they don't meet code requirements for some jobs. Splice boxes are required for all wire junctions.

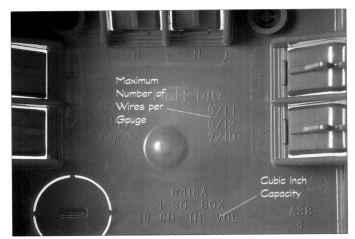

The inside of a nonmetallic electrical box is labeled with the cubic-inch capacity of the box as well as the maximum permitted number of wires per gauge.

Plastic Boxes

The most common type of plastic box is the single-gang, nail-on box. It has two integral nails that fasten it to stud framing. This type of box is commonly used in new construction and is available in several depths—the deepest having the greatest capacity. Make certain not to purchase ones that are too shallow even if you must shop at several stores to find them.

Box Placement. When attaching nail-on boxes to studs, leave enough of the box edge protruding to bring the box flush with the finished wall. If you don't know the depth of the finished wall, use an adjustable box. Once installed, this box can be moved in and out on a slider to match the finished wall depth. The slider also allows you to change from a single box to a double without ripping apart the wall. You just unscrew and remove the single box, cut the opening to the new size, and insert the new box on the slider.

All plastic boxes must be installed carefully because they can be easily damaged. If a plastic box is hit with a hammer or if nails are driven in too far, the box will distort or break. Drive nails until they are snug, but no farther.

You'll sometimes need more than one switch in a single location. For these occasions, double, triple, and quad boxes are available. Be aware that a quad box may require an additional stud for support. Also note that quad switching can be very confusing because of the number of switches involved.

Ceiling Boxes. Ceiling pan boxes are typically used for ceiling fixtures. Named for its shape, a ceiling pan box may be designed to hold a fixture, such as a ceiling fan/light, weighing up to 35 pounds. If this is the case, it will be labeled. This type of box can be screwed or nailed directly into a ceiling joist. It is preferable, though, to screw the box into a wooden support such as a flat 2×6 spanning between two joists. A box having integral nails can break easily and will not support weight well. A fixture that weighs more than 50 pounds, such as a chandelier (35 for a paddle fan), cannot be suspended from a box. Instead, it must be supported independently from the box. Another way to mount an overhead fixture is by using an approved box with an adjustable bar hanger attached to it. Mounted between two overhead joists, this type of box can be positioned anywhere along the bar between the two joists.

Plastic Box Types

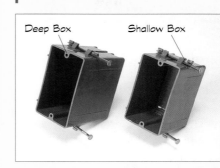

Deep Box   Shallow Box

Plastic nail-on boxes are available in many sizes, shallow or deep. Use the deepest box that can fit your space when installing receptacles, switches, and wires.

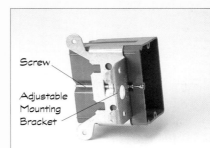

Screw

Adjustable Mounting Bracket

Adjustable boxes provide for variations in finished wall thicknesses, even after they are installed. Turning a screw on the face of the box adjusts it in or out.

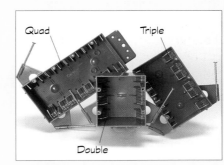

Quad   Triple

Double

Multiple-switch boxes—double, triple, and quad. A quad box should be attached to two framing studs, one on each side, to prevent wobbling.

ACCEPTABLE FOR FAN SUPPORT
SCREWS PROVIDED MUST BE USED
2 PCS - #8 x 3 1/2" (P/N G429)
2 PCS - #8 x 1" (P/N G430)
PATENT NO. 5522577   LBL720

Fixture Supporting Label

Ceiling Pan Box

Ceiling pan boxes for overhead fixtures bolt to framing. If a fixture weighs up to 50 lbs., the box must be marked "For Support"; if it weighs more, it must be supported independently.

Some ceiling-fixture boxes are supported between joists with an adjustable bar hanger. You adjust the fixture location by sliding the box along the bar.

Most plastic boxes, regardless of purpose, have internal clips that clamp onto the NM cable where it is inserted into the box. Open these clips using a flat-blade screwdriver before inserting the cable. Use a screwdriver to push the clips aside if you need to pull the cable out again.

Metal Boxes

Though more expensive and harder to work with than plastic boxes, metal boxes have some advantages. For one, they are available in more configurations than plastic boxes because they have been around longer. Basic boxes include the switch or receptacle box (rectangular) and the fixture or equipment outlet box (square or octagonal). One of the greatest advantages of metal boxes is that they are much stronger than plastic boxes. Because they can stand up to greater abuse, they are suitable for use in exposed locations such as unfinished basements and garages. To accommodate different finished wall thicknesses, some metal boxes have a built-in depth gauge.

Another important advantage is that some metal boxes have removable sides that allow additional boxes to be added, or ganged, to accommodate more than one device. A single-gang box, for instance, can be expanded to become a quad box.

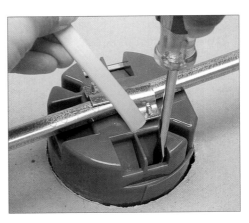

Most plastic boxes have internal clips that automatically clamp NM cables in place. You need to pry the clips with a screwdriver to insert cables in the box.

A depth gauge marked on an electrical box tells the installer where to align the box on a framing stud so that its face will be flush with the finished drywall.

CRE▲TIVE HOMEOWNER®   **SMART TIP**

Adding Space to a Metal Gangable Box

1 To add space to a gangable box, use a screwdriver to remove the retaining screw on the side of the existing box to be expanded, and take out the side panel.

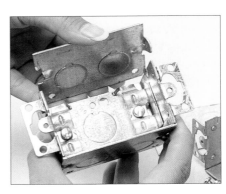

2 Remove the opposite panel from a second, add-on box.

3 Remove the retaining screw from the open side of the second box, and align the screw slot over the retaining screw on the open side of the first box.

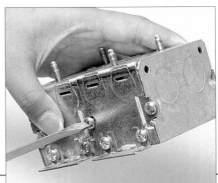

4 Tighten the retaining screw, creating one double-size box.

Bringing NM Cable into a Metal Box

To bring NM cable into a metal box, you must first remove one of the knockouts on the box. Some boxes have a pryout built into them that can easily be removed using a flat-blade screwdriver. Others have a circular knockout that must be punched out using a hammer and a screwdriver or knockout punch. Once the knockout hole is open, a cable clamp can be inserted into the opening. The clamp secures the cable in place and protects it from chafing against the sharp metal edges of the box opening.

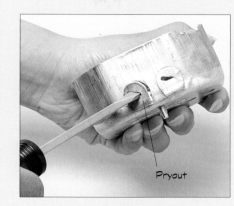

Some metal boxes have pryouts that can be removed using the flat blade of a screwdriver.

Pryout

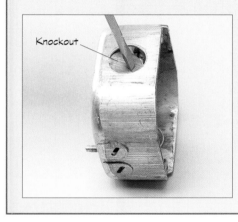

Knockout

Other boxes have knockouts that must be punched out with a hammer and screwdriver or with a special tool called a knockout punch.

Cable Clamp

A cable clamp screws into the pryout or knockout opening to secure the cable entering the box and protect it from chafing against the sharp edges of the opening.

Weatherproof Boxes

Boxes mounted outdoors must be watertight. One way to achieve this is by recessing a standard box with a watertight lid in an outside house wall. Another is to mount a watertight box with a watertight lid on the surface of the exterior wall.

The problem with either method is that once the lid is opened, the box is no longer watertight; the interior is exposed. The NEC requires that when unattended equipment is left plugged into an exterior outlet, a special box or lid must be used that will keep the outlet weatherproof even while the plug is in place [Section 410-57(b)].

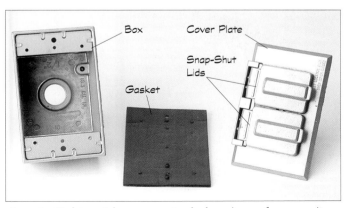

Box Cover Plate Snap-Shut Lids Gasket

A watertight outdoor-receptacle box has a foam sealing gasket and a cover with snap-shut receptacle lids. The box is watertight only when the lids are shut.

Protective Lid Cord Notch

A weatherproof box must remain watertight even while the receptacle is in use. This type of box must have a lid that closes over the plug-in cord.

Special Boxes

Special types of electrical boxes include pancake and cut-in boxes. Pancake boxes are commonly used to mount outside entrance lights. Because of their low silhouette, they can be attached to the surface of an exterior wall yet remain hidden beneath the dome of the exterior light.

Retrofit cut-in boxes are available in metallic and non-metallic forms. Both types have flat lips, or drywall ears, on the front and some type of adjustable wing on the back. The wings expand outwardly, grabbing the back of the finished wall surface, while the metal ears on the front keep the box from falling into the opening. Metal cut-in boxes are not as popular as fiberglass or plastic because they are more expensive, must be grounded, and often have limited room for wires.

▶ *Old-work, or cut-in, boxes are for retrofits and are designed for installation in existing walls. Once inserted into a wall opening, screws are adjusted to expand side wings that grasp the back of finished drywall or plaster. Cut-in boxes come in the same shapes and sizes as standard electrical boxes and are made of metal, plastic, or some other composite material like fiberglass. Ceiling cut-in boxes should not be used to support heavy fixtures, however, because drywall is their only support.*

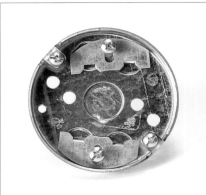

Pancake boxes are aptly named because of their flat, round shape. They contain minimal cubic volume and are designed to fit under the dome of an exterior light.

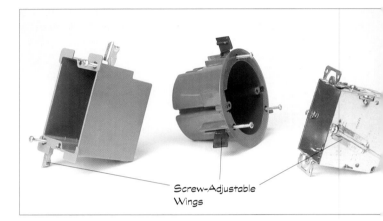

Screw-Adjustable Wings

Installing a Cut-In Box

To install a receptacle, switch, or ceiling cut-in box, first trace a template of the box on the surface of the wall or ceiling. Using a keyhole or saber saw, cut the opening for the box. Insert the box in the opening; then adjust and tighten the wings against the back of the drywall.

1 Trace a template of the box on the wall or ceiling surface, and cut the opening for the box.

2 Insert the box in the opening, and adjust the side wings.

3 Tighten the adjusting screws to bring the wings firmly against the back of the finished wall (view from inside the wall).

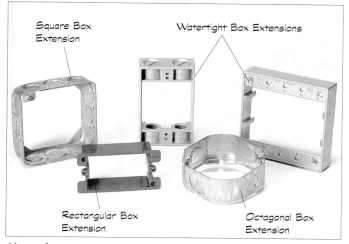

Use a box extension to increase the volume available for wiring inside an electrical box. Watertight box extensions are also available for outdoor work.

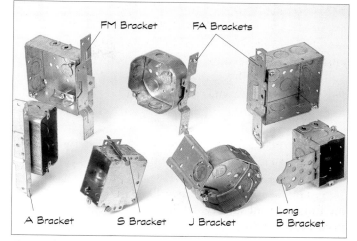

Several types of brackets exist for mounting metal electrical boxes—some are designed for specific functions, while others have multiple uses.

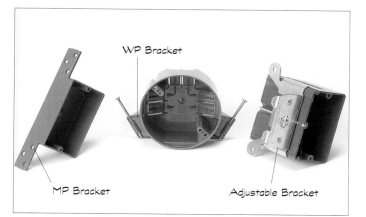

Fewer bracket styles are available for plastic than for metal boxes. Most have nailing spurs that permit them to be securely fastened to stud framing.

Box Extensions

Box extensions, or extension rings, are used to add wiring capacity to a box. If a finished ceiling or wall surface lies beyond a box front or more space is needed for wiring within the box, simply add an extension ring. A watertight box extension can be used when tapping into an existing outdoor receptacle or junction box for power.

Mounting Brackets

Brackets exist for mounting every type of metallic and nonmetallic box under a wide variety of installation conditions. Though some brackets are used for only one purpose, others may be used for several types of boxes. Each bracket type attaches a box differently. An A bracket, for example, attaches to the face and side of a stud, while a B bracket only attaches to the face and a D bracket only to the side of a stud. Metal framing-stud mounting brackets

such as the MS snap-in bracket are also available. Other brackets are used for gangable boxes and boxes that must be backset or offset from stud work. Mounting brackets for plastic boxes are available in fewer styles. Because of they are less durable, nonmetallic boxes are more likely to have nailing spurs than actual brackets. Whether you are using metallic or nonmetallic boxes, discuss your wiring plans with your electrical supply retailer to be sure you are getting the type of brackets you need.

Receptacles

Duplex Receptacles

Different types of receptacles are manufactured for a variety of residential purposes. Standard duplex receptacles are the most common type available and are used to power fixtures, appliances, and residential equipment rated for 110 to 125 volts. This type of duplex receptacle has a long neutral slot, a short hot slot, and an arch-shaped grounding hole. This slot configuration guarantees that a plug can only be inserted into the receptacle one way—so it will be properly polarized and grounded.

Nongrounded Receptacles

In an older home, you may encounter receptacles that are likely to have only two slots and no grounding hole. If the two slots are identical, then the receptacle is neither grounded nor polarized. If one slot is long and the other short, then the receptacle is not grounded but is polarized. On a nonpolarized receptacle, the neutral and hot wires can be connected to either screw terminal.

Appliance Receptacles

Other types of receptacles have slot configurations that limit their use to specific appliances or groups of appliances. For example, the hot slot on a large 20-amp appliance or tool receptacle is T-shaped, while the hot and neutral slots on an air-conditioner receptacle are horizontal instead of vertical. Appliances that draw high currents, like clothes dryers and ranges, use a single dedicated receptacle. Each type has a slot configuration designated only for the particular appliance being powered. The amperage and voltage are clearly marked on the receptacle, along with the number assigned by the National Electrical Manufacturers Association (NEMA) and the listing mark of the Underwriters Laboratories (UL). The NEMA code ensures that you are buying the correct receptacle for the appliance, and the UL-listing label indicates that the receptacle has passed rigorous testing standards.

Isolated-Ground and GFCI Receptacles

An isolated-ground receptacle is a specialized, orange-colored device. It has an insulated grounding screw and is primarily used to protect sensitive electronic equipment, like computers, from disruptive or damaging electrical power surges. A GFCI (ground-fault circuit-interrupter) receptacle is a special duplex receptacle that protects you from electrical shock. When incoming and returning current are unequal, the GFCI cuts off the circuit in a fraction of a second, before you can feel a shock. This type of receptacle is required by code in wet locations, such as bathrooms, kitchens, basements, garages, and outdoors.

Receptacle Types

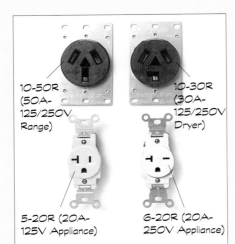

Terminal Screws

Push-In Terminals

Standard duplex receptacles have terminal screws for connecting wires. Some also have push-in terminals where 14-gauge wires can be inserted, but these connect less securely and are not recommended.

Older receptacles have only two slots. If both are the same size, as in these outlets, the receptacle is neither grounded nor polarized. If one slot is longer than the other, the receptacle is polarized but not grounded.

10-50R (50A-125/250V Range)

10-30R (30A-125/250V Dryer)

5-20R (20A-125V Appliance)

6-20R (20A-250V Appliance)

High-voltage appliance receptacles have specific slot configurations that are designed to prevent you from plugging an appliance into the wrong circuit.

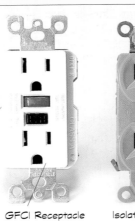

GFCI Receptacle

Isolated-Ground Receptacle

A GFCI receptacle protects the user against electric shock, while an isolated-ground receptacle protects sensitive equipment from power surges.

Switches

Types and Designations

A switch controls the flow of power in an electrical circuit. When a switch is on, electricity flows through the circuit from its source to the point of use. The standard switch used in residential work is the toggle switch, sometimes called a snap switch. Other types include dimmer, pilot-light, timer, and electronic switches. Switches are further categorized by quality and usage. The standard, or construction grade, switch is rated for 15 amps and is the grade and type most commonly found in homes. Also available are tech, commercial, and industrial-grade switches, which are higher in quality and cost.

Toggle Switches

Toggle switches have evolved over time. Now you can perform many functions throughout a home with them. But the basic function of a toggle switch remains the same—that of closing a circuit to apply power and opening it to cut off power. A standard, single-pole toggle switch turns a light on from only one location. But switches may also control a circuit from two (three-way switch) or three (four-way switch) locations. A single-pole switch has two terminal screws. Only this one switch can control the circuit. The hot wire connects to one terminal, and the outgoing wire to the other. A three-way switch has three terminals. One is marked COM or "common"; the hot wire connects to this terminal. The other terminals are switch leads. A four-way switch has four terminals. One four-way switch and two three-way switches can be used to control

Some of the switches you can buy include toggle, pilot light, clock-timer, time delay, automatic, programmable, and motion sensor.

one outlet or fixture from three different places. A similar-looking switch, the double-pole switch, is used to control 240-volt appliances and is differentiated from the four-way switch by the ON and OFF markings on the toggle. Switches also come with different terminal positions for side, end, front, and back wiring. Back-wired switches have terminal holes instead of screws.

Dimmer Switches

A dimmer switch is used to control the brightness, or intensity, of light emitted from a light fixture by increasing or decreasing the flow of electricity to the fixture. Dimmers may have standard toggle switches, rotary dials, sliders, or automatic electronic sensors that respond to the level of ambient light in a room and adjust accordingly. They can also be either single-pole or three-way switches.

CRE**A**TIVE
HOMEOWNER®

SMART TIP

Reading a Switch

Switches must be marked with labels that represent different ratings and approvals. These labels convey important information about safety and usage. The designation UND. LAB-INC. LIST, for example, means that the switch has been listed by the Underwriters Laboratories, an independent testing agency. AC ONLY indicates that the switch can only handle alternating current. CO/ALR specifies that the switch can be connected to either copper or aluminum wires. A switch marked CU can be used only with copper and not with aluminum wires. The amp and voltage ratings are given by designations like 15A–120V, which means that the switch is approved for use with circuits that carry 15 amps of current at 120 volts.

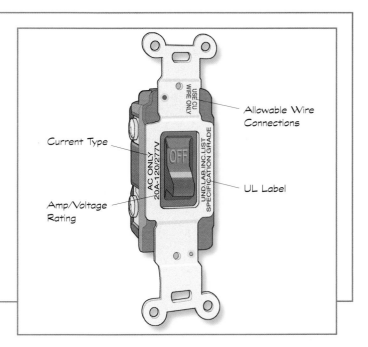

Switch Types

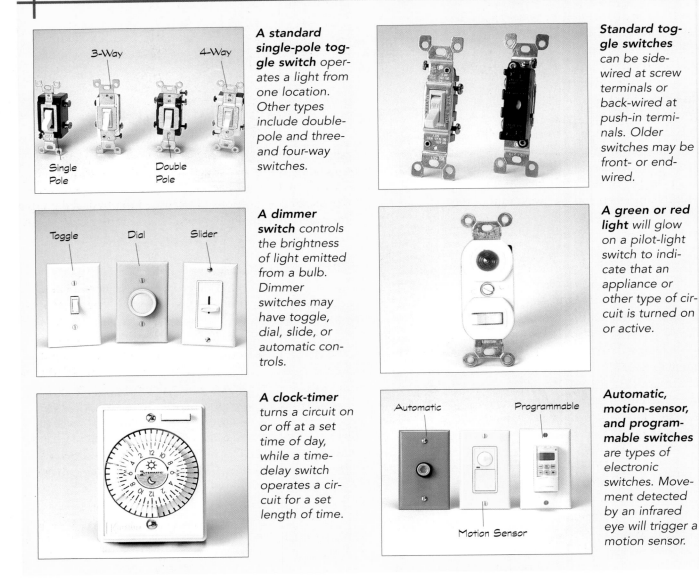

A standard single-pole toggle switch operates a light from one location. Other types include double-pole and three- and four-way switches.

3-Way   4-Way
Single Pole   Double Pole

A standard single-pole toggle switch operates a light from one location. Other types include double-pole and three- and four-way switches.

Standard toggle switches can be side-wired at screw terminals or back-wired at push-in terminals. Older switches may be front- or end-wired.

Toggle   Dial   Slider

A dimmer switch controls the brightness of light emitted from a bulb. Dimmer switches may have toggle, dial, slide, or automatic controls.

A green or red light will glow on a pilot-light switch to indicate that an appliance or other type of circuit is turned on or active.

A clock-timer turns a circuit on or off at a set time of day, while a time-delay switch operates a circuit for a set length of time.

Automatic   Programmable
Motion Sensor

Automatic, motion-sensor, and programmable switches are types of electronic switches. Movement detected by an infrared eye will trigger a motion sensor.

Pilot-Light Switches

Pilot-light switches are usually found on appliances but are especially useful for controlling remote fixtures, like porch, attic, basement, and garage lights, because they can let you know whether or not a light is on or off. When a fixture or appliance is turned on, the pilot light is illuminated.

Timer Switches

Timer switches come in two varieties: clock and time delay. A clock-timer can be set to turn on a fixture or other device at a preset time of day. An example would be a thermostat set to turn down the heat during the day when no one is home. Another example would be a switch that turns on security lights in your home after dark or when you are away on vacation. This type of switch can also be used to operate a lawn-sprinkler system. In contrast, a time-delay switch is designed to allow a fixture or appliance to operate for a set period of time and then shut off. An example would be a heat lamp or exhaust fan in a bathroom.

Electronic Switches

Electronic switches offer automatic control of lights and other devices. As a matter of safety, they can be overridden by using manual switch levers. An automatic switch allows a user to simply wave a hand in front of the switch to turn it on or off. An infrared beam emitted from the switch detects the movement of the user's hand and activates an electronic signal to operate the switch. A motion-sensor switch operates the same way but is designed for security lighting. When someone or something passes in front of the infrared eye, the light is activated. When the motion ceases, the light will turn itself off after a set period of time has elapsed. Outdoor perimeter or garage lighting is commonly on this type of switch. A programmable switch is a digitally controlled version of the clock-timer. It can be programmed to turn lights and other devices on and off several times a day at specified or random times. For security, this type of switch is especially advantageous when you are away from home.

Low-Voltage Transformers
Types and Applications

Many types of household fixtures and equipment require much less power to operate than is provided by standard 120-volt house current: door chimes, low-voltage outdoor and pool lights, telephones, antennas, and thermostats are just a few examples. (See Chapter 6, "Low-Voltage and Specialty Lighting," pages 166–183.) A low-voltage transformer steps down 120-volt house current to 30 volts or less. Some fixtures may come with a built-in transformer that serves only that device. A remote transformer is externally connected and can control several devices. A special weatherproof transformer is used to power low-voltage lighting outdoors. The most common type of transformer used in residential work, however, is a simple box-mounted transformer that attaches to a junction box. Both the supply and device wires are connected to the transformer wires inside the junction box. The current is stepped down by the transformer before proceeding to the equipment.

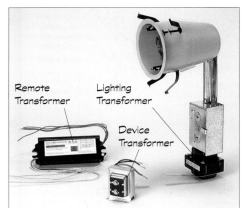

Low-voltage transformers may be installed separately or come as an integral part of a fixture, but they all step down line voltage.

Raceways and Conduit
Raceway Application

In residential construction, raceways house surface wiring. This eliminates fishing cable through existing walls, allowing wire to be run along masonry surfaces. Raceways protect cable in enclosed plastic or metal casings that are permanently attached to walls, baseboards, ceilings, or floors. Raceway wiring includes receptacles, switches, and ceiling fixtures. Special connectors turn corners, providing intersections to extend branches. Raceways are grounded by an equipment-grounding conductor, a metal casing, or both. (See Chapter 4, "Wiring Methods," pages 68–119.) The NEC limits raceway use to dry locations not exposed to physical damage. Raceways are permitted to contain a certain number and size of wires for each intended use. (Section 352).

Raceway Components

Raceway components are available in metal or plastic and must be joined mechanically and electrically to protect wires. Raceway fasteners must be flush with the channel surface so that they don't cut the wires. Like metal, plastic raceways must be flame-retardant; resistant to moisture, impact, and crushing; and installed in a dry location. Components include channel sections, elbows, T-connectors, and electrical boxes.

Raceway wiring is connected in the same way as conventional wiring. A backing plate and extension fit over the electrical box, and the switch or receptacle mounts on the plate.

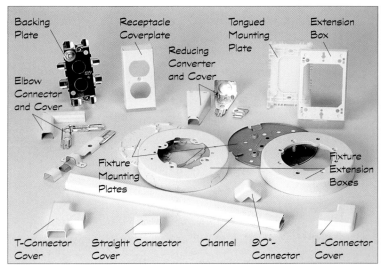

Typical raceway components include straight channel sections, elbows, T-connectors, extension boxes, plates, and covers.

► **Raceway receptacles** are conventionally wired. An existing box is extended with a plate and extension frame to accommodate the raceway channel.

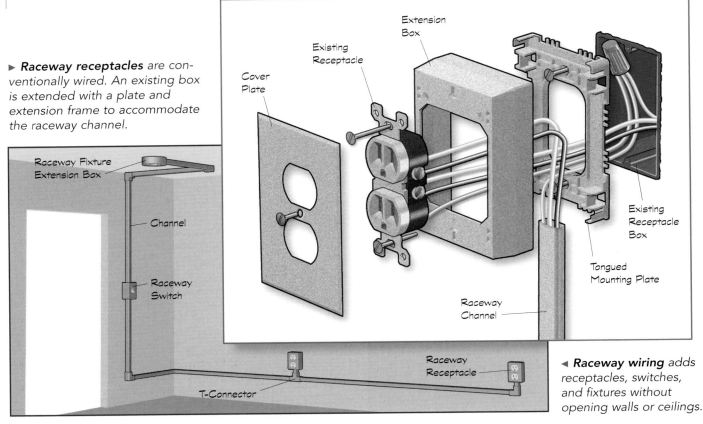

Cover Plate

Existing Receptacle

Extension Box

Raceway Fixture Extension Box

Channel

Raceway Switch

Existing Receptacle Box

Tongued Mounting Plate

Raceway Channel

T-Connector

Raceway Receptacle

◄ **Raceway wiring** adds receptacles, switches, and fixtures without opening walls or ceilings.

Conduit Types and Applications

Conduit in residential wiring protects service-entrance cable, outdoor cable, and wiring exposed to physical damage. Several types of metallic and nonmetallic conduit are manufactured. Each serves a different application. Metallic conduit used in residential work includes rigid metallic (steel or aluminum) conduit, intermediate metallic conduit (IMC), electrical metallic tubing (EMT), flexible metallic conduit in a liquid-tight polyvinyl chloride (PVC) cover, and helically wound flexible metallic conduit. Nonmetallic PVC conduit includes rigid nonmetallic and electrical nonmetallic tubing (ENT). Regardless of the type, make all your wiring connections in an accessible electrical box.

Conduit Components

Each conduit type uses connectors and fittings made only for that type. Rigid metallic conduit is threaded on both ends, with a preattached coupling on one end. The metal is usually galvanized and may be finished in enamel or plastic for use in corrosive environments. Rigid metallic conduit must be supported every 10 feet and within 3 feet of any connected junction box. Various straps are made for this purpose. Other fittings include compression connectors, elbows, couplings, and locknuts. Although its walls are thinner, IMC is similar to rigid metal conduit and uses the same connectors and fittings. EMT is thinner than rigid metallic conduit and IMC. Unlike rigid metal, it is not threaded and can only be used with its own connectors and fittings. Both IMC and EMT follow the same code requirements as rigid metallic conduit. Helically wound flexible metallic conduit is used in locations demanding tighter turns and where equipment vibrations occur. Liquid-tight flexible metallic conduit is used in locations subject to liquids and vapors, including burial underground, if so rated. Flexible metallic conduit must be supported every 4½ feet and within 1 foot of electrical boxes. Because it has higher resistance than rigid metal, it is independently grounded with an internal wire. Flexible metallic conduit requires special connectors and fittings.

Rigid nonmetallic conduit is used for underground wiring because it is lightweight and resistant to corrosion and moisture. ENT is permitted in wet indoor areas, in concrete slabs, or in any building, but must be concealed behind fire-rated drywall. Both types are toxic when burned, so check local codes to see whether they are permissable. Connectors and fittings for nonmetallic conduit are attached using approved cement. Bend the conduit by heating it with hot air or an infrared heater. Never use an open flame. Use a hacksaw to cut it. Code requires that nonmetallic conduit be supported every 3 to 8 feet, depending on size (NEC Table 347-8), and within 3 feet of a junction box.

Conduit Components

Several metallic and nonmetallic conduit types are generally used in residential work. Each type has specific uses and installation requirements.

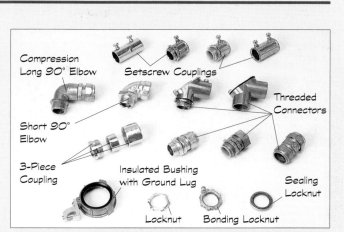

Connectors, elbows, couplings, locknuts, and bushings for rigid metallic and intermediate metallic conduit (IMC) must be made of metal.

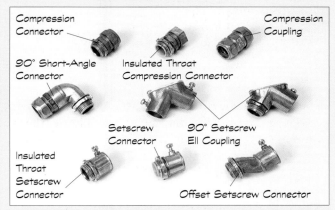

The connectors and fittings used to install electrical metallic tubing (EMT) are different from those used for rigid metallic and intermediate metallic conduit.

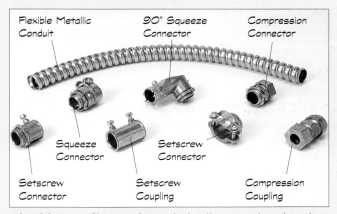

Flexible metallic conduit is helically wound and is also available in a liquid-tight version that is impervious to moisture. Like EMT, it must also use its own special connectors and fittings.

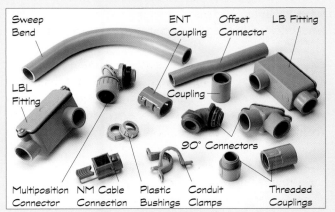

Some special connectors and fittings are required for rigid nonmetallic conduit and electrical nonmetallic tubing (ENT).

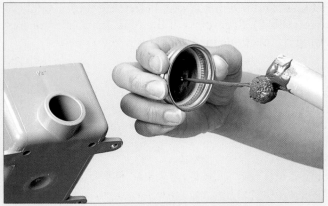

Nonmetallic conduit connectors and fittings are welded in place using a particular type of solvent called conduit cement.

Materials and Equipment

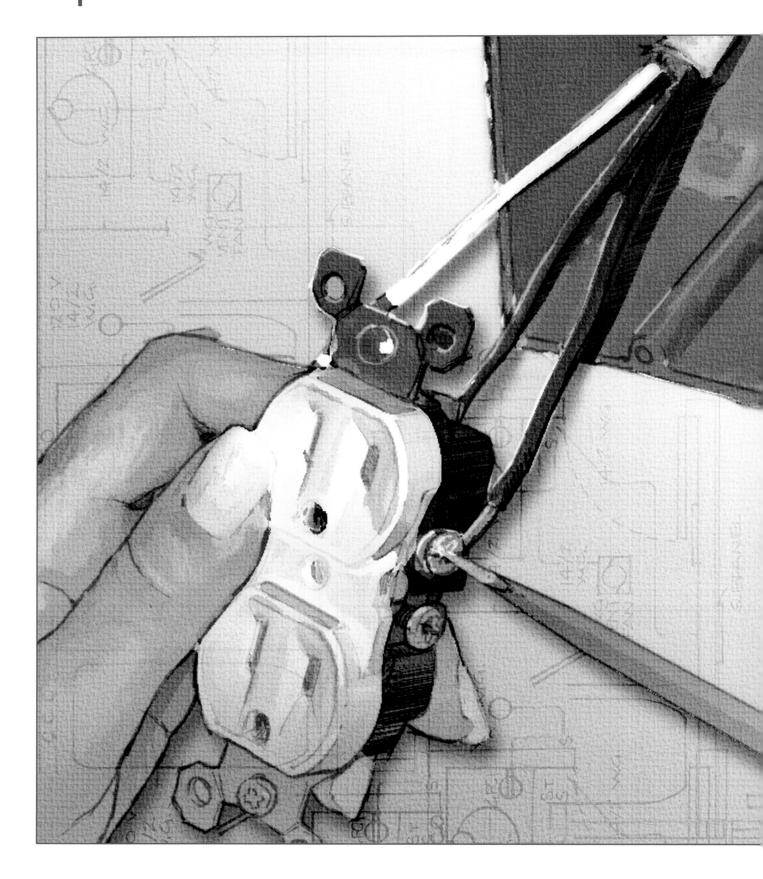

CHAPTER 4

Wiring Methods

Now that you've learned the fundamentals of electricity and acquainted yourself with the tools, materials, and equipment that you may need to complete an electrical project, it's time to acquire some basic wiring skills. Before you begin any wiring project, however, remember that safety comes first. Working on a given circuit means first knowing to which breaker or fuse the circuit is connected. If it hasn't already been done, this is a good time for you to chart the circuits in your home. (See page 70.)

Fuse and Circuit Breaker Capacities

Fuse or Circuit Breaker	Wire Gauge Capacity	Load Capacity
15-Amp Fuse / 15-Amp Circuit Breaker	14/2G	15 Amps
20-Amp Fuse / 20-Amp Circuit Breaker	12/2G	20 Amps
30-Amp Fuse / 30-Amp Circuit Breaker	10/2G	30 Amps

Basic Circuitry

Charting Circuits

Whether working with fuses or circuit breakers, you must know which switches, receptacles, fixtures, or equipment are on the circuits they control. You must also know how they work. There are many types of fuses and circuit breakers, each with its own function. The purpose of fuses and circuit breakers is to protect the wiring—not the appliance. Keep this in mind as you chart circuits, verifying that no fuse or circuit breaker has more amperage than the wire it is protecting. The maximum allowable current a wire can carry, measured in amps, is called its *ampacity*.

While you are inspecting your fuse box or breaker panel, look for any obvious problems. For example, if you unscrew a fuse from a fuse box, examine both the fuse and its screw shell. (To be safe, first pull the main fuse.) Check the fuse or the screw shell for any damage from arcing or burning.

Once you are certain that there is no damage to your fuse box or breaker panel, you may begin to chart your circuits. A plug-in radio will come in handy, as will an assistant, if you can find one. If necessary, you can do the work alone—it will just take a bit longer.

Inspect your main panel to be certain that no fuse or circuit breaker exceeds the capacity of the wires it protects.

Checking for Damage

You can easily diagnose a blown fuse element by looking through the fuse glass. A burned element suggests an overload; a broken element and darkened glass suggests a short circuit.

A damaged plug fuse will clearly show marks caused by burning and arcing.

When a plug fuse is blown, the fuse shell may also be damaged. Check it for signs of burning and arcing.

Burn flashes in a circuit breaker panel are a telltale sign of serious damage.

HOW TO: *Chart Your Circuits*

Difficulty Level: 🗲

Tools and Materials

- Felt-tip pen and marker
- 1½x2-inch self-stick notepad
- Graph paper
- Stick-on labels (optional)

Make a Sketch, and Number the Circuits. Using a black or blue felt-tip pen, make a scaled floor plan of each room in your home. **(Photo 1)** Use a separate sheet of graph paper for each space, noting the location of each receptacle, switch, fixture, and direct-connect appliance. At your main service panel, note the number next to each circuit breaker. **(Photo 2)** You can either use this number or you can write your own number next to or over it. If you have a fuse box, then write your numbers adjacent to each fuse, using a felt-tip marker. As an alternative, use adhesive labels.

Turn Off the Power, and Turn On the Radio. Turn off all of the circuit breakers in your breaker panel or, if you have a fuse box, unscrew all of the fuses. **(Photo 3)** Do this during daylight, or use a high-beam 9-volt flashlight with a backup to avoid working in the dark. Select a

starting point, such as your kitchen; then plug in your radio. Turn the volume up high enough so that you will be able to hear it from the main panel. **(Photo 4)**

Switch on a Circuit. Switch on the power to only one circuit at a time. If you don't hear the radio, switch that circuit off again, and turn on a different one. Continue this process until you can hear the radio. Once you can hear it, record the appropriate circuit number on your sketch plan. **(Photo 5)** Use this method to check every receptacle. For switches and fixtures, you may need an assistant to help you to verify whether or not they are on a given circuit.

Check Large Appliances. For a large appliance like a dishwasher, turn it on; then turn on the circuit breaker or fuse. When you hear the appliance running, record the circuit. Some equipment, like a stove, may not make any noise. A stove, however, will have a light that turns on (bake light, for example) or a clock that will run as it receives power. **(Photo 6)** It should also be on a 40- or 50-amp double-pole breaker. A typical electric water heater will be on a 30-amp double-pole circuit in the panel. Heat pumps are also normally on a 30-amp double-pole breaker. To verify a heat-pump circuit, you may have to adjust the thermostat.

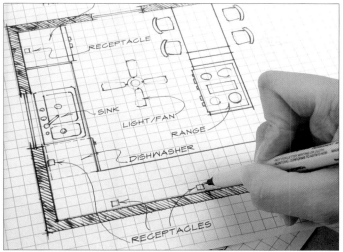

1 Sketch a plan to record the circuits that control each switch, receptacle, and fixture in your home.

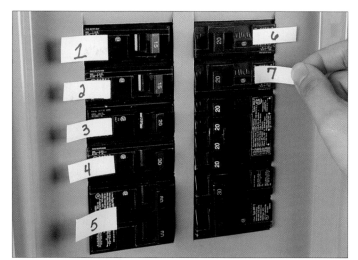

2 Numbering each breaker or fuse in your panel box simplifies the process of charting circuits.

3 Working on circuits can be dangerous. Be sure power is off before you begin tracking circuits.

4 A loud radio is one way to tell from a distance whether or not a receptacle is on a given circuit.

5 After verifying power to a receptacle, record the circuit number on your sketch plan.

6 A 30- to 50-amp circuit breaker or fuse powers a large appliance or mechanical equipment.

Wiring Methods

Calculating Circuit Ampacity

An overloaded circuit is a real danger in any electrical system and can easily lead to a blown fuse or tripped circuit breaker. Worse, it poses a potential fire hazard and can be a threat to both your life and property. The NEC requires that the demand on a given circuit be kept below its safe capacity (Section 220-4).

To calculate the total amperage of the circuit, add up those loads of which you know the amperage. For those loads that are listed in wattage instead of amperage, divide the wattage by the circuit voltage to get the amperage (amps = watts/volts), and add the values to the other amperage loads. This total amperage load for the circuit should not exceed 80 percent of the breaker or fuse rating. If you cannot find the amperage or wattage of the appliance, use the maximum approximate ratings found in the table "Appliance Wattage," page 17.

This product label provides information about the amperage used by the device.

Basic Wiring

Height and Clearance Requirements

New-construction wiring proceeds from a power or lighting plan. Use these floor plans to lay out what is known as rough-in work. This includes installing the outlet boxes, running the wiring through the rough framing, stripping the wires inside the electrical boxes, and connecting the grounding wires. Because the electrical inspector will review the construction site and approve or reject the rough-in wiring, it is necessary to follow NEC requirements when installing wiring and electrical fixtures.

Clearance requirements are especially important to reduce the potential for fire hazards. For example, recessed fixtures not approved for contact with insulation must be spaced at least ½ inch from combustible materials (NEC Section 410-66). When locating receptacles and switches, adhere to specific height requirements both for reasons of safety and accessibility. Switches, for instance, are not permitted to be any higher than 6 feet 7 inches above the floor or working level (Section 380-8).

Installing Electrical Boxes

Both for ease of use and aesthetics, receptacle and switch boxes should be kept at a uniform height above the finished floor or work surface. A general rule of thumb is to center receptacle boxes 12 inches above the floor—18 inches for handicapped accessibility. Center receptacle boxes over countertops 4 feet above the fin-

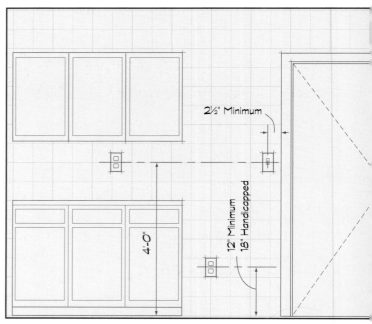

Receptacles should be centered 12 in. above the finished floor—18 in. for handicapped accessibility. Receptacles over countertops should be centered 4 ft. above the finished floor. Switches are generally centered at this same height, which is the maximum for handicapped accessibility.

ished floor, as well as receptacle boxes in bathrooms and garages. Laundry receptacles are placed at a height of 3½ feet. Switch boxes, on the other hand, are normally centered 4 feet above the finished floor—the maximum for handicapped accessibility.

A common type of electrical box used in residential work today is a nonmetallic (plastic or fiberglass) box that may include integral nails for fastening it to stud framing. Nonmetallic boxes such as this are inexpensive and easy to install. You place the box against a stud, bring the face of the box flush to where the drywall will be after it is installed, and then nail the box in place. Be sure to purchase boxes that have enough depth—at least $1\frac{1}{4}$ to $1\frac{1}{2}$ inches. This will give you approximately 23 cubic inches of interior box volume in which to tuck your wires. Using cable staples, secure the nonmetallic cable no more than 8 inches from the single-device electrical box. Make sure that at least $\frac{1}{4}$ inch of fully insulated cable will be secured inside of the box after the wires are stripped. Many switch boxes have gauge marks on their sides that allow you to position the box on a framing stud without having to measure depth. Recess boxes no more than $\frac{1}{4}$ inch from the finished wall surface. Mount boxes flush with the surface of combustible materials, such as wood.

Another type of electrical box is the handy box: a single-switch/receptacle box that is often screwed directly to a framing member, using a portable electric drill with a screwdriver bit. They sometimes come with a side-mounting flange to aid in installation. One danger, however, is that most handy boxes do not have adequate depth and can, therefore, only accommodate one cable safely. Misuse of this type of box is a code violation and should be avoided.

On masonry surfaces, attach boxes with masonry anchors and screws. Simply drill anchor holes in the masonry; then insert the anchors, and mount the box.

Maximum Wires in a Box

Box Type and Size	Maximum Number of Wires Permitted						
	18 GA	16 GA	14 GA	12 GA	10 GA	8 GA	6 GA
4"x1¼" Round or Octagonal	8	7	6	5	5	4	2
4"x1½" Round or Octagonal	10	8	7	6	6	5	3
4"x2⅛" Round or Octagonal	14	12	10	9	8	7	4
4"x1¼" Square	12	10	9	8	7	6	3
4"x1½" Square	14	12	10	9	8	7	4
4"x2⅛" Square	20	17	15	13	12	10	6
3"x2"x2" Device Box	6	5	5	4	4	3	2
3"x2"x2½" Device Box	8	7	6	5	5	4	2
3"x2"x2¾" Device Box	9	8	7	6	5	4	2
3"x2"x3½" Device Box	12	10	9	8	7	6	3
4"x2⅛"x1½" Device Box	6	5	5	4	4	3	2
4"x2⅛"x1⅞" Device Box	8	7	6	5	5	4	2
4"x2⅛"x2⅛" Device Box	9	8	7	6	5	4	2
3¾"x2"x2½" Device Box	9	8	7	6	5	4	2
3¾"x2"x3½" Device Box	14	12	10	9	8	7	4

Electrical boxes must be of sufficient size to safely contain all enclosed wires. (Table 370-16a, NEC)

HOW TO: *Install a Junction Box*

Difficulty Level:

Tools and Materials

- Multipurpose tool
- Electrician's hammer
- Neon circuit tester
- Wire connectors
- Screws/nails
- Insulated screwdrivers
- Grounding pigtail & screw
- Junction box
- Cable clamps
- Cable

Check the Power, and Prepare the Box. Be sure that the circuit you are working on is turned off and tagged at the main panel. Use a circuit tester to test for power in any wires to be spliced inside the junction box, avoiding contact with potentially live wires until after they are tested. **(Photo 1)** Using a hammer and screwdriver or a knockout punch, remove one knockout on the box for each cable entering the box. **(Photo 2)**

Attach the Box, and Clamp the Cable. Using an insulated screwdriver or electrician's hammer, screw or nail the junction box to the framing, making certain that the box is centered at the appropriate location on the wall, ceiling, or framing member. **(Photo 3)** Pull each cable through a cable clamp so that at least ¼ inch of full insulation will extend into the junction box. Then tighten the cable clamps, and screw them into the box. Secure the clamps with locknuts. **(Photo 4)**

Splice the Wires, and Close the Box. Splice the hot (black) wires, then neutral (white) wires, using twist-on wire connectors. **(Photo 5)** Be sure to pigtail the green grounding wires to the grounding screw terminal inside the metal junction box. Carefully tuck the wiring into the box, verifying that there is adequate free space to comply with code requirements. Secure the cover plate to the box, and restore power to the circuit at the main panel. **(Photo 6)**

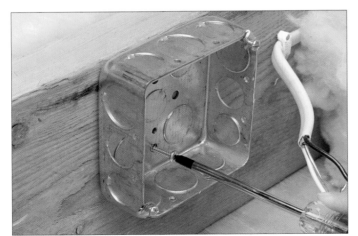

1 *Carefully check disconnected cable splices for power before resplicing them in a junction box.*

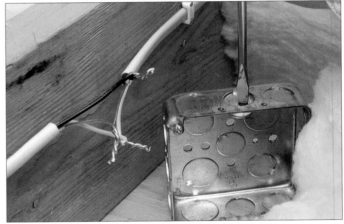

2 *Electrical boxes have various knockouts that can be removed to permit the safe entry of cable for splicing.*

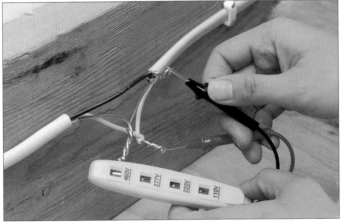

3 *Using an insulated screwdriver or electrician's hammer, screw or nail the box to the framing.*

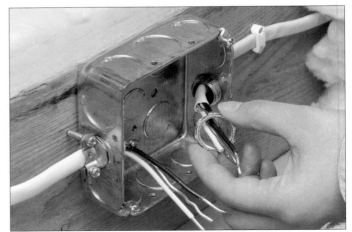

4 *Use a locknut to secure the clamped cable—friction from movement can cause fraying.*

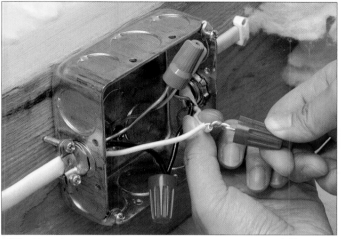

5 Use the correct-size wire connectors to carefully splice wires inside the electrical junction box.

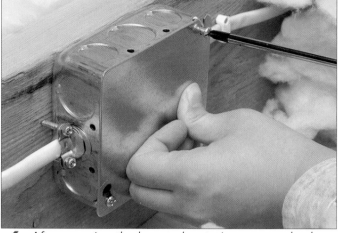

6 After covering the box and restoring power, check the receptacles, switches, and fixtures on the circuit.

Surface Wiring

Conditions exist where concealed wiring isn't possible—for example, a basement having exposed concrete or masonry walls. In this case, surface wiring is the only option. Surface-mounted conduit, or raceway, provides a rigid flat metal or plastic pipe to convey wire across instead of inside a wall or ceiling. Special receptacle and fixture boxes are used in conjunction with raceway to offer a safe way to install surface wiring. A plastic raceway requires the inclusion of a separate grounding wire; a metal raceway connected to a properly wired and grounded electrical box is self-grounding.

▼ **Raceway channels** protect exposed wire along a wall or ceiling surface.

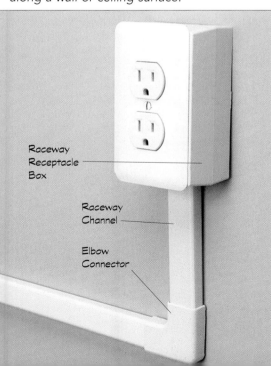

Raceway Receptacle Box

Raceway Channel

Elbow Connector

Running Cable through Framing

Installing wiring through new construction is relatively easy. The most common electrical installations are those in which outlet boxes are mounted alongside a stud or joist, although this is not always possible. Once electrical boxes are in place, run the cable through the framing members. Do this by drilling ¾-inch holes directly through the center of the studs or joists. Center the holes at least 1⅝ inches in from the edge of the framing member. If you must drill closer, then attach a wire shield to the outer edge of the framing to prevent nails or screws from penetrating the hole and causing damage to the cable during the course of future work.

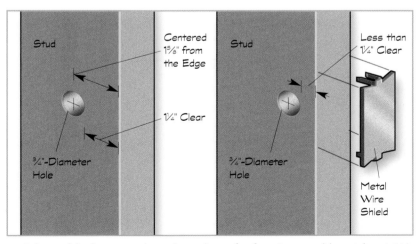

Stud · Centered 1⅝" from the Edge · Stud · Less than 1¼" Clear · 1¼" Clear · ¾"-Diameter Hole · ¾"-Diameter Hole · Metal Wire Shield

▲ **A bored hole** must clear the edge of a framing stud by at least 1¼ in. A ¾-in. hole, for example, must be centered at least 1⅝ in. in from the outer edge of a wall stud. If the hole edge is closer to the stud edge than this, it must be protected by a metal wire shield (NEC Section 300-4).

Wiring Methods

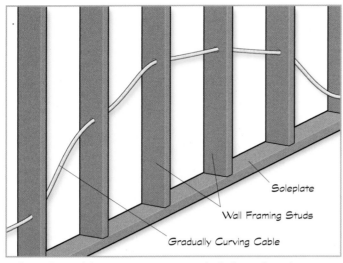

Allow the cable to sag or curve slightly, rather than extending it horizontally through a stud wall, to prevent potential kinks, sharp bends, or overstretching of the wire.

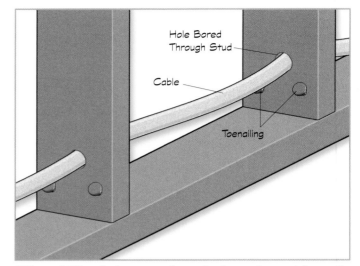

When drilling holes near the soleplate of a stud-framed wall, steer clear of toenailing and other metal fasteners that may snag your drill bit.

If you cannot drill holes through framing because the framing cavity contains ductwork or plumbing, you may have to resort to surface wiring to do the job properly. (See "Surface Wiring," page 75.)

Avoiding Damage. Be careful not to jerk the wire cable violently as you pull it through the drilled holes in the framing. The friction from pulling cable through rough-cut wood can cause the cable sheathing to tear, exposing the wires to serious damage. You should also avoid making sharp bends or kinks in the cable, as these too can damage the wiring. In addition, be careful when running cable along the bottom of a wall—there are likely to be toenailed fasteners near the bottom of each wall stud.

Getting around windows and doors can also be a problem. If there are cripple studs above the header, then you can drill holes through them for cable. However, you can't drill through the length of a solid-wood header. If possible, you can go over or under such obstacles. As a last resort, use a router to cut a channel deeply enough across the surface of the header to accommodate a cable; protect the cable by installing a metal plate over it.

Holes and Notches. If you bore holes through ceiling and floor joists, the holes must be located so that they will not undermine the structural integrity of the framing. (See illustration on next page.) This is also a concern if you notch the wood along the top or bottom edge to run cable perpendicular to the joists. In this instance, you must install metal wire shields to protect the cable from damage. Even cable that runs parallel with framing

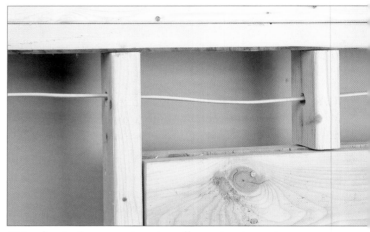

Cripple studs over a header offer a simple and convenient path for wiring around a door or window opening.

The best way to go around a solid header is to run your wiring through the ceiling joists above or the floor joists below the rough opening.

SMART TIP

Routing a Solid Header

Channel Cut
by Router

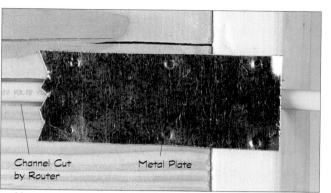

Channel Cut
by Router

Metal Plate

◀ **Use a router** to cut a cable channel across a solid header only if you have no other alternative. **Attach a metal plate** (shown as cutaway, above) over the routed cable channel to protect the cable from potential nail damage.

should not be left vulnerable or hanging loosely in a wall or floor space. Use cable staples to secure it in place along the center of the stud, joist, or rafter.

Attic Runs. To run cable in an attic requires advance planning. You must run the cable where it won't be exposed to damage. Usually this means running the cable along the edge plate around the perimeter of the building or within a concealed floor or wall space. Where the framing is open, place two guard boards over the top of the joists; then run the cable between them. If you access your attic by ladder, be careful when laying cable around the hatchway door, as protection must be provided withing 6 inches of the opening.

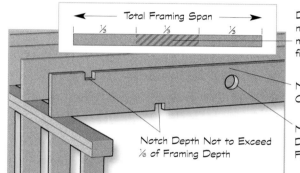

Total Framing Span

⅓   ⅓   ⅓

Do not cut any notch within the middle third of the framing span.

Minimum 2-Inch Clearance to Edge

Notch Depth Not to Exceed ⅙ of Framing Depth

Maximum Hole Diameter = ⅓ Framing Depth

▲ **Follow the guidelines** illustrated above whenever it is necessary to bore a hole or cut a notch in structural joists.

▼ **To run cable** perpendicular to framing joists in an unfinished attic, construct a channel space along an edge wall, using two 1x4 furring strips as guard boards, as shown.

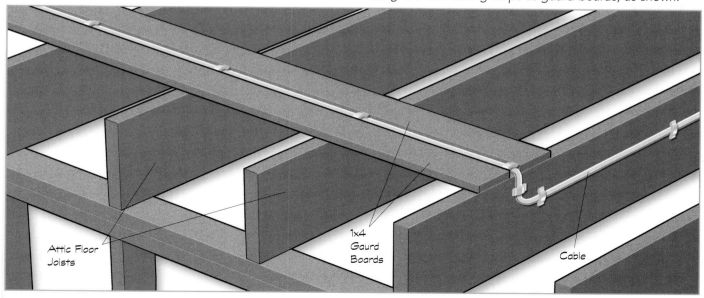

Attic Floor
Joists

1x4
Gaurd
Boards

Cable

Crawl Space Runs. Although you may seldom enter your crawl space, you should be as careful when you install cable here as anywhere else—maybe more so. Because maneuvering space is limited, you do not want to have any loose wires where they may snag your clothing as you move through the space. If it is 8 gauge (three-wire) or larger, fasten cable to the bottom edge of the joists. For smaller cable, either bore holes or staple the cable to a furring strip run along the bottom edge of the joists.

Preparing for Inspection. Once new framing walls are ready to be wired and electrical boxes have all been put in place, carefully begin pulling the cable through the framing. When you insert a cable end into an electrical box, leave a minimum of 6 inches of extra cable, cutting away the excess. Using a cable staple, secure the cable at a maximum of 8 inches above the single-device box. After you have run all cables through the framing and into the electrical boxes, rip back and remove the sheathing from the cable ends in each box; then strip the individual wires. Before a rough-in inspection can be done, you must also splice together the grounding wires using either green wire connectors or wire crimping ferrules. Then place the wires securely in their boxes.

After a rough-in inspection is performed, install the receptacles and switches. Wait until the drywall is in place before doing this work. When the walls are completed and all of the boxes wired, you can install cover plates and turn on the power. Check each receptacle, using a plug-in receptacle analyzer, to verify that all of the wiring has been properly done. Install the light fixtures; then confirm that they are all working. Once you have completed all of this, your work will be ready for final inspection. The inspector will reexamine your work, performing many of the same circuit tests as you.

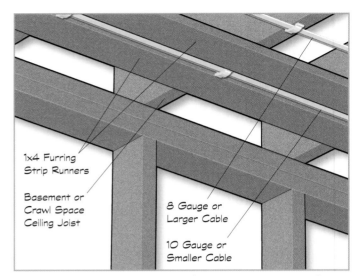

1x4 Furring Strip Runners

Basement or Crawl Space Ceiling Joist

8 Gauge or Larger Cable

10 Gauge or Smaller Cable

To run cable perpendicular to framing joists in an unfinished basement or crawl space, construct a runway using a 1x4 furring strip along the bottom edge of the framing or bore holes in the joists. You can staple cable containing three 8-gauge conductors or larger directly to the underside of the joists.

Green Wire Connector

Pigtail

This grounding setup is common practice, and what you're likely to see when you work with existing wiring. This configuration is shown throughout the book.

CRE**A**TIVE HOMEOWNER® | **SMART TIP**

Splicing Grounding Wires

In existing wiring you're likely to come across the pigtail method of splicing grounding wires (in the photo above right), so that's the method demonstrated throughout this book. However, grounding wire connectors are manufactured with a hole at the top so that wires can be spliced as shown at far right. This is the method actually preferred by electricians these days.

Grounding Screw

Ground from Branch-Circuit Cable

Pigtail to Box

Pigtail to Switch

Ground from Fixture Cable

Grounding Screw

Ground (from Branch-Circuit Cable) to Box

HOW TO: *Strip Wires and Cables*

Difficulty Level:

Tools and Materials
+ Multipurpose tool
+ Wire stripper (optional)
+ Cable ripper
+ Cable

Cut the Sheathing. Center the cable ripper carefully over the nonmetallic cable, as shown; then slide it down to a point about 8 inches from the end. Grasp the tool tightly, and squeeze the handles, allowing the cutting tip to pierce the center of the cable without damaging the insulated wires inside. **(Photo 1)** Using a firm grip, draw the ripper toward the end of the cable, cutting open the plastic cable sheathing. **(Photo 2)** Carefully strip back the ripped cable sheathing to expose the insulated wires inside the cable, and then pull back the paper insulation wrapped around the wires inside the cable. **(Photo 3)**

Cut the Wires, and Strip the Insulation. Use a multi-purpose tool to cut away the excess cable sheathing and paper insulation. **(Photo 4)** Use a multipurpose tool or wire cutter to cut the insulated wires to the appropriate length for splicing. **(Photo 5)** Select the proper gauge opening on the wire stripper or multipurpose tool; then strip the insulation from the individual wires inside the cable. **(Photo 6)** Be careful not to gouge or scratch any of the exposed wires.

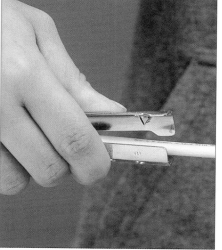

1 Firmly clench the cable ripper to pierce the cable sheathing.

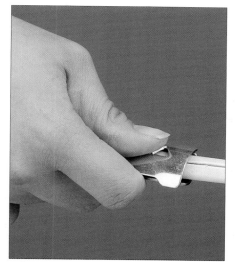

2 Pull the cable ripper toward the end of the cable.

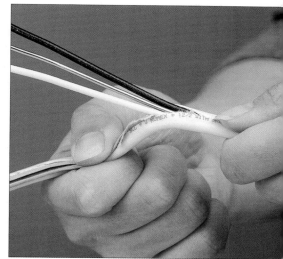

3 Before you can wire a box, you must expose the individual wires.

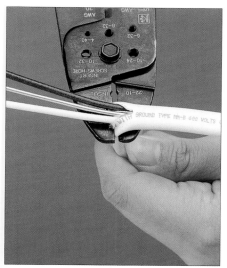

4 Remove enough sheathing so you can cut and strip the wires.

5 Use a wire cutter or multipurpose tool to trim the exposed wires.

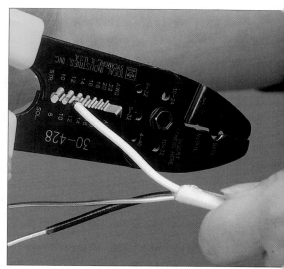

6 Strip just enough wire to make a secure connection.

Opening and Closing Walls

Running cables through existing walls and joist spaces is a lot more complicated than running cables in new construction. Because you cannot see into finished framing cavities, fishing cables through walls and ceilings requires great patience and more than a little skill.

When wiring in an existing home, you may have to cut a series of access holes in the drywall so that you can route the cable through the framing.

If you have access to walls from a basement or attic, you can get power into walls by fishing the cable vertically instead of horizontally through the structural framing. In many cases, running cable the long way around to complete a circuit may be the easiest route, even if you have to spend more money for cable. The cost of the cable is likely to be much less than that of ripping into walls and ceilings. If you must run cable across existing framing, for example, you may have to cut into drywall in order to position the cable properly. It is a good idea to take time initially to explore alternative routes the cable might follow. Try to determine the best route; then make a rough sketch or map of the cable route. This will undoubtedly save you time and money later.

Before running cable, first decide where to locate your new switch, outlet, or junction box; then determine which walls or ceilings, if any, need to be opened to efficiently route the cable to this point. You can cut openings in drywall using a utility knife, mini-hacksaw, or keyhole or saber saw. After you make your cut, either remove the scrap or knock it back between the framing members.

In an unfinished basement, you may encounter hollow concrete-block walls or poured steel-reinforced solid concrete walls. Although it is possible to cut into a hollow concrete block wall, it isn't practical. For block and concrete walls, it is best to install metal surface raceways or electrical conduit, and surface-mount your electrical boxes and wiring. Use a masonry bit on your power drill to make pilot holes for masonry anchors; then anchor the boxes and conduit clamps directly to the wall. An alternative is to pack out the wall using 2×4 furring lumber, either on flat or on edge, spaced at 16 inches on center. If you install the furring flat, you will have to use special electrical boxes that are made to fit within a 1½-inch wall cavity. Avoid using handy boxes because these do not have enough room to contain properly spliced wires.

Fishing Cable

One way to get cable into an existing stud wall is by running it down from an already functioning electrical box, into a basement or crawl space, and over to the location in the wall of the new electrical box. From here you can fish the wire up into the appropriate wall cavity.

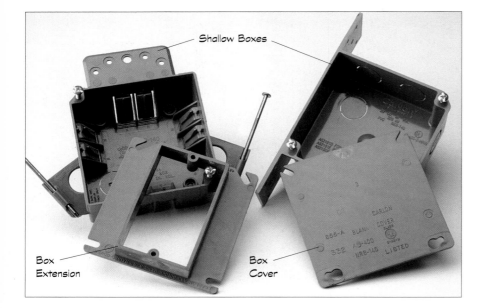

Shallow Boxes

Box Extension

Box Cover

Flat square electrical boxes are specially made to fit in shallow furred-out wall cavities.

HOW TO: *Fish Cable from Below the Floor*

Difficulty Level: 🦇🦇

Tools and Materials

- Keyhole or saber saw
- ⅟₁₆- or ⅛-inch bit
- Fish tape (nonmetallic)
- Cordless drill
- Guide wire
- ¾-inch spade or wood bit

Cut the Box Opening, and Drill a Guide Hole. Using a keyhole or saber saw, cut an opening where the new receptacle or switch box will be installed in the wall. **(Photo 1)** Directly in line with the opening for the new electrical box, drill a ⅟₁₆- to ⅛-inch hole at the base of the wall. **(Photo 2)** If you have carpeting, cut a small X to prevent unraveling. If possible, remove the baseboard, and drill as close to the wall as you can; then insert a thin guide wire down the hole.

Locate the Guide Wire and Soleplate. Go down into your basement or crawl space; then locate the end of the guide wire you inserted through the floor. Use the guide wire to establish the location of the soleplate at the bottom of the stud wall above. **(Photo 3)** The position of the plate should be conspicuous because of the protruding nails visible just a short distance away from the guide wire. Mark a spot for drilling along the centerline of the soleplate. **(Photo 4)**

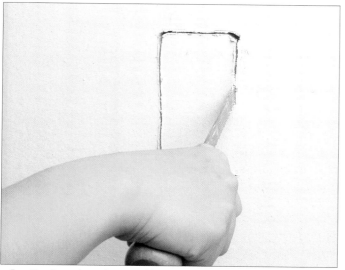

1 Outline the electrical box on the wall; then cut the drywall along the outline using a keyhole saw.

2 Drill a small hole in the floor below a new box cutout and drop a guide wire through the hole.

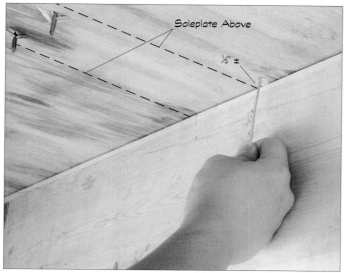

3 Find the guide wire in the ceiling below. This will help you locate the soleplate in the wall above.

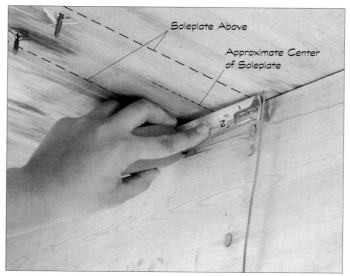

4 Mark the center of the soleplate—approximately 2 inches behind the guide wire.

Drill through the Soleplate. Using a ¾-inch spade or wood bit, drill a hole up through the soleplate, about 2 inches behind the the guide wire. The hole should extend into the wall cavity between framing studs. **(Photo 5)**

Fish the Cable. Push the cable up into the wall. If you are installing a low wall receptacle, you should be able to reach the cable from above and grab it. **(Photo 6)** If you need to push the cable up high in the wall to reach a new switch location, use fish tape.

If there is no attic, basement, or crawl space, fishing wire may require that you cut access openings along the length of a wall. Although this method requires extensive repair work, you may have no alternative, unless you can run your wiring behind a baseboard.

Soleplate Above

5 Drill a hole up through the soleplate large enough to accommodate the passage of a cable connector.

6 Push the cable up into the wall, and fish it out through the box opening.

HOW TO: *Run Cable Behind a Baseboard*

Difficulty Level:

Tools and Materials

- Pencil
- Metal paint scraper
- Straightedge
- Electrician's hammer
- Nail set
- Wire shields
- Wood shim
- Utility knife
- Wood chisel
- Backsaw
- Finishing nails
- Fish tape
- Measuring tape
- Cable

Mark the Wall, and Loosen the Baseboard. If your baseboard can be removed without damaging it, trace a light pencil mark on the wall along the top edge of the baseboard to use as your reference line. **(Photo 1)** Using a utility knife, cut between the top edge of the baseboard and the wall to break the paint seal. **(Photo 2)** This will prevent paint from being pulled away from the wall when you remove the baseboard.

Remove the Baseboard, and Mark a Cut Line. Cut the section of baseboard with a backsaw. Using a steel paint scraper or a chisel, carefully pry the section away from the wall. Slip a wood shim behind the scraper or chisel to prevent any damage to your wall. **(Photo 3)** Pencil a secondary reference line ½ inch below your primary reference line. **(Photo 4)** Use this as a guideline to cut and remove the drywall.

Cut and Remove the Drywall, and Notch the Studs. Make your cut along the secondary reference line, using a straightedge and a utility knife; then remove the cutout section of drywall. **(Photo 5)** Saw a notch in the face of each exposed stud at the bottom of the wall, using a backsaw and chisel, or drill holes through the studs to make a raceway channel for your cable. **(Photo 6)** If you make notches, place wire shields as you run the cable to protect it from damage.

Replace the Drywall and the Baseboard. Measure and cut a new section of drywall to replace the one that you removed. Then carefully nail it in place. **(Photo 7)** Reinstall the baseboard trim using a hammer and finishing nails. Set the nails, putty the holes, and restore the damaged wall and baseboard finishes to match the existing adjacent surfaces. **(Photo 8)**

1 Outline the top edge of your baseboard. You can safely cut the drywall ½ in. below this mark.

2 To protect the drywall from damage, score a line behind the baseboard before removing it.

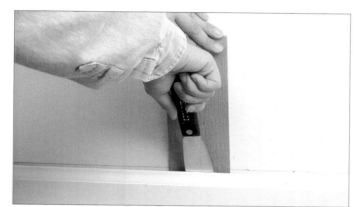

3 Cut the baseboard past the existing box at one end and the new box at the other end. Pry it off.

4 Measure ½ in. down from your original reference line; then draw a new cut line.

5 Cut away the drywall at the bottom of the wall, exposing the stud framing in the space behind it.

6 Either notch the face edge of each stud or make a ¾-in. hole through each stud; then run the cable.

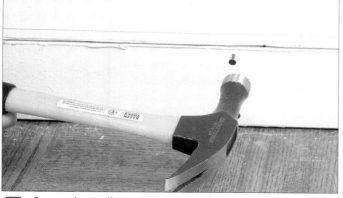

7 Cut and install a new section of drywall to seal the access opening in the wall.

8 Restore the cut baseboard to its original position, and refinish the wall and trim.

Wiring Methods

Use a special long and flexible bit to drill through studs in a concealed wall cavity. These bits reduce or eliminate the need for cutting access holes in a finished wall. (The long section of drywall in this photo has been removed for clarity.)

If removing your existing baseboard is not a reasonable option, you will simply have to cut out a limited section of visible drywall in order to gain access to the stud framing. The resulting wall damage can probably be minimized if you use a specialized flex-drill—one that is long and flexible—to bore through several adjacent framing studs, rather than having to notch them all at the wall surface. Nevertheless, some patching and repair work, as well as refinishing, will still be necessary.

CREATIVE HOMEOWNER® | SMART TIP

Wiring around an Existing Doorway

If an existing doorway is in the path of your cable, you will have to run the cable up and around the door frame. In this situation, rather than cutting out sections of the drywall, you may be able to take advantage of the shim space. Remove the molding from around the door, gently prying it away from the wall. Use a rigid paint scraper with a scrap piece of wood under it to protect the wall. If you cannot remove the trim without causing it damage, you may have to replace the molding. If the molding is irreplaceable, you may wish to reconsider using this method to route the cable around your door. Once the shim space is exposed, notch out the shim spacers just enough to accommodate the cable. String the cable around the shim space; then cover the notched areas, using metal wire shields.

You can run cable around an existing door through cutouts in the drywall. An alternative is to take advantage of the shim space between the door frame and the jamb studs.

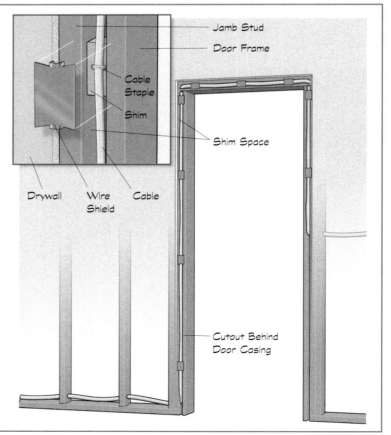

Jamb Stud

Door Frame

Cable Staple

Shim

Shim Space

Drywall   Wire Shield   Cable

Cutout Behind Door Casing

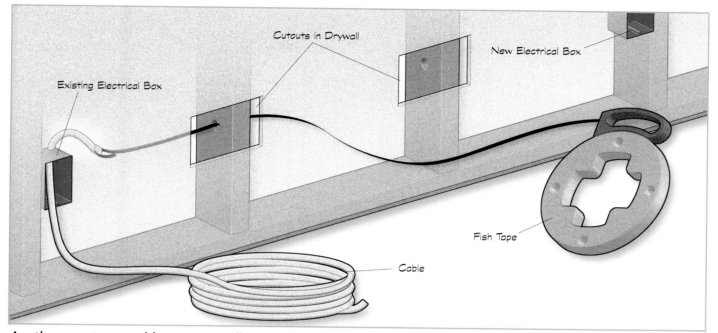

Existing Electrical Box

Cutouts in Drywall

New Electrical Box

Fish Tape

Cable

Another way to run cable across a wall *is to make several cutouts in the drywall to expose the stud framing, and bore holes through the studs. Fish the cable gradually from the existing box to the new location.*

Running cable through an existing but inaccessible ceiling may require that you cut both a ceiling and a wall opening in order to fish the cable from a vertical wall cavity to a horizontal ceiling cavity. Once the ceiling is opened, use fish tape to get the cable across to the new electrical box.

HOW TO: *Fish Cable across a Ceiling*

Difficulty Level: 🐾🐾

Tools and Materials

◆ Stepladder	◆ Utility knife
◆ Keyhole or saber saw	◆ Pencil and straightedge
◆ Chisel	◆ Plumb bob
◆ Cordless drill	◆ ¾-inch spade bit
◆ Fish tape (nonmetallic)	◆ Electrical tape
◆ Wire shields	◆ Electrician's hammer
◆ Safety glasses	◆ Dust mask

Cut the Ceiling Opening. Using a keyhole or saber saw, cut a hole in the ceiling where you wish to locate the ceiling box. **(Photo 1)** From the ceiling hole, make a visual reference line running perpendicular to the wall where the cable will turn downward; then mark a reference line on the wall at the point of intersection. **(Photo 2)**

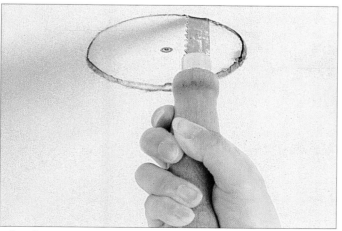

1 *If your ceiling is not open from above, use the ceiling cutout for your new box as an access hole.*

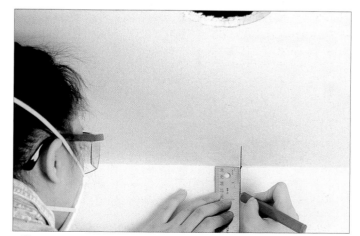

2 *Site a line from the opening to the wall where the cable will turn down. Mark the intersection.*

Cut Access Holes, and Notch the Top Plate. At the point of intersection, use a utility knife to make adjoining 2×4-inch openings in the drywall, one in the ceiling and in the wall. **(Photo 3)** From the 2×4-inch ceiling cutout, bore a ¾-inch hole down through the double top plate, or use a chisel to notch the outer face of the top plates to receive the cable. **(Photo 4)**

Fish the Tape. Through the new opening that you cut for the ceiling box, feed a long fish tape through the joist space in the ceiling until it reaches across to the ceiling

cutout made previously at the top of the adjoining wall. Tie a plumb bob or other weight to the end of the fish tape, and drop it down into the wall cavity. **(Photo 5)**

Pull the Cable. Cut an access hole near the bottom of the wall; then grab and pull the fish tape through the hole. Fasten the cable to the fish tape, **(Photo 6)** and pull the cable up through the wall, across the ceiling, and then out the hole that you cut previously to house the ceiling box. **(Photo 6 inset)** Cover the exposed cable with metal plates.

3 At the spot marked, cut adjoining access openings in both the ceiling and the wall.

4 Cut a ¾-in.-wide and 1-in.-deep notch through the top plate to serve as a raceway for the cable.

5 Feed the fish tape across the ceiling and down the wall to an access opening at the bottom of the wall.

6 Secure the cable to the fish tape at the bottom of the wall, and pull the tape back up to the ceiling hole.

Receptacles

Duplex Receptacles

Although there are two basic types of receptacles—single and duplex—only duplex receptacles are commonly found in modern homes. A duplex receptacle accommodates two plugs at the same time. Originally, receptacles were neither grounded nor polarized; later, they became polarized but not grounded. Today, receptacles include a screw terminal for a grounding connection. These receptacles have a total of five terminal screws: two brass screw terminals on the right side, for black/red hot-wire connections; two silver screw terminals on the left side for white neutral-wire connections; and one green screw terminal on the left side for a bare copper or green grounding-wire connection. How many wires are connected to a receptacle is determined by whether the connection occurs at the end or in the middle of a wiring run. An end-of-run receptacle will have only one cable entering the box, while a middle-of-run receptacle will have two.

▶ **Early receptacles** had two nonpolarized connections (**A**). For this type of receptacle, the colored wires could go to either screw terminal. Later, manufacturers made polarized receptacles (**B**). These require that a specific color wire be connected to a specific screw terminal, but they are not grounded. Today, receptacles also include a green grounding screw terminal (**C**).

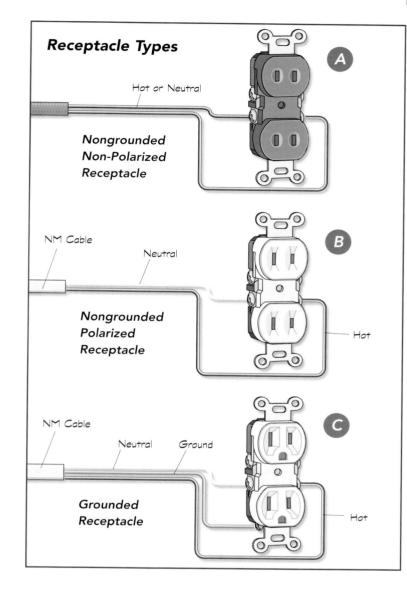

Receptacle Types

Hot or Neutral

A

Nongrounded Non-Polarized Receptacle

NM Cable

Neutral

B

Nongrounded Polarized Receptacle

Hot

NM Cable

Neutral   Ground

C

Grounded Receptacle

Hot

Wiring Methods

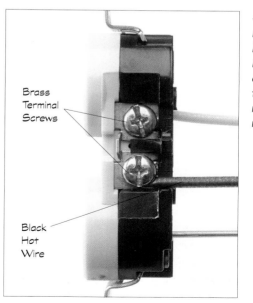

Brass Terminal Screws

Black Hot Wire

◀ **Receptacle, right side.** The hot black or red wires are connected to the brass terminal screws on a receptacle.

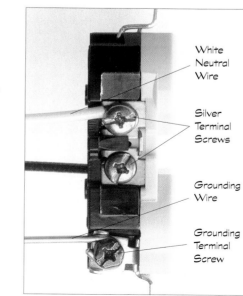

White Neutral Wire

Silver Terminal Screws

Grounding Wire

Grounding Terminal Screw

◀ **Receptacle, left side.** The silver terminal screws on a receptacle receive the white neutral wires, while the green terminal screw receives the grounding wire.

HOW TO: *Wire an End-of-Run Receptacle*

Difficulty Level: 🖐

Tools and Materials

For metal boxes

- Insulated screwdriver
- Receptacle box
- Green wire connector
- Long-nose pliers
- Multipurpose tool (optional)
- Cable clamps*

- Duplex receptacle
- 12/2G NM cable
- Diagonal-cutting pliers
- Wire stripper
- Cable ripper
- Grounding pigtail and screw*

Pull the Cable End, and Strip the Wires. After installing the receptacle box, bring the end of the wire cable into the box. **(Photo 1)** Secure the cable, using cable clamps. Rip the sheathing back on the cable, remove the excess, and strip the inside wires. **(Photo 2)**

Wire and Ground the Receptacle. Connect the black hot wire to a brass screw terminal and the white neutral wire to a silver screw terminal. **(Photo 3)** Using a green wire connector, splice together the cable grounding wire and two pigtail grounding wires—one from the receptacle, and another from the grounding screw (if you are using a metal box). **(Photo 4)**

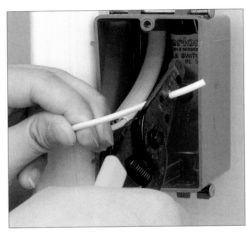

1 Pull approximately 6 in. of wire cable into the receptacle box to allow enough wiring to complete your work.

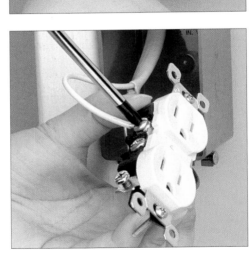

2 Strip the cable sheathing no closer than ½ in. from the clamp inside the receptacle box.

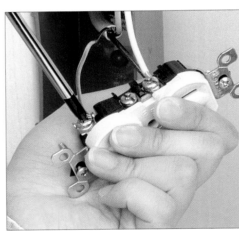

3 Loop the stripped wires clockwise two-thirds of the way around their respective screw terminals; then tighten the screws.

4 Secure the grounding wire to the grounding screw on the receptacle.

The conventional way to wire a middle-of-run receptacle is to connect all of the wires to the receptacle, letting it act as the splice between the connecting black or white wires. Wiring a receptacle this way is easy but connects all of the devices on the circuit in series—if you temporarily remove one receptacle, the current to the rest of the line will be cut. As an alternative, wire the receptacles on the circuit independently. Splice each pair of hot and neutral wires using wire connectors; then connect a pigtail from each splice to the appropriate receptacle terminal. Only current drawn by the appliance plugged into it will flow through the receptacle. If you remove the receptacle from the circuit, the rest of the circuit will continue to work. This type of connection is necessary where three or more cables must be spliced together because more than one wire is not permitted under a single screw terminal.

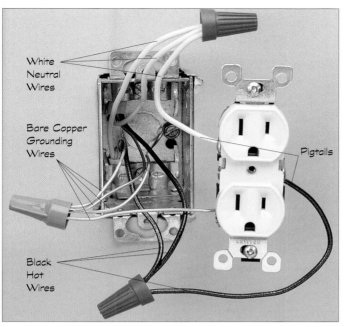

White Neutral Wires

Bare Copper Grounding Wires

Pigtails

Black Hot Wires

This type of connection, using a metal box, allows the receptacles on a circuit to be wired independently.

HOW TO: *Wire a Middle-of-Run Receptacle*

Difficulty Level: 🐟

Tools and Materials — *For metal boxes*

- Insulated screwdriver
- Receptacle box
- Green wire connector
- Multipurpose tool (optional)
- Wire stripper
- Cable clamps*

- Duplex receptacle
- 12/2G NM cable
- Diagonal-cutting pliers
- Long-nose pliers
- Cable ripper
- Grounding pigtail and screw*

Pull the Cable Ends, and Strip the Cable and Wires.
After installing the receptacle box, bring the ends of the two cables into the box. Secure the cables with cable clamps if the box isn't self-clamping. **(Photo 1)** Rip the sheathing back on the cable, removing the excess and paper insulation, and strip the inside wires. **(Photo 2)**

Wire and Ground the Receptacle. Connect the two black hot wires to the brass screw terminals and the two white neutral wires to the silver screw terminals. **(Photo 3)** Using a green wire connector, splice together the cable grounding wires and two pigtail grounding wires—one from the receptacle, and another from the grounding screw (if you are using a metal box). **(Photo 4)**

1 Thread the cables through cable clamps, pull enough of each for 6 in. of free conductor into the receptacle box, and then lock the clamps.

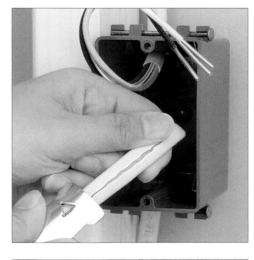

2 Remove the cable insulation back to within ½ in. of the cable clamps, and then strip ½ in. of insulation from each wire end.

3 Loop the bare wire ends counterclockwise two-thirds of the way around their respective terminal screws.

4 Splice the grounding wires together, and pigtail them to the grounding screw in the receptacle box (if it is metal).

Wiring Methods

Sequential 120-Volt Duplex Receptacles

Start- or middle-of-run receptacles are connected to all wires from both directions. End-of-run receptacles are the last on the circuit and have only two terminations and a ground connection.

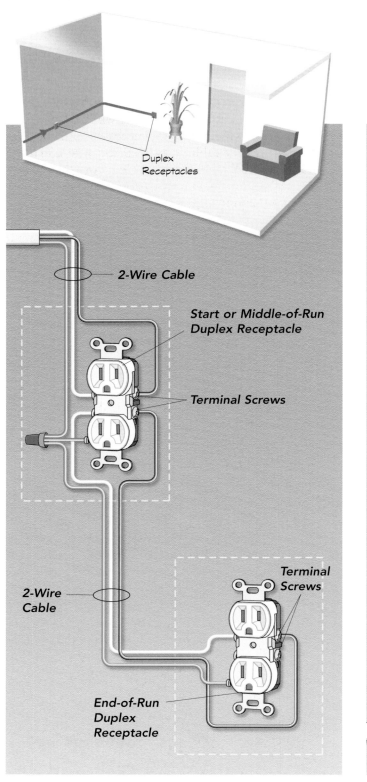

2-Wire Cable

Start or Middle-of-Run Duplex Receptacle

Terminal Screws

2-Wire Cable

Terminal Screws

End-of-Run Duplex Receptacle

Duplex Receptacles

Multiple 120-Volt Duplex Receptacle Circuit

On multiple 120-volt receptacle circuits, three-wire cable is used to connect all but the last receptacle. The white neutral wire is shared by both circuits.

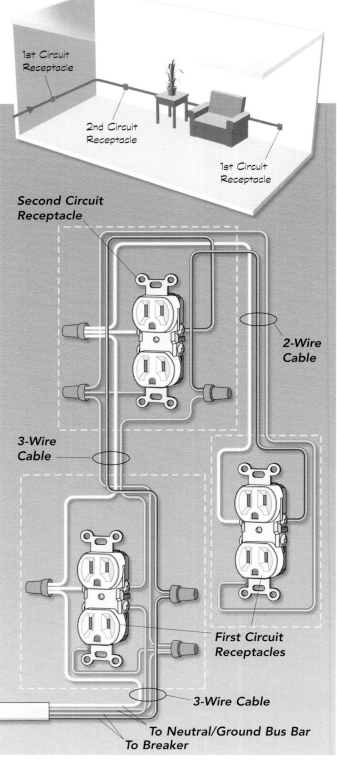

1st Circuit Receptacle

2nd Circuit Receptacle

1st Circuit Receptacle

Second Circuit Receptacle

2-Wire Cable

3-Wire Cable

First Circuit Receptacles

3-Wire Cable

To Neutral/Ground Bus Bar

To Breaker

Split Circuit Receptacles

The metal tabs connecting the screw terminals on each side of a receptacle can be removed. By breaking the connection between the brass screw terminals you can wire the top outlet of the receptacle independently from the bottom. The silver tabs are normally left intact. This type of split-circuit wiring, which is similar to that for a switch-controlled receptacle, permits two appliances that would otherwise draw too much current from one circuit to be powered by different circuits.

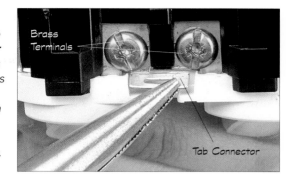

Removing the tab connector between brass terminal screws allows you to wire outlets on a duplex receptacle independently.

Brass Terminals

Tab Connector

HOW TO: *Wire a Split-Circuit Receptacle*

Difficulty Level: 🦃

Tools and Materials
For metal boxes

- Insulated screwdriver
- Receptacle box
- Green wire connector
- Multipurpose tool (optional)
- Wire stripper
- Cable clamps*

- Duplex receptacle
- Cable ripper
- 12/3G NM cable
- Diagonal-cutting pliers
- Long-nose pliers
- Grounding pigtail and screw*

Wire the Split Circuit. Install the receptacle box, secure and rip the cable, and strip the wires. Then remove the tab connector on the receptacle and connect the wiring. The cable contains three wires and a ground. Connect the hot black and red wires to separate brass screw terminals and the white neutral wire to a silver screw terminal. **(Photo 1)**

Ground the Split Circuit. Using a green wire connector, pigtail the grounding wire to the grounding screw terminal on the receptacle and to the grounding screw in the receptacle box if the box is metal. **(Photo 2)**

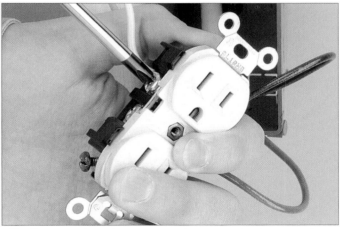

1 Remove the tab connector between the brass, or hot, terminal screws; then wire the receptacle.

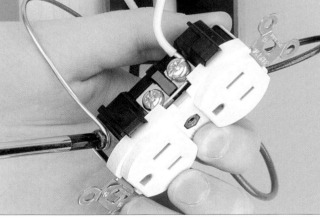

2 Pigtail the receptacle grounding wire to the cable grounding wire and the grounding screw in the box.

Wiring Methods

CRE▲TIVE HOMEOWNER®

SMART TIP

Avoid Push-In Terminals

Some receptacles have wire holes instead of screw terminals. On this type of receptacle, the end of each stripped wire (14-gauge copper only) is pushed into the appropriate hole to complete the connection. Although simple to use, these kinds of connections can be problematic and are not recommended.

Some types of receptacles have push-in terminals— you simply insert the end of each wire into an appropriate hole to complete the connection.

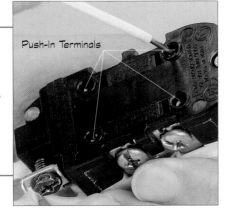

Push-In Terminals

Switch/Receptacle Combinations

Combine a grounded receptacle with a single-pole wall switch to make up for a lack of receptacles in a room. You can wire a switch/receptacle combination in one of two ways—either the switch controls the receptacle or, more commonly, the receptacle remains constantly active while the switch powers a separate fixture. This type of circuit must occur in the middle of a run.

HOW TO: *Wire a Switch/Receptacle*

Difficulty Level: 🐷

Tools and Materials
For metal boxes

- Insulated screwdriver
- Electrical box
- Green and red wire connectors
- 12/2G NM cable
- Wire stripper
- Cable clamps*

- Switch/receptacle
- Cable ripper
- Long-nose pliers
- Diagonal-cutting pliers
- Grounding pigtail and screw*

Connect the Hot and Neutral Wires. Once the box is installed, cables pulled, and wires stripped, connect the hot wires. Connect the black wire that feeds power to the device to one of the two dark screw terminals that are linked by a tab. Attach the black wire that powers the fixture or appliance to the single brass screw terminal on the other side of the switch/receptacle. **(Photo 1)** Using a red wire connector, splice together the white neutral wires from each cable, pigtailing them to the silver screw terminal on the switch/receptacle. **(Photo 2)**

Connect the Grounding Wires. Using a green wire connector, splice together the bare copper grounding wires from each cable, pigtailing them to the green grounding screw terminal on the switch/receptacle and to the green grounding screw if in a metal box. **(Photo 3)**

Alternative Connection. To have the switch control the receptacle, reverse the two hot black wires, so that the power-feed is attached to the brass screw terminal that doesn't have a tab connector. **(Photo 4)**

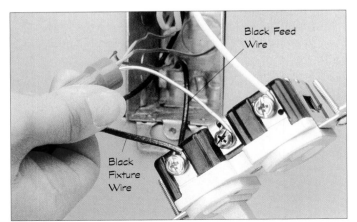

1 Connect the black fixture wire to the brass screw and the black feed wire to a dark screw on the switch.

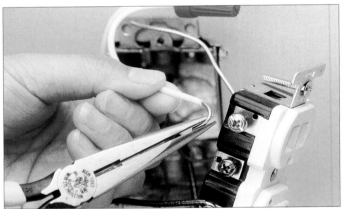

2 Connect the white neutral wires together, and pigtail them to the silver switch/receptacle screw.

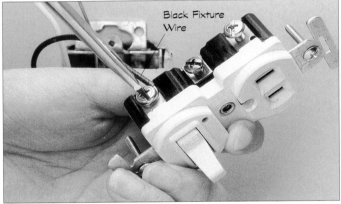

3 Connect the grounding wires, and pigtail them to the box (if metal) and switch/receptacle grounding screws.

4 To control the receptacle with the switch, reverse the black wires. The receptacle is hot when the switch is on.

Single-Pole Switch with Light Fixture and Duplex Receptacle

Wire a middle-of-run light fixture through a single-pole switch using two-wire cable to power the switch and three-wire cable from the switch to the fixture. Continue the circuit to an end-of-run receptacle using two-wire cable.

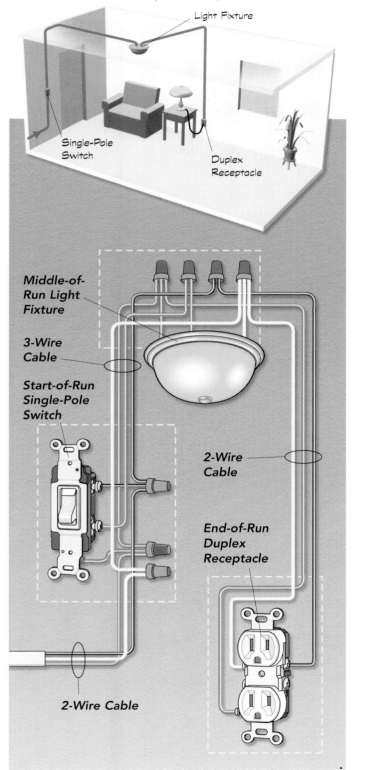

Light Fixture

Single-Pole Switch

Duplex Receptacle

Middle-of-Run Light Fixture

3-Wire Cable

Start-of-Run Single-Pole Switch

2-Wire Cable

End-of-Run Duplex Receptacle

2-Wire Cable

Split Receptacle Controlled by End-of-Run Switch

In this configuration, one-half of a split receptacle (tab removed) is powered by a switch located at the end of the circuit run. The other half of the receptacle is constantly powered. Mark the white neutral wire with black tape to indicate that it is hot.

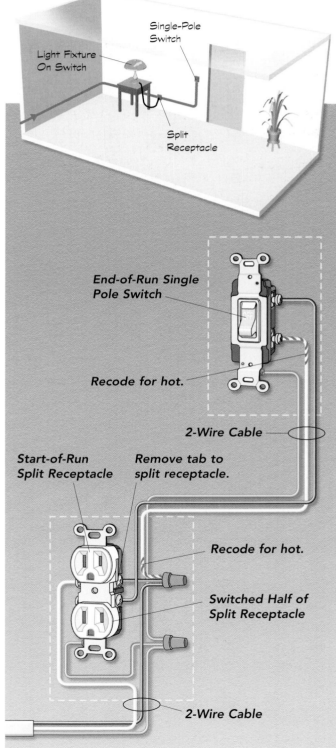

Single-Pole Switch

Light Fixture On Switch

Split Receptacle

End-of-Run Single Pole Switch

Recode for hot.

2-Wire Cable

Start-of-Run Split Receptacle

Remove tab to split receptacle.

Recode for hot.

Switched Half of Split Receptacle

2-Wire Cable

Wiring Methods

Duplex Receptacle with Split Receptacle Controlled by Start-of-Run Switch

To install a split receptacle controlled by a switch, remove the tab on the receptacle. Using two-wire cable, connect the switch to the power source. One hot wire from the switch connects to each half of the receptacle.

Duplex Receptacle with Split Receptacle Controlled by End-of-Run Switch

In this combination, the split receptacle is located at the start of the cable run. One-half of the receptacle is controlled by the switch. The other half of the receptacle is always hot and feeds the remainder of the circuit.

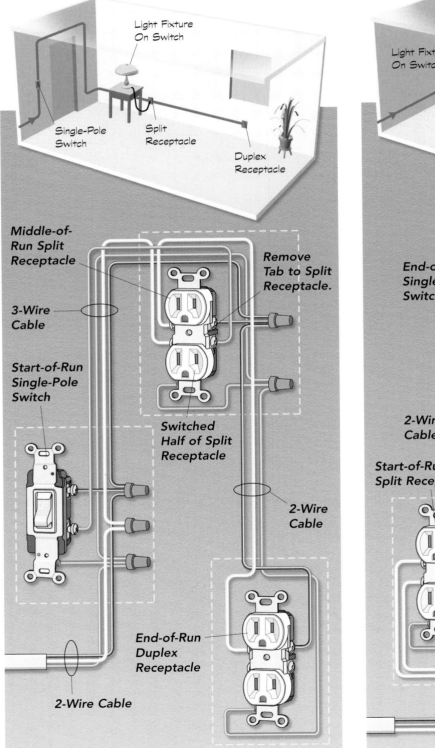

Light Fixture On Switch

Single-Pole Switch

Split Receptacle

Duplex Receptacle

Middle-of-Run Split Receptacle

3-Wire Cable

Start-of-Run Single-Pole Switch

Remove Tab to Split Receptacle.

Switched Half of Split Receptacle

2-Wire Cable

End-of-Run Duplex Receptacle

2-Wire Cable

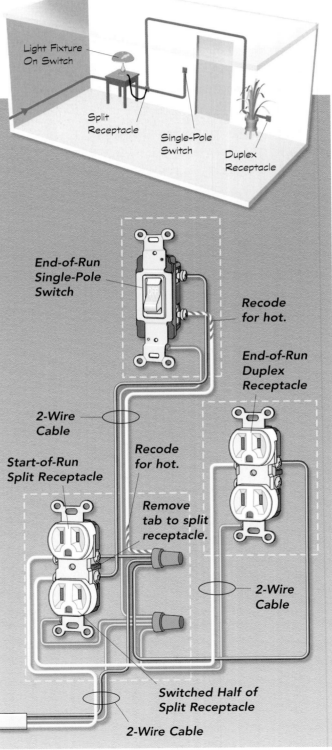

Light Fixture On Switch

Split Receptacle

Single-Pole Switch

Duplex Receptacle

End-of-Run Single-Pole Switch

Recode for hot.

End-of-Run Duplex Receptacle

2-Wire Cable

Start-of-Run Split Receptacle

Recode for hot.

Remove tab to split receptacle.

2-Wire Cable

Switched Half of Split Receptacle

2-Wire Cable

Interpreting a Receptacle

The labels or markings that appear on a receptacle convey important information about safety and usage. A UL label, for instance, means that the device has been certified for safety by the American Underwriters Laboratories, while a CSA label indicates approval by the Canadian equivalent—the Canadian Standards Association. Also shown are amperage and voltage ratings, which state the maximum permitted for the device. You should be especially alert to the acceptable wire usage designation, which indicates what kind of wire is safe to connect to the receptacle. A CU label means that only copper wire can be used; CO/ALR indicates that aluminum wires are acceptable; and CU/AL specifies copper or copper-clad aluminum wires only.

The screw terminal colors on a receptacle also denote specific information. Use the brass screw terminals for black/red hot wires, the silver screw terminals for white neutral wires, and the green terminal screw for the grounding connection.

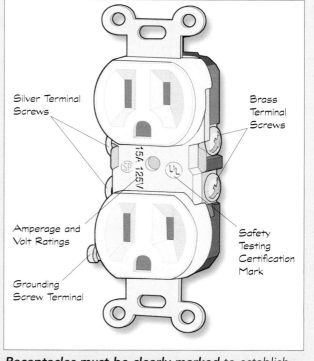

Receptacles must be clearly marked to establish proof of safety, to indicate amperage and voltage, and the proper type of wire.

High-Voltage Receptacles

Large appliances in a home often draw significantly more current than smaller appliances. For this reason, contemporary homes usually have two types of receptacles—one type provides low-voltage power (115 to 125 volts), and the other provides high-voltage power (220 to 250 volts). Appliances that are rated for 240 volts—such as cooking ranges, clothes dryers, and air conditioners—are required to be connected to a single circuit. Though some high-voltage appliances incorporate their own electrical box and must be directly hard-wired, most are connected to either a flush- or surface-mounted receptacle box. A nonmetallic sheathed cable containing two hot wires, each carrying 120 volts, and a grounding wire typically form an end-of-run connection within the receptacle box, which must be located within the length of the appliance cord. Because no neutral wire is needed, the white wire is coded, using black tape, to indicate that it is hot. However, a high-voltage circuit that also requires 120-volt current to operate clocks, timers, and lights does need to have a white neutral wire connected to the receptacle—so that the appliance can split the entering current between 120 volts and 240 volts. These circuits use three-wire cable.

A 240- (250) volt receptacle uses a two-wire cable with ground; the white wire is taped black. The grounding wire is pigtailed to the receptacle and the electrical box if metal.

Wiring Methods

All receptacles for high-voltage appliances have specific slot configurations that can only mate with the corresponding type of plug. (See the table, "High-Voltage Receptacle Patterns," below.) Note that such plugs are labeled with X and Y to designate connections for the current-carrying wires, W for the white grounding wire connection, and the G for the receptacle grounding wire connection.

▶ *Older three-slot 120/240- (125/250) volt receptacles use a three-wire cable with ground; the black and red wires are connected to brass setscrew terminals, and the white wire goes to neutral. Newer four-slot receptacles include a ground connection.*

Bare Copper Grounding Wire

Red Hot Wire

White Neutral Wire

Black Hot Wire

High-Voltage Receptacle Patterns

Slot Configuration	NEMA No.	Amps	Volts	Phase	Poles	Wires	With Grounding	Without Grounding
	5-30R	30A	125V		2	3	x	
	6-30R	30A	250V		2	3	x	
	7-30R	30A	277V		2	3	x	
	10-30R	30A	125/250V		3	3		x
	14-30R	30A	125/250V		3	4	x	
	15-30R	30A	250V	3	3	4	x	
	18-30R	30A	120/208V	3	4	4		x
	5-50R	50A	125V		2	3	x	
	6-50R	50A	250V		2	3	x	
	7-50R	50A	277V		2	3	x	
	10-50R	50A	125/250V		3	3		x
	14-50R	50A	125/250V		3	4	x	
	18-50R	50A	120/208V	3	4	4		x
	14-60R	60A	125/250V		3	4	x	

The National Electrical Manufacturer's Association (NEMA) assigns a number to each receptacle slot pattern. All NEMA receptacle numbers end with the letter R. The corresponding plug number ends with the letter P. These numbers are universal and identify compatible receptacles and plugs, irrespective of manufacturer.

240-Volt Appliance Receptacle

Wire a 240-volt appliance receptacle using a two-wire cable with a ground. Connect the white wire to one brass terminal and the black wire to the other. Tape the white wire black to indicate that it is hot. Pigtail the grounding wire to both the receptacle and box grounding screws.

120/240-Volt Appliance Receptacle

Red and black wires in a three-wire cable provide 240-volt power to this type of appliance receptacle. Either wire, combined with the white wire, provides 120-volt power. The receptacle has no ground terminal. Connect the grounding wire to the grounding screw in the receptacle box.

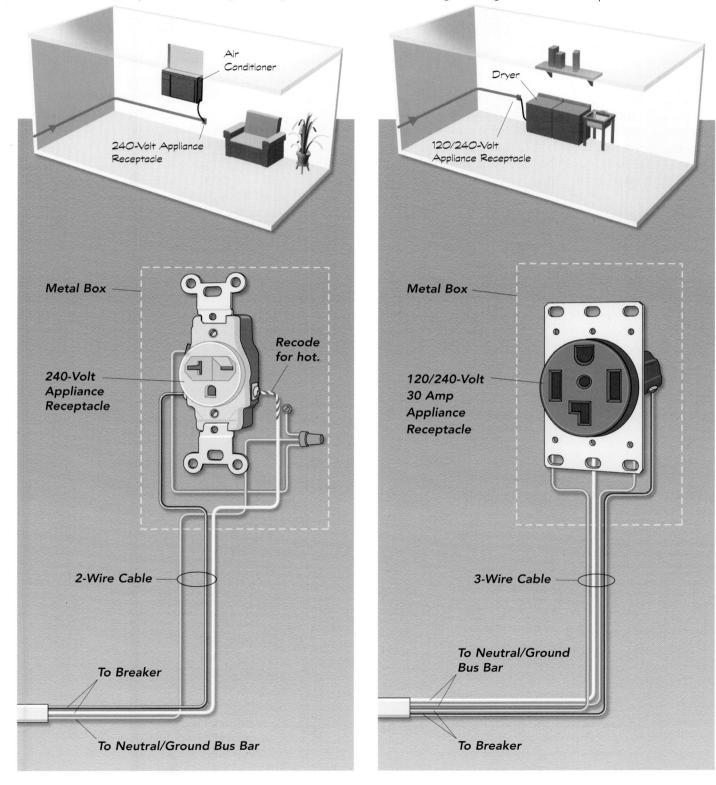

Air Conditioner

240-Volt Appliance Receptacle

Dryer

120/240-Volt Appliance Receptacle

Metal Box

240-Volt Appliance Receptacle

Recode for hot.

Metal Box

120/240-Volt 30 Amp Appliance Receptacle

2-Wire Cable

3-Wire Cable

To Breaker

To Neutral/Ground Bus Bar

To Neutral/Ground Bus Bar

To Breaker

GFCI Receptacles

A ground-fault circuit interrupter (GFCI) is an electrical device that prevents electrocution caused by an accident or equipment malfunction. In a general-purpose, 120-volt household circuit, current moves along two insulated wires—one white and one black. Power is brought to the device or appliance by the black wire and returns from it by the white wire. As long as these two current flows remain equal, then the circuit operates normally and safely. However, if a portion of the return current is missing, or "faulted," a GFCI will immediately open the circuit in $\frac{1}{25}$th to $\frac{1}{30}$th of a second—25 to 30 times faster than a heartbeat. In this fraction of a second, you may receive a mild pinprick of a shock, rather than the dangerous or potentially lethal shock that would otherwise occur in a circuit without the protection of a ground-fault circuit interrupter.

A GFCI receptacle, however, is not foolproof. For a ground-fault circuit interrupter to succeed, a ground-fault must first occur. This happens when current flows out of the normal circuit to a ground pathway, causing the imbalance between the black and white wires mentioned earlier. In this instance, if you place your body between the black and white wires, and you are not grounded, the GFCI will not function properly because it has no way of distinguishing your body from any other current-drawing device. The number of electrons entering the circuit is equal to the number of electrons returning from the circuit, except that they are passing first through the resistance within your body—causing your heart to go into defibrillation, beating erratically. If your heartbeat is not quickly restored to normal, then you will die. Even if the circuit is connected to a breaker panel, the breaker will not trip unless the internal current exceeds 15 or 20 amps—2,500 times more than is necessary to cause electrocution. A breaker or fuse is only designed to protect your household wiring against excessive current—it is not designed to protect you.

Required GFCI Locations. Even though GFCI circuits are not foolproof, they are nevertheless required in certain locations within a dwelling unit, specified by the NEC (Section 210-8). These locations include, but are not strictly limited to, bathrooms, garages, outbuildings, outdoors, crawl spaces, unfinished basements, kitchens, and wet-bar sinks. A good general rule to follow is that if you are working in a damp or wet environment, then the receptacle you use should be GFCI-protected. If no GFCI receptacle is located nearby, then use an extension cord that has a built-in GFCI.

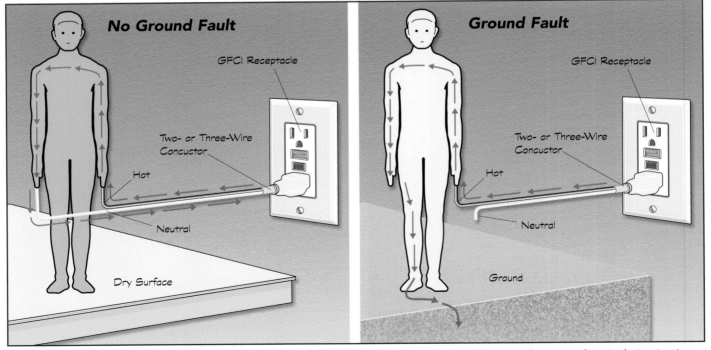

If an electrical current flows through your body from a hot wire to a neutral wire, this completes an electrical circuit—just as though you were an appliance or fixture. In this case, a ground-fault circuit interrupter cannot save you from being electrocuted because it cannot distinguish you from your microwave. If you hold only one wire, however, the resulting imbalance in current entering and leaving the circuit will trip the GFCI and protect you from serious shock or electrocution.

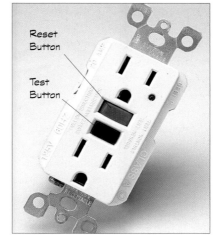

A GFCI receptacle has both TEST and RESET buttons. When a ground fault occurs or a test is made, the RESET button will pop out. Once a fault is eliminated or the test completed, press the button back in to reset the circuit.

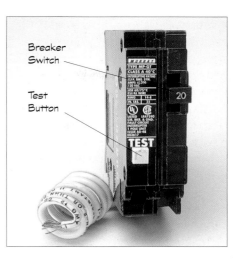

A GFCI circuit breaker has a TEST button, but no RESET button. To reset a GFCI breaker, first push the switch to the OFF position; then flip it back to the ON position.

A GFCI receptacle resembles a conventional receptacle, except that it has built-in RESET and TEST buttons. A GFCI can also be directly installed at the panel box as a circuit breaker. This type of ground-fault circuit interrupter has a TEST button only; when tripped, the switch flips only halfway off to break the circuit. To reset the circuit, the breaker must be switched completely off and then flipped back on again. A GFCI receptacle is less expensive than a breaker-type GFCI and has the advantage of letting you reset a circuit at the point of use. Although ground-fault circuit interrupters can be wired to protect multiple devices, they are most effective when limited to protecting a single location.

HOW TO: *Install a GFCI Receptacle*

Difficulty Level: 🦇🦇

Tools and Materials
For metal boxes

- Insulated screwdriver
- Receptacle box
- Wire connectors
- Long-nose pliers
- 12/2G NM cable
- Wire stripper
- Cable clamp*

- GFCI receptacle
- Cable ripper
- Neon circuit tester
- Copper grounding wire
- Diagonal-cutting pliers
- Grounding pigtail and screw*

Connect the GFCI Hot and Neutral Wires. After installing the receptacle box, pull and rip the cable, and strip the inside wires. Using a wire connector, splice the black hot wires; then pigtail them to the GFCI receptacle at the terminal screw labeled HOT LINE. **(Photo 1)** Using another wire connector, splice the white neutral cable wires; then pigtail them to the GFCI receptacle at the terminal screw labeled WHITE LINE. **(Photo 2)**

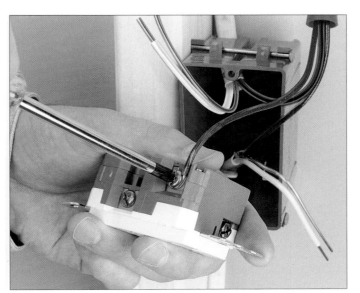

1 Splice the black hot wires and pigtail them to the HOT LINE terminal screw on the GFCI receptacle.

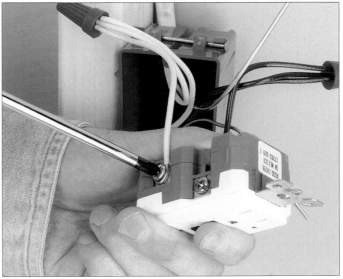

2 Splice the white neutral wires and pigtail them to the terminal screw labeled WHITE LINE on the receptacle.

Connect the GFCI Grounding Wires, and Install the Receptacle. Splice the bare copper cable grounding wires together, and then pigtail them to the green GFCI receptacle grounding screw. **(Photo 3)** Install the GFCI receptacle box and coverplate, and then turn on the power. Using a neon circuit tester, test the circuit for power. Press the TEST button to see whether or not the GFCI is operational; then reset it. **(Photo 4)**

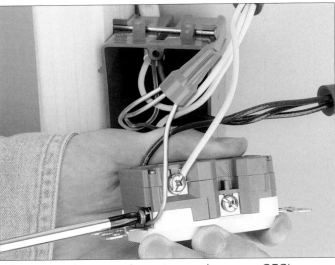

3 Pigtail the grounding wires to the green GFCI receptacle grounding screw.

Reset Button

Test Button

4 Check the RESET button on the receptacle by pushing in the TEST button; the RESET button should pop out.

Protecting Multiple Locations. If you want several receptacles farther down circuit, or *downstream,* from the GFCI receptacle to also have GFCI protection, then use the method of wiring for multiple locations. Wire the receptacle using a middle-of-run configuration, connecting the downstream hot and neutral wires to the screw terminals labeled LOAD. In this type of connection, any *upstream* receptacles will not be protected.

GFCI Breaker. To install the circuit breaker type of GFCI, simply insert the device into the panel box in the same way as a conventional circuit breaker; then connect the wires from the circuit you wish to protect. Connect the white corkscrew wire attached to the GFCI circuit breaker to the white neutral bus in the panel.

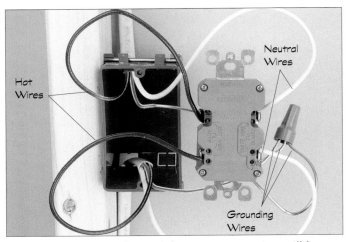

Hot Wires

Neutral Wires

Grounding Wires

A GFCI receptacle for multilocation protection will have one set of hot and neutral wires connected to the LINE terminal screws and the other to the LOAD terminal screws.

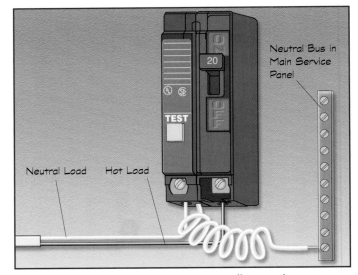

Neutral Bus in Main Service Panel

Neutral Load   Hot Load

A GFCI circuit breaker is easy to install—simply connect the black and white load wires to the appropriate screw terminals on the breaker; then connect the white "corkscrew" wire to the panel neutral bus.

Single-Location GFCI Receptacle Circuit

All kitchen countertop and bathroom receptacles—and receptacles within 6 ft. of a wet-bar sink—must be GFCI protected. To protect a single location using a GFCI receptacle, connect the feed cable to the LINE terminals. Receptacles downstream will remain unprotected.

Multiple GFCI Receptacle Circuit

In some locations the electrical code may require more than one protected receptacle where multiple receptacles must be GFCI protected, such as over kitchen counters. They should be wired for single-location protection. This will require both two- and three-wire cables.

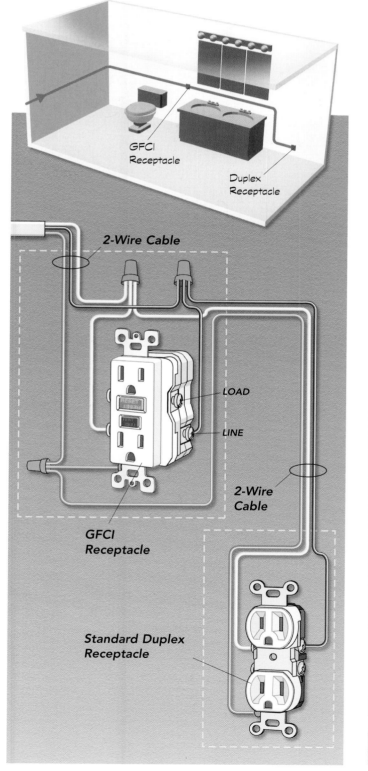

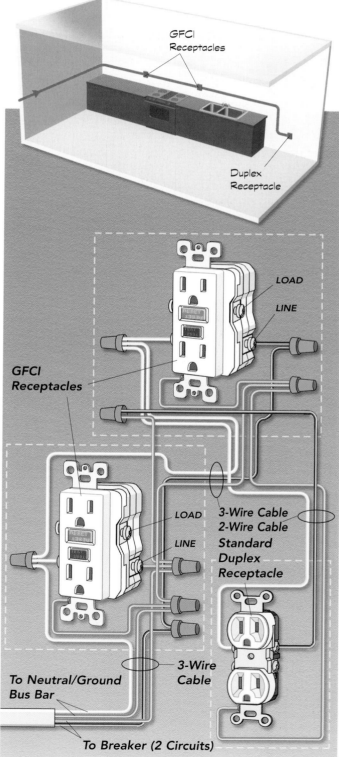

Switches

Single-Pole Switches

An electrical switch controls the flow of power in an electrical circuit. It provides an open circuit in the OFF position and acts as a short, or closed, circuit in the ON position. A switch having two screw terminals is known as a single-pole switch; it can control a circuit from one location only. Most residential switches are single-pole switches. Power is connected to one side of the switch at all times. When the switch is on, electricity flows from the wire attached to the powered screw terminal, through the switch, and into the fixture or appliance wiring connected to the other screw terminal. If the switch is at the end of a circuit, power will flow through the black hot wire and return through the white neutral wire, taped black to classify it as hot. (Neutral current in the white wire equals that in the black wire; in the ON position, either wire can cause an electric shock.) If the switch is in the middle of a run, two black hot wires connect to the switch and the two white neutral wires are spliced together with a wire connector in the switch box. Splice together the bare copper grounding wires, and then pigtail them to the green grounding screw on the switch and in the box, if it is metal.

HOW TO: Wire a Middle-of-Run Single-Pole Switch

Difficulty Level: 🦇🦇

Tools and Materials
*For metal boxes

- Insulated screwdriver
- Switch box and switch
- Long-nose pliers
- 12/2G NM cable
- Cable clamps*
- Wire connectors
- Multipurpose tool
- Cable ripper
- Grounding pigtail and screw*

Connect the Switch Hot and Neutral Wires. After you've installed the box, pulled the cable, and stripped the wires, connect the black hot wires to the switch. **(Photo 1)** Loop each wire left to right over the screw terminals to prevent them from unraveling. Splice the white neutral wires in the switch box. **(Photo 2)**

Install and Test the Switch. Splice together the bare copper grounding wires and pigtail them to the green grounding screw on the switch or in the box, if it is metal. **(Photo 3)** Screw the switch into the box, with the ON in the up position, install the cover plate, and turn on the circuit. Test the switch to be sure that it operates the connected fixture. **(Photo 4)**

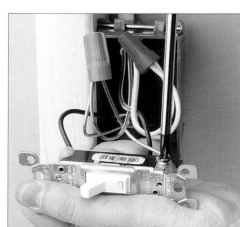

1 In a middle-of-run switch circuit, connect both of the black hot wires to the screw terminals on the switch.

2 Splice together the white neutral wires in a middle-of-run switch circuit inside the switch box.

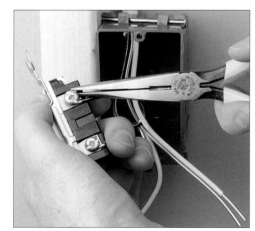

3 Braid the grounding wires together; then pigtail them to the switch and metal box grounding screw.

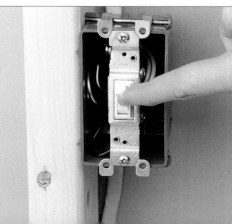

4 Push the wiring and the switch carefully into the switch box, screw the switch in place; then test the circuit.

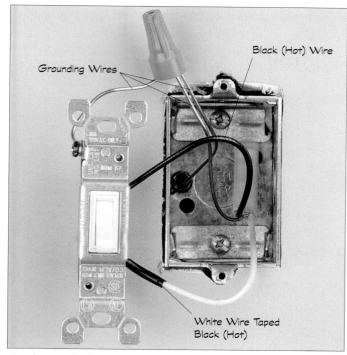

At the end of a circuit, both the black and white wires connecting to a switch are hot. To indicate this, wrap the white wire with black tape.

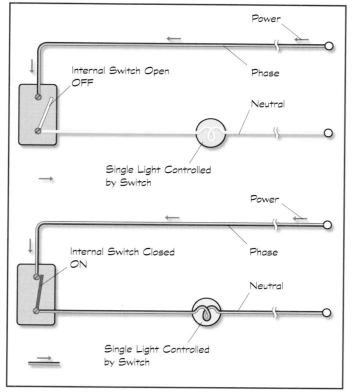

A single-pole light switch has one operable contact and one fixed contact. In the OFF position, the switch is open; in the ON position, the switch is closed and the circuit is complete.

Single-Pole Switch to Light Fixture

In a standard lighting circuit, the power is supplied by a two-wire cable with a grounding wire. In this configuration, the light fixture is located at the end of the cable run.

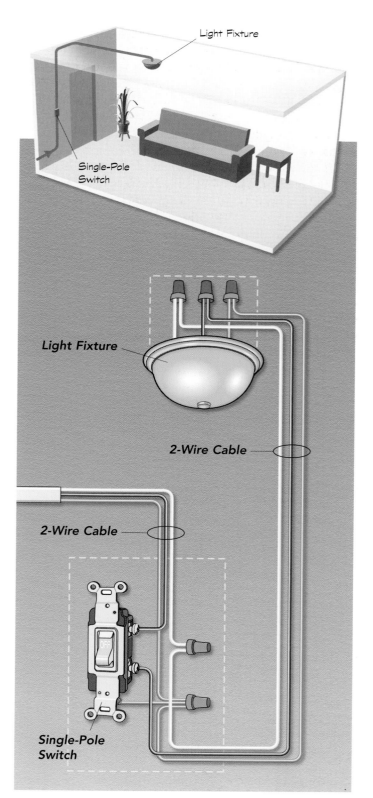

Wiring Methods

Light Fixture to an End-of-Run Single-Pole Switch

Use two-wire cable to wire a light fixture where the switch comes at the end of the cable run. This configuration is known as a switch loop. Mark the white neutral wire with black tape to indicate that it is hot.

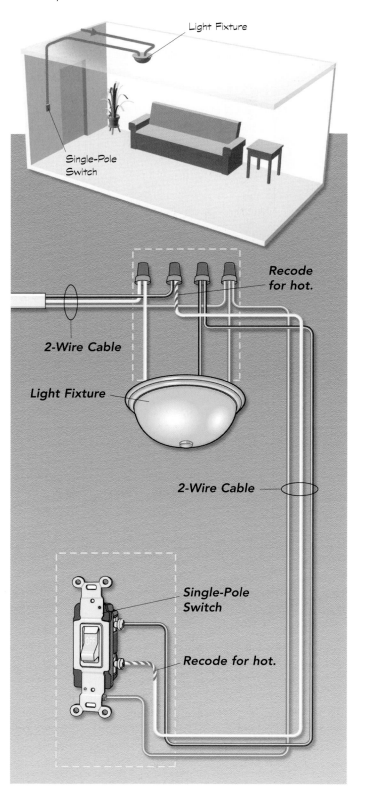

Light Fixture

Single-Pole Switch

Recode for hot.

2-Wire Cable

Light Fixture

2-Wire Cable

Single-Pole Switch

Recode for hot.

Double-Ganged Switches to End-of-Run Light Fixtures

In this setup, power is fed first through the switches and then to the light fixtures. Only two-wire cable is needed for the wiring connections. The switches occupy one double-ganged electrical box.

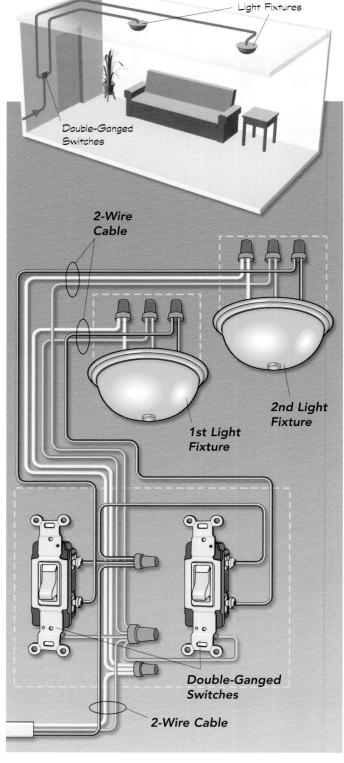

Separately Switched Light Fixtures

Double-Ganged Switches

2-Wire Cable

2-Wire Cable

2nd Light Fixture

1st Light Fixture

Double-Ganged Switches

2-Wire Cable

Three-Way Switches

Like a single-pole switch, a three-way switch controls the flow of power in an electrical circuit, but from two different locations instead of just one. This type of switch is useful, for example, when you want to be able to turn on a stairway light from either the top or bottom of the stairway, or a detached garage light from either the house or the garage. Such switching requires special three-conductor or three-way switch cable with ground. This type of cable is usually round, rather than flat like conventional nonmetallic (NM) cable, and it contains an additional, insulated conductor—a red wire.

Three-way switches also differ from single-pole switches in that they have three screw terminals instead of two: a COM terminal (dark screw), and two traveler screws to connect wires that run between switches. The switch also has a grounding screw. The switch does not have

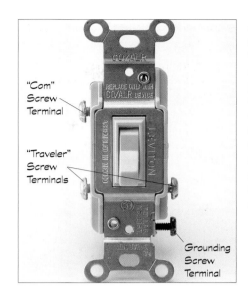

A three-way switch has three terminal screws and no ON/OFF positions. The dark colored screw terminal screw is the COM, or common, terminal. The two light screw terminals are switch leads, known as "travelers."

"Com" Screw Terminal

"Traveler" Screw Terminals

Grounding Screw Terminal

either an ON or an OFF marked position because the COM terminal alternates the connection between two different switch locations, allowing either position to potentially close the circuit.

You must consider three different cables when wiring a three-way switch: the feeder cable, the fixture cable, and the three-wire cable. The typical wiring method is to run the two-wire hot feeder cable into the first switch box, and then the three-way switch cable between the first and the second switch box. You can then run a second two-wire fixture cable between the second switch box and the fixture box. An alternative method is to run the hot feeder into one switch box; then run the three-way switch cable from the first switch box to the light fixture and then to the second switch box. Either method initially requires that you run the hot feeder to a switch box. It's also possible to run power first to the light fixture, but this method is not preferred because it's more difficult to troubleshoot if there's a problem in the circuit.

HOW TO: *Wire a Three-Way Switch*

Difficulty Level: 🐾🐾🐾

Tools and Materials

- Insulated screwdriver
- Switch boxes
- Wire connectors
- Two-wire cable
- Wire stripper
- Cable ripper
- Long-nose pliers
- Three-way switches
- Cable clamps
- Three-way switch cable
- Copper wire
- Diagonal-cutting pliers
- Multipurpose tool (optional)

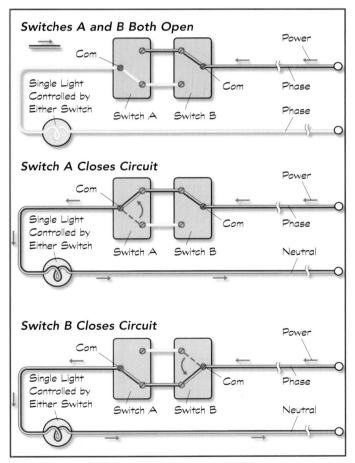

Switches A and B Both Open

Com
Single Light Controlled by Either Switch
Switch A   Switch B   Com
Power
Phase
Phase

Switch A Closes Circuit

Com
Single Light Controlled by Either Switch
Switch A   Switch B   Com
Power
Phase
Neutral

Switch B Closes Circuit

Com
Single Light Controlled by Either Switch
Switch A   Switch B   Com
Power
Phase
Neutral

A three-way light switch has one operable contact and two fixed contacts. In the first position, the switch is open; in the second position, the switch is closed and the circuit is completed through switch box A; in the third position, the switch is also closed but the circuit is completed through switch box B.

Wiring Methods

Connect the Feeder Cable, and Splice the Neutral Wires. After you have installed the switch boxes, pull the cables into the boxes. Rip back and remove enough sheathing and paper insulation to expose the insulated wires. Then strip the wires. Connect the black hot wire in the feeder cable to the COM terminal (the dark, oxidized "common" screw terminal) on the first three-way switch. The feeder cable is a two-wire cable and ground coming from the power source. **(Photo 1)** Splice the white neutral wire from the feeder cable to the white neutral wire in the three-way switch cable that goes to the second three-way switch. **(Photo 2)**

Connect the Black and Red Traveler Wires. Connect the black traveler wire in the three-way switch cable from one traveler terminal (light-color screw) on the first switch to one traveler terminal on the second. The traveler wire provides uninterrupted power between the first and second three-way switches. **(Photo 3)** Next, connect the red traveler wire in the three-way switch cable from the other traveler terminal on the first switch to the remaining traveler terminal on the second. This traveler wire also maintains continuity of power between the three-way switches. **(Photo 4)** The wires between COM terminals power the fixture.

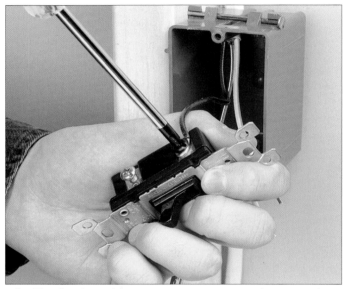

1 *The feeder cable contains two wires and a ground; it supplies power to the first switch.*

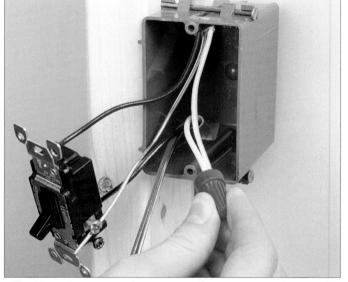

2 *The white neutral wires in a three-way switch circuit must run continuously through the entire circuit.*

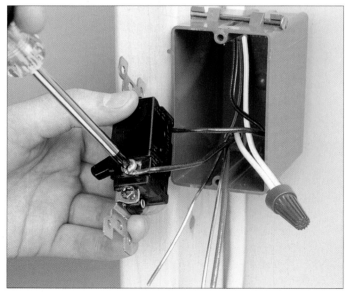

3 *The black traveler wire maintains continuity of power between the first and second three-way switch.*

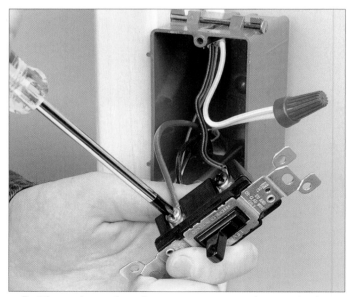

4 *The red traveler wire connects a traveler terminal on the first switch to one on the second switch.*

Connect the First and Second Switch Grounding Wires. Using a green wire connector, in the first switch box, splice the grounding wires from the feeder cable, the first switch, and the traveler cable going to the second switch. Pigtail these to the green grounding screw in the first switch box (if it is a metal box). **(Photo 5)** In the second switch box, splice together the grounding traveler wire from the first switch box, the bare copper grounding wire from the second switch, and the grounding wire from the light fixture box (a two-wire cable). Pigtail these to the green grounding screw inside the second switch box (if it is a metal box). **(Photo 6)**

Splice the Traveler Neutral Wires, and Wire the Fixture. Inside the second switch box, splice the neutral traveler wire in the three-way switch cable coming from the first switch box and the neutral wire in the two-wire cable coming from the light fixture box. **(Photo 7)** In the fixture box, splice the white neutral wire from the second switch box and the white neutral wire coming from the light fixture. Do the same with the black wire coming from the COM terminal on the second switch and the black wire coming from the light fixture; then connect the fixture grounding wire to the green grounding screw in the box, if it is metal. **(Photo 8)**

5 *Feeder line and traveler switch grounding wires must be pigtailed to the grounding screw in the first switch.*

6 *Fixture and traveler switch grounding wires must pigtail to the grounding screw on the second switch.*

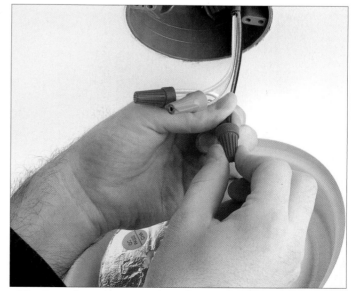

7 *Continue neutral wiring through the second switch, connecting the traveler neutral to the fixture neutral.*

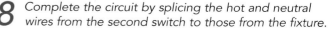

8 *Complete the circuit by splicing the hot and neutral wires from the second switch to those from the fixture.*

Three-Way Switches with Fixture at End-of-Run

In this switch circuit, power goes from the first switch box through the second, and then to the light fixture. A three-wire cable with ground is run between the switches and a two-wire cable runs between the second switch and the fixture.

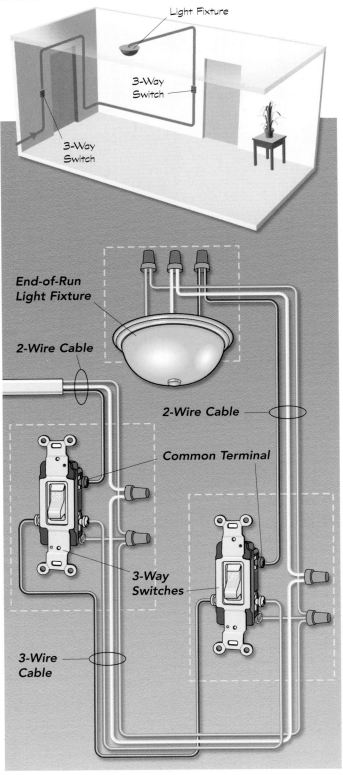

Light Fixture

3-Way Switch

3-Way Switch

End-of-Run Light Fixture

2-Wire Cable

2-Wire Cable

Common Terminal

3-Way Switches

3-Wire Cable

Three-Way Switches with Fixture at Start-of-Run

In this setup, power enters the light fixture on a two-wire grounded cable. It proceeds to the three-way switches and then returns to the fixture. Two-wire cable connects the fixture to the first switch and three-wire cable runs between the switches.

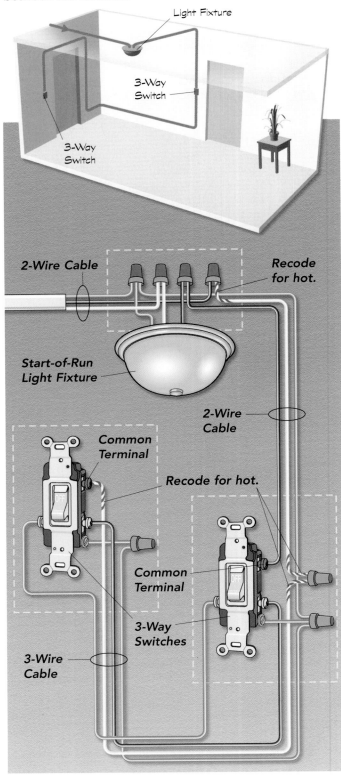

Light Fixture

3-Way Switch

3-Way Switch

2-Wire Cable

Recode for hot.

Start-of-Run Light Fixture

2-Wire Cable

Common Terminal

Recode for hot.

Common Terminal

3-Way Switches

3-Wire Cable

Three-Way Switches with Fixture at Middle-of-Run

Here, the light fixture is positioned between the two three-way switches. Power comes to the first switch on a two-wire grounded cable. It passes through the light fixture, proceeds to the second switch, and then returns to the fixture on three-wire cable.

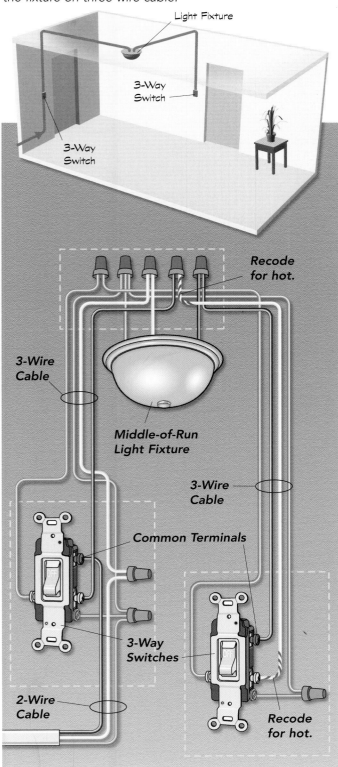

Light Fixture

3-Way
Switch

3-Way
Switch

Recode
for hot.

3-Wire
Cable

Middle-of-Run
Light Fixture

3-Wire
Cable

Common Terminals

3-Way
Switches

2-Wire
Cable

Recode
for hot.

Start-of-Run Fixture between Three-Way Switches

In this hookup, power comes to the light fixture box and is then connected to the three way switches, which are powered on separate lines from opposite sides of the fixture. The white feeder wire connects directly to the silver screw terminal of the fixture.

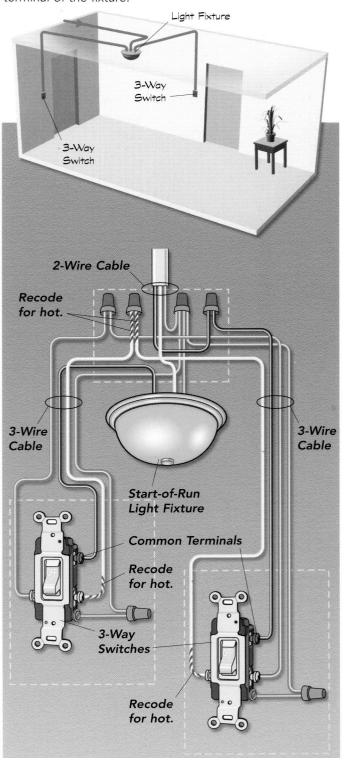

Light Fixture

3-Way
Switch

3-Way
Switch

2-Wire Cable

Recode
for hot.

3-Wire
Cable

3-Wire
Cable

Start-of-Run
Light Fixture

Common Terminals

Recode
for hot.

3-Way
Switches

Recode
for hot.

Wiring Methods

Four-Way Switches

A four-way switch can be connected between two three-way switches to allow you to control a light from three different locations. A four-way switch is installed in line or "series" with the travelers between the two three-way switches. A three-wire cable should be run from the first three-way switch to the four-way switch and from the second three-way switch to the four-way switch. The red and black wires from the first switch connect to the brass-color screws, and the black and red wires from the second switch connect to the dark- or copper-color screws. The white neutral conductor is carried all the way through all switches. Pigtail the grounding wires to the green grounding screw inside the metal switch box.

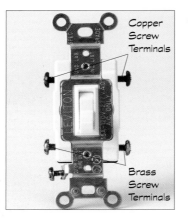

A four-way switch has four terminal screws. It looks similar to a double-pole switch, but does not have any dedicated ON or OFF position. A four-way switch controls an outlet or fixture from three separate locations, in tandem with two three-way switches; it must always be located between the other two switches on the circuit.

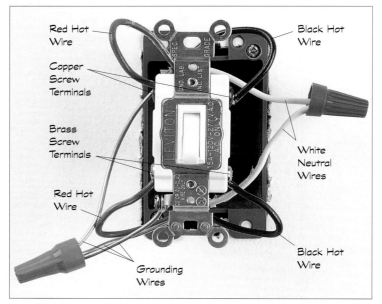

The internal levers in a four-way switch either connect the screw terminals in a straight vertical configuration or in a diagonal X pattern. In combination with the two three-way switches, this permits the circuit to be completed or broken by any one of the three switches.

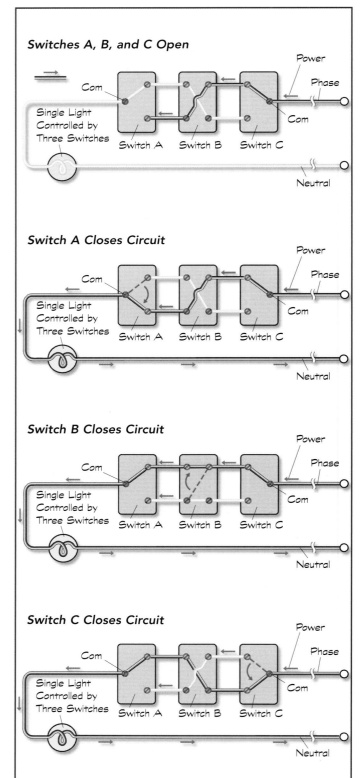

A four-way light switch has two operable contacts and two fixed contacts. In the first position, the switch is open; in the second position, the circuit is completed to switch box A; in the switch is also closed but the circuit completed to switch box B; and in the fourth position, the circuit is closed to switch box C.

Four-Way Switch

A four-way switch must be combined with two three-way switches to control a light fixture from three or more locations. Two-wire cable feeds power through the fixture to the first three-way switch. The four-way switch is connected to the other switch using three-wire cable.

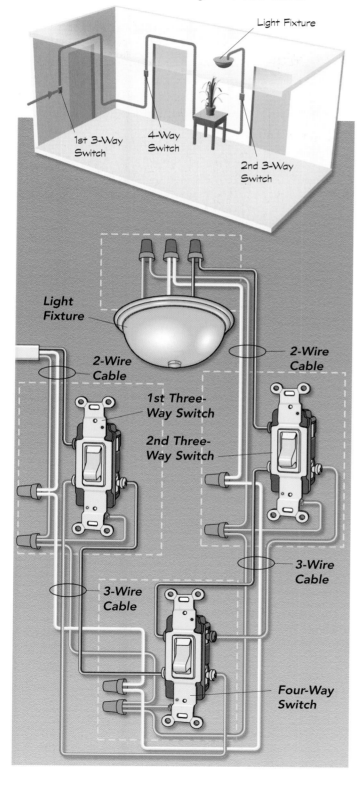

Light Fixture

1st 3-Way Switch

4-Way Switch

2nd 3-Way Switch

Light Fixture

2-Wire Cable

2-Wire Cable

1st Three-Way Switch

2nd Three-Way Switch

3-Wire Cable

3-Wire Cable

Four-Way Switch

Dimmer Switches

A dimmer switch allows you to regulate luminosity, or brightness, of light emanating from a light fixture—either to set a mood or conserve energy. Dimmer switches can be single-pole or three-way switches. In a three-way configuration, only the dimmer switch regulates brightness, while the paired toggle switch merely turns the fixture on or off. Though not commonly used, dimmer switches are also available for fluorescent lighting.

Dimmer switches are controlled by a solid-state device within the switch that alternately turns the current on and off as many as 120 times per second. By restricting the flow of current, the switch dims the light. The longer the current is off, the dimmer the light. Standard dimmer switches are rated for 600 watts.

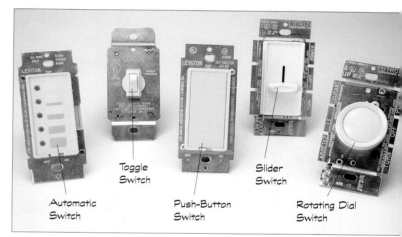

Toggle Switch

Slider Switch

Automatic Switch

Push-Button Switch

Rotating Dial Switch

Dimmers are available *in a variety of types, from conventional toggle switches to rotating dials or switches that slide up and down. Automatic dimmers are operated by electronic sensors. Others have faces that light up in the dark.*

In an end of run switch, *the travelers are a red wire and a white wire taped black, or a black wire and a white wire taped black.*

A middle-of-run *dimmer switch has traveler wires that are either both black or one red and the other black.*

HOW TO: *Wire a Single-Pole Dimmer Switch*

Difficulty Level: 🐿️

Tools and Materials

- Insulated screwdriver
- Neon circuit tester
- Wire stripper
- Multipurpose tool
- Dimmer switch
- Wire connectors
- Long-nose pliers

Turn Off Power, and Disconnect the Circuit Wires.
Turn off power to the existing switch circuit, remove the cover plate on the switch box, and pull out the switch. Using a neon circuit tester, check the circuit to be sure that the power is turned off, taking care not to touch the wire terminals while doing so. **(Photo 1)** Disconnect the circuit wiring to the old single-pole switch; then discard the switch. Check for damage to the wire or box. **(Photo 2)**

Strip the Circuit Wires, and Connect the Dimmer Switch. Clip off the stripped ends of the existing circuit wires; then strip them again—leaving about ½ inch of exposed wire at the ends. **(Photo 3)** Using red wire connectors, splice the lead wires from the dimmer switch to the existing circuit wires in the switch box. Because they are interchangeable, either of the dimmer wires may be spliced to either of the hot circuit wires. **(Photo 4)** However, be certain that the white circuit wire is taped black to label it as a hot wire. If there was a bare copper grounding wire connected to the old switch, then pigtail it to the grounding screw in the switch box if it is a metal box. Place the dimmer switch inside the switch box and replace the cover plate.

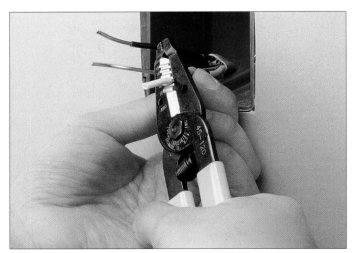

1 Before pulling out a switch, check the circuit with a neon circuit tester to be sure that the power is off.

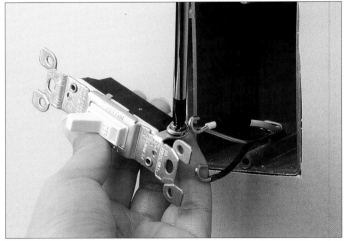

2 After disconnecting and discarding the old switch, examine the existing wiring and box for any damage.

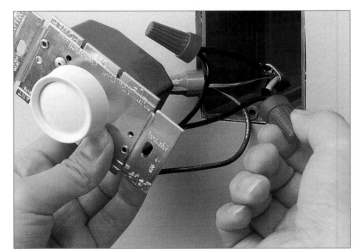

3 To make a crisp, new connection, cut away damaged wire ends, and restrip the circuit wires.

4 Splice the wires from the new switch to those from the circuit; either lead can connect to either circuit wire.

SMART TIP

Testing a Switch

When you flip on a switch and the switch circuit doesn't work, the problem may not be with the switch. It could be a blown fuse, a tripped circuit breaker, or a faulty fixture. First check the service panel; then test the switch. Begin by removing the fuse or setting the breaker on the switch circuit to the OFF position; then remove the switch coverplate. Apply the probes on a multi-tester to the black and white wire terminal screws to verify that the power is turned off; then turn on the switch. Next, touch the probe and clip of a battery-operated continuity tester to the wire terminals. If the switch is good, then the tester will either light up or buzz. Finally, turn off the switch. If it is good, then the tester should no longer light up or buzz. Replace the switch if it fails any of these tests. If the switch is good, the fault must be in the fixture.

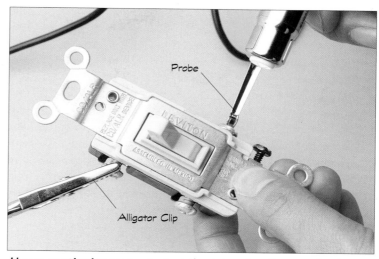

Use a continuity tester to test the integrity of an unwired or disconnected switch. Attach the alligator clip to one terminal screw and touch the probe to the other. If the switch is good, the probe will light when you turn the switch on, but will not light when you turn it off.

Plugs, Cords, and Sockets

Standard Plugs

Plugs come in a variety of different styles and shapes, including flat- or round-corded, grounded, polarized, and quick-connect. Round-corded plugs are typically used on larger appliances that require three-pronged, grounded plugs; smaller appliances commonly use flat-corded plugs. A polarized plug has one wide and one narrow prong and can only be inserted into a receptacle so that the neutral and hot cord wires properly align with the neutral and hot receptacle wires.

Some homeowners may still be using fixtures that have older-style, permanently attached cords and plugs. Because such cords and plugs no longer meet

NEC standards, it is simply cheaper and safer for you to replace them, rather than attempting to repair them. When you do replace a plug or cord, be sure that the new device meets current code requirements (NEC Article 400). If your existing cord is in good condition, but the plug needs to be replaced, cut the cord just behind the plug, and strip the insulation off the end of the cut wires. Then properly reconnect them to the new plug.

Plugs come in various configurations for different purposes; be sure that the replacement plugs you buy are appropriate for the appliances, receptacles, or wires to which they will be connected.

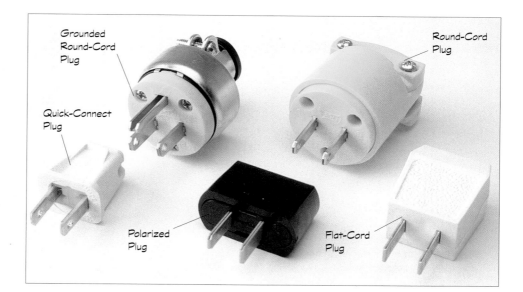

Grounded
Round-Cord
Plug

Round-Cord
Plug

Quick-Connect
Plug

Polarized
Plug

Flat-Cord
Plug

HOW TO: *Replace a Standard Round-Cord Plug*

Difficulty Level:

Tools and Materials

- Insulated screwdriver
- Wire stripper or multipurpose tool
- Replacement plug
- Diagonal-cutting pliers
- Long-nose pliers

Cut the Cord; Strip and Knot the Wires. If the plug cannot be easily detached from the cord, then use diagonal cutting pliers to cut the plug away from the cord. **(Photo 1)** Using a wire stripper or multipurpose tool, strip away ½ inch of insulation from the cut ends of the cord wires. **(Photo 2)** Thread the stripped wires through the new plug; then you can tie the black and white wires together, using an Underwriters' knot (page 116), but it's not necessary. **(Photo 3)**

Wire the Plug, and Install the Insulator. Pull the knot tight to the base of the plug; then attach the cord wires to the terminal screws. Wrap the black hot wire clockwise around the brass screw and the white neutral wire clockwise around the silver screw; then tighten the terminal screws. Next, attach the grounding wire to the plug grounding screw. **(Photo 4)** Slip the insulating plate over the plug prongs to protect the wires. **(Photo 5)**

1 Disconnect or cut the plug cleanly from the wiring.

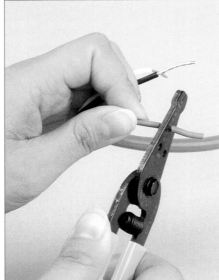

2 Restrip the wire ends to make a clean connection to a new plug.

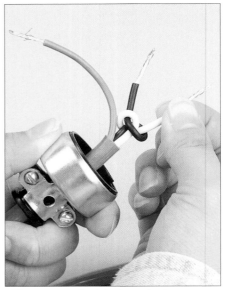

3 Secure the black and white wire ends using an Underwriters' knot.

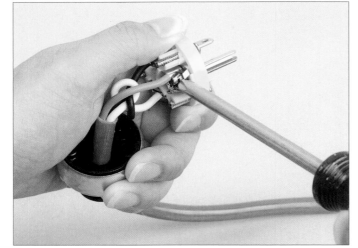

4 Attach the neutral wire to the silver screw and the hot wire to the brass screw. Then attach the ground.

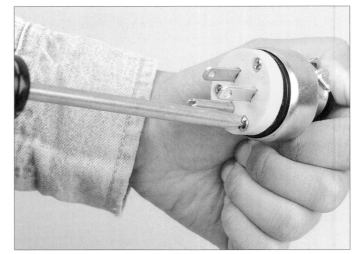

5 If an insulator came with the plug, slip it over the prongs to protect the wiring.

Many newer-style plug replacements are the quick-connect type—you simply squeeze together the prongs, pull to release the core from the plug casing, cut and insert the flat-cord ends, and replace the core in the casing. The wires do not need to be stripped because barbs on the inside of the plug core pierce the cord wires to complete the connection.

HOW TO: Install a Quick-Connect Plug

Difficulty Level:

Tools and Materials
- Quick-connect plug
- Diagonal-cutting pliers

Cut the Flat-Cord Wire. Use a diagonal cutting pliers or aviation snips to cleanly cut the plug away from the existing flat-cord wire. **(Photo 1)**

Insert the Cord. Squeeze the prongs on the quick-connect plug to remove the plug core; then insert the cut wire ends through the plug casing and into the opened core. **(Photo 2)**

Secure the Quick-Connect Plug. Squeeze the plug prongs together again to pierce the cord wires. Once the wires are pierced, snap the plug core back into its casing. **(Photo 3)** The quick-connect plug is now ready for use.

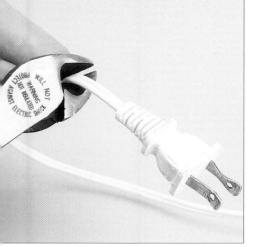

1 On flat cord, simply disconnect or cut away the old plug.

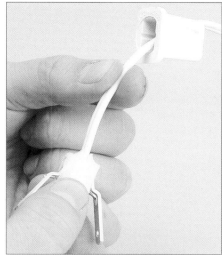

2 Insert unstripped wires into the prongs of a quick-connect plug.

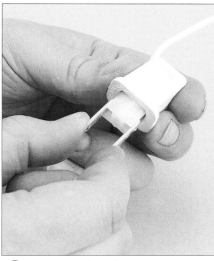

3 Squeeze the plug prongs together and secure the cover.

Lamp and Appliance Cords

Whenever you replace a plug, you should also check the cord. If its worn or damaged, then replace it too. Several different types of cords are available for lamps and appliances. Although a cord with an integral plug is preferable, you can purchase appliance cord by the foot and attach a plug to it. This alternative lets you choose the length of cord you want. In either case, select a cord that is appropriate for the appliance and that matches the original type of cord—do not use a light-duty cord in place of a heavy-duty one. Also, if the appliance is metal, the cord should contain a green grounding wire.

Before checking an old cord, be sure it is unplugged. Examine the wire carefully for cracking, fraying, and dryness. Replace all worn or damaged cords.

HOW TO: *Replace a Lamp Cord*

Difficulty Level: ✎

Tools and Materials
- Insulated screwdriver
- Utility knife
- Lamp cord
- Wire stripper

Remove the Old Cord, and Thread the New Cord.
Unplug the lamp, remove the lampshade and bulb, and separate the brass shell and insulation jacket from the socket. Disconnect the old cord, and pull it through the lamp base, unknotting it if necessary. **(Photo 1)**

Pull the new cord up through the lamp base and socket base, separate the last 2 inches of the cord wires, and strip at least ½ inch of each wire end. **(Photo 2)**

Knot the Wires, and Rewire the Socket. Using an Underwriters' knot, tie the wire ends together. (This is also known as a Hartford loop.) **(Photo 3)** Tighten the knot, and then pull the cord snugly into the socket base. Loop the bare wire ends clockwise around their respective screw terminals, and tighten the screws. **(Photo 4)** Replace the socket, put in a new bulb, and plug in the lamp. (See "How to Replace a Light Socket and Switch," next page.)

1 Turn off the power. Pull the old cord through the center pipe and out through the lamp base.

2 Pull the cord through the lamp base, and insert it into the socket base. Strip the ends of the wires.

3 Using an Underwriters' knot, tie the wire ends, tuck them into the socket base, and connect the wires.

4 Attach the copper wire to the brass terminal and silver wire to the silver terminal. Reassemble the socket.

Light Sockets and Switches

Occasionally, you may have a problem with a faulty light socket or switch. To test a socket, first unplug the lamp. Next, remove the socket from the lamp; then separate it from its outer shell and insulating sleeve. Clip a continuity tester to the socket shell; then touch the probe to the neutral (silver) terminal screw. If the tester lights, the continuity of the circuit is unbroken. To test the switch, clip the tester to the brass terminal screw; then touch the probe to the brass tab inside the socket shell. If the tester does not light in either switch position, the switch needs to be replaced.

HOW TO: *Replace a Light Socket and Switch*

Difficulty Level: ✎

Tools and Materials

* Insulated screwdriver
* Utility knife
* Lamp socket and switch
* Multipurpose tool

Remove the Socket and Insulator, and Disconnect the Wires. Unplug the lamp, remove the lampshade and bulb, and separate the brass shell and insulation jacket from the socket. **(Photo 1)** To free the socket, loosen the terminal screws; then disconnect the wires from the switch. **(Photo 2)** If the cord is damaged, replace it.

Wire the New Socket, and Reassemble the Socket and Switch. Twist the wire strands tightly together; then wire the new socket. Be sure the wire ends are secured with an Underwriters' knot. Connect the hot copper or black insulated wire to the brass terminal screw and the silver or white insulated wire to the silver terminal screw. **(Photo 3)** Connect the green grounding wire to the metal of the lamp. Replace the insulation jacket over the socket; then reinstall the brass shell. **(Photo 4)** When this is done, replace the bulb and the shade. Plug in the lamp.

1 Squeeze the brass sleeve above the base cap, and slip off both the sleeve and the inside insulator (often cardboard).

2 Loosen the terminal screws, disconnect the wires, and remove the old switch.

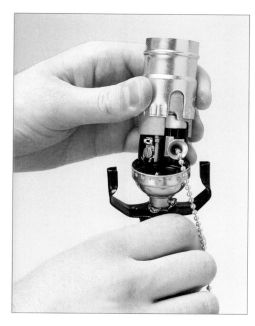

3 Connect the hot wires to the new socket. The wires should fit snugly under the terminal screws; if not, then re-twist them.

4 Place the insulator and brass shell over the socket. Tighten the setscrew holding the cord in the socket, if there is one, and replace the harp.

Wiring Methods

To test a socket, *clip a continuity tester to the socket; then touch the probe to the silver (neutral) terminal screw.*

To test the switch, *clamp the tester to the brass (hot) terminal screw, and touch the probe to the brass tab in the socket. The tester will light if connections are not broken.*

Socket and Switch Anatomy

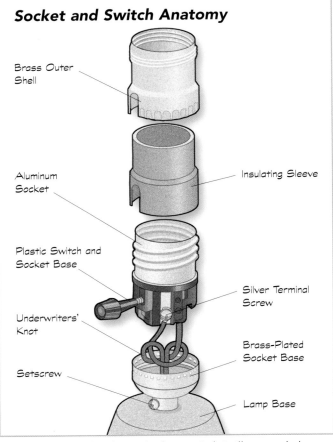

Brass Outer Shell

Aluminum Socket

Insulating Sleeve

Plastic Switch and Socket Base

Silver Terminal Screw

Underwriters' Knot

Brass-Plated Socket Base

Setscrew

Lamp Base

A lamp socket that has a built-in switch is illustrated above. If either the socket or the switch is faulty, it is best to replace them both; if the cord is damaged, then replace it too.

If a lamp requires no ground, then a nongrounded zip cord may be used to wire its socket and switch. This type of cord has one ribbed side and one smooth side; the ribbed side contains the neutral wire and connects to the silver terminal screw. The smooth side contains the hot wire and connects to the brass screw terminal. This difference aids in maintaining the correct polarity of all the wiring and fixture components—neutral to neutral, hot to hot. A reversal of polarity can result in a shock hazard, even when the lamp is switched off.

Multi-Socket Switches

Lamps that have two sockets are generally controlled by a single ON/OFF switch. In contrast, a three-socket lamp may have either a single switch or multiple switches.

In a two-socket lamp, the sockets are commonly soldered together, in which case the wiring is run internally. Because the switch operates both bulbs simultaneously, if one socket doesn't light, then you will first need to undo the wire connectors splicing together the switch and the power wires before you will be able to connect a new switch. If the two sockets are independently wired, then each can be replaced separately. Because both bulbs are still operated simultaneously, by one switch, the socket wiring is more complicated. In this instance, each power wire must be spliced to both sockets. Aside from the additional jumper wires, the switch can be replaced using the same method as before.

Lamps that have three sockets may have either a separate switch for each bulb or one four-way switch. In the case of separate switches, each socket will have jumper wires that are spliced together with the power wires. You can simply disconnect the jumper wires from the socket screw terminals and replace the faulty socket and switch. If a three-socket lamp has only one switch, then that switch will have three positions. The first position will operate the first socket only; the second position will operate both the second and third sockets; and the third position will operate all three sockets. A black wire attaches the switch to the line cord. A wire-connector splice connects the switch to a black jumper wire from the first socket, while a second splice connects the switch to black jumper wires from both the second and third sockets. Each socket may be individually replaced by disconnecting the wires from the terminal screws. To replace the switch, disconnect the wire-connector splices between the lamp cord and the socket.

Repairing Multi-Socket Switches

Soldered Double Socket

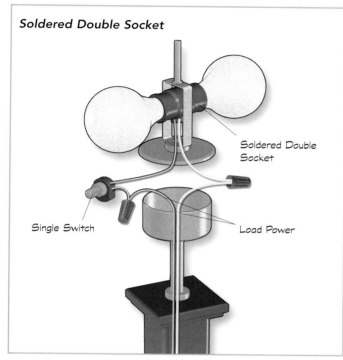

Soldered Double Socket

Single Switch

Load Power

To replace a soldered double socket, simply remove the wires from the socket terminal screws. To replace the switch, disconnect the wire-connector splice between the switch and the socket.

Separate Sockets

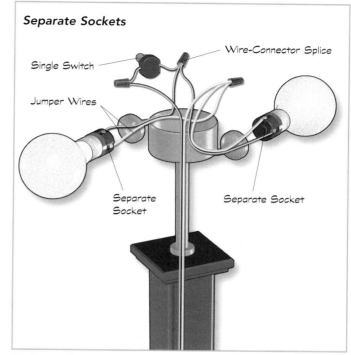

Single Switch

Wire-Connector Splice

Jumper Wires

Separate Socket

Separate Socket

If the sockets are separated, then you can replace them independently. Replace the switch by disconnecting the wire-connector splice between the switch and the black jumper wires.

Multiple Sockets with Separate Switches

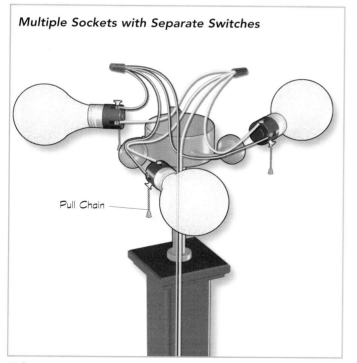

Pull Chain

When every socket has its own switch—for example, pull-chain switches for each lightbulb—each one can be easily disconnected at its own socket terminal screws for repair or replacement.

Multiple Sockets on a Four-Way Switch

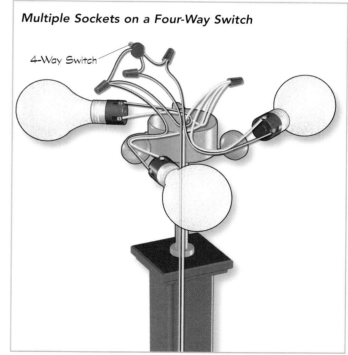

4-Way Switch

Multiple sockets on a four-way switch can also be disconnected at their terminal screws. Replace the four-way switch by undoing the wire-connector splice between it and the three black jumper wires.

Wiring Methods

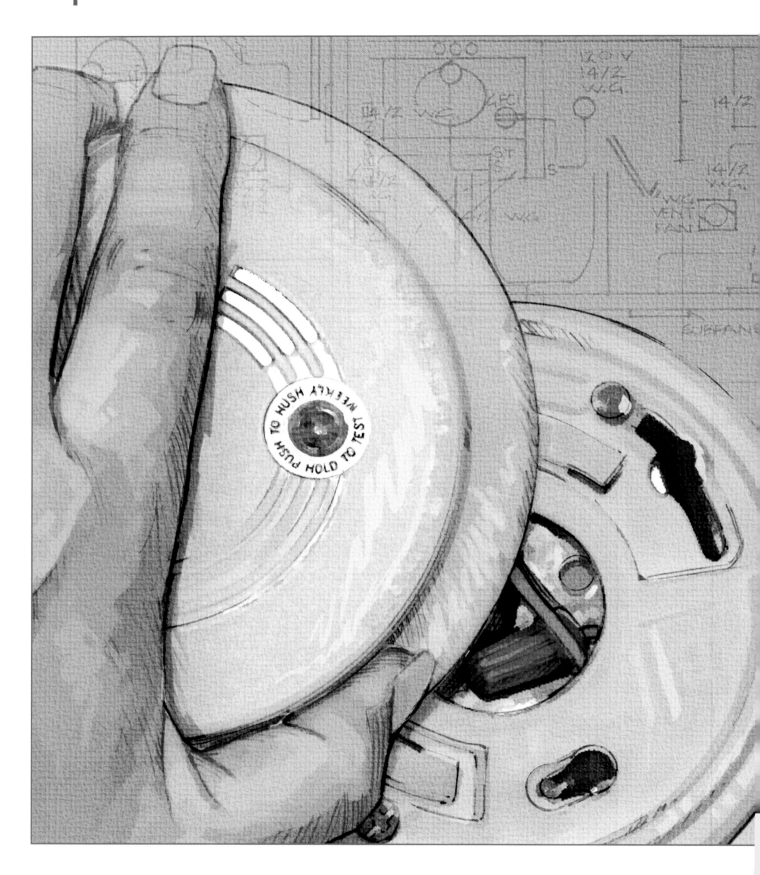

CHAPTER 5

Fixtures, Appliances, and Equipment

If you are an average do-it-yourself homeowner, you will seldom find yourself lacking in opportunities to apply basic wiring skills. Whether you are adding new fixtures, appliances, and equipment, or repairing existing ones, you will use many of the basic wiring techniques learned earlier in this book—including the handling of wires, switches, receptacles, and other electrical devices—to complete these projects. Refer to these techniques as you proceed through the steps covered in this and subsequent chapters, and always check with the local building or electrical inspector to determine what code requirements will govern your project.

Lighting Fixtures

Incandescent

Artificial lighting is the primary illumination we use to perform tasks. Lighting also provides ambient, or general, lighting and decorative, or accent, lighting. The quantity and quality of light produced will depend on the type of lightbulb you use. Incandescent, fluorescent, and high-intensity discharge bulbs (including mercury-vapor lamps) provide the three major sources of artificial light. A standard incandescent lightbulb produces light when electricity is passed through a thin wire, or filament. As a result of heating, the filament emits a visible light called incandescence. Incandescent lightbulbs come in a variety of shapes and styles to match fixtures that are freestanding, wall or ceiling mounted, or recessed. The term luminaire describes the entire assembly of lamp, fixture, housing, and attached electrical wires.

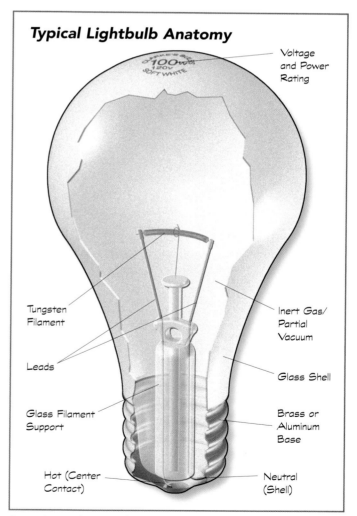

Typical Lightbulb Anatomy

100w
120V
SOFT WHITE

- Voltage and Power Rating
- Tungsten Filament
- Leads
- Inert Gas/ Partial Vacuum
- Glass Shell
- Glass Filament Support
- Brass or Aluminum Base
- Hot (Center Contact)
- Neutral (Shell)

In an incandescent lightbulb, electrical energy is used to produce heat, or incandescence, in a tungsten filament. The incandescence is apparent as visible light.

If a luminaire isn't working, you will usually see signs of a faulty plug, switch, or cord. A defective plug normally has visible damage, such as cracks in the plug housing or loose, broken, or bent prongs. A bad switch may feel loose when you turn it on and off, or the bulb may flicker when the switch is jiggled. Damaged cord will often look frayed or worn. Sometimes a broken wire within the cord causes problems. You can check for this, as explained below, but don't do so if the cord seems frayed or if any bare wire is exposed. Cords in this condition should always be replaced. You can use the table on page 123 to troubleshoot some of the more-common problems encountered with incandescent light fixtures.

HOW TO: *Test a Lamp Cord for Broken Wires*

Difficulty Level: 🐾

Tools and Materials

- Continuity tester
- If required: plug, socket, or cord replacements
- Insulated screwdriver
- Utility knife
- Multipurpose tool

Turn On the Fixture. Plug the lamp into a receptacle, and turn on the switch. Flex the cord back and forth over its entire length. Flexing the cord will separate the ends of any broken section of wire. If the bulb flickers, a wire in the cord is broken. **(Photo 1)** Cord most commonly breaks at the plug end, the shell, and at the junction where the cord enters the lamp base.

Incandescent lightbulbs are designated by letters and numbers that represent their shapes and diameters.

Test the Cord. If flexing the cord does not cause the bulb to flicker, use a continuity tester to evaluate the integrity of the wire. **(Photo 2)** Check the prongs on the plug end and the socket itself—including both the shell and center contact. Be sure the switch is turned on but the power is off. Place the clip on the continuity tester on one prong and touch the probe to one exposed wire at the end of the cord, then the other wire. Do the same with the other prong. If the circuit is complete, the tester will light. You can also perform this test while flexing the cord. If the cord is defective, the broken wire ends will make intermittent contact, causing the meter reading to jump wildly up and down. If you find a faulty plug, switch, or line cord, replace the defective part.

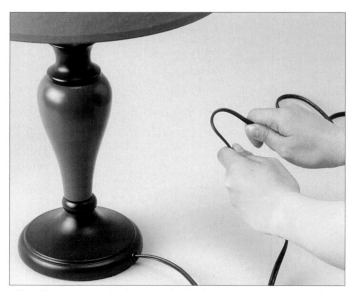

1 Flex the cord while the light fixture is turned on. If the bulb flickers, the cord is defective.

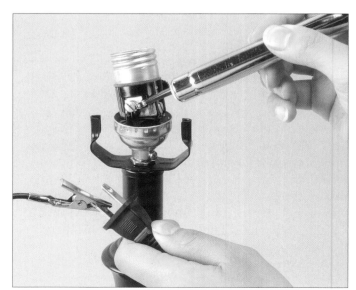

2 To evaluate the integrity of a wire, use a continuity tester to check the plug prongs and the lamp socket.

Lightbulb Burnout

A typical incandescent lightbulb has a life span of approximately 900 to 1000 hours. At roughly five hours per day, that's about six months. If your lightbulbs seem to have a shorter life span, the problem may be with the fixture. Some fixtures have loose contacts. A loose center contact on a lamp can overheat, melting the lead weld on the glass filament support. If the fixture doesn't appear to be the problem, check the lightbulb for the following:

An Overheated Lightbulb. If bulb wattage is too high and there's too little space around the fixture, the bulb will burn out due to improper air circulation.

Vibration. Bulbs can vibrate in loose fixtures or a wall that bounces.

Excessive Line Voltage. If the line voltage equals or exceeds 135 volts, have it checked out by your power company.

Lightbulbs rated 130-volts are superior to standard lightbulbs but may not last as long as a commercial-grade bulb.

The plastic coating on a rough-service lightbulb will contain the glass shards should it explode.

If none of these is the cause of your bulb burnout, the bulb may be inferior. Be sure to purchase the best bulbs you can. Look for commercial- or industrial-grade lightbulbs because they last much longer than standard lightbulbs. Bulbs rated at 130 volts are better than standard lightbulbs but do not necessarily last longer. This is also true of rough-service bulbs that have a plastic coating on the surface and are designed to withstand vibration and will prevent shattering if the bulb explodes.

Troubleshooting Incandescent Light Fixtures

Problem	Diagnosis	Solution
Bulb Doesn't Light	Plug has been pulled from receptacle.	Push plug back into receptacle.
	Bulb is loose; isn't making contact with socket.	Tighten bulb.
	Bulb is burned out.	Replace bulb.
	Cord is damaged.	Replace cord.
	Switch is defective.	Replace switch.
	Receptacle is defective.	Replace receptacle.
Bulb Flickers	Bulb is loose; barely makes contact with socket.	Tighten bulb.
	Loose wire at socket terminal.	Turn off power to circuit or unplug fixture; then secure wire.
	Switch is defective.	Replace switch.
	Receptacle is intermittent.	Replace receptacle.
	Receptacle wire is loose.	Reconnect or splice wires.
	Socket contact is dirty or corroded.	Turn off power; clean contact.
Fixture Blows a Fuse or Trips Circuit Breaker	Short circuit in cord.	Replace cord.
	Plug is defective.	Replace plug.
	Socket is defective.	Replace socket.

Problems with incandescent light fixtures can often be identified by checking a trouble-shooting table and using a process of elimination.

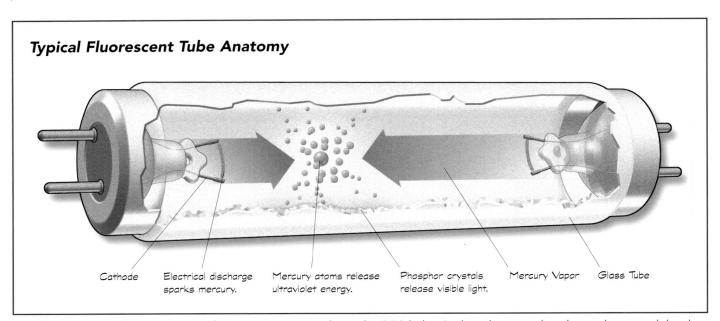

Typical Fluorescent Tube Anatomy

Cathode | Electrical discharge sparks mercury. | Mercury atoms release ultraviolet energy. | Phosphor crystals release visible light. | Mercury Vapor | Glass Tube

In a fluorescent tube, mercury and argon gases emit ultraviolet (UV) light. A phosphor powder glows when struck by the UV light, making the light visible.

Fluorescent

In a fluorescent tube, electrical current jumps from an electrode at one end of the tube and flows through the tube to an electrode at the other end. This current flow causes mercury and argon gases in the tube to emit ultraviolet (UV) light, which is not visible to the human eye. To make the ultraviolet light visible, the tube is coated with a phosphor powder that glows, or fluoresces, when it is struck by the light. When the fixture is turned off, the mercury/gas mixture within the tube does not conduct electricity. When power is first applied, several hundred volts are emitted from the ballast to initiate the release of electrical energy. Once this occurs, however, a much lower voltage is all that is required to maintain power—usually less than 100 volts for fluorescent tubes under 30 watts and 100 to 175

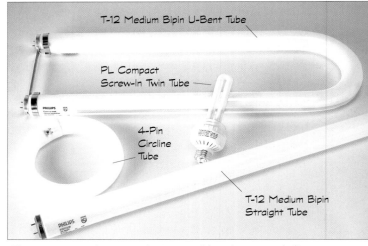

T-12 Medium Bipin U-Bent Tube

PL Compact Screw-In Twin Tube

4-Pin Circline Tube

T-12 Medium Bipin Straight Tube

Fluorescent tubes are designated by shape and diameter, just as incandescent lightbulbs.

Fluorescent Tube Types

Fluorescent tubes provide a wide spectrum of light, including warm white, cool white, tinted, and black light.

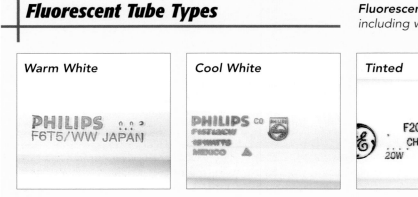

Warm White	Cool White	Tinted	Black
PHILIPS F6T5/WW JAPAN	PHILIPS	F20T12-C50 CHROMA 50 20W USA	F20T12-BLB BLACK LIGHT 20W USA

volts for tubes of 30 watts or more. When the higher voltage breaks down the gas and current begins to flow through it, the gas emits a great quantity of ultraviolet light but not much visible light. Only when the UV light hits the phosphor coating does the tube begin to glow. Different phosphors are used to achieve the light spectrum required for the fluorescent tube's intended designation—cool white, warm white, colored, or black light.

Fluorescent bulbs are about two to four times more efficient at light production than incandescent bulbs. They also last a lot longer—10,000 to 20,000 hours vs. 900-1000 hours for a typical incandescent. However, this does not take into account the expense of replacing a fluorescent light ballast when one fails. Nevertheless, not all fluorescent bulbs require ballasts, and they are more energy-efficient than incandescents, providing two to four times more light per watt and using fewer watts than standard bulbs. They are also fairly maintenance-free.

One way to start a fluorescent light is to use a starter switch, sometimes known as a glow switch. The switch turns on when it is activated by an electric current. Inside it is a contact and a bimetal strip that provides the initial current surge that warms the bulb's cathode (electron-emitting electrode). After the initial warm-up, the starter permits the electrical current to energize the gases in the tube. There are three types of starters: preheat, rapid start, and instant start. In preheat starters, the electrodes are heated before high voltage is affected to the bulb. This type of starter is a replaceable twist-in module. Rapid-start fixtures have electrodes that are constantly heated by low-voltage coiled wires (windings), and instant-start bulbs rely on step-up transformers for a short burst of high voltage to start up. The latter two types of starters are built into the ballast and cannot be independently replaced. The ballast is an enclosed com-

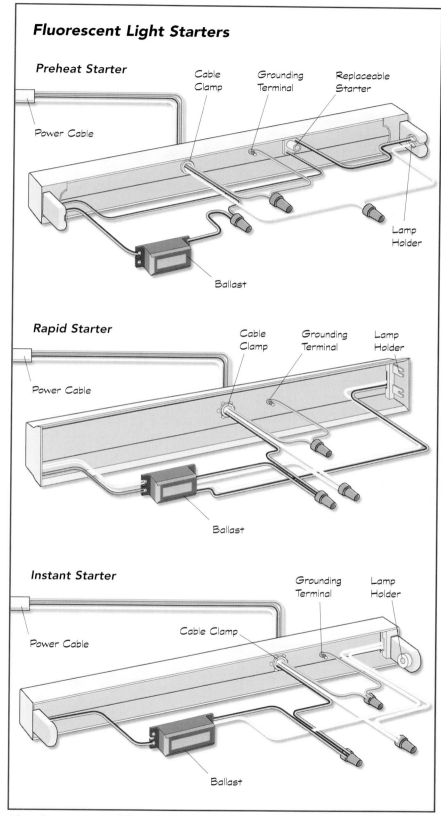

Fluorescent Light Starters

Preheat Starter

Cable Clamp · Grounding Terminal · Replaceable Starter · Power Cable · Lamp Holder · Ballast

Rapid Starter

Cable Clamp · Grounding Terminal · Lamp Holder · Power Cable · Ballast

Instant Starter

Grounding Terminal · Lamp Holder · Cable Clamp · Power Cable · Ballast

The three types of fluorescent light starters are preheat, rapid start, and instant start. Preheat starters are twist-in modules about ¾ inch in diameter. Rapid starters are integrated with the ballast, and instant starters use step-up transformers to provide an initial surge in start-up power.

Fixtures, Appliances, and Equipment

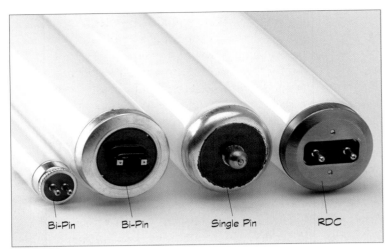

Base-pin configurations are generally single pin, bi-pin (two-pin), or recessed double contact (RDC).

Bi-Pin   Bi-Pin   Single Pin   RDC

include transformers as well as choke coils. With this type of ballast, when the light is turned on, a transformer momentarily steps up the voltage.

Another important aspect of fluorescent tubes is their pin configuration. The pins are the protrusions on each end that hold the tube in the fixture and transfer power to the tube. Fluorescent light fixtures commonly installed in homes use 4-foot-long bi-pin (two-pin) lamps. The two narrow pins on each end make these lamps difficult to install but easy to be loosened by normal vibrations. Once the base pins become loosened, the tube contacts disconnect, causing the light to flicker or go out.

A more reliable configuration is found on 8-foot-long tubes. These have a large pin on each end, and one is spring-loaded. They are equipped with an instant starter. They are easy to install and present few problems. Having one large connection on each end of the lamp eliminates the light flickering and corrosive tendencies of the smaller bi-pin tubes. In areas needing even more light, special fixtures with high-output tubes can be used.

ponent, that governs the electric current—holding it to the level required to operate a fluorescent light properly. There are two types of ballasts: choke and therma-protected. Choke ballasts limit the amount of current flowing through the fluorescent tube. Fixtures that hold long fluorescent tubes use thermal-protected ballasts that

Troubleshooting Fluorescent Light Fixtures

Problem	Diagnosis	Solution
Bulb Doesn't Light	Bulb is loose; pins aren't making contact with fixture terminals.	Reinstall lamp.
	Bulb is burned out.	Replace bulb.
	Terminals are corroded.	Clean terminals.
	Lamps are dirty.	Remove lamps and wash them.
	Bulb is cold.	Remove old ballast and install cold-rated ballast.
	End pins are broken or bent.	Replace bulb.
	Starter/ballast is defective.	Replace starter/ballast.
Bulb Flickers	Bulb is loose; pins aren't making contact with fixture terminals.	Reinstall lamp.
	Bulb is cold.	Allow enough time for ballast to warm up.
	Starter/ballast is defective.	Replace starter/ballast.
Bulb Discoloration	Bulb is worn out.	Replace bulb.
	Starter/ballast is defective.	Replace starter/ballast.
Humming	Loose ballast wires.	Secure wire connectors.
	Ballast is incorrect.	Replace with correct ballast type.

Though most problems with fluorescent fixtures involve loose tubes or poor contacts, consult the table above to check for problems other than these.

Check discoloration on a fluorescent tube to determine its condition and remaining life expectancy.

Tube Near Burnout

Tube Used but Still Good

New Tube

Loose bulbs or connections are common problems with fluorescent fixtures. Test a fixture using a bulb known to be working. Inspect connection terminals, and clean off dirt or corrosion. Typical fluorescent lights are designed for warm areas, and their ballasts may not function below 50 degrees Fahrenheit. For unheated spaces it's best to install cold-rated ballasts. Another common problem is a broken or bent tube pin or fixture terminal. Also, dirt and dust affects the phosphorous coating and may cause the lamps not to work. Excessively dirty lamps should be removed, washed with soapy water, rinsed, dried, and reinstalled about every 6 months. Inspect ballasts and starters, too. If a bulb flickers or won't turn on, the ballast may be defective or the starter module may have failed. In either case, replace the defective part.

HOW TO: *Replace a Fluorescent Ballast*

Difficulty Level: 🪝

Tools and Materials
- Ballast replacement
- Insulated screwdriver
- Diagonal-cutting pliers
- Electrical tape
- Neon circuit tester
- Wrench (optional)
- Wire connectors

Remove the Defective Ballast. Disconnect power to the circuit at the main panel. Remove the light diffuser, fluorescent bulb or bulbs, and the metal fixture cover. **(Photo 1)** Using a neon circuit tester, verify that the power is turned off. **(Photo 2)** Disconnect or cut the ballast wires at the fixture sockets. **(Photo 3)** Carefully supporting the ballast, use a screwdriver or wrench to loosen the locking nuts that hold it in place. Make certain that the replacement ballast matches the one removed.

1 Disconnect the power; then remove the light diffuser, fluorescent lamp, and the metal cover plate.

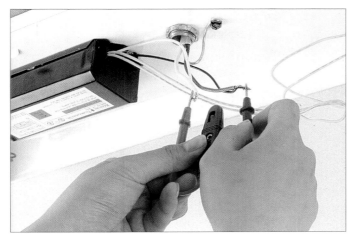

2 Remove the end sockets to access the wires. Use a neon circuit tester to verify that the power is off.

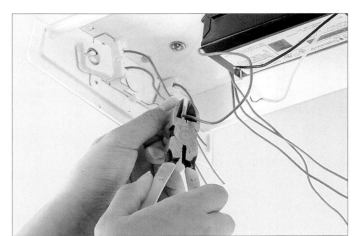

3 Disconnect or cut the wires extending from the end sockets to the ballast device. Remove the old ballast.

Fixtures, Appliances, and Equipment

4 *Supporting the new ballast with one hand, install the locking nuts.*

Install the New Ballast. Support the replacement ballast with one hand, while leaving your other hand free to fasten it in place. Line up the new ballast so it will be positioned in the same location as was the old ballast. Once the ballast is accurately positioned, tighten the locking nuts. **(Photo 4)** Using appropriately-sized wire connectors, splice together the ballast and socket wires, making certain to twist-connect the like-color wires. **(Photo 5)** For added safety, wrap the wire connectors with electrical tape. Also tape the wires securely in place along the entire length of the channel, so they won't be inadvertently pinned beneath the cover when it is put back in place. **(Photo 6)** Next, reattach the cover, install the fluorescent tube, and then replace the light diffuser. As a final step, turn on the power to the circuit, and test the light fixture.

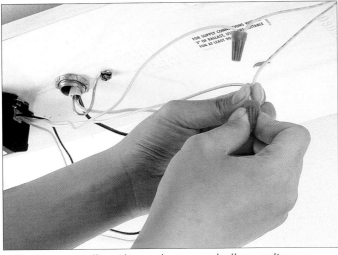

5 *After installing the replacement ballast, splice together the fixture and ballast wires.*

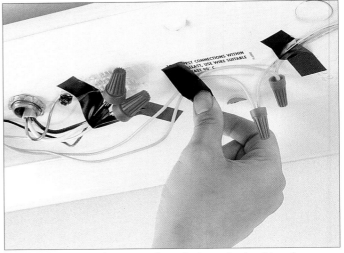

6 *To prevent the wires from being pinched by the cover, tape the wires in place along their length.*

HOW TO: *Replace a Fluorescent Fixture*

Difficulty Level: 🐾

Tools and Materials

- ◆ Fluorescent fixture replacement
- ◆ Long-nose pliers
- ◆ Wire connectors
- ◆ Insulated screwdriver
- ◆ Neon circuit tester
- ◆ Multipurpose tool

Remove the Old Fixture. Turn off the circuit and switch to the existing fluorescent light fixture. Remove the light diffuser and fluorescent tube, and take off the fixture cover. **(Photo 1)** Using a neon circuit tester, verify that the power is off. **(Photo 2)** Disconnect the fixture wiring, and unscrew the cable clamp. **(Photo 3)** Loosen the fasteners holding the fixture in place, and carefully remove the fixture from its mounting. **(Photo 4)**

Install the New Fixture. Locate the new fixture over the mounting, and pull the branch-circuit cable through the center hole. **(Photo 5)** Mount the fixture securely to the mounting bracket or structural framing. Connect the fixture wires to the branch-circuit wires, following the manufacturer's instructions. Be sure that like-color wires are properly matched and spliced, using wire connectors. **(Photo 6)** Reattach the cover, replace the fluorescent bulbs and light diffuser, and turn on the power. Patch the ceiling, if necessary, and test the circuit.

1 Turn off power to the circuit; then remove the light diffuser, lamps, and cover plate.

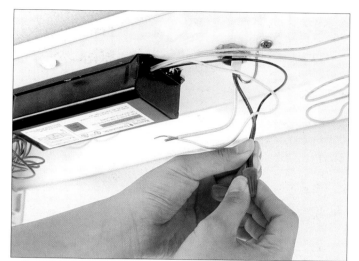

2 Using a neon circuit tester, verify that power is off. Then disconnect the fixture wiring.

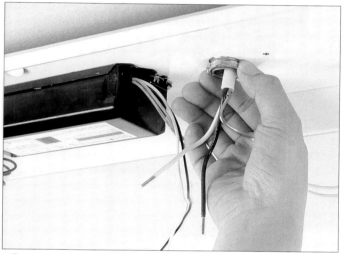

3 Unscrew and remove the cable clamp holding the power cable.

4 Loosen the screws holding the fixture, and remove the fixture from its mounting.

5 Position the new fixture over the electrical box, and mount it on the ceiling.

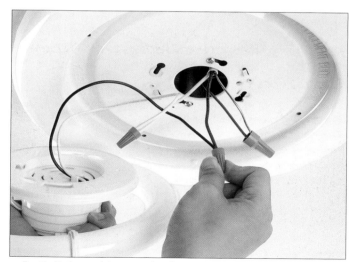

6 Pull the cable into the fixture's electrical box, and splice the fixture wires to the branch-circuit wires.

Fixtures, Appliances, and Equipment

Quartz Halogen

Quartz halogen lamps have become very popular in recent years. However you must be extremely careful using any light fixture that employs a quartz halogen bulb. This type of bulb gets extremely hot and can easily cause a fire. Never allow anything flammable to come near the glass covering on the bulb. Even an extension cord placed too close to the lamp can heat up and ignite. Do not use quartz halogen bulbs where children or pets may be in danger of knocking them over or coming into contact with the bulb. Exposed skin will burn immediately if it comes into contact with the glass. Though advertised as having a long life span, quartz halogen bulbs sometimes last only for minutes and have been known to explode within a fixture. Use extreme caution if you decide to use this type of bulb.

HOW TO: *Replace a Quartz Halogen Bulb*

Difficulty Level:

Tools and Materials

✦ Quartz halogen bulb replacement	✦ Insulated gloves

Remove the Burned-Out Bulb. Turn off the switch to the existing halogen light fixture. Allow the bulb to cool for several minutes before attempting to replace it. Remove the light diffuser and fixture cover. Be sure to keep the bulb glass absolutely clean, and never touch it with your fingers. Oil from the skin causes "hot spots"

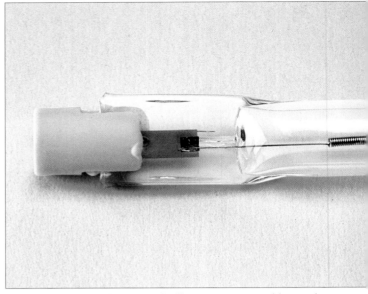

Although quartz halogen bulbs are protected by a glass tube, they must nevertheless be used with extreme caution because of the intense heat they generate.

on the lamp when lit, which destroys the lamp. One side of the bulb holder is typically spring-loaded. Reach in with gloved hands, and push the bulb toward the spring-loaded end while lifting out the bulb. **(Photo 1)**

Install the New Bulb. Install a new quartz halogen bulb by simply pushing it toward the spring-loaded end of the bulb holder and snapping it into place. **(Photo 2)** Reattach the fixture cover and light diffuser, turn the power on again, and test the bulb.

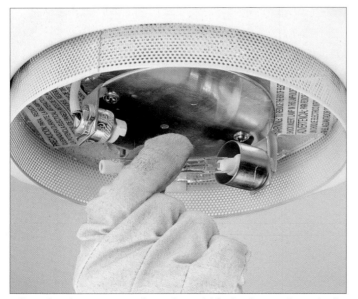

1 *After letting it cool, push and lift the burned-out bulb toward its spring-loaded end.*

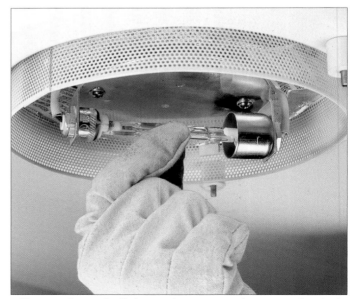

2 *Install new bulb by pushing it into the spring-loaded end and snapping the other end into place.*

Recessed

Recessed lights are characteristically used where spot lighting is needed and/or low-hanging fixtures are not desirable. Most commonly used in kitchens and living areas where they provide concealed lighting, recessed light can also illuminate a specific area. Some recessed lights rotate and focus at an angle to illuminate or bathe a particular object—a favorite painting, sculpture, or antique—in light.

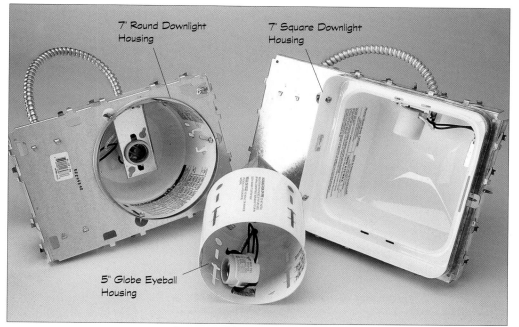

Recessed lamp housings come in various sizes and shapes. They may or may not be designed for insulation contact. Be sure to check the labels. (See photos below.)

Recessed light fixtures fall into two categories: insulated ceiling (IC) and non-insulated ceiling (NIC). It is best to opt for IC light fixtures so that you can put insulation right up against the metal fixture housing in an attic floor or cathedral ceiling. Non-insulated ceiling fixtures require, for fire safety, a minimum clearance of 3 inches between the housing and insulation and a clearance above the fixture so as not to entrap heat (NEC Section 410-66). Most housings have two adjustable arms that are mounted to adjoining ceiling joists. The exposed surface of the fixture is extended below the joists just far enough to be flush with the finished ceiling. A decorative cover is snapped into place when the ceiling is finished. After the fixture has been mounted, the power branch-circuit cable is run into the electrical box attached to the housing.

Recessed lights don't draw much electrical current, so they can be wired into a standard light or receptacle circuit. They can be wired using either 14- or 12-gauge wire.

A recessed ceiling fixture has its own prewired box attached. You need only bring the power cable into the box and splice the wires.

◄ *A fixture* rated for a non-insulated ceiling (NIC).

► *A fixture* rated for an insulated ceiling (IC).

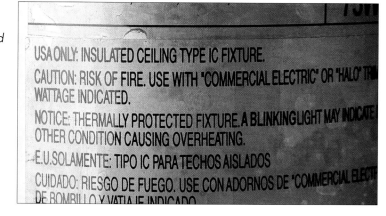

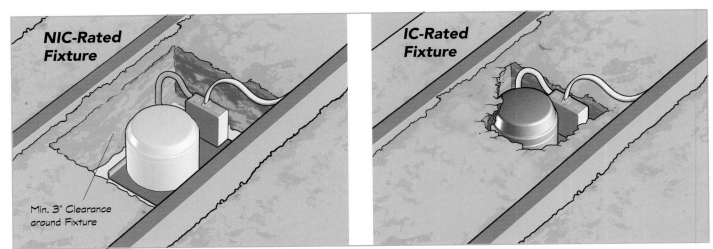

NIC-Rated Fixture

Min. 3" Clearance around Fixture

IC-Rated Fixture

Recessed light housings are either rated for non-insulated ceilings (NIC) or insulated ceilings (IC). For fire safety, NIC housings must be at least 3 in. clear of any insulation, while IC housings are permitted to be in direct contact with insulation.

HOW TO: *Install a Recessed Light Fixture*

Difficulty Level: 🐾

Tools and Materials

- Recessed lamp housing
- Electrician's hammer
- Power drill
- Long-nose pliers
- Cable clamps
- Insulated screwdrivers
- Nails or screws
- Cable ripper
- Multipurpose tool
- Wire connectors

Install the Lamp Housing. Once you have determined where the housing will be mounted, pull out the extension bars on the lamp housing to reach the adjoining ceiling joist. **(Photo 1)** Make final adjustments on the housing position by sliding the fixture along the bars. Be sure that the face of the unit extends below the framing so that it will be flush with the finished ceiling. Then, using nails or screws, fasten the extension bars to the joists. **(Photo 2)**

Prepare the Electrical Box. Take the cover off the electrical box attached to the lamp housing. Using a screwdriver, remove a knockout for the switch-leg cable. **(Photo 3)** Pull the cable into the box, and secure it into place using a cable clamp. **(Photo 4)** Leave about 10 inches of cable in the box. Rip the cable sheathing to within ¾ inch of the cable clamp, and remove ripped-back sheathing. Then using a multipurpose tool, strip the wires in the cable and cut away excess wire. Repeat this procedure for each cable entering the box.

Wire the Electrical Box. Using wire connectors, splice the white switch-leg wire to the white wire from the fixture. Next, connect the black switch-leg wire to the black wire from the fixture. **(Photo 5)** Pigtail the grounding wires from the switch-leg and fixture cables to the green grounding screw terminal in the electrical box, and attach the box cover. **(Photo 6)** When the ceiling is finished, install the decorative housing cover.

1 Install the bracket for the lamp housing, positioning it between two joists.

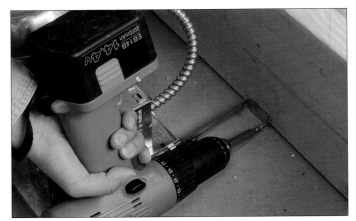

2 Adjust the housing, and fasten the extension bars to the adjoining joists.

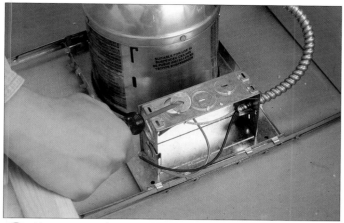

3 Use a screwdriver to remove one of the knockouts to accommodate the power cable.

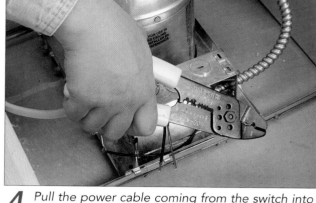

4 Pull the power cable coming from the switch into the junction box, and clamp it securely in place.

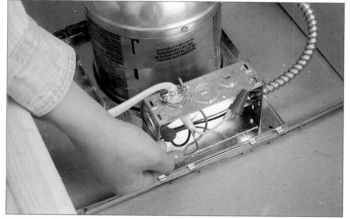

5 Splice the black hot wires and white neutral wires from the switch-leg cable and fixture.

6 Pigtail the ground wires to the green grounding screw in the electrical box. Attach the cover.

Surface-Mounted

Surface-mounted fixtures are usually installed on a ceiling or wall. They may use incandescent, fluorescent, or quartz halogen bulbs. Wall sconces, globe lights, above-vanity strip lighting, and ceiling fixtures are all examples of this type of lighting. Surface-mounted lights are generally attached to lighting outlet boxes.

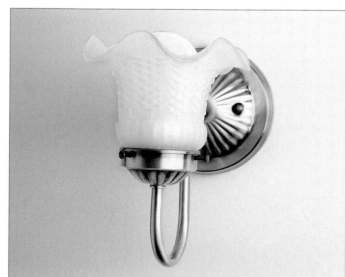

Surface-mounted fixtures *come in a variety of styles appropriate for ceiling or wall installation.*

Fixtures, Appliances, and Equipment

HOW TO: Install a Ceiling-Mounted Fixture

Difficulty Level: 🐾

Tools and Materials

- Surface-mounted light fixture
- Mounting strap
- Knockout punch
- Long-nose pliers
- Cable clamps
- Insulated screwdriver
- Electrical box
- Threaded nipple
- Cable ripper
- Wire stripper
- Wire connectors

Prepare the Electrical Box. After turning off the power, use a neon circuit tester to confirm that no power is at the light circuit. Pull the cable from the switch into the electrical box, secure it in place, rip the cable sheathing, and strip the wires in the cable. **(Photo 1)** If the box does not have a built-in hanger stud, attach a mounting strap to the box tabs. **(Photo 2)** Screw a threaded nipple into the collar of the crossbar to support the weight of the light fixture. **(Photo 3)** Make certain that it will extend through the suspended fixture to engage the mounting nut.

Wire the Fixture. Using wire connectors, splice the hot black wire from the switch to the hot black lead wire from the fixture. Next, connect the neutral white wire from the switch to the neutral white wire from the fixture. Then, splice together the grounding wires, and pigtail them to the green terminal screw in the electrical box or on the mounting strap. **(Photo 4)** Push the completed wiring neatly into the box, and install the fixture cover over the threaded nipple. Lastly, tighten the mounting nut. **(Photo 5)**

1 Pull the cable into the box, and strip the insulated wires.

2 If needed, attach a mounting strap to the ceiling box.

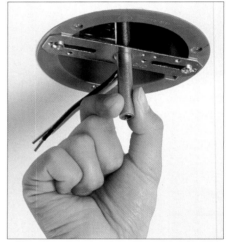

3 Screw a threaded nipple into the collar of the support.

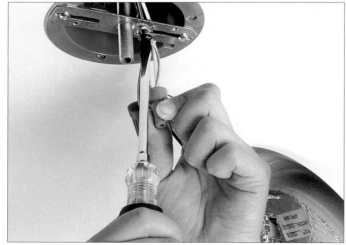

4 Splice the fixture wires to the power wires, pigtailing the grounding wires to the grounding screw.

5 Place the fixture cover over the nipple, and tighten the mounting nut.

Track-Mounted

Track lighting is used primarily to focus light on a particular object or work surface. Because the light fixtures can be moved to any point along a modular power track, this type of lighting affords the homeowner a great deal of flexibility in lighting design. Noted for ease of installation, track lighting can be powered off an existing or new switch-controlled electrical box. The wiring remains concealed as the exposed lighting track runs along the wall or ceiling surface. Track sections are connected straight from the outlet (or electric) box and can branch off in different directions with the aid of special connectors.

HOW TO: Install Track Lighting

Difficulty Level: 🐾

Tools and Materials

- Track lights
- Track connectors and covers
- Neon circuit tester
- Pencil
- Insulated screwdrivers
- Multipurpose tool
- Molly bolts or wood screws
- Track
- Power connector plate
- Power-box cover
- Measuring tape
- Straightedge
- Long-nose pliers
- Wire connectors
- Power drill

Lay Out and Wire the Track Lighting. Turn off power to the electrical box where the track lighting will be connected. Use a neon circuit tester to verify that the power is off, and disconnect the existing fixture wiring. Measure and draw guidelines out from the ceiling box to

Installing a track light *is a simple way to provide flexible, multiple-task lighting, using only one electrical box.*

center the new track lighting. **(Photo 1)** Then, wire the track lighting power connector to the electrical box. **(Photo 2)** Using wire connectors, splice the neutral white wire from the cable to the neutral white fixture wire and the hot black switch wire to the hot black fixture wire. Next, splice together the grounding wires, and pigtail them to the green terminal screw in the electrical box, if the box is metal. Secure all of the wires in the box. (Some nonmetallic boxes are provided with a grounding plate and green terminal screws.)

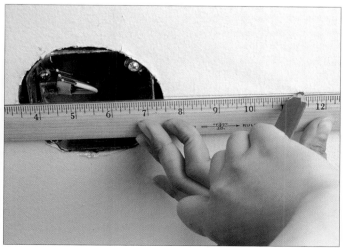

1 Measure and draw guidelines for the precise placement of your track lighting.

2 Wire the track-light power connector directly into a ceiling or wall-mounted electrical box.

Fixtures, Appliances, and Equipment

Install the Track Lighting. Fasten the power connector plate to the electrical box, and screw or bolt the first section of lighting track temporarily into place. **(Photo 3)** Insert the power connector into the first section of track. Twist-lock the connector in place, and attach the power-box cover. **(Photo 4)** Install additional lengths of track to the first section, using T-connectors and L-connectors, if needed. **(Photo 5)** Cover all connections using connector covers. Mark the positions for screws or Molly bolts on the ceiling. Then take down the temporary track sections, and drill pilot holes as needed. Install the track, and tighten all fasteners. Set the lighting fixtures into the track, slide them into place, and lock them in position. **(Photo 6)**

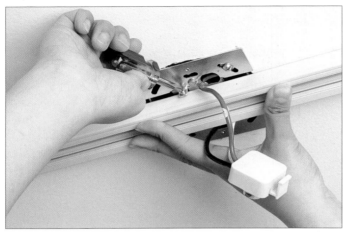

3 Fasten the power-connector plate to the electrical box, then attach the first section of track.

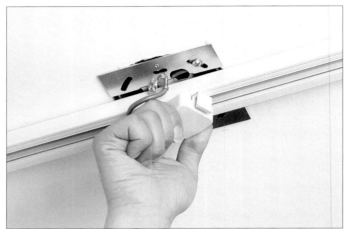

4 Twist-lock the connector in place, and attach the power-box cover.

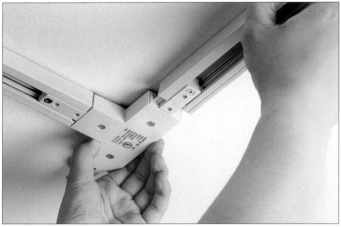

5 Install additional connectors and track sections, as needed, using the appropriate connectors.

6 Slide the lighting fixtures into the track, and lock them into the desired position.

Chandeliers

Hanging a chandelier differs from installing a ceiling-mounted light fixture because of the added weight of the fixture. This requires modifying the ceiling box to accommodate the extra weight. Special chandelier-hanging hardware is used for this purpose, including a threaded stud and nipple, a hickey, and locknuts.

The added weight of a chandelier must be supported by the ceiling box. (See NEC Section 410-16.)

HOW TO: *Install a Chandelier*

Difficulty Level: 🦇🦇

Tools and Materials
- Chandelier
- Collar nut
- Threaded nipple
- Stud
- Insulated screwdrivers
- Ratchet wrench
- Wire connectors
- Escutcheon plate
- Hickey
- Locknuts
- Neon circuit tester
- Long-nose pliers
- Multipurpose tool

Prepare the Ceiling Box. After turning off the power, use a neon circuit tester to confirm that there is no power at the light circuit. **(Photo 1)** Remove the fasteners holding the old light fixture to the ceiling box. Carefully support the fixture, or have someone else do it as you disconnect the lead wires from the box. Screw a short threaded stud into the center knockout at the top of the electrical box to support a hickey. Inside the box, screw a hickey onto the stud. Then screw a threaded nipple into the hole at the bottom of the hickey. Secure the hickey and threaded nipple using locknuts. **(Photo 2)**

Wire and Install the Chandelier. Pull the chandelier wires through the nipple and into the electrical box. Using a wire connector, splice the black hot wire from the chandelier to the black hot wire in the ceiling box. Do the same with the white neutral wires. To complete the wiring, pigtail the ground wires to the green grounding screw in the electrical box. **(Photo 3)** Tuck the wiring in the box. Then screw the chandelier support to the threaded nipple, and slide the escutcheon plate up to the ceiling box. Thread the chandelier's collar nut onto the nipple protruding from the box, and tighten it to secure the escutcheon plate and support the chandelier. **(Photo 4)**

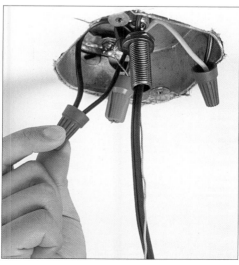

1 Turn off power at the main panel before disconnecting wires on the existing fixture.

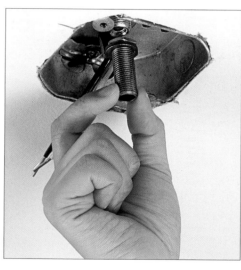

2 Install a stud in the box. Then screw a hickey onto the stud and a threaded nipple into the hickey to support the chandelier.

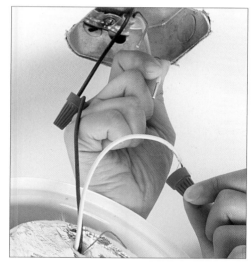

3 Pull the chandelier wires into the box through the nipple, and wire the fixture. Install the chandelier and escutcheon plate.

4 Thread the chandelier's collar nut onto the nipple, and tighten the nut.

Indoor Lighting Design

Use lighting the way an artist uses a brush, to downplay or highlight elements in a room. Lighting focused on an object will draw the eye to that object in contrast to its background. For example, lighting the corners in a room makes it seem larger, as the eye takes in its entirety. In comparison, a soft pool of light created around a sofa will focus attention on the piece of furniture. The remainder of the room recedes into shadow, making it seem smaller.

Not everyone reacts to light in the same way. Some people are more photosensitive than others, preferring a lower field of general lighting. To others, the toned-down lighting suitable to photosensitive people may be depressing. Consider the personal preferences of all family members when you design your lighting system.

The functions of lighting divide into three basic categories: to provide general or ambient lighting, task lighting, and accent or decorative lighting.

General Lighting. General or ambient lighting provides overall brightness for an area. Furnishing background illumination, it can vary with day and night, winter and summer, or different moods and activities.

Task Lighting. Task lighting makes it easier to see what you are doing. Individual fixtures concentrate light in specific areas for chores such as preparing food, reading, or doing crafts.

Accent Lighting. Accent or decorative lighting highlights an area or object, emphasizing that aspect of a room's character. These mood-makers of lighting, to be effective, must contrast with their background of ambient lighting.

▲ **Widely dispersed recessed lights** present one way to create aesthetically pleasing ambient lighting.

◄ **Ceiling fixtures** wash an entire wall in light or focus on a single item. Unusual lamps provide decorative accents.

This living space effectively uses recessed ceiling lights to create ambient lighting and wall washers to accent the fireplace and entryway. A freestanding fixture provides both task and decorative lighting.

An elegant chandelier on a dimmer switch provides both ambient mood and task lighting.

Wall sconces provide task lighting as well as a decorative flourish to this bathroom. [See NEC Section 370-27(a).]

Fixtures, Appliances, and Equipment

Indoor Lighting Design, cont'd.

Avoid eyestrain by providing adequate ambient lighting, thereby reducing the harsh contrasts of task lighting. Determine the level of light needed for a particular activity or task, then relate this to the available light. Design ambient, task, and accent lighting to match the specific needs for a given space. Eyes that feel little strain during 20 minutes at a computer, for example, will need more light when subjected to an intensive three-hour computer session in a home office.

▲ *Flexible-neck fixtures* on this decorative headboard supply easily-directed reading light.

◄ *A suspended track* concentrates light where it is needed, while a pendant fixture provides fixed light.

Individual wall-mounted decorative fixtures supply task lighting over the counters in this kitchen.

Wall sconces provide functional lighting above while foot-lighting delineates the toe space below this bathtub.

Carefully placed recessed ceiling fixtures *in this kitchen/dining area deliver task as well as general lighting. The pendant lights provide accent and task lighting, as well as a visual focus over the cooktop island.*

Appliances

Dishwasher

Before installing a dishwasher, you must first install a dedicated circuit to provide power to the appliance. The dishwasher can be hardwired, with the cable wire going directly to the appliance's power junction box, or it can be wired using a cord and plug that's connected to a dedicated receptacle normally installed below a kitchen counter and near the sink. If the wiring will go directly to the dishwasher's junction box, be certain to leave adequate wiring between the wall and the box. The most likely mistake a homeowner will make is to merely extend the cable to the box and wire it. But if you ever have to slide the dishwasher forward to work on it, there won't be enough slack in the wire to permit movement of the appliance. Always leave an adequate length of wire (3 to 4 feet) looped behind the dishwasher before extending it to the junction box. Characteristically, the power junction box will be mounted behind the dishwasher's kick panel. To expose the box, simply remove the panel.

Many dishwashers have a built-in electric dryer. The dryer is an ordinary heating element. It's a circular device made of metal that's found at the inside bottom of the dishwasher. This type of dryer draws a great deal of current because it uses the same 120-volt circuit that feeds the dishwasher. For this reason you should use 12-gauge wire and run the dishwasher on its own circuit.

*A **dishwasher** requires its own circuit and can be hardwired to the junction box or simply plugged into a designated receptacle.*

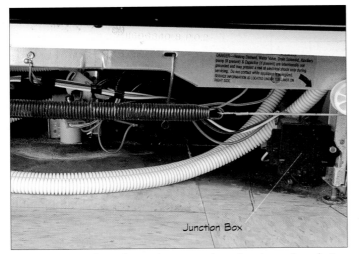

*Most **dishwashers** have their own junction box already in place behind the kick panel. Gain access for wiring simply by removing the panel.*

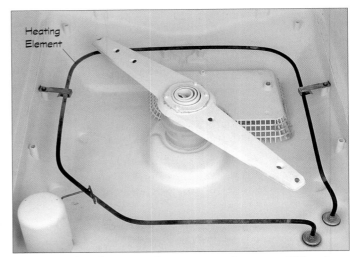

*A **dishwasher heating element** uses the same 120-volt circuit as the dishwasher. For this reason, the dishwasher should be on a separate circuit.*

HOW TO: *Direct-Wire a Dishwasher*

Difficulty Level: 🦫

Tools and Materials

- Dishwasher
- Cable ripper
- Knockout punch
- Multipurpose tool

- 12/2G NM cable
- Insulated screwdrivers
- Long-nose pliers
- Wire connectors

Pull the Cable. The internal wiring of a dishwasher is terminated in the power junction box, just behind the dishwasher's kick panel. The connecting wires are black, white, and green. A green grounding screw is sometimes substituted for the green wire. Using a knockout punch, remove a knockout on the dishwasher's junction box, and pull the 12/2G NM branch-circuit cable into the box. Be sure to leave extra wire (3 to 4 feet) looped behind the dishwasher so that the appliance can be pulled away from the wall for later servicing. **(Photo 1)** Rip back the cable sheathing, cut away the excess, and secure the cable in the box using a cable clamp.

Wire the Box. After exposing them, strip the insulated wires from the branch-circuit cable, and wire the junction box. Using wire connectors, splice the black hot wire from the branch-circuit cable to the black hot wire from the dishwasher. Then, do the same with the white neutral wires. Lastly, splice the bare copper grounding wire to the green appliance wire, or connect it to the green grounding screw in the junction box to complete the appliance wiring. **(Photo 2)**

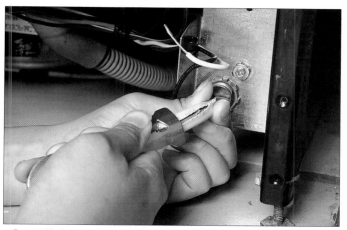

1 Pull the power cable into the dishwasher's junction box. Leave a wire loop behind the dishwasher.

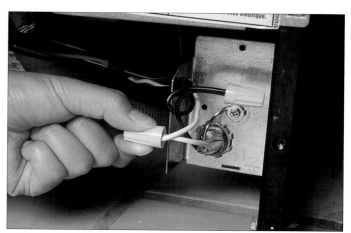

2 Splice the black to black and white to white wires. Then connect the ground wire to the grounding screw.

Range Receptacle

In the past, cable for kitchen ranges included two hot wires and a stranded ground/neutral. This type of cable is called service-entrance conductor (SEU) cable. The range receptacle for this kind of cable accommodated a three-prong plug configuration. The problem with this arrangement was that the current-carrying neutral was also used as the grounding conductor for the appliance frame. Today, cables for kitchen ranges are still required to carry two hot conductors, but the neutral wire must also be insulated, and the grounding conductor can be either bare or insulated. It is a four-conductor cable containing three insulated wires and one grounding conductor. Usually, the two hot wires are black or black and red, the neutral wire is white or gray, and the grounding wire is green or bare. This category of cable is called service entrance round (SER) cable. The size used for a kitchen range is usually 6/3G SER copper or aluminum cable. A range receptacle must accept a 4-prong plug configuration for this type of cable.

Of the four wires in SER cable, the two hot wires carry the 240 volts required to power the heating elements. The 120-volt power is carried across the neutral to either of the two hot wires—it doesn't matter which one. The 120-volt power is used to run the timer, clock, buzzer, etc. Drawing the neutral current away from the grounding conductor causes the return current to flow safely through an insulated conductor rather than through a bare copper grounding wire. The 4-slotted female receptacle into which the SER cable is wired can be surface- or flush-mounted. For the average homeowner, a surface-mounted receptacle is often preferred because it is easier to wire. When a range is not hardwired but has a cord and plug, the plug must have four prongs to match the receptacle, as mentioned earlier, so that the neutral and grounding conductor will remain separate.

HOW TO: *Install a Range Receptacle*

Difficulty Level: 🦃

Tools and Materials

- ◆ Keyhole or saber saw
- ◆ Cable staples
- ◆ 50A or 60A 125/250V range receptacle (NEMA 14-50R or 14-60R)
- ◆ Insulated screwdrivers
- ◆ Cable ripper
- ◆ Multipurpose tool
- ◆ Fish tape (nonmetallic)
- ◆ 6/3G SER copper cable
- ◆ 50A or 60A double-pole circuit breaker
- ◆ Knockout punch
- ◆ Long-nose pliers
- ◆ Cable clamp

Fish the Cable. Turn off the main breaker at the service-entrance panel. Locate the position on the wall for mounting the range receptacle, and cut an opening to fish the cable. Run an adequate length of 6/3G SER copper cable from the main panel to the receptacle opening. **(Photo 1)** Staple the cable to structural framing at intervals of 54 inches on center and at least once within 12 inches of the panel. Using fish tape, pull the cable out the wall opening. (See "Fishing Cable," in Chapter 4, page 80.) Install the cable into the receptacle housing through one of the knockouts, and secure it in place using a cable clamp. Install the receptacle housing in the wall opening. Rip the sheathing from the cable, cut away the excess, and strip the inside wires.

Wire and Mount the Receptacle. Connect the hot red and black wires to the brass screw terminals on the receptacle. Then connect the white neutral wire to the silver screw terminal and the green or bare copper grounding wire to the green grounding screw terminal. **(Photo 2)** Mount the housing on the wall, and install the receptacle cover.

Wire the Breaker Panel. At the main panel, wire the range cable to its own dedicated 50- or 60-amp double-pole circuit breaker. Connect the hot wires (red and black) to each of the brass screw terminals on the breaker. Then connect the white neutral wire and the green or bare copper ground wire to the neutral/grounding bus bar in the panel. **(Photo 3)** Restore power to the panel, and test the circuit.

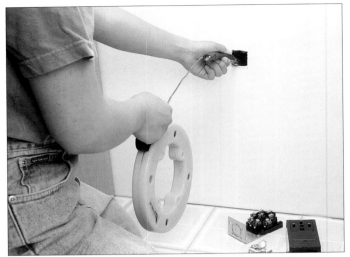

1 *Cut a wall opening at the location of the appliance. Fish 6/3G SER copper cable from the main panel.*

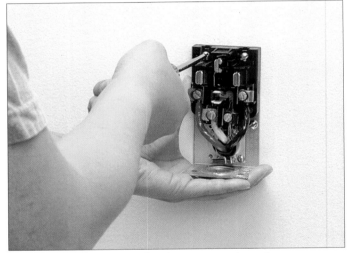

2 *Insert the wires under their appropriate clamps, tighten the screws, and mount the receptacle housing.*

3 *Connect the red and black wires to a 50-amp breaker; the white and bare wires to the neutral/grounding bus.*

Range and Dryer Receptacle Types

Range Receptacles

Older range *receptacles had only three slots, combining the current-carrying neutral with the appliance's frame grounding.*

Modern range *receptacles have four slots, for three insulated wires and a grounding conductor or wire, either bare or insulated.*

Dryer Receptacles

An older-style dryer *receptacle had two angled slots for hot wires and a third elbow-shaped slot for the grounding/neutral.*

Newer dryer *receptacles have four slots to provide independently for the two hot wires, the neutral, and the grounding wire.*

Dryer Receptacle

Like an electric range, an electric dryer uses both 120- and 240-volt power and requires a four-conductor cable. The greater voltage supplies only the heating element while the lesser voltage powers the motor timer and buzzer. Also like ranges, dryers were once powered by two-conductor cable with a ground. Such dryers were fed with 10/2G NM copper cable containing a black hot wire, a white neutral wire, and a bare copper grounding wire. 10 gauge NM cable is still used, but it must now have three conductors—red, black, and white wires—plus a bare copper grounding wire. This 10/3G NM cable must be connected to a dedicated female four-slot receptacle rated at 30 amps. The cord on the dryer must have a four-prong male plug and the neutral must not be connected to the dryer frame. The receptacle is usually surface-mounted but can be flush-mounted. When the dryer is shipped to a distributor, the plug and cord are not sent with it. The distributor must install the cord onto the dryer. Before you have a dryer delivered to your home, ask the distributor to install an extra-long rather than standard-length cord. The extra cord will permit you to pull the dryer away from the wall for servicing. It is also a good idea to install the plug high enough on the wall so that you will not have to bend far to unplug it.

CRE**A**TIVE
HOMEOWNER®

SMART TIP

Choosing a Dryer

Purchasing a clothes dryer often means choosing between a gas- or an electric-heated model. Gas dryers are slightly more expensive to purchase and maintain but less expensive to operate. For some homeowners, however, gas may not be an option. Regardless, you can consider other options. Older dryers, for example, rely on timers or thermostats to sense when clothing is dry. Newer models gauge humidity in a dryer, allowing precise heat control to protect clothing from damage. Another option is a wrinkle-gaurd. When heat turns off, this keeps clothing tumbling until it's removed from the dryer. If you want clothing dried in a hurry, consider a larger dryer. Extra air space between clothing exposes more fabric surface, resulting in faster drying times. For aesthetics, think about built-in units that blend with the room's decor. If you lack space, look at combination or stackable washer/dryers. Also, take into account ease of use. If lifting is a problem, choose a unit with angled or large doors, or down- or side-opening doors. Select electronic controls for more cycle options and custom programming.

Fixtures, Appliances, and Equipment

HOW TO: Install a Dryer Receptacle

Difficulty Level: 🦇

Tools and Materials

- Keyhole or saber saw
- Cable staples
- 30A 125/250v dryer receptacle (NEMA 14-30R)
- Knockout punch
- Long-nose pliers
- Cable clamp
- Conduit straps
- Masonry screws
- Fish tape (nonmetallic)
- 10/3G NM copper cable
- 30A double-pole circuit breaker
- Insulated screwdrivers
- Cable ripper
- Multipurpose tool
- EMT conduit (for masonry walls)

Fish the Cable. Turn off the main breaker at the service-entrance panel. Locate a position on the wall for the dryer receptacle, and cut an opening in the drywall to fish the cable. **(Photo 1)** Run 10/3G NM copper cable from the main panel to the dryer receptacle location. Fasten the cable to the framing at intervals not to exceed 54 inches and within 12 inches of each end or joint. Using fish tape, pull the NM cable up through the wall and out the cut opening. (See "Fishing Cable," in Chapter 4, page 80.) If you're mounting the receptacle on a basement masonry wall, run the cable in EMT conduit, and attach the conduit to the wall using conduit straps and masonry screws. Pull the cable into the receptacle housing through one of the knockouts, and secure it in place using a cable clamp. Rip the sheathing from the cable, remove the excess, and strip the inside wires.

Wire and Mount the Receptacle. Connect each of the hot red and black wires to either of the brass screw terminals on the receptacle. (They are interchangeable.) Next, connect the white neutral wire to the silver screw terminal and the green or bare copper grounding wire to the green grounding screw terminal on the receptacle housing. **(Photo 2)** Mount the housing on the wall, and install the receptacle cover.

Wire the Breaker Panel. At the main service-entrance panel, wire the dryer cable to its own dedicated 30-amp double-pole circuit breaker. **(Photo 3)** Connect the hot red and black wires to each of the two brass screw terminals on the breaker. Then connect the white neutral wire and the green or bare copper grounding wire to the neutral/grounding bus bar in the breaker panel. Turn on the power to the panel by flipping the switch at the main breaker, and test the dryer circuit.

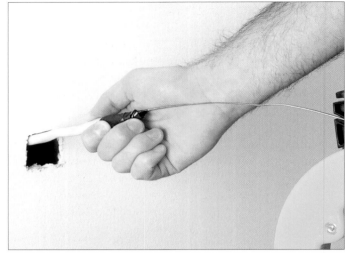

1 Cut a wall opening at the location of the dryer. Fish 10/3G cable from the main panel.

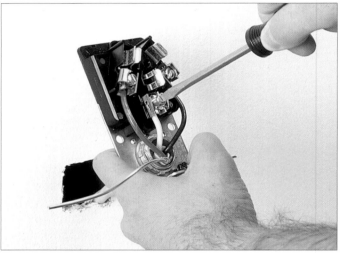

2 Wire the dryer receptacle, mount the receptacle housing on the wall, and install the cover plate.

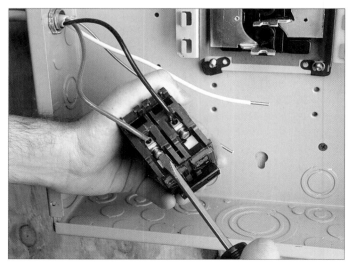

3 At the main panel, connect the dryer cable wires to a 30-amp circuit breaker designated for the dryer only.

Waste-Disposal Unit

A kitchen waste-disposal unit is fairly easy to wire, but you will also need to install a switch to operate the appliance. Ordinarily, you should mount a disposal-unit switch on the wall off to one side of the kitchen sink. However, if the disposal unit is an add-on, you must choose between the expense of mounting the switch on the wall or simply placing it in the cabinet beneath the sink. Some homeowners choose the latter because it is simpler and less expensive. However, should you need to shut off the disposal unit in an emergency, having the switch readily accessible is safer and more convenient. To mount your switch on the wall, follow the instructions below.

HOW TO: *Wire a Waste-Disposal Unit*

Difficulty Level:

Tools and Materials

- Waste-disposal unit
- 12/2G NM cable
- Long-nose pliers
- Cable clamps
- Knockout punch
- Single-pole switch
- Insulated screwdrivers
- Cable ripper
- Multipurpose tool
- Wire connectors
- Switch box

Wire the Switch. To install a wall switch for a waste-disposal unit, you will still need to bring the power cable up through the wall from the sink cabinet below. In the back wall of the sink base cabinet, open a hole directly below where you want the switch. Above the opening, cut a hole in the wall the size of the electrical switch box. Then fish both the power cable and the disposal-unit

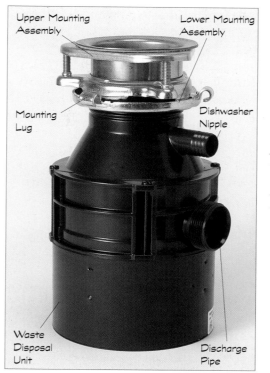

Upper Mounting Assembly · Lower Mounting Assembly · Mounting Lug · Dishwasher Nipple · Waste Disposal Unit · Discharge Pipe

A waste-disposal unit can be safely controlled by a switch mounted on the wall to the side of your kitchen sink or within the sink's base cabinet.

cable up and into the hole for the switch box. **(Photo 1)** Insert the cables into the box, clamp them in place, and install the box. Rip the cable sheathing, strip the wires, and wire the switch. Connect the black hot wire from the branch-circuit cable to one screw terminal on the switch and the black load wire from the disposal-unit cable to the other screw terminal. Using a wire connector, splice the neutral wires directly through the box. Pigtail the bare copper grounding wires to the grounding screw on the switch. **(Photo 2)** When the switch is turned on, the power will be applied directly to the disposal unit.

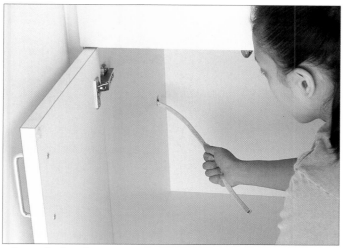

1 Fish the disposal-unit cable from the sink cabinet to the switch box. Fish the power cable separately.

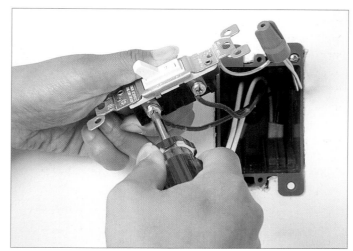

2 Wire the switch, tuck in the wires, and then install the switch-box cover plate.

Fixtures, Appliances, and Equipment

Wire the Unit. Although waste-disposal units can be plugged into dedicated receptacles, they're usually wired directly into a switch box. Remove the cover plate at the bottom of the unit to expose the wiring. **(Photo 3)** Bring the switch cable through the knockout on the unit, and clamp it in place. **(Photo 4)** Splice the switch wires to the appliance wires, white to white and black to black. Then connect the bare copper grounding wire to the grounding screw terminal on the disposal unit. **(Photo 5)** Be sure to keep all of the cables away from the drain and water lines. Tuck the wires into the bottom of the disposal unit, and replace the cover plate. **(Photo 6)**

3 Remove the cover plate from the splice box at the bottom of the waste-disposal unit.

4 Pull the power cable into the splice box, and clamp it securely in place.

5 Splice the switch and appliance wires, and connect the grounding wire to the grounding screw.

6 Tuck the wires carefully into the box, and replace the splice box cover plate.

CRE▲TIVE HOMEOWNER® **SMART TIP**

Waste-Disposal Unit Safety

- Limit waste to non-fibrous foods such as meats, eggshells, coffee grounds, rinds, and peels. Avoid fibrous foods like celery and asparagus, and bones over ½-inch in diameter.

- Install a ½ hp unit for light use; ¾ hp for heavy use.

- Never pour chemical drain cleaners into a unit.

- Run water while grinding food to ensure that particles are properly flushed into the sewer system.

- When dismantling the unit or working on electrical connections, shut off power at the main panel.

- Never put your hands into a disposal unit; use tongs to remove objects.

Waste-Disposal-Unit Wiring

Although it may be easier to position a retrofit waste-disposal-unit switch in a sink cabinet, the best location is at the side of the sink where it can be quickly reached in an emergency. Bring a two-wire power cable into the switch box; then from the box to the disposal unit.

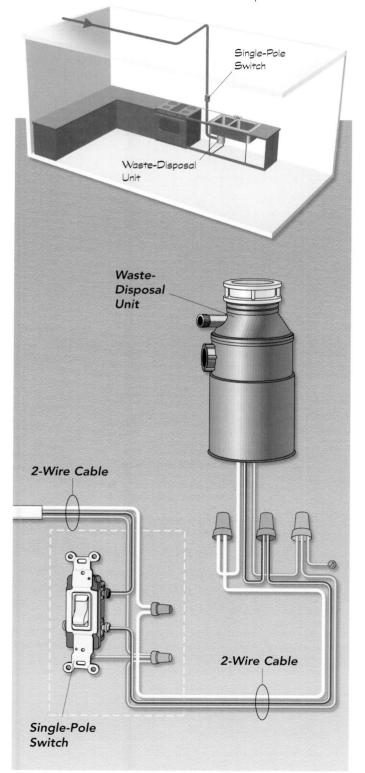

Heating and Ventilating Equipment

Ceiling Fans

When it comes to installing ceiling (paddle) fans, homeowners commonly assume that a fan can be suspended from an existing ceiling box. This is often not the case. A ceiling-suspended fan weighing up to 35 pounds, for example, requires an electrical box that is approved for the weight of the fixture. [NEC Section 422-18(a)] If it does not have this approval, an existing box must be replaced with one that does. The electrical box must be firmly secured to the structural framing. If the box is not completely rigid, the fan will wobble. A fan weighing more than 35 pounds must be supported independently of the electrical box. [NEC Section 422-18(b)]

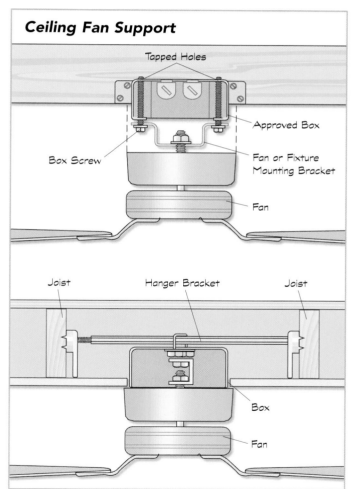

The NEC requires that a ceiling-suspended fan be supported by one of two methods, depending upon the weight of the fixture (Section 422-18). If the fixture weighs up to 35 lbs., it can be supported by an electrical box listed for that purpose. If it weighs over 35 lbs., the fixture must be supported independently of the electrical box.

Adding a light kit to a ceiling fan is a popular option among homeowners, but be aware that some light kits produce only enough illumination for general-purpose lighting and not for task lighting.

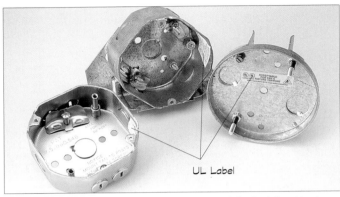

A ceiling fan's electrical box must be labeled (by Underwriters Laboratories) to carry the weight of the fixture.

If you place a light kit on your ceiling fan, you can install wall switches to control the fan and light independently.

HOW TO: *Wire a Ceiling Fan/Light*

Difficulty Level: 🦇🦇

Tools and Materials

- Ceiling fan/light
- 12 or 14/2G NM cable
- Cable ripper
- Multipurpose tool
- Wire connectors
- Knockout punch
- Hanger Bracket (for fans over 35 lbs.)
- Fan switch

- Insulated screwdrivers
- 12 or 14/3G NM cable
- Long-nose pliers
- Cable clamps (if boxes are metal)
- Approved ceiling-fixture box
- Square light-switch box
- Light switch

Install the Electrical Boxes. Cut an opening in the wall for the light-switch box and another in the ceiling for the fan/light box. Fish 12 or 14/2G NM cable from the breaker panel to the switch-box opening and 12 or 14/3G NM cable from the switch box to the fan/light-box opening in the ceiling. (See "Fishing Cable," in Chapter 4, page 80.) Install the switch box, and pull both cables into the box. **(Photo 1)** Rip open 10 inches of each cable, and remove the excess sheathing. Secure the cables in the box, and strip the wires. Do the same for the cable in the fan/light box. The three-wire cable from the switch box to the fan/light box allows you the option of controlling the light and fan independently. **(Photo 2)** If you decide that you do not want to have independent control, run the three-wire cable anyway so you will preserve the option for later.

Wire the Electrical Boxes. Although there are two ways to run power to a ceiling fan/light—through the ceiling box or through the switch box—the preferred way is to

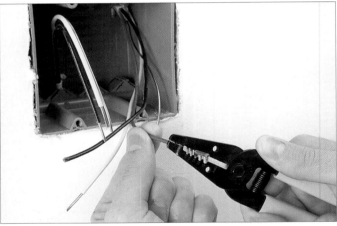

1 Install the switch box, and fish the cables from the panel and fixture to the box.

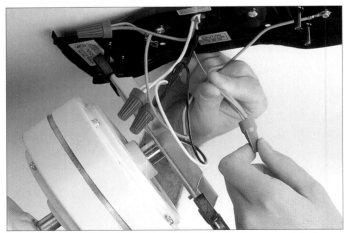

3 In the fan/light ceiling box, splice the fan and light switch wires to the fixture wires.

bring power to the fan/light through the switch box. This makes trouble-shooting easier and minimizes crowding wires in the ceiling box. Using wire connectors, in the fan/light ceiling box, splice together the black hot wire from the fixture and the hot black lead wire from the fan switch. Connect the hot red wire from the fan/light to the hot black lead wire from the light switch. Next, connect the white neutral wire from the switch box and the white neutral wire from the fixture. Then splice the green grounding wire from the fixture to the bare copper grounding wire from the switch box. **(Photo 3)** In the switch box, pigtail the hot black feeder wire to both switches, and connect the white neutral feeder to the white neutral from the fixture. Then connect the hot wires from the fixture to their respective switches. **(Photo 4)** Push the switch wires into the box, screw the switches in place, and install the cover plate. Then install the mounting plate and ceiling fixture in accordance with the manufacturer's directions. (See "How to Install a Chandelier," page 137.)

2 Install the fan/light box, and secure and strip the three-wire cable from the switch box.

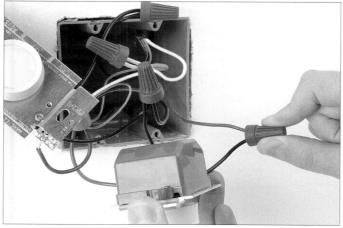

4 In the switch box, splice the fixture wires to the fan and light switch wires.

End-of-Run Ceiling Fan/Light Wiring

In this arrangement, a two-wire cable feeds power into a start-of-run double-ganged switch box. It then proceeds to the end-of-run combination ceiling fan/light along a three-wire cable. The fan/light fixture is controlled by separate speed-control and light dimmer switches.

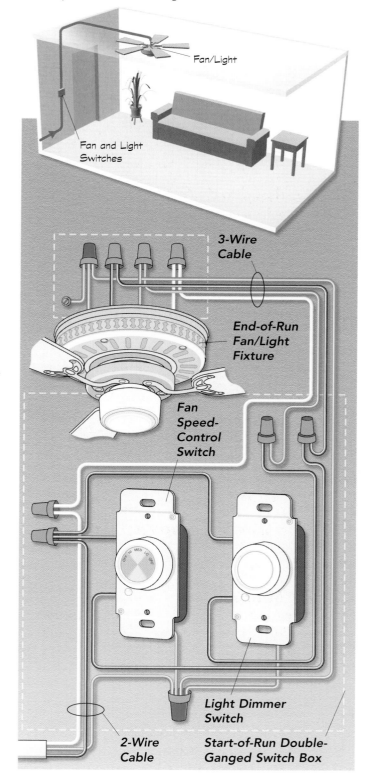

Fan/Light

Fan and Light Switches

3-Wire Cable

End-of-Run Fan/Light Fixture

Fan Speed-Control Switch

Light Dimmer Switch

2-Wire Cable

Start-of-Run Double-Ganged Switch Box

Fixtures, Appliances, and Equipment

Start-of-Run Ceiling Fan/Light Wiring

Following a switch-loop configuration, in this layout power flows first to the fan/light fixture through two-wire cable. It then proceeds to the double-ganged end-of-run switch box and back to the fixture along a three-wire cable.

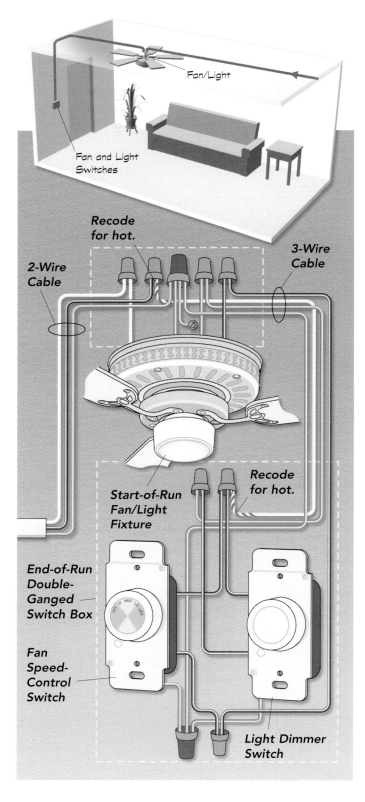

Fan/Light

Fan and Light Switches

Recode for hot.

2-Wire Cable

3-Wire Cable

Start-of-Run Fan/Light Fixture

Recode for hot.

End-of-Run Double-Ganged Switch Box

Fan Speed-Control Switch

Light Dimmer Switch

Whole-House Fans

Installing a whole-house fan in an attic floor is a great way to remove excess heat buildup in your home. The volume of air moved by a fan is measured in cubic feet per minute (CFM). The fan capacity you need is determined by the cubic volume of your home. The CFM rating of the fan also determines the amount of venting area you will need to prevent air pressure from building up in your attic space. As an alternative, a whole-house fan can be installed in an attic gable, but you will still need a louver in the attic floor. It is better to put the entire unit in the floor and use the gable ends and eaves for ventilation. In either case, the size of the fan and venting area must be calculated on the basis of the volume of space being vented. (See "Calculating Fan/Vent Sizes," page 155.) The airflow drawn through screened windows and doors must be at least equal to the airflow through the ventilation system.

A properly sized whole-house *fan is capable of changing the air in your home within one to three minutes.*

HOW TO: *Install a Whole-House Fan*

Difficulty Level: 🦇🦇

Tools and Materials

◆ Whole-house fan	◆ Screened louver vents
◆ Stepladder	◆ Keyhole saw
◆ Measuring tape	◆ Pencil
◆ Circular saw	◆ Carpenter's hammer
◆ 2x joist lumber	◆ Bracing lumber
◆ ½ in. plywood panels	◆ Nails
◆ 1½ in. rigid foam board	◆ Insulated screwdrivers
◆ Multipurpose tool	◆ Long-nose pliers
◆ 12/2G and 12/3G NM cable	◆ Junction box
	◆ Switch box
◆ Speed-control fan switch	◆ Wire staples
◆ Wire connectors	◆ Work gloves
◆ Safety glasses	◆ Dust mask

Frame the Fan Opening. Choose a suitable location for your whole-house fan, and mark an outline for the cutout on the ceiling. A hallway or other central location is best. In a two-story home, locate the fan where it will be able to draw air up from the first floor with minimal interference, for instance at the top of a stairway. Using a keyhole saw, cut away the drywall, and expose the framing joists in the ceiling. **(Photo 1)** Brace the ceiling joists, and cut the opening for the fan frame. Using two-by joist lumber to match the existing framing, install double headers and trimmer joists to frame the opening for the fan. Be sure to follow the manufacturer's directions when measuring the rough opening required. **(Photo 2)**

Build the Fan Enclosure. Install the fan in the rough opening following the fan manufacturer's instructions. In the attic, build an insulated plywood-box enclosure around the fan. **(Photo 3)** Make the enclosure high enough to clear the fan housing, and include a cover for the box. Attach rigid insulation to the attic surfaces of the box and cover. Do not fasten the cover to the top of the box—it will be used to seal the fan box when it is not in use during the winter months. From the hallway below, screw the metal louver in place on the ceiling side of the fan opening. Be sure the louver blades are not warped or bent and that they open and close freely. **(Photo 4)**

1 In a suitable location, mark and cut out a ceiling opening for the fan framing.

2 Using two-by joist lumber, frame the rough opening to support the fan and ceiling louver.

3 Build an insulated plywood-box enclosure with a removable cover to house the fan.

4 From the ceiling below, screw the fan louver squarely into the framed fan opening.

Fixtures, Appliances, and Equipment

Wire the Fan. Shut off the power at the main panel, and install a junction box outside the fan enclosure. **(Photo 5)** Run 12/2G NM cable from the panel to the junction box, stapling it to the framing along the way. Pull the cable into the box and secure it. Rip and remove 10 inches of cable sheathing and strip the exposed wires. Using wire connectors, in the junction box, splice the black hot wire from the branch-circuit cable to the white wire (coded black) from the switch. Connect the white neutral from the branch-circuit cable to the white neutral from the fan. Splice the red wire from the fan to the red wire from the switch and the black wire from the switch to the black wire from the fan. **(Photo 6)**

Wire the Switch Loop. Using appropriately-sized wire connectors in the switch box, splice the black hot wire from the switch leg to one of the black hot wires from the switch. Connect the switch-leg white wire to the other black wire from the switch. Mark the white wire with black tape to indicate that it is hot. Connect the red wires. Next, splice the switch-leg bare copper grounding wire to the grounding wire on the switch. **(Photo 7)** If the box is metal, pigtail the grounding wires to the grounding screw terminal in the switch box. Tuck the wires in the switch box, and install the cover plate. **(Photo 8)** Turn on the breaker at the main panel, and test the circuit.

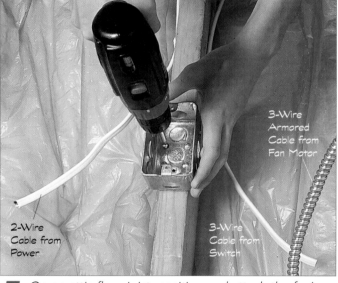

3-Wire Armored Cable from Fan Motor

2-Wire Cable from Power

3-Wire Cable from Switch

5 On an attic floor joist, position and attach the fan's junction box near the plywood-box fan enclosure.

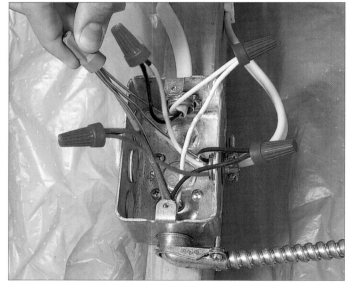

6 Wire the fan, switch, and power cables inside the junction box.

7 Install the switch box and wire the two-speed fan switch. Mark the white wire with black tape.

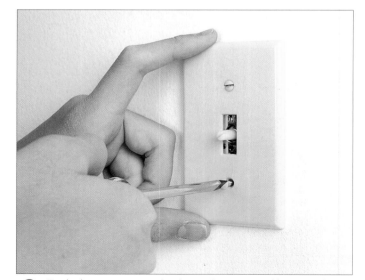

8 Tuck the wires into the box; then screw the switch's cover plate onto the switch box.

Whole-House Fan Wiring

In this wiring layout, two-wire cable feeds power into a junction box mounted near the whole-house fan. Three-wire cable takes power on to the fan speed-control switch box and then returns to the junction box. A three-wire armored cable powers the fan motor.

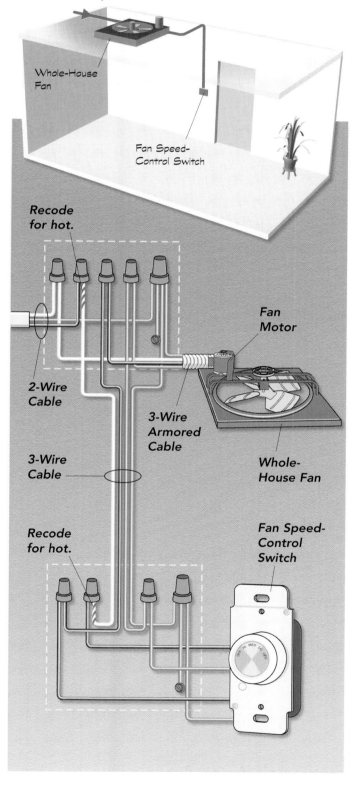

Whole-House Fan

Fan Speed-Control Switch

Recode for hot.

2-Wire Cable

3-Wire Cable

Recode for hot.

Fan Motor

3-Wire Armored Cable

Whole-House Fan

Fan Speed-Control Switch

Calculating Fan/Vent Sizes

To determine fan size, first calculate the total volume of all the rooms in your house. Multiply the length x width x height of each room, and add them all together. An ideal airflow would be one air change per two minutes. Simply divide the total room volume by 2 to obtain airflow in cubic feet per minute (CFM). A 2,000 sq. ft home with an 8 ft. ceiling height, for example, would have a volume of 16,000 cu. ft. Ideal airflow would be 16,000 ÷ 2 = 8,000 CFM. For such a house, you would need a fan having an airflow rate of 8,000 CFM. The venting area would be about 1 sq. ft of unobstructed space per 750 CFM of airflow. In this example, that would be almost 11 sq. ft. For ¼ in. screen multiply this by a factor of 1.00; for ⅛ in. screen, 1.25; and for ¹⁄₁₆ in. screen, 2.00.

Fan Sizes and Exhaust Ratings

Fan Size	Typical Exhaust Rating in CFM
24"	3,500–5,500
30"	4,500–8,500
36"	8,000–12,000
42"	10,000–15,000
48"	12,000–20,000

An effective fan will change the air in a house at least once a minute. Check the manufacturer's exhaust rating in cubic feet per minute (CFM) to determine whether a fan has the capacity you need.

Baseboard Heating

Electric baseboard heaters, also called resistance heaters, are extremely popular because of their low cost and ease of installation. They are manufactured in sizes ranging from 2 to 10 feet in length, 7 to 8 inches in height, and approximately 2 to 3 inches in depth. Electricity is supplied to a heating element running the length of the baseboard heater. Aluminum fins attached to the heating element absorb the heat and radiate it out into the surrounding space. Electrical current enters a baseboard heater from either end. Most units require 240 volts and draw about 1 amp or

250 watts per linear foot of baseboard. Units using 120 volts are also available. Be aware, however, that if they are wired to a 240-volt line, they will severely overheat and breakdown and could cause a fire. They also draw twice as much current as a 250-volt heater, making them extremely inefficient and requiring larger and more expensive cable to power them.

Although baseboard-heating units can be powered separately, you do not need to run a separate cable for each heater. One cable can feed several heaters in parallel, provided that the circuit capacity is not exceeded. The branch-circuit cable connects to one heater and is then circuited to the next in line so that all the heaters are wired in parallel—not in series.

Twelve-gauge cable is most commonly used to wire baseboard heaters. However, even though 12-gauge cable can carry 20 amps of current, you cannot power 20 linear feet of baseboard heating on a wire of this size. Such a heater, if run continuously for three or more hours, will load the cable to its maximum capacity. It should not be loaded beyond 80% of its capacity, which would be 16 amps, or 16 linear feet of baseboard heating.

You can install baseboard heaters in virtually any room in a house. In new construction, they are typically installed after the walls are painted and the finished flooring is down. Preferably, place baseboard heating on the coldest walls in a room—usually the outside walls

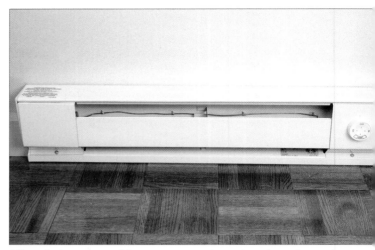

Electric baseboard heaters come in various lengths and can be installed individually or in parallel, as long as circuit capacity is not exceeded.

below window openings, where furniture is not likely to be placed. However, don't locate the heating units below wall receptacles because rising heat can cause a cord hanging across a heater to become brittle, resulting in wire damage and the potential for a short-circuit hazard. On walls that already have or require receptacles, install heaters in short sections, placing the receptacles on the wall between the heaters. An alternative is to purchase baseboard heaters that have built-in receptacles wired on a separate cable. The separate cable is necessary because you are not permitted to split the 240-volt line by putting both the receptacle and the heater on the same circuit.

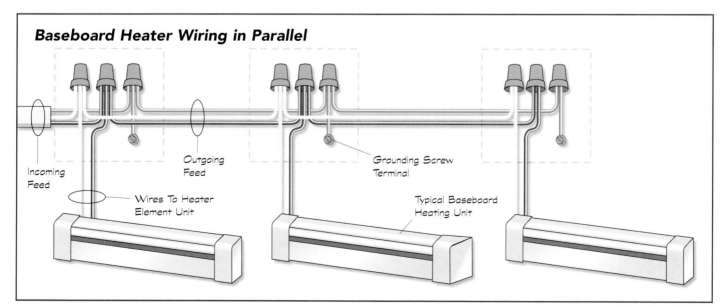

Baseboard Heater Wiring in Parallel

Incoming Feed

Outgoing Feed

Grounding Screw Terminal

Wires To Heater Element Unit

Typical Baseboard Heating Unit

Baseboard heaters can be wired in parallel, provided that the maximum amount of electrical current allowed per circuit is not exceeded.

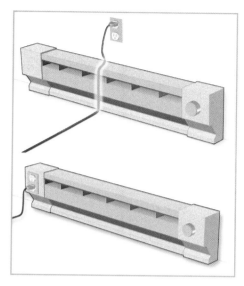

◄ *Baseboard heaters* should not be placed below existing receptacles. A cord draped over a heater may become brittle and deteriorate, causing a short circuit to the heater. Baseboard heaters can be purchased with a built-in receptacle wired on a separate cable.

HOW TO: *Wire a Baseboard Heater*

Difficulty Level: 🦇🦇

Tools and Materials

- Baseboard heating unit
- Power drill
- Knockout punch
- Long-nose pliers
- Wire stripper
- 12/2G NM cable
- Double-pole thermostat (in-heater or wall-mounted)
- Keyhole or saber saw
- Cable ripper
- Insulated screwdrivers
- Electrical tape
- Cable clamp
- TEK-head screws
- Electrical box (for wall-mounted thermostat)
- Wire connectors

Pull the Cable. Wiring for a baseboard heater can be brought directly into the heater from below the floor or from the wall behind the unit. In either case, try to align the cable coming with the knockouts on the heater. Cut a hole in the floor or wall, and pull the cable through the opening. **(Photo 1)** Using a knockout punch, remove a knockout from the baseboard unit (two, if the unit is in the middle of a run). Bring the 12/2G NM cable into the box, and secure it in place using a cable clamp. **(Photo 2)** Rip back the cable sheathing; cut away the excess; then strip the cable wires. Using a power drill and TEK-head self-drilling screws, attach the heater to the structural framing in the wall. The cutting tip on the TEK-head screws will allow you to easily drill them through the metal box, should the predrilled holes in the heating unit not line up with any of the wall studs. Unless the manufacturer specifies otherwise, keep a clearance of approximately 1 inch below the unit rather than letting it sit on the floor. **(Photo 3)**

1 Fish the power cable from the main panel to the heater location.

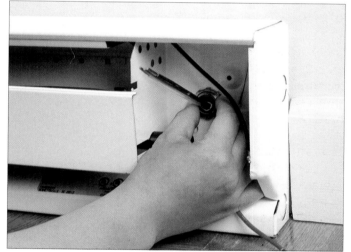

2 Pull the cable into the heater's junction box, and securely clamp it in place.

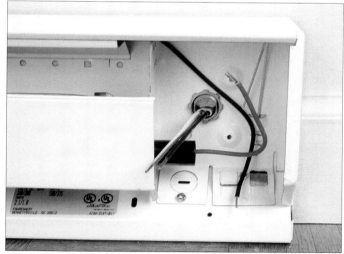

3 Mount the baseboard heater to the wall. (Some units may require 1-in. floor clearance.)

Fixtures, Appliances, and Equipment

Wire the Built-In Thermostat. A thermostat is needed to control a baseboard heater's on-off cycle. Though single-pole and double-pole thermostats are available, the single-pole type is not recommended for a 240-volt circuit because it leaves power applied to the baseboard even when it's not on. A person working on the heater may think the power isn't connected just because the heater isn't running. If you work on any type of heater, always switch the power off at the breaker panel or fuse box. Thermostats can be installed in the heater itself or wall-mounted. Mounting it on the wall eliminates the inconvenience of having to bend over when you want to adjust the temperature, but mounting it in the heater saves time and expense. To mount a thermostat in the heater, connect the black hot wire from the heater to one of the black wires on the thermostat and the red wire

from the 240-volt heating element to the other black wire on the thermostat. Then connect the black hot wire from the incoming power cable to one of the red wires on the thermostat and the white wire from the cable to the other red wire on the thermostat. Wrap black tape around the white wire to signify that it is hot. Next, pigtail the grounding wire from the incoming branch-circuit cable to the grounding screw in the heater. **(Photo 4)** Screw the thermostat into the heater box, replace the cover plate on the box, and install the thermostat's temperature control dial.

Alternative Wiring: Wire the Wall-Mounted Thermostat. To mount a thermostat on a wall, install a wall box, and pull the branch-circuit cable and a traveler cable from the heater into the box. **(Photo 5)** Secure the cables, rip the sheathing, cut away excess, and strip the inside wires. Then connect the black hot wire from the branch-circuit cable to one of the black wires on the thermostat and the white wire from the branch-circuit to the other black wire on the thermostat. Wrap the white wire with black tape to indicate that it is hot. Next, connect the black wire from the traveler cable to one of the red wires on the thermostat and the white wire from the traveler cable to the other red wire on the thermostat. Wrap the white wire with black tape to indicate that it is hot. Pigtail the bare copper grounding wires to the green grounding screw terminal on the thermostat. In the heater box, splice the black traveler (power transfer) wire to the black hot wire in the heater and the white traveler wire to the black wire coming from the 250-volt heating element. Again, wrap the white wire with black tape. **(Photo 6)** Connect the traveler ground wire the grounding screw in the heater box. Install the cover plates on both boxes.

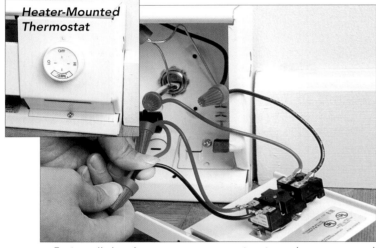

 Install the thermostat, connecting it to the power and heater wires.

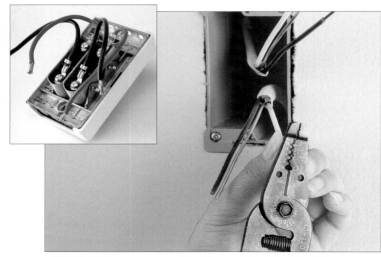

5 Pull the power and heater cables into the thermostat's electrical box.

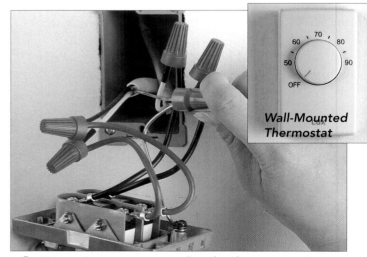

6 Using wire connectors, splice the thermostat wires to the power and heater wires.

Baseboard Heater Wiring

In this setup, 250-volt baseboard heaters are laid out in series and controlled by a wall-mounted thermostat. Two-wire cable extends through the thermostat to power the heaters. Only one cable connects to the last heater in the series.

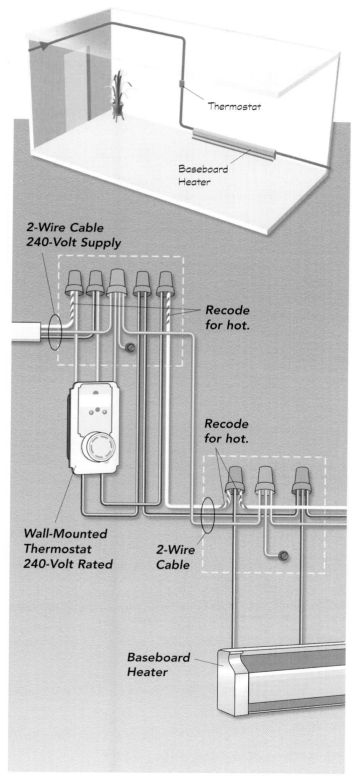

2-Wire Cable
240-Volt Supply

Recode for hot.

Recode for hot.

Wall-Mounted Thermostat
240-Volt Rated

2-Wire Cable

Baseboard Heater

Recessed wall heaters *provide spot heat in small areas like bathrooms. The heaters can be operated by a thermostat or a timer.*

Recessed Wall Heater

A recessed wall heater is ideal for spot-heating small areas not easily reached by other types of heaters, such as a mudroom or bathroom. This type of heater is preferred over a combination ceiling unit that includes a fan, light, and heater because it places the heat closer to the floor, and it can be operated by a thermostat. If desired, use a wall-mounted timer instead of a thermostat to operate the fan. It is best to install a 250-volt unit because it will draw less current than a 125-volt heater. A 125-volt heater may also short circuit, creating a fire hazard, if it is attached to a 240-volt line.

A recessed wall heater is typically mounted inside a simple metal box. The metal box is then mounted vertically or horizontally inside a stud space. Recessed wall heaters come in various sizes ranging from 750 to 1,000 watts for smaller units, to 1,500 watts for larger ones. Using 1 amp per 250 watts as a rule of thumb, you can see that a 1,500-watt heater draws about 6 amps of current. As long as the total circuit current doesn't exceed 16 amps, the heater can be added to another heater circuit. If wired by itself, the cable gauge should be No. 12 because the heat produced corresponds to the amount of voltage accessed by the heater. The less voltage the unit gets, the less heat it produces and the more inefficient it becomes. Smaller-gauge wire reduces the amount of accessible voltage, making it impossible to install a larger heating unit later on, should you want one.

Fixtures, Appliances, and Equipment

HOW TO: *Install a Recessed Wall Heater*

Difficulty Level:

Tools and Materials

- Recessed wall heater
- Measuring tape
- Carpenter's hammer
- Knockout punch
- Long-nose pliers
- Multipurpose tool
- 12/2G NM cable
- Power drill
- Electrical box (for wall-mounted thermostat)
- Keyhole or saber saw
- Pencil
- Cable ripper
- Insulated screwdrivers
- Electrician's tape
- Cable clamp
- Fish tape (nonmetallic)
- TEK-head screws
- Wire connectors
- 2x framing members

Install the Heater Box. Between two studs, mark the position of the recessed heater on the wall, using the heater box as a template. Keep one side of the unit flush to a vertical stud. Cut the opening, fish the cable through the cutout, and clamp it into the heater box. **(Photo 1)** Most heaters require a 20-amp circuit and 12/2G NM cable. Check the manufacturer's literature for specific wiring requirements. If you tap into an existing circuit, be sure it can handle the extra load. Next, add horizontal framing above the box so that it can be supported on two edges. Using a power drill and TEK-head screws, attach the box to the structural framing. **(Photo 2)**

Wire the Heater. Rip back 10 inches of cable sheathing, and cut it away, exposing the insulated wires. Trim excess sheathing. Strip ¾ inch of insulation from the wires; then wire the heater. Connect the grounding wire from the branch-circuit cable to the green grounding screw in the heater box. Then connect the black hot wire from the branch-circuit cable to one of the heater's lead wires and the white wire from the branch-circuit cable to the other lead wire from the heater. Be sure to wrap the white wire with black electrician's tape to specify that it's hot. **(Photo 3)** Then insert the heater assembly into the heater box, screw it in place, and install the decorative cover. Lastly, attach the control knob to the switch/thermostat shaft protruding through the cover. **(Photo 4)** (See page 158 for how to install a wall thermostat.)

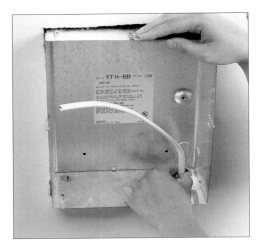

1 Fish cable into a wall opening cut for the recessed heater box.

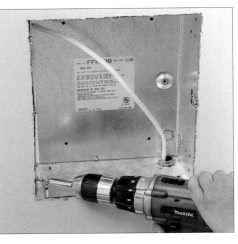

2 Install a cross-brace to support the heater box between wall-framing studs.

3 Seat the heater in its box, and splice the power and heater wires.

4 Mount the decorative heater grille. Attach the heater control knob or dial, if it is not built-in.

Range Hood

Range hoods come in two styles: ducted and ductless. A ducted hood removes heated air by exhausting it outside, while a ductless hood filters smoke and odor from the air and returns the air directly to the room. An average-size range hood circulates or removes 400 to 600 cubic feet of air per minute (CFM). The fan rating will determine the size duct you need for a ducted system. Because installation steps vary for each manufacturer, be sure to follow the specific instructions given by each for installing ductwork and wiring.

HOW TO: *Wire a Ducted Range Hood*

Difficulty Level: 🦇🦇🦇

Tools and Materials

- Ducted range hood
- Duct elbow (if needed)
- Aviation snips
- Pencil
- Reciprocal saw
- Insulated screwdrivers
- Multipurpose tool
- Cable clamp
- Power drill
- Wire connectors
- Silicone caulking or roofing compound
- Ducting
- Wall or roof cap
- Measuring tape
- Carpenter's hammer
- Cable ripper
- Long-nose pliers
- NM cable
- Fish tape (nonmetallic)
- TEK-head screws
- Caulking gun
- Aluminum flashing

A range hood may be ducted or ductless. A ducted system exhausts air to the outside, while a ductless system recirculates filtered air.

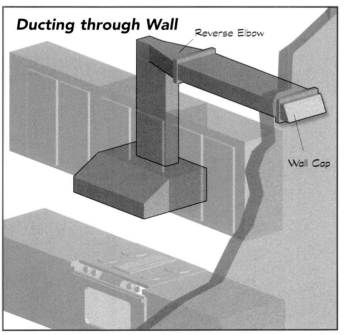

Ducting through Wall

Reverse Elbow

Wall Cap

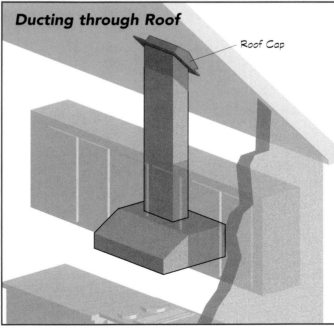

Ducting through Roof

Roof Cap

Ductwork can go directly through an exterior wall or up through the kitchen ceiling and out the roof. Either method requires capping the duct with a backdraft louver so exhaust cannot reenter the home and wind can be kept out.

Install the Ductwork. Measure and mark the proposed location for the metal ductwork. The ductwork may exit the range hood from the rear and extend directly through an outside wall, or it may exit from the top and then either elbow out through the wall or extend to the roof and then out. Cut the opening as required, carefully following the manufacturer's written instructions, and install the ductwork and a roof or wall cap. Be sure to flash and caulk around any exterior openings to ensure a good weathertight and waterproof seal. **(Photos 1–4)**

Attach and Wire the Range Hood. Fasten the hood assembly to the wall and/or cabinets using the screws or toggle bolts provided. Adhere carefully to the manufacturer's installation recommendations and requirements. **(Photo 5)** Then, fasten the branch-circuit cable to the range-hood junction box using a cable clamp. Splice the white cable wire to the white range-hood wires and the black cable wire to the black range-hood wires. **(Photo 6)** Next, connect the branch-circuit grounding wire to the grounding screw in the range-hood junction box, and cover the box. Restore power, and test the unit.

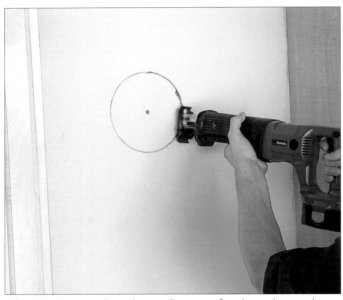

1 Measure and mark a wall cutout for the exhaust duct, and then cut the opening.

2 Extend the ductwork from the range hood to the exhaust outlet.

3 If the duct goes through the wall, install a wall cap over the duct.

4 If the duct goes through the roof, cover it with a metal roof vent cap.

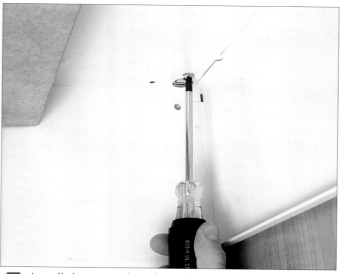

5 Install the range-hood unit by attaching it to the cabinet above using the appropriate fasteners.

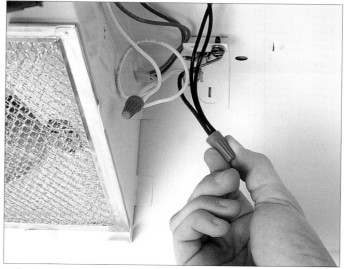

6 Run power to the range-hood box, and wire the fan. Then turn on power, and test the unit.

Safety Equipment
Hardwired Smoke Detectors

Though battery-powered smoke detectors are widely used and readily available, most building codes now require hardwired smoke detectors (with battery backup) in a home. In addition, all hardwired residential smoke detectors must be interconnected so that when one alarm sounds, they all sound. If you purchase any smoke detectors, be certain that they have these capabilities—many don't. Continue to use your battery-powered detectors as a backup system, remembering to change the batteries at least twice a year.

Most building codes now require homes to have hardwired smoke detectors. Use battery-powered detectors only as a backup.

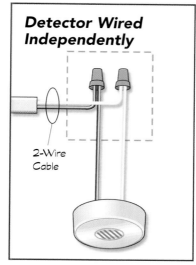

Detector Wired Independently

2-Wire Cable

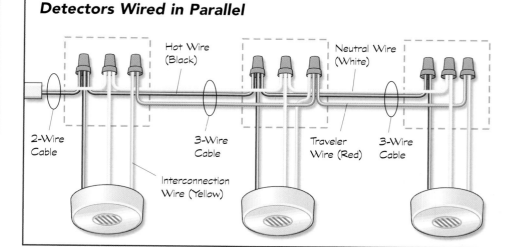

Detectors Wired in Parallel

Hot Wire (Black)

Neutral Wire (White)

2-Wire Cable

3-Wire Cable

Traveler Wire (Red)

3-Wire Cable

Interconnection Wire (Yellow)

Smoke detectors can be wired independently or in parallel. To wire in parallel, use a three-wire smoke detector. When one alarm sounds, they will all sound.

HOW TO: *Hard-Wire Smoke Detectors*

Difficulty Level:

Tools and Materials

- Smoke detectors
- Cable ripper
- Long-nose pliers
- 14/2 or 12/2 NM cable
- 14/3 or 12/3 NM cable
- Cable clamps (as needed)
- Ceiling boxes
- Insulated screwdrivers
- Multipurpose tool
- Wire stripper
- Fish tape (nonmetallic)
- Wire connectors

Install the Ceiling Boxes. Cut ceiling openings, and fish 14/2 or 12/2 NM branch-circuit cable to the first opening in the series. Run the 14/3 or 12/3 NM traveler cable between the remaining ceiling openings, and install ceiling boxes. **(Photo 1)** Pull the cables into the boxes. If they are not self-clamping, use cable clamps to secure the cable in each box. Rip back about 10 inches of the cable sheathing, and cut away the excess to expose the insulated wires. Then strip ¾ inch of insulation off the ends of the wires.

Wire the First Detector. To hard-wire the detectors in parallel, first splice the hot black branch-circuit wire to the black traveler wire and the black wire from the first detector's wiring module. Next, connect the white branch-circuit wire (neutral) to the white traveler wire and the white wire from the first detector's wiring module. Then splice the red traveler wire to the oddly-colored wire (in this case, the yellow wire) from the wiring module. Usually, there is no grounding wire. The oddly-colored third wire connects the parallel-wired detectors so that when one alarm sounds, they will all sound. For this reason, be sure to use a three-conductor cable between alarms. **(Photo 2)**

Wire the Remaining Detectors. Wire the rest of the detectors by simply splicing together the like-color wires in each box. Then attach each of the detector mounting brackets to the ceiling. Plug the wiring modules into each of the smoke detectors, and mount the foam gaskets and detectors on the ceiling. **(Photo 3)** Turn the power on at the main panel, and test the system by pushing the test button.

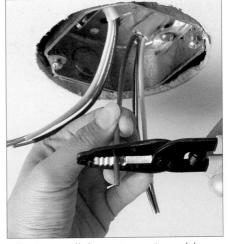

1 In parallel, run two-wire cable into the first detector and three-wire cable between detectors.

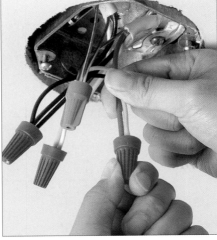

2 Splice two-wire cable to the first smoke detector and three-wire cable to the next detector.

3 Wire the remaining detectors, plug in the wiring modules, and mount the detectors.

Carbon Monoxide Detectors

A carbon monoxide (CO) detector is as important to life safety as a smoke detector. Carbon monoxide can accumulate from any number of sources, including clogged chimneys, gas or wood-burning stoves, portable kerosene or gas heaters, or even a car left running in a garage. A carbon monoxide detector is absolutely essential in a home with a gas heating and hot-water system or other gas appliances. It must be relied upon to detect harmful levels of carbon monoxide gas, which is odorless and colorless, yet deadly. Like smoke detectors, carbon monoxide detectors can be battery operated. However, for greater protection, these should also be hardwired, leaving battery-operated detectors as a backup system. Wiring is similar to that for smoke detectors and can be done in parallel.

Every home with a gas furnace or other gas appliance should have a hardwired carbon monoxide (CO) detection system.

HOW TO: *Hard-Wire Carbon Monoxide (CO) Detectors*

Difficulty Level:

Tools and Materials

- Carbon monoxide (CO) detectors
- Insulated screwdrivers
- Multipurpose tool
- 14/3 or 12/3 NM cable
- 14/2 or 12/2 NM cable
- Fish tape (nonmetallic)
- Wall or ceiling boxes
- Cable ripper
- Long-nose pliers
- Wire connectors
- Cable clamps (if boxes are metal)

Install the Electrical Boxes. Cut the openings needed for the wall or ceiling boxes, and fish 14/2 or 12/2 NM branch-circuit cable into the first opening. Fish the 14/3 or 12/3 NM traveler cable between the remaining openings, and install the electrical boxes. **(Photo 1)** Pull the cables into the boxes, and secure them in place. Using a cable ripper, rip back about 10 inches of the cable sheathing on each cable, and cut away the ripped sheathing, exposing the insulated wires. Strip ¾ inch of insulation off the end of each wire.

Wire the First Detector. To hard-wire the carbon monoxide detectors in parallel, first splice the hot black branch-circuit wire to the black traveler wire and the black wire from the first detector's wiring module. Next, connect the neutral white branch-circuit wire to the white traveler wire and the white wire from the first carbon monoxide detector. Then splice the red traveler wire from the three-conductor cable to the oddly colored wire (in this case, the yellow wire) from the detector. No grounding wire is necessary in this configuration. **(Photo 2)** The oddly colored third wire connects the parallel-wired detectors, ensuring that when one alarm sounds, they will all sound.

Wire the Rest of the Detectors. Wire the remaining detectors by splicing together the like-color wires in each successive electrical box. **(Photo 3)** Attach each of the detector mounting brackets to the wall or ceiling. Next, install the foam gaskets, and plug the wiring modules into each of the carbon monoxide detectors. Then mount the detectors on the support brackets. Turn the power on at the main panel, and test the system by pushing the test button.

1 Locate the electrical boxes for carbon monoxide detectors on a wall or ceiling.

2 Using 14/2 or 12/2 NM cable, bring power into the first detector box from the main panel.

3 Wire the remaining detectors in parallel, using 14/3 or 12/3 NM cable.

Fixtures, Appliances, and Equipment

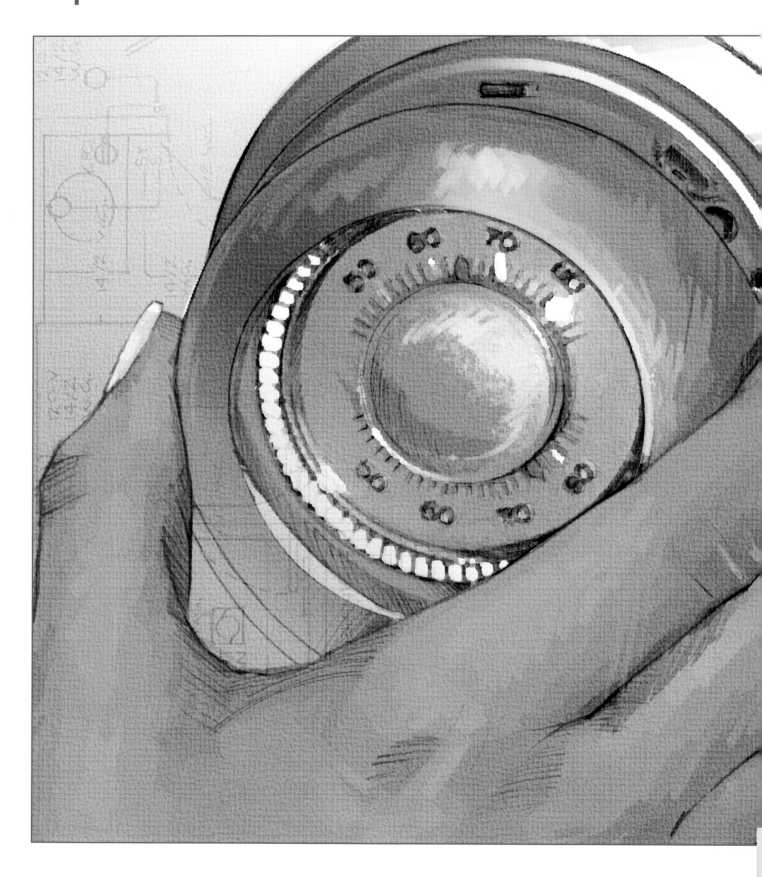

CHAPTER 6

Low-Voltage & Specialty Wiring

So far standard 120- and 240-volt residential circuits have been discussed . Many devices used in contemporary homes, however, require much less voltage to operate. Such devices include but are not limited to bells, chimes, timers, sensors, alarms, thermostats, antennas, and telecommunications equipment. Because low-voltage wiring presents few hazards, it is barely touched upon by the NEC, except as it pertains to recreational vehicles and RV parks.

Low-Voltage Power

What It Is and How It Works

Low-voltage power is defined as 30 volts or less supplied through a transformer, a device that reduces standard 120-volt house current to the current required to power low-voltage equipment. A transformer may be mounted near or be directly attached to a junction box. In either case, the low-voltage wiring is connected to the transformer, which is in turn connected to the 120-volt wiring in the junction box. The current is converted as it passes from the box through the transformer and proceeds from the transformer to the low-voltage switch and/or device.

Specialty devices, like timer controls and heat detectors, use standard 120-volt current. Low-voltage devices, such as chimes, telephones, and thermostats, use 30 volts or less.

Low-Voltage Transformers

Transformers are usually composed of two tightly wound coils of wire. Because the coils, known as primary and secondary windings, are close together, as a current passes through the primary winding, magnetic flow produces another current in the secondary winding. In a low-voltage or step-down transformer, the primary coil—rated at 120 volts—has more windings than the secondary coil. A reduction in windings results in a proportional reduction in voltage, with the secondary coil usually providing from 8 to 24 volts.

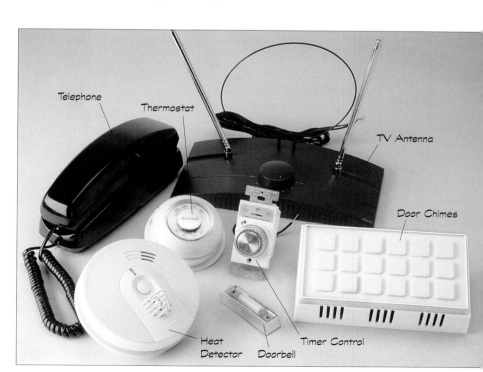

Telephone

Thermostat

TV Antenna

Door Chimes

Heat Detector

Doorbell

Timer Control

24-Volt Transformer

16-Volt Transformer

8- to 24-Volt Transformer

◄ **Power is provided** to low-voltage equipment by means of a step-down transformer that reduces standard 120-volt current to the lower voltage required.

HOW TO: *Install a Low-Voltage Transformer*

Difficulty Level: 🦇

Tools and Materials

- Insulated screwdrivers
- Knockout punch
- No. 14/2G NM cable
- Mounting bracket and screws or nails
- Octagonal junction box
- Cable ripper
- Electrician's hammer
- Long-nose pliers
- Cable clamp
- Transformer with locknut
- Wire connectors
- Wire stripper

Install and Wire the Junction Box. Install an octagonal junction box and mounting bracket on the appropriate wall stud. Next, using a screwdriver and hammer, remove the knockouts for the wire cable and low-voltage wires. **(Photo 1)** Pull the wire cable through the cable clamp and into the junction box, securing 6 inches of cable in the box. Tighten the cable clamp, rip the cable, strip the cable sheathing back to within ½ inch of the clamp, and strip the cable wires to ¾ inch. **(Photo 2)**

Mount and Wire the Transformer. Screw the transformer into the junction box, lock it in place, and pull the transformer wires into the box. **(Photo 3)** Splice the two black transformer wires to the black and white circuit wires. Connect the green transformer grounding wire to the bare copper circuit grounding wire; then pigtail them to the grounding screw terminal in the junction box. **(Photo 4)** Screw on the cover plate to finish the job.

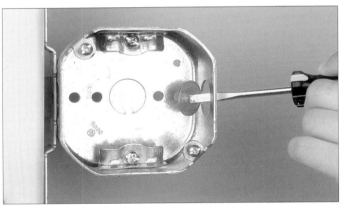

1 First, install a junction box; then remove two knockouts to accommodate the transformer and circuit wires.

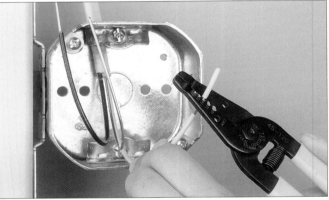

2 Pull the circuit cable into the junction box, secure it in place, and strip the cable wires.

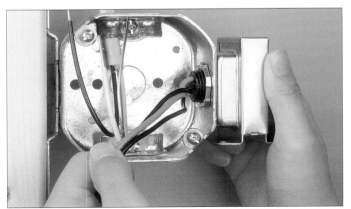

3 Attach the low-voltage transformer to the junction box. Pull the transformer wires into the box.

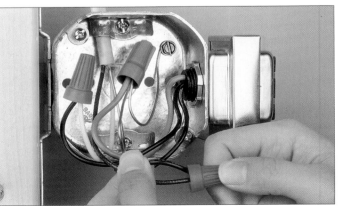
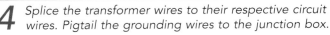

4 Splice the transformer wires to their respective circuit wires. Pigtail the grounding wires to the junction box.

Low-Voltage Wire

Because it carries such low secondary power, low-voltage wiring requires only a thin layer of plastic insulation. Low-voltage wiring may consist of a single conductor or multiple conductors wrapped in cable. This type of wiring encompasses a variety of uses from connecting simple bells and chimes to wiring sophisticated home theater, telecommunications, and computer networking systems. (See the table, below, "Low-Voltage Wire and Cable.") Typically, low-voltage wires extend in size from 14 gauge down to 24 gauge (AWG) and even smaller. The NEC does not permit this type of wiring to run in the same raceways, conduits, or cables as wires carrying normal voltage (Article 725). In addition, low-voltage wires may not occupy any electrical box containing higher voltage wiring, unless the box is properly partitioned. Low-voltage wires must generally be separated from higher-voltage wiring by 2 inches or more.

CREATIVE HOMEOWNER®

SMART TIP

Routing Low-Voltage Wire

Because high-voltage AC wiring can cause severe interference in low-voltage wire signals, it is important to carefully plan the layout of any low-voltage wiring system. Low- and high-voltage wires should never run closely together and parallel with one another unless absolutely necessary. Where it is necessary, such runs may occur for distances of 6 feet or less. It is acceptable, however, to run high- and low-voltage wires across one another at 90-degree angles. Generally, it's good practice to try to keep high- and low-voltage wires at least one stud bay apart, and run them on opposite stud sides. Never place low-voltage and high-voltage AC wires in the same electrical box.

Low-Voltage Wire and Cable

Wire Type	Description	Gauge	Typical Usage
Lamp Cord *Zip Cord*	Two insulated wires that can be pulled or "zipped" apart	18	Lamps, small appliances, cords
Flat Ribbon Cable	Several insulated, color-coded wires that can be "zipped" apart	24	Computer circuit/ serial bus connections for keyboards, scanners, printers
Bell Wire	Single or multistranded, insulated, color coded	18	Bells, chimes, thermostats, timers, control circuits
Video Coaxial Cable	A single insulated wire wrapped by a foil and braided shield	RG-59 *22-Gauge Core*	Television antenna connections, home entertainment
	Quad-shielded cable containing 2 foil shields, 2 braided shields	RG-6 *18-Gauge Core*	Cable, satellite television antenna connections, home entertainment
D-Station Cable	Cable containing four insulated, color-coded wires	24–28	Permanent, indoor, home-telephone wiring
Category 5 Cable	Cable containing four pairs of insulated, color-coded wires	24	Increased circuit capacity for home computer, telecommunications

Low-voltage wires and cables are available in a variety of types and gauges that are suitable for different purposes, including wiring bells and chimes, telecommunications equipment, and home theater.

▶ *A doorbell circuit* consists of three connections—one between the transformer and the push-button doorbell switch, a second from the transformer to the chimes, and a third between the chimes and the doorbell switch.

Low-voltage wires can be fished, stapled, and spliced the same way as conventional wiring. Just as full-voltage wire must be joined at screw terminals or be spliced inside a junction box, low-voltage wires must be connected or spliced inside a terminal jack or other type of specialized coupling device. Today, most electronic equipment comes with its own specialized wiring and terminal connectors to make properly insulated splices. Common connectors are also available and are usually color-coded red for 22- to 18-gauge wire and blue for 16- to 14-gauge wire.

Wiring Applications

Bells and Chimes

Although modern homes are more likely to have chimes than doorbells or buzzers, their wiring systems are essentially the same. Because a doorbell or chime needs less than 120 volts of power to operate, you will have to install a step-down transformer to reduce house voltage to 24 volts. A system connecting multiple signal devices will require a transformer that can provide this much power. Some systems, however, may need as little as 15 volts. If you haven't already installed a transformer, then see "How to Install a Low-Voltage Transformer," on page 168. Be sure to use a transformer that is right for the signal system you are installing.

Once a low-voltage transformer is in place, you must make three separate connections to complete the doorbell or chime circuit. The push button is the switch that, when pressed, completes the circuit by ringing the signal.

HOW TO: *Install Door Chimes*

Difficulty Level: ✎

Tools and Materials

◆ Power drill and ⅜" bit	◆ Long-nose pliers
◆ Insulated screwdrivers	◆ Low-voltage bell wire
◆ Continuity tester	◆ Multipurpose tool
◆ Multi-tester	◆ Toggle or molly bolts
◆ Fish tape (nonmetallic)	as required
◆ Two doorbell push	◆ Caulking gun and
button switches	silicone caulk
◆ Door chimes	

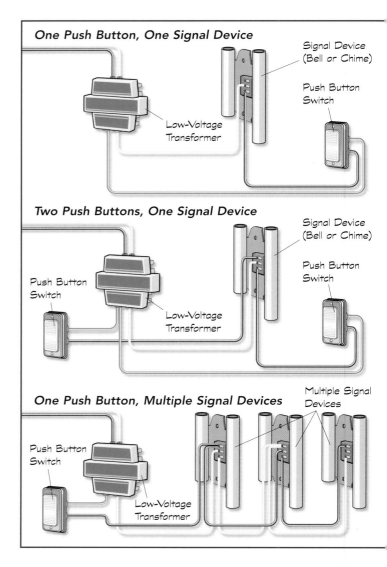

One Push Button, One Signal Device

Signal Device (Bell or Chime)

Push Button Switch

Low-Voltage Transformer

Two Push Buttons, One Signal Device

Signal Device (Bell or Chime)

Push Button Switch

Push Button Switch

Low-Voltage Transformer

One Push Button, Multiple Signal Devices

Multiple Signal Devices

Push Button Switch

Low-Voltage Transformer

Mount the Chimes. Select a suitable location for the chimes, or signal device; then mount it on the wall. **(Photo 1)** If the wall finish is drywall, use toggle or molly bolts to anchor the chimes. If the wall is masonry, use masonry anchors or screws with expansion sleeves.

Wire the Switches. Fish bell wire from the transformer to each doorbell switch location, then from the chimes unit to each doorbell switch location, labeling each wire appropriately. Drill a ⅜ inch hole through the exterior siding, and fish the wires to each doorbell switch. **(Photo 2)** Test the doorbell switches with a continuity tester; then wire the doorbell switches.

Wire the Transformer and the Chimes. Be sure that the power has been turned off to the transformer. Next, strip the two wires coming to the transformer from the front and rear doorbell switches, removing about ½ inch of insulation from each wire; then connect both wires to one of the screw terminals on the transformer. **(Photo 3)** Strip the labeled wires coming to the chimes from the push-button switches; then connect each wire to the appropriate screw terminal, marked either REAR or FRONT. **(Photo 4)** Connect a wire to the terminal screw, marked TRANS, on the chimes. **(Photo 5)** Fish the loose end of this wire to the low-voltage transformer; then connect it to the remaining screw terminal on the transformer.

Complete the Project. After using a multi-tester to check the system, carefully caulk around the exterior holes; then install the doorbell switches. Set the cover plate over the chimes. **(Photo 6)** Repair and finish the damaged drywall as required.

1 *Securely mount your chimes where they are mostly likely to be heard throughout your home.*

2 *Locate a push-button switch at each house entrance. Caulk around each switch to keep out moisture.*

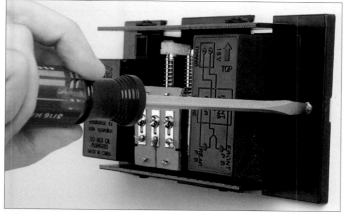

3 *Attach a red wire from each switch to a screw terminal on the low-voltage transformer.*

4 *Connect red wires from the switches to the matching screw terminals on the chimes.*

5 *Connect a wire between the chimes transformer and the unused terminal on the low-voltage transformer.*

6 *Install the chimes and switch cover plates; then repair any damage and refinish the wall as needed.*

SMART TIP

Testing Door Chimes

Once you have successfully installed the chimes unit, turn on the power to the circuit. (See "HOW TO: Install Door Chimes," page 170, for installation instructions.) Press each push-button switch to determine whether or not it is functional. If the chimes sound, then the installation is complete. If the push-button switches don't work, the problem is probably with either the transformer or the wiring between the transformer and the chimes. If one button works but the other doesn't, the trouble is in either the switch or the wiring connecting the switch to the chimes unit. If the transformer makes no humming sound, it may be faulty or the circuit may be dead. To test the circuit, touch the probes on a multi-tester to the ends of the circuit wires; then have someone turn on the circuit. If the multi-tester does not detect power within 2 volts of its rating, replace the transformer; if it does, then have a licensed electrician inspect the circuit.

Timers

Timers can turn on your porch light at dusk or control your thermostat when you're not home during the day. Also, timers operate electrical devices for a set length of time—turning off a heat lamp or exhaust fan when its task is completed. State-of-the-art digital timers can be programmed to perform even more sophisticated automation tasks, such as random security switching—turning several lights and other devices on and off during the course of a day to simulate your presence while you're away from home. Clock-type switches operate by trippers that rotate on an electronically motorized dial. When the tripper reaches a preset time, a set-pin switches the circuit on or off. A digital timer does essentially the same thing, switching on and off electronically at the times set by using push-button controls. Time-delay switches, on the other hand, are usually wound manually and driven by a spring mechanism. When installing a clock-timer switch you wire the device you wish to control into the switch box. A clock-timer switch must be wired in the middle of a run.

HOW TO: Wire a Clock-Timer Switch

Difficulty Level: 🐾

Tools and Materials

- Insulated screwdrivers
- Wire stripper
- Switch box
- Red and green wire connectors
- Long-nose pliers
- Cable ripper
- Clock-timer switch
- No. 14/2G NM Cable

Pull the Cables. Bring the wire cables into the switch box, and secure them in place, leaving 8 inches of cable. There should be two separate cables entering the box—one from the power source and another from the device or fixture that will be controlled by the timer. Rip the cable sheathing, and strip the wires entering the box. **(Photo 1)**

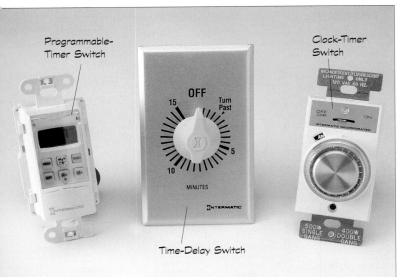

Many types of switching devices perform specialized functions, such as programmable-timer and clock-timer switches.

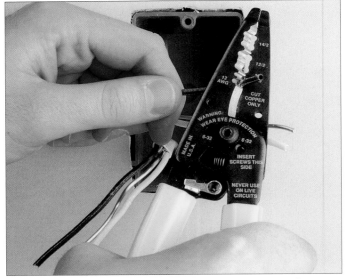

1 Clock-timer switches require two cables—one from the power source and one from the controlled device.

Connect the Hot and Neutral Wires. The clock-timer switch will have three wire leads attached to it. Using a red wire connector, splice the hot black lead wire to the black hot circuit wire inside the electrical switch box. Then connect the hot red wire from the clock-timer switch to the black hot wire going to the fixture. **(Photo 2)** Using a red wire connector, splice the two white neutral circuit wires inside the box to the white neutral wire from the clock-timer switch. **(Photo 3)**

Pigtail the Grounding Wires, and Mount the Timer Switch. Using a green wire connector, splice together the grounding wires coming from the power source and the fixture that will be controlled by the timer. **(Photo 4)** If you are using a metal box, then pigtail these to the green grounding screw inside the switch box. Push all the spliced wires carefully into the switch box; then screw the clock-timer switch securely to the switch box. **(Photo 5)**

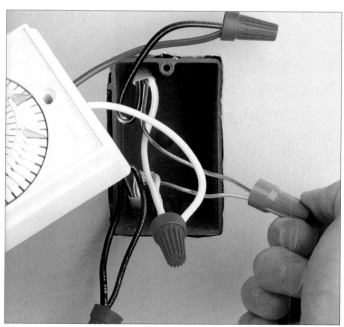

2 Splice the hot wires from the switch to those from the power source and the device being controlled.

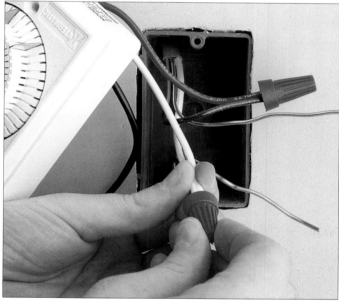

3 Splice the timer-switch neutral wire to the supply and device neutral wires inside the switch box.

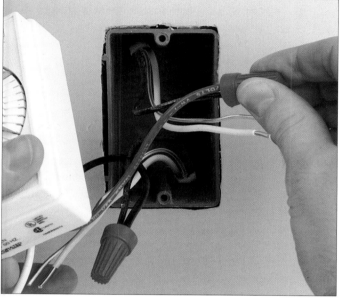

4 Splice the grounding wires from the source and the fixture. If the box is metal, pigtail them to the box.

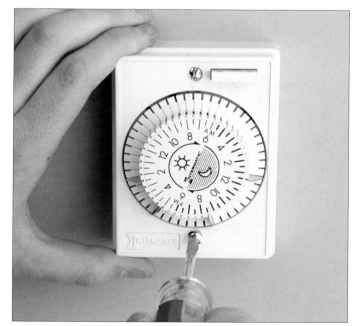

5 Carefully secure the wiring in the switch box; then mount the timer switch to the box.

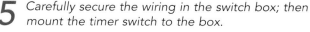

Wiring a Time-Delay Switch. Because a time-delay switch, unlike a clock-timer switch, does not require a neutral connection, it can be installed either in the middle or at the end of a wire run. Instead of three wires coming off the switch, there will only be two. Connect the black lead wires from the timer to the black hot wires from the circuit and fixture cables; then splice the two neutral circuit wires. Pigtail the bare copper grounding wires from the cables to the grounding screw in the switch box, if the box is metal. A digital-control switch is typically installed in the same way.

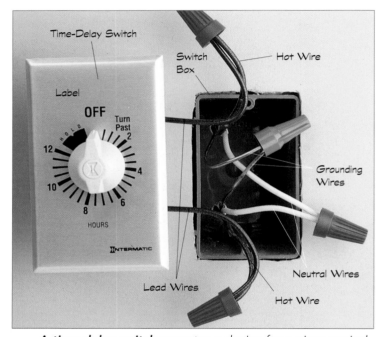

*A **time-delay switch** operates a device for a given period of time, as opposed to operating it at a specified time.*

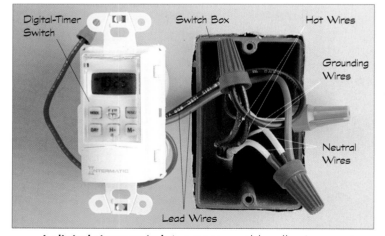

*A **digital timer switch** is programmable, allowing you to set multiple on/off cycles during the day. Cycles may be set at either regular or random intervals.*

Sensors and Alarms

The same type of low-voltage circuiting that is used to wire bells and chimes is also used to wire various types of sensors and alarm systems. Low-voltage wiring has the advantages of being relatively hazard-free and easy to install—making it ideal for the homeowner who wants to set up his or her own security or alarm system.

Different types of sensors are available that can detect motion, smoke, flame, heat, gas, and even human occupancy. A passive infrared (PIR) motion detector, for example, can sense the heat emitted from a human body. Such devices are often used to detect intruders moving through a security zone. When motion is detected, a light will turn on and remain on until the motion stops. The light will stay on for a set length of time; then it will turn itself off.

Smoke detectors are designed to set off an alarm before smoke and fire become intense enough to overwhelm the occupants of a home. Ionization smoke detectors contain electrically charged molecules that cause a flow of current within the detection chamber. Smoke particles attracted to the ions reduce the current flow, thereby triggering the alarm. Photoelectric smoke detectors, on the other hand, use a photocell that is sensitive to light. When smoke interrupts the source light, a broken signal causes an alarm to sound. Infrared flame detectors respond to high-frequency radiant energy emissions that are characteristic of flickering flames. Fixed-temperature heat detectors set off alarms when either a metal having a low melting point reaches the temperature at which it will melt, breaking a circuit, or a metal that expands in heat touches a terminal to com-

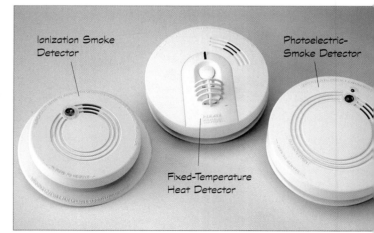

Heat, smoke, and flame detectors sense fire by ionization of charged molecules, photoelectric reflection of smoke particles, temperature, or transmission of infrared beams.

plete a circuit. Rate-of-temperature heat detectors can measure a minute rise in temperature by calibrating the expansion of air.

An occupancy detector uses either a passive infrared or an ultrasonic sensor. Ultrasonic sensors emit high-frequency sounds—setting off an alarm when they sense a change in the frequency of reflected sound. Several different types of sensors are combined to create a comprehensive home security system.

HOW TO: *Wire a Motion Sensor*

Difficulty Level:

Tools and Materials

- ◆ Insulated screwdrivers
- ◆ Wire stripper
- ◆ Switch box
- ◆ Red and green wire connectors
- ◆ Long-nose pliers
- ◆ Cable ripper
- ◆ Motion sensor
- ◆ No. 14/2G NM cable

Mount the Switch Box. Select an appropriate location for the sensor; then mount the switch box. **(Photo 1)** Pull the cable into the box. A motion sensor can be installed either in the middle or at the end of a run.

Wire and Mount the Sensor. Using red wire connectors, connect one of the black lead wires from the sensor switch to the hot black circuit wire; then connect the

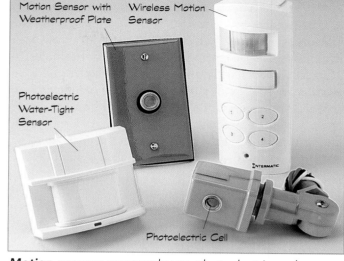

Motion sensors commonly use photoelectric and passive infrared detection methods and may also employ ultrasound. Other types include vibration, acoustic, and thermal sensors.

other black lead wire to the hot black fixture wire. **(Photo 2)** Next splice together the neutral white circuit and fixture wires. No neutral connection is required to the sensor. Splice together the grounding wires. If you are using a metal box, then add a pigtail from the grounding wires to the grounding screw in the switch box. Mount the motion sensor on the switch box. **(Photo 3)** Set the time-delay and sensitivity controls; then test the manual override switch.

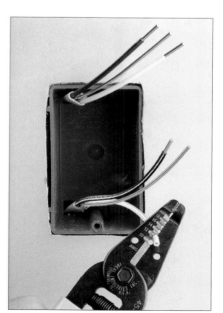

1 Locate a motion sensor where it will strategically detect the passage of an intruder.

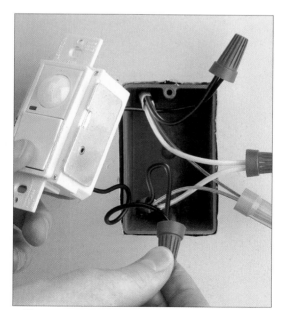

2 Splice the hot, neutral, and grounding wires from the motion sensor to the corresponding circuit wires.

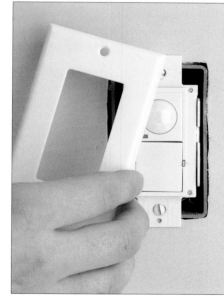

3 Secure the wiring, and attach the sensor box. Set and test the controls.

Thermostats

Thermostatic controls work off low-voltage or line-voltage wiring, depending on the type of heating, ventilating, and air-conditioning system (HVAC) you have in your home. Low-voltage thermostats typically control central HVAC systems, while line-voltage thermostats control multi-zone systems. As a thermostat senses a temperature change, it signals the HVAC equipment to kick on or off. A low-voltage thermostat, powered by a transformer that reduces 120-volt current to 24 volts, may require up to six wires to transmit this signal. A line-voltage system typically has four wires and is powered by a 240-volt circuit. Today, most thermostats are programmable, allowing you to raise or lower the temperature in your home at preset times. Lowering the temperature while you are at work on a winter day, for example, reduces energy consumption significantly, saving money on heating bills.

HOW TO: Wire a Low-Voltage HVAC Thermostat

Difficulty Level: ✎

Tools and Materials

◆ Insulated screwdrivers	◆ Long-nose pliers
◆ Wire stripper	◆ Circuit cable
◆ Low-voltage transformer	◆ Cable clamps
◆ Red and green wire connectors	◆ Low-voltage programmable thermostat
◆ Octagonal electrical box	

Mount the Electrical Box. Install an octagonal electrical box in the desired location of the thermostat. Pull the feeder cable into the box, and clamp it in place. Then rip the cable, and strip the branch-circuit wires. **(Photo 1)**

Attach and Wire the Transformer. Attach the low-voltage transformer to the electrical box; then splice together the transformer and feed wires. (See "How to Install a Low-Voltage Transformer," page 168.) **(Photo 2)** Pigtail the transformer and branch-circuit grounding wires to the electrical box grounding screw; then screw the cover plate to the box. Connect the hot red wires from the HVAC unit and the thermostat to the terminal screws on the low-voltage transformer.

Wire the Thermostat. Pull the HVAC and transformer wires through the thermostat base; then mount the base on the wall. Attach the red transformer wire to the terminal screw labeled Rh and a jumper wire from Rh to terminal screw Rc. Connect the remaining HVAC wires to the screw terminals designated for them by the thermostat manufacturer. **(Photo 3)** Paint the screw heads to match the wires for future reference; then install the thermostat and cover plate.

1 Determine where to mount your thermostat—a centrally located interior wall is usually the best place.

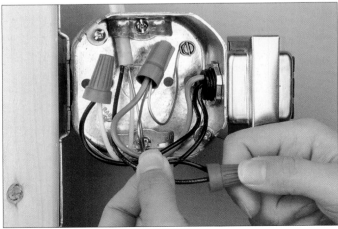

2 Mount a low-voltage transformer on the junction box; then splice the lead wires to the power source.

3 Pull the HVAC wires into the thermostat base; then connect each to its designated screw terminal.

HOW TO: *Wire a Line-Voltage Heater Thermostat*

Difficulty Level: 🐾

Tools and Materials

- Insulated screwdrivers
- Wire stripper
- Line-voltage thermostat
- Yellow and green wire connectors
- Long-nose pliers
- No. 14/2G NM cable
- Electrical tape
- Rectangular electrical box
- Cable ripper

Mount the Electrical Box. Install a rectangular electrical box where the thermostat will be located. Pull the branch-circuit cable into the box, secure it in place using the internal clamps, and then strip the wires. **(Photo 1)**

Wire the Thermostat. Using yellow wire connectors, splice the red LINE wires from the thermostat to the black and white hot branch-circuit wires. Wrap the white wire with black tape to designate it as hot. Connect the black LOAD wires from the thermostat to the black and white wires from the heating unit, again using black tape to mark the white wire. **(Photo 2)** Splice the grounding wires. If you are using a metal box, then pigtail them to the grounding screw in the box.

1 Mount an electrical box, and pull branch-circuit cable into the box. Remove 6 in. of cable sheathing; then strip the wires.

2 Connect the thermostat LINE wires to the branch-circuit cable and LOAD wires to the heating unit. Splice the grounding wires. If the box is metal, pigtail the grounding wires to the box.

Antennas

Antennas are used to transmit and receive electromagnetic waves. When a transmitted wave is received by a television antenna, for example, a current is produced in the antenna. This current travels through the lead-in wires to your television set where it provides enhanced signal reception. The quality of that reception depends largely upon the type of antenna used and the strength of the signal received. Older, mast-style antennas, commonly seen on residential rooftops, have many technical limitations and code restraints. The NEC specifies what materials are used to construct antennas and lead-in

Keep mast antennas a safe distance from overhead wires, and be sure that they are connected to a grounding rod driven into the earth at least 8 ft.

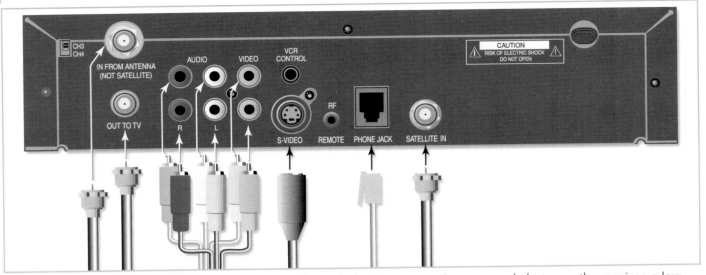

For a digital-satellite-system television receiver, color-coded wiring connections are made between the receiver, a low-noise amplifier or blocker, and an antenna. These are connected, in turn, to the satellite dish antenna.

wires, as well as their size and how they are spliced and supported (Article 810). Most importantly, mast antennas must be located and installed to avoid potential contact with live wires. These radio and television antennas must also be grounded to protect against lightning.

Because so many variables determine the quality of signal received by a conventional mast antenna, improvements to this system are often employed. Today, many antenna systems use coaxial-cable lead-in wires to improve reception. Other choices include preamplifiers, high-sensitivity receivers, and directional antennas that can be rotated by remote-control motors. A rotating antenna is commonly operated by a simple low-voltage plug-in transformer that reduces 120-volt power to 24 volts—enough power to control the rotational motor. Where available, most homes today have cable television connections that provide direct-wired reception through a cable company antenna. This type of antenna typically uses RG6 quad-shielded coaxial cable, which consists of two foil shields, each covered with a second braided shield. The shielding helps to prevent loss or degradation of the signal at higher electromagnetic frequencies.

Many homeowners who don't have access to cable television or who simply prefer another option now use satellite systems to receive television programming. Satellite television offers a wider selection of programming than cable and often provides better-quality reception. A home satellite television (HSTV) system consists of a transmitter that beams microwaves at a communications satellite, the satellite itself, a receiving antenna dish, and a satellite television receiver, known as a TVRO (Television Receive Only). Once it receives a signal, the satellite

responds by transmitting it back to earth (transponding), where it may be received by any digital satellite antenna aimed toward the satellite and tuned to the right frequency. A device called a feedhorn at the focal point of the parabolic (bowl-shaped) antenna dish focuses imprecise satellite signals and conveys them to a low-noise block converter (LNB). (See the illustration on page 180.) The signals are then greatly magnified and sent to the digital satellite system (DSS) receiver that sits on your television set. Audio/video tuning is handled by an A/V receiver that sits on or near your television set.

HOW TO: Install a Satellite TV System

Difficulty Level:

Tools and Materials

- Satellite dish
- Low-noise amplifier/ blocker/connector
- RG-6 quad-shielded coaxial cable
- DSS receiver
- Fish tape
- AV receiver
- Insulated screwdrivers
- Multipurpose tool

For a large dish antenna you will also need an antenna positioner, antenna motor cable, and polarization motor cable.

Mount the Satellite Dish. Choose a location for your satellite dish that is readily accessible and at the shortest possible wiring distance from your television. Avoid placing it on your roof, unless you have no other choice, and stay away from any metal that may interfere with signal reception or pose an electrical hazard. Follow the antenna manufacturer's instructions for mounting the satellite dish and its components. **(Photo 1)**

Wire the Antenna. Wire the antenna equipment according to the directions given by the manufacturer. There will be two coaxial cables coming from the low-noise amplifier. On a large dish, there will also be one cable from a polarization motor, and one from an antenna-positioning motor. Plan your wire routing before you purchase any cables because they come with connectors already attached and should not be cut or spliced. **(Photo 2)**

Wire the DSS Receiver. Wire the receiver according to the manufacturer's directions. If your antenna dish is mounted in the yard, install the direct-burial cables in a trench 1 to 2 inches wide and 6 to 8 inches deep. Connect the two coaxial cables from the low-noise blocker to the Digital Satellite Receiver (DSS) receiver. For large dish antennas, the cable from the polarization motor will contain three wires that are color-coded red, white, and black. Connect these to the properly designated terminals on the DSS receiver. A cable from an antenna positioning motor will contain four color-coded wires (brown, blue, green, and orange). Connect these to their respective terminals on the DSS receiver. **(Photo 3)**

Position the Antenna. Connect the digital satellite system receiver to your television set; then use the signal strength meter displayed on your TV screen to guide you in, properly positioning the satellite dish antenna for the best possible signal reception. **(Photo 4)**

1 Parabolic, or bowl-shaped, antenna dishes must be precisely aimed at a satellite that is positioned in a fixed orbit around the earth.

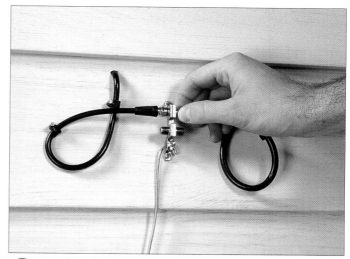

2 Carefully follow the manufacturer's directions when wiring your satellite system, especially if it includes polarization and antenna motors.

3 Connect the coaxial cables for the low-noise blocker (LNB). If included, do the same for the polarization and antenna motor cables.

4 Wire the satellite receiver to your television, and then position the antenna for best reception. Follow the manufacturer's directions to connect peripheral devices.

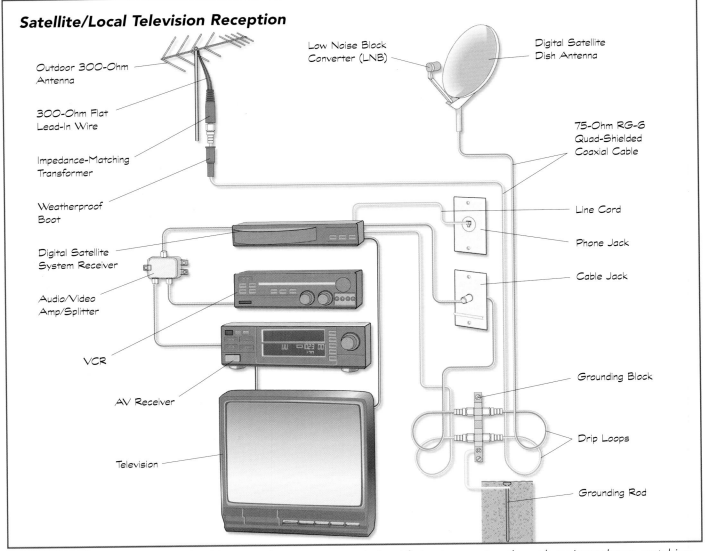

Satellite/Local Television Reception

Outdoor 300-Ohm Antenna

300-Ohm Flat Lead-In Wire

Impedance-Matching Transformer

Weatherproof Boot

Digital Satellite System Receiver

Audio/Video Amp/Splitter

VCR

AV Receiver

Television

Low Noise Block Converter (LNB)

Digital Satellite Dish Antenna

75-Ohm RG-6 Quad-Shielded Coaxial Cable

Line Cord

Phone Jack

Cable Jack

Grounding Block

Drip Loops

Grounding Rod

An RG-6 quad-shielded coaxial cable is used to connect a twin-lead flat antenna wire, through an impedance-matching transformer, to a digital satellite receiver. Reception from a 300-ohm flat lead-in antenna may be enhanced by connecting a 75-ohm RG-59 coaxial lead-in cable between a matching transformer and your TV receiver.

Telecommunications

Telecommunications wiring includes both conventional telephone and data transmission wiring for computers. In this chapter, discussion is limited to telephone wiring. (See Chapter 9, pages 228–245, "Home Automation," for more information.) Before you attempt to do any telephone wiring in your home, be sure to check with your state public service commission and local telephone company concerning rules and regulations that may apply to your work. National regulations, set by the Federal Communications Commission (FCC), also define your responsibilities with regard to system maintenance and hookup. For example, the telephone company may be responsible for central wiring to your home, while you are responsible for all of the wiring beyond the point of entrance, commonly called the

point of demarcation. A modular wiring jack must also be provided that allows you to disconnect everything on your side of the demarcation point from everything on the other, public side of the telephone network.

Telephone wiring is commonly available as four-conductor line cord and telephone station cable. Line cord is the flat cord that connects your telephone equipment to a telephone jack. It should not be used for anything else. Telephone station cable for residential use typically consists of D-station wire that is color-coded for easy identification. Most home telephone systems require only four conducting wires (two-pair wire), with one pair for the phone and the remaining pair for a secondary line for a fax machine or modem. Color codes for telephone wire

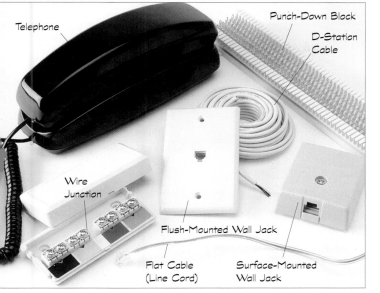

A **basic telephone system** consists of a service entrance, a wire junction, telephone station cable, a surface- or flush-mounted wall jack, flat cable, and a telephone.

CREATIVE HOMEOWNER® SMART TIP

How Many Phones?

Although local telephone companies generally provide you with enough power to ring five telephones on a single line, the actual number you can install is determined by the amount of power required by the particular telephone—some phones require more power than others. The power required is represented by a number, called a ringer equivalency number (REN). The total number of telephones that you can install on your line is determined by adding up the RENs on your phones. If the number is less than five, you will not have any problems. If the number exceeds five, your phones will still work, but not all phones on the line will ring. Either reduce the number of phones on the line or replace one or more with phones having a lower REN.

may consist of solid colors or two-color banding. The standard solid colors are red, green, yellow, and black. Banded colors are more varied. The telephone station cable variations shown in the phone-jack illustration below consist of alternating bands of green and white, orange and white, and blue and white.

The diagram shows how to wire two- or three-pair telephone jacks. Each pair includes a tip and a ring wire. The tip wire on a single-phone line is usually green, while the ring wire is usually red. In any case, it is important to connect like-color wires together throughout any telephone wiring system.

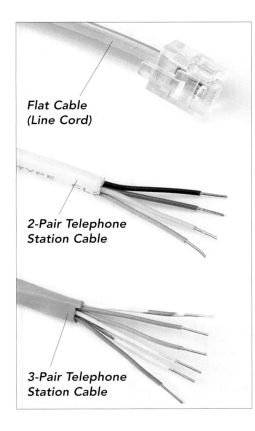

Flat Cable (Line Cord)

2-Pair Telephone Station Cable

3-Pair Telephone Station Cable

◄ **Use telephone station wire** between wire junctions and modular telephone jacks. Use flat wire or line cord to connect telephone or data transmission equipment to the jacks.

► **This phone-jack diagram** illustrates a standard 3-pair color scheme for telephone wiring. A 4-pair scheme would also have a white wire with brown banding and a brown wire with white banding. The slot numbers apply to 4- and 6-terminal telephone jacks only and would not apply to a fourth pair of wires. In a pair of telephone wires, each wire is identified by a tip (+) or a ring (-) polarity. Each pair of wires is further coded by a color scheme consisting of a primary color or a primary and secondary color.

3rd Pair
2nd Pair
1st Pair

T or (+) = Tip
R or (-) = Ring

Slot Number   1 2 3 4 5 6

Solid-Color Wire

2-Color Banded Wire

You can route telephone wires from the network junction box, independently to each jack, in a straight line connecting the jacks in an open loop, or in a closed loop that returns to the junction box. A wire break to an independent jack will only cut service to the phone on that one line. A break in an open-loop system cuts service to any phones beyond the break. But a break in a closed-loop system won't stop a signal from traveling to the break point from either direction.

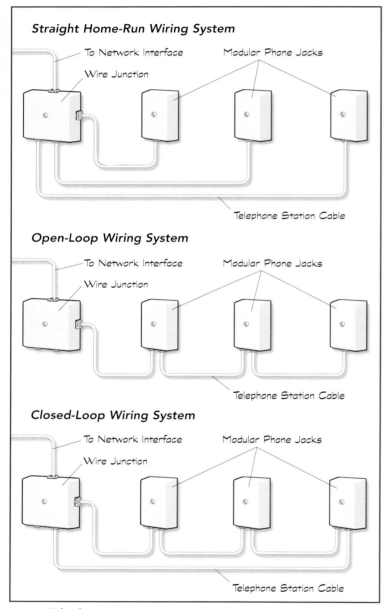

Straight Home-Run Wiring System

Open-Loop Wiring System

Closed-Loop Wiring System

Telephone wiring can be run using either a home-run system, in which each telephone jack is directly wired to a wire junction, or a loop system, in which wiring runs from jack to jack in an open or closed loop that returns to the wire junction and provides a second wiring path. Up to three jacks may be wired to one wire junction.

HOW TO: **Wire a Telephone Jack**

Difficulty Level:

Tools and Materials

◆ Long-nose pliers	◆ Fish tape (nonmetallic)
◆ Wire stripper	◆ Insulated screwdrivers
◆ Telephone jack	◆ Telephone line tester
◆ D-station telephone cable	◆ Cable staples
	◆ Telephone wire junction

Wire the Telephone Junction. Remove 2 inches of sheathing from the end of a length of D-station telephone cable, exposing the insulated wires inside. Be sure that the cable is long enough to reach the location of your new telephone jack. No jack should be more than 200 feet from the telephone service entrance. If your wire junction, or connecting block, has color-coded screw terminals, then strip the cable wires, and connect them to the appropriately colored terminals in the wire junction. **(Photo 1)**

Run the Telephone Cable. Run the telephone cable from the wire junction to the location of your new telephone jack. Be careful not to run telephone wiring within 6 inches of parallel circuit wiring or within 5 feet of any bare wiring. Also, avoid running telephone wire near receptacles or other potential causes of electrical interference.

Wire and Mount the Jack. Fish the phone cable through a hole cut in the wall where the jack will be mounted. **(Photo 2)** Remove 2 inches of sheathing from the cable; then strip the telephone wires. **(Photo 3)** Connect the telephone wires and jack leads to the matching color-coded screw terminals in the telephone jack, replace the cover, and mount the jack on the wall. **(Photo 4)**

Test the Jack. After the outlet has been mounted, the jack is ready for testing. Insert the plug end of a telephone line tester into the jack. **(Photo 5)** If the jack is correctly wired, then the LED on the box will glow green; if not, it will glow red. The line tester will not light if no connection has been made.

Test the Telephone. Plug the telephone into the jack; then listen for a dial tone. **(Photo 6)** If there is no tone, disassemble the jack and recheck the wiring. If there is a dial tone, then try dialing a number. The dial tone should cease after you begin to dial. If it does not, then the wires must be reversed. Reconnect the wires in the proper sequence.

1 Connect station wires to screw terminals or a punch-down block in a telephone wire junction.

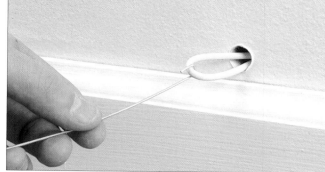

2 Fish the telephone cable through the wall to where the telephone jack will be mounted.

3 Pull telephone cable through a hole cut in the wall, rip the cable sheathing, and strip the telephone wires.

4 Mount the telephone jack, connect the lead (spade tip) wires to the jack, and attach the jack cover plate.

5 Using a telephone line tester, test the polarity of the telephone jack. A green light indicates correct wiring.

6 Plug a telephone receiver into the jack; then listen for a dial tone. If there's no tone, recheck the wiring.

Newer phone systems, instead of screw-terminal junction blocks, use punch-down, or connection, blocks. They are also known as insulation displacement connectors (IDCs). A standard M, or 66, block has connections for 25 pairs of wires. Additional blocks can be added if needed. A special punch-down tool presses the telephone wires into a 66 block, eliminating the need to strip the wires before connecting them to the block.

*A **punch-down,** or impact, tool presses wires into a 66 punch-down block. Because the system is self-connecting, the wires need not be stripped before being punched.*

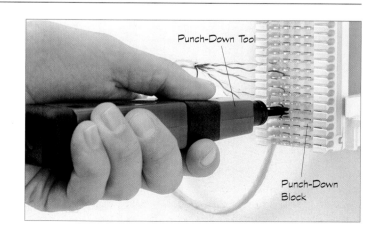

Punch-Down Tool

Punch-Down Block

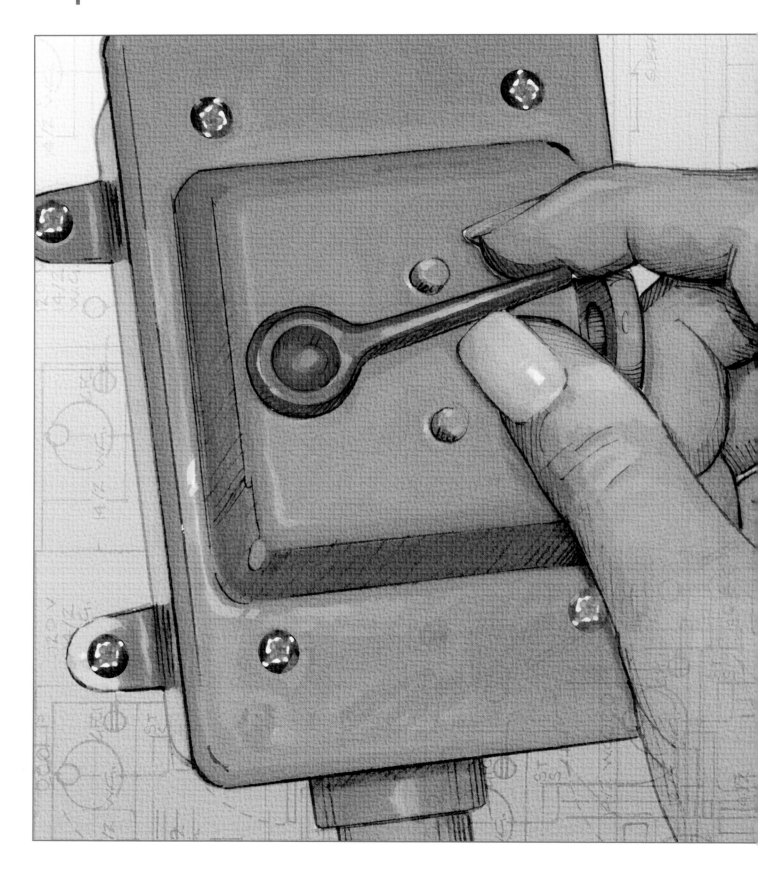

CHAPTER 7

Outdoor Wiring

Outdoor power and lighting enables you to light walkways, driveways, pools, patios, and yards to maintain the safety and security of your home. You will need exterior receptacles to power outdoor appliances, tools, and equipment. Before providing this power and lighting, however, you must be aware of how it differs from interior power and lighting and be familiar with the different code requirements. Some communities require a licensed electrician to do outdoor wiring, while others simply demand that the work be inspected by one before you use it.

What Makes It Different

Circuiting

Underground or overhead outdoor wiring needs protection from the elements. It's subjected to wet and icy conditions, drastic changes in temperature, corrosion, frost heaves, yard tools, and excavation equipment. Overhead cable must be kept high enough not to pose a hazard to anyone or anything passing beneath it. Generally, a height of 12 feet is adequate for residential work, but not always practical, and does nothing to guard against dangers like falling tree limbs and swinging lad-

10'
- SIDEWALK
- PLATFORM

MAX. 150V TO GROUND

12'
- RESIDENTIAL PROPERTY
- DRIVEWAYS
- NON-COMMERCIAL TRAFFIC

MAX. 300V TO GROUND

15'
- PUBLIC STREETS
- ALLEYS
- ROADWAYS WITH NO TRUCK TRAFFIC

300 TO 600V TO GROUND

18'
- PUBLIC STREETS
- ALLEYS
- ROADWAYS SUBJECT TO TRUCK TRAFFIC
- NON-RESIDENTIAL DRIVEWAYS

MAX. 600V TO GROUND

For wires of up to 600 volts, the NEC mandates acceptable clearances from the ground for overhead cable spans (Section 225-18).

Underground Cable Depth Requirements

Condition	Direct-Burial Cable	Rigid Nonmetallic Conduit (PVC)	Rigid and IMC Conduit
In open soil-pedestrian traffic only	24"	18"	6"
In trenches below 2" of concrete	18"	12"	6"
Under streets, highways, roads, alleys, driveways, and parking lots	24"	24"	24"
1- & 2-family dwelling driveways and outdoor areas; used for dwelling related purposes only	18"	18"	18"

The NEC requires that there be a minimum distance between the topmost surface of an underground cable or conduit and the top surface of the finished grade or other cover above the cable or conduit (NEC Table 300-5).

ders. To avoid the worry of maintaining overhead wire, you'll probably to want bury your outdoor cable or conduit underground. Burying underground cable in a protective conduit is one choice. Or, if identified for such use, cable can be buried directly in the ground.

Underground feeder and branch-circuit cable, known as UF cable, is designated for outdoor wiring because it is weatherproof and suitable for direct burial. UF cable looks somewhat like ordinary NM cable, so be sure that the UF designation is clearly written on the sheathing.

Outdoor Conduit and Cable Types

◄ **Flexible nonmetallic conduit** offers limited protection for underground cable or conductors.

◄ **Rigid conduit** affords extra protection for underground cable, but water penetration and eventual corrosion remain an inevitable problem.

ENT (Electrical Nonmetallic Tubing)

EMT (Electrical Metallic Tubing)

Rigid Metal Conduit

Rigid Nonmetallic Conduit

▶ **Type UF (underground feeder) cable** is designed for direct burial underground. The sheathing label indicates whether it is also sunlight and corrosion resistant.

▶ **UF cable** doesn't have paper insulation between the wires and outer sheathing. A thermoplastic coating encases the wires, making them water resistant but difficult to strip.

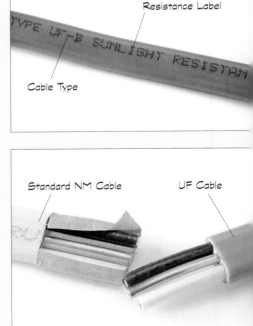

Resistance Label

Cable Type

Standard NM Cable

UF Cable

The wires are molded into plastic rather than wrapped in paper and then sheathed in plastic, like NM cable wires. Aboveground UF cable must be protected with conduit.

Direct-burial cable must be buried deeply enough to be protected from routine digging, yet not so deeply that trenching may interfere with existing water or power lines. The NEC specifies minimum depth requirements for underground cable: 24" for direct-burial cable; 18" for rigid nonmetallic conduit; 6" for rigid and intermediate metal conduit (Table 300-5). If your cable is powered from a ground-fault breaker, you may be permitted to trench less deeply, but this is not recommended—you might someday plant a tree or shrub over the cable and risk cutting it while digging.

Any special characteristics of newer types of cable insulation will be identified on the sheathing, such as sunlight and corrosion resistance. Note that the plastic sheathing on UF cable encases the insulated conductors inside it, making the individual wires somewhat difficult to strip, even using a utility knife.

Weatherproofing

Outdoor electrical materials and equipment, such as fixtures, electrical boxes, receptacles, connectors, and fittings must be manufactured not only to meet code requirements but to resist the elements. Outdoor electrical equipment must be weatherproof and, in some cases, watertight. For these reasons, you use different materials and equipment for outdoor electrical work than for indoor work.

Materials and Equipment

Outdoor Electrical Boxes

Outdoor electrical boxes are either rain-tight or watertight. Rain-tight boxes typically have spring-loaded, self-closing covers, but they are not waterproof. This type of box has a gasket seal and is rated for wet locations as long as the cover is kept closed. It is best to mount a rain-tight box where it cannot be penetrated by driving rains or flooding. Watertight boxes, on the other hand, are sealed with a waterproof gasket and can withstand a soaking rain or temporary saturation. These boxes are rated for wet locations.

▶ **Watertight receptacle boxes** are sealed with waterproof foam gaskets. Receptacle covers snap shut over each outlet. Switch covers have watertight levers. (See page 189.)

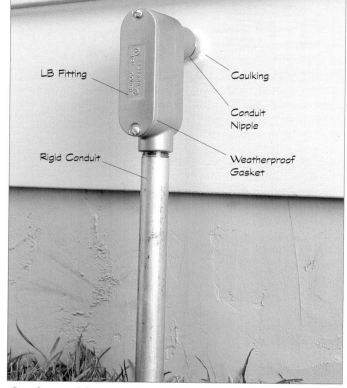

Outdoor cable run underground must be protected in rigid conduit where it enters or emerges from the trench.

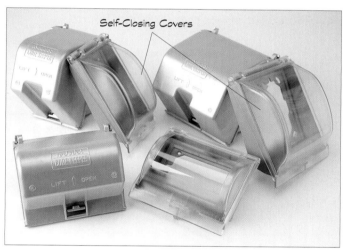

A rain-tight electrical box is not waterproof. It is rated for wet locations only if the cover remains closed.

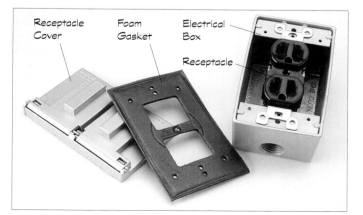

Outdoor Wiring

Receptacles and Switches

Any receptacles that provide outdoor power for a residential dwelling, even if they are in an outbuilding, must have ground-fault-circuit-interrupter protection [NEC Section 210-8(a)]. Although GFCI receptacles may be used, they tend to nuisance-trip when exposed to the weather. It is better to have your outdoor branch circuit powered by a cable connected directly to a GFCI circuit breaker.

Every residence must have at least one receptacle installed at the front and back of the house. These receptacles must be within 6½ feet of the finished grade [Section 210-52(e)]. In addition, any outdoor receptacle that will be in unattended use, such as one that supplies power to a pump motor, must have a weatherproof box and a cover that protects the box even when the plug is in the receptacle [Section 410-57(b)]. Receptacle covers are available for both vertical and horizontal installations and are either on the device in the box or attached to the box itself.

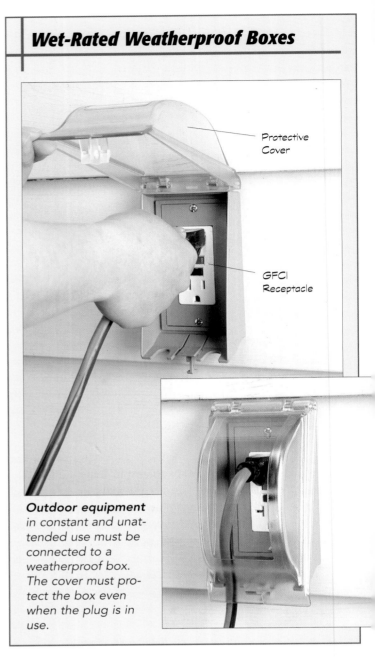

Wet-Rated Weatherproof Boxes

Protective Cover

GFCI Receptacle

Outdoor equipment in constant and unattended use must be connected to a weatherproof box. The cover must protect the box even when the plug is in use.

Snap-Shut Covers

Device-Mounted Cover Plates

Box-Mounted Cover Plates

Flip-Top Cover

Receptacle coverplates for vertical or horizontal boxes may be box- or device-mounted. The cover types can be snap-shut, screw-cap, or flip-top.

An outdoor receptacle may be mounted on a wall, post, or any secure location. If you choose to screw a receptacle box onto a wooden post, then be sure that the post is pressure-treated to inhibit rotting. You can also mount a weatherproof electrical box on the end of a ½-inch-diameter section of galvanized rigid metal conduit that is threaded on one end and anchored in concrete at the other. A two-gallon bucket can be filled with concrete to form the anchor. Burial depths vary across the country.

A freestanding receptacle box supported by rigid metal conduit must be mounted at least 12 inches, but no more than 18 inches, above the ground. It should have secondary support, such as a second conduit (not shown).

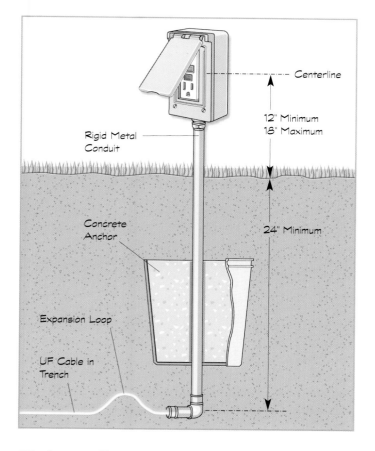

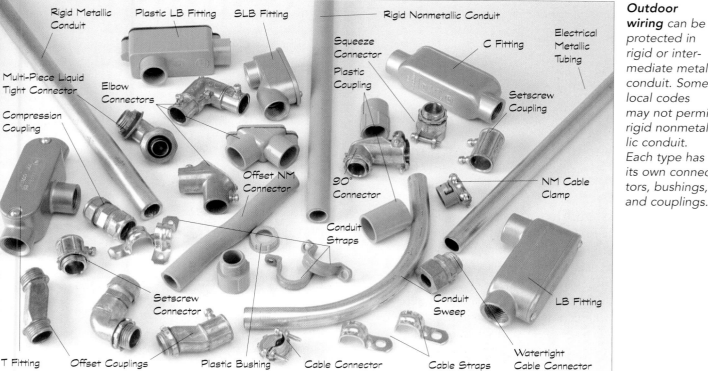

▲ **Weatherproof boxes and cover plates** are available for single-pole, double-pole, and three-way switches. Covers also exist for switch/pilot lights or switch/receptacles.

◄ **A concrete-anchored, rigid metal conduit** may be used as a support on which to mount a weatherproof outdoor receptacle (with secondary suport). Check local code for above-grade minimum and maximum height requirements.

Conduit, Connectors, and Fittings

As mentioned above, under "Circuiting" (page 185), outdoor wiring is typically protected by rigid conduit—both aboveground and wherever it enters or emerges from underground trenching. Rigid and intermediate metallic conduit (IMC) are most commonly used, but most local

Weatherproof boxes and covers are also required to protect outdoor switches from exposure to the elements. Covers to single-, double-, and triple-gang boxes operated by toggle levers are available for outdoor switches, and there is also a cover for a combination single-pole switch with a duplex receptacle.

Outdoor wiring can be protected in rigid or intermediate metal conduit. Some local codes may not permit rigid nonmetallic conduit. Each type has its own connectors, bushings, and couplings.

Outdoor Wiring

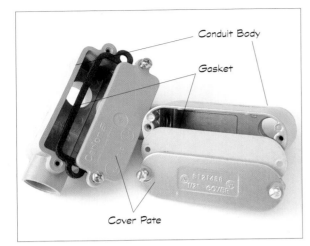

Conduit Body

Gasket

Cover Pate

◀ *An LB fitting* protects cable at the junction of interior NM cable and exterior UF cable. The fitting directs cable in rigid conduit to a cable trench.

▶ *A box extension* is often used to increase the interior size of an existing electrical box to accommodate tap-in wiring for a new circuit.

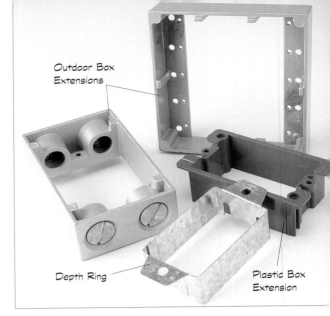

Outdoor Box Extensions

Depth Ring

Plastic Box Extension

codes permit the use of rigid nonmetallic conduit, which is made of Schedule 80 polyvinyl chloride (PVC). Regardless of which type of rigid conduit you are permitted to use, you will have to make a variety of connections. To do this, you will need special connectors. These are available for metal and nonmetallic conduit, including bushings for straight pieces and elbow connections, locknuts, offsets, and various couplings. Be sure that the connectors you select match the material and category of conduit you are using.

At the point where cable runs through the exterior wall of your home, you will need a special L-shaped connector called an LB conduit body. An LB encloses the joint between your indoor cable and the outdoor UF cable running down the side of your house and into an underground trench. LB conduit bodies are fitted with a gasket that seals the cable connection against the weather.

Another type of fitting that you may find useful is a box extension, or extender, which is used to increase the volume of an existing outdoor receptacle or junction box when you need to tap into it to bring power where it is required. This is often done to avoid extensive rewiring and/or renovation work.

Lamps and Yard Lights

The NEC requires that all residential dwellings have switch-controlled exterior lighting outlets to provide illumination at outdoor entrances or exits accessible from grade level, at attached garages, and at detached garages with electrical power (Section 210-70). In addition to such required lighting, you may wish to highlight a pond, garden, flower bed, or other feature in your yard. Whatever your purpose, you should be familiar with currently available types of outdoor lighting.

For general-purpose outdoor lighting, either type R (reflector) or type PAR (parabolic aluminized reflector) lamps are suitable. These long-lasting lamps have a reflective interior surface that maintains a bright light and resists weathering. Although PAR lamps are not affected by inclement weather, not all type R lamps are acceptable for outdoor use, so check the package labeling carefully. To mount lamps of this kind, you must install weatherproof lamp sockets. Outdoor lamp sockets for single-, double-, and triple-lamp installations are available on both rectangular and round electrical-box lamp mounts. Some mounts can also accommodate a motion-sensor control switch.

For accent or yard lighting, both 120-volt and low-voltage lighting can be used, depending upon your purpose. You can mount a 120-volt light fixture on a post or on a ground spike containing a built-in extension cord. If you choose low-voltage lighting, then you will also need to install a 120- to 12-volt outdoor step-down transformer on the exterior wall of the house.

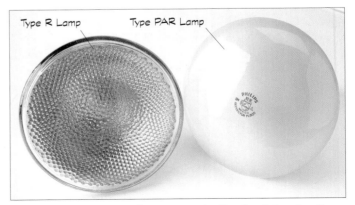

Type R Lamp

Type PAR Lamp

Type R (reflector) and PAR (parabolic aluminized reflector) lamps are typically used for general purpose outdoor illumination and floodlighting.

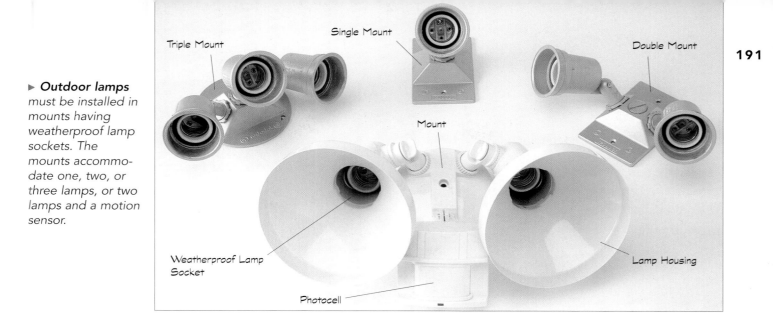

▶ **Outdoor lamps** *must be installed in mounts having weatherproof lamp sockets. The mounts accommodate one, two, or three lamps, or two lamps and a motion sensor.*

Triple Mount

Single Mount

Double Mount

Mount

Weatherproof Lamp Socket

Photocell

Lamp Housing

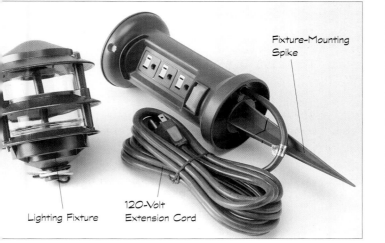

Fixture-Mounting Spike

Lighting Fixture

120-Volt Extension Cord

▲ **Outdoor 120-volt lights** *are available that can be spiked into the ground as far from an outdoor receptacle as the length of the pre-attached extension cord.*

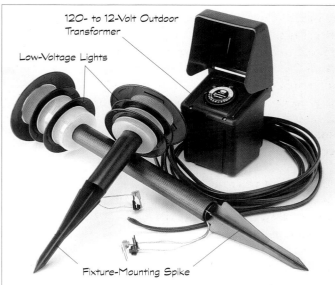

120- to 12-Volt Outdoor Transformer

Low-Voltage Lights

Fixture-Mounting Spike

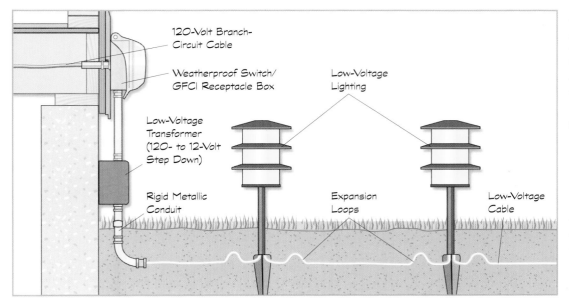

120-Volt Branch-Circuit Cable

Weatherproof Switch/ GFCI Receptacle Box

Low-Voltage Transformer (120- to 12-Volt Step Down)

Rigid Metallic Conduit

Low-Voltage Lighting

Expansion Loops

Low-Voltage Cable

▲ **Low-voltage lights,** *powered by outdoor step-down transformers, are commonly strung along a path or drive to provide safe low-level accent or guide lighting.*

◀ **Use low-voltage lighting** *to illuminate a driveway or walkway. You need to wire it to a low-voltage step-down transformer.*

Outdoor Lighting

Outdoor lighting is an essential part of any home lighting system, whether it is used to add interest to a landscape, accent design elements on and around the house, or provide illumination for the safe movement and security of a homeowner or guest.

▲ **Strategically placed uplighting** invites the viewer to enter this tree-lined walkway.

▲ **A simple porch light** near an entryway provides a warm welcome to visitors.

▼ **Decorative bollards** highlight these deck walks, while the individual step lights provide additional safety.

▲ **Low-voltage lighting** lends interest to this home and accentuates its pathways, outdoor areas, and landscaping.

▼ **Strings of mini-lights** set off these exterior steps, emphasizing their presence to the unwary walker.

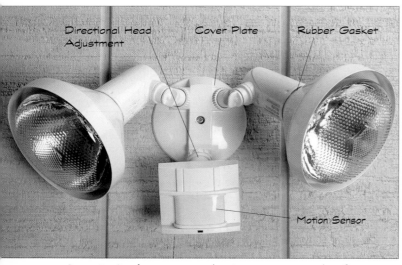

Directional Head Adjustment

Cover Plate

Rubber Gasket

Motion Sensor

An exterior lamp mount having an extra socket for a motion sensor can play an important part in any home-security system.

Sensors and Timers

As an added security measure, you can combine outdoor lighting with devices that sense motion or operate off a timer-switch. Infrared motion detectors trip on the lights whenever an object passes within a given field of vision. The detector is usually attached to a special socket on an outdoor lamp mount that also houses sockets for type R or PAR lamps. A photocell prevents the device from tripping during daylight hours, and a timing mechanism determines the length of light operation in the absence of continued motion. You can use a manually operated indoor switch to override the automatic control.

You can also control outdoor lighting by using an indoor timer-switch in place of a conventional switch. There is a drawback to this, however: you must be aware of which types of lamps are permitted for use with a particular timer switch. Some switches can only be used with incandescent lamps. Timer switches using type R and PAR lamps may be unable to prevent potential damage to the timer in the event of an overload and should be limited to 150 watts.

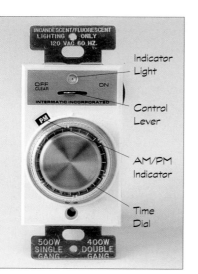

Indicator Light

Control Lever

AM/PM Indicator

Time Dial

Setting your exterior lights to work on a timer is a good way to enhance your security system, especially during times when you are away from home.

Wiring Preparation

Planning

Whatever your intentions are for outdoor power and lighting, you should first plan your work; then follow certain precautions before you actually begin it. As with interior wiring, it is a good idea to make a diagram indicating where and how you want to locate receptacles, switches, lighting fixtures, pump and sprinkler motors, trenches, and cable runs. Your plan should also show the location of major elements like pools or ponds, outbuildings, patios, and yard equipment. It should also include other important items, especially known hazards, such as large trees, boulders, and rock outcroppings, and underground hazards like pipes, cables, and septic systems. In fact, you should contact your utility company and municipal government to get help in locating underground utilities before you even sketch out your final plan. To avoid potentially dangerous consequences and unnecessary expenses, it is better to be forewarned than to be surprised.

Extending Service

Extend power from your interior service entrance panel to the outside either through a basement/crawl space or a roof overhang. Exiting from a basement or crawl space requires mounting an LB conduit body on the side of your house. Run a rigid-metal conduit nipple through the wall to link the interior junction box to the LB fitting. For power exiting through an eave, mount an outdoor junction box on the surface of your soffit; then run Schedule 80 PVC or rigid metallic conduit from there down to a ground trench. If possible, run your conduit alongside a downspout so that it will be less conspicuous.

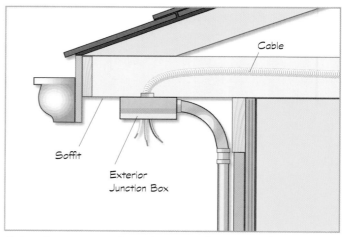

Cable

Soffit

Exterior Junction Box

Extend power outdoors by mounting an outdoor junction box on an exterior wall accessible from your basement or in a roof soffit accessible from the attic.

HOW TO: *Extend Power Outdoors*

Difficulty Level:

Tools and Materials

- Insulated screwdrivers
- Measuring tape
- Long-nose pliers
- 14/2G NM cable
- Mounting bracket
- Rigid conduit
- Conduit compression connector (if metal)
- Caulking compound
- Masonry or spade bits
- Handheld sledgehammer
- Masonry anchors
- Electrician's hammer
- Drill
- Cable clamps
- Cable staples
- Junction box
- LB fitting
- Conduit sweep bend
- Conduit nipple
- Pipe straps
- Star drill
- Safety glasses
- Work gloves
- Knockout punch

Locate and Cut a Cable Exit. Select the location where you wish to extend electrical power to the outside of your home. This point should not be too far from your service entrance panel. Exit through the wall at least 3 inches away from the nearest joist, sill plate and subflooring to allow centering clearance for a junction box. **(Photo 1)** Using a spade bit slightly larger in diameter than your conduit, drill a hole through the exterior header joist where you'll mount the junction box. **(Photo 2)** If your exterior walls are masonry, measure from a common reference point to mark the exit location on the outside of your basement or crawl-space wall. Wearing work gloves and safety glasses, use a masonry bit or star drill and handheld sledgehammer to make an access hole. Avoid the top course of block on a concrete-block wall. This course is usually grouted solid to form a structural bond beam.

Install a Junction Box and LB Fitting. Inside the house, mount a junction box and mounting bracket over the access hole. **(Photo 3)** Next, using a knockout punch, remove the knockouts for the cable and low-voltage wires, pull the branch-circuit cable into the box, and secure it using a cable clamp. From outside, insert a conduit nipple (long enough to reach the box) through the access hole, screw it into the junction box, and screw the LB fitting into the conduit nipple. **(Photo 4)** Seal the joint around the LB fitting using caulk.

1 Mark an access hole to extend power outdoors at least 3 in. from any structural framing.

2 Using a spade or masonry bit, drill an access hole through the exterior wall or header joist.

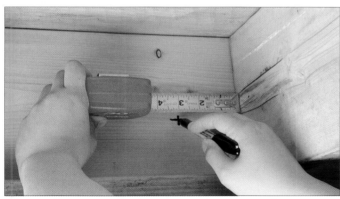

3 Mount the junction box over the access opening, and bring the branch-circuit cable into the box.

4 Use a short length of conduit (conduit nipple) to make a connection between the LB fitting and junction box.

Outdoor Wiring

Attach a Conduit Sweep Bend. Attach a straight length of threaded rigid metallic (or Schedule 80 PVC) conduit, long enough to reach down into the cable trench, to the underside of the LB fitting. Then anchor the conduit to the house or foundation wall using pipe straps and self-tapping screws or masonry anchors. **(Photo 5)** Using a compression connector, attach a conduit sweep bend to the end of the straight length of conduit. The sweep bend should lead deeply enough into your trench to protect the Type UF cable. **(Photo 6)**

5 Connect a length of conduit from the LB fitting into the cable trench.

6 A conduit sweep bend safeguards the cable as it goes underground. A bushing at the end prevents chafing.

Trenching

Digging a trench without first knowing what is underneath can be extremely dangerous. If you excavate randomly, you may unwittingly cut into a sewer or water pipe, or a telephone, cable TV, or electrical power line. Before you do any digging, be sure to check with your local utility company and have it mark the location of any underground utility lines where you plan to dig. In most areas, you are required by law to inform your utility company and secure its approval before you do any excavating. Once you are cleared to excavate, you can dig your trench using a shovel, mattock, backhoe, trencher, or any other suitable equipment. Keep your trenches as short and narrow as possible to reduce expenses and keep landscaping damage to a minimum. Also, when you run UF cable in a trench, always be sure to leave a slack loop for expansion wherever the cable enters or leaves the pipe (conduit). (See table, "Underground Cable Depth Requirements," page 186.) Pulling the cable tight will result in damage or even a complete break because of the soil pressure against the cable.

Always leave a slack loop for cable expansion wherever cable enters or leaves a conduit to avoid potential damage from soil pressure and ground heaving.

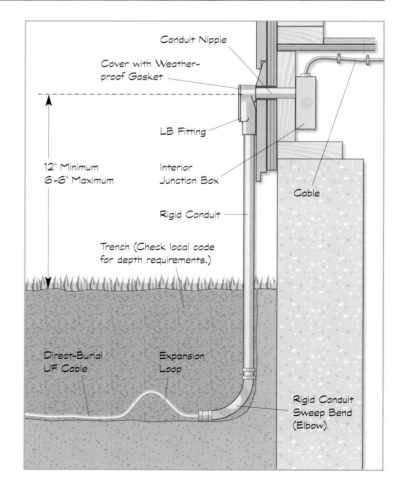

Conduit Nipple

Cover with Weather-proof Gasket

12" Minimum
6-6" Maximum

LB Fitting

Interior Junction Box

Cable

Rigid Conduit

Trench (Check local code for depth requirements.)

Direct-Burial UF Cable

Expansion Loop

Rigid Conduit Sweep Bend (Elbow)

HOW TO: *Install UF Cable*

Difficulty Level: 🔨🔨

Tools and Materials

- Round-head shovel
- Backhoe (optional)
- Adjustable pliers
- 6-mil plastic sheeting
- Conduit compression connectors and bushings
- Work gloves
- Handheld sledgehammer
- Wooden stakes
- Chalk-line box
- Mason's string
- UF direct-burial cable
- LB fitting
- Rigid conduit

Lay Out and Excavate the Trench. Beginning directly below the outdoor-power-extension LB fitting location, chalk an outline of your proposed trench, using a chalk-line box. Using a handheld sledgehammer, drive wooden stakes to mark the length of the trench just outside each chalk line; then run mason's string between the driven stakes. **(Photo 1)** Using a round-head shovel, remove the upper layer of sod between the string guidelines, and store it on a sheet of plastic or tarp. Lay down another sheet of plastic or a tarp along the entire length of the trench. Use this second sheet to catch the excavated dirt as you remove it from the trench. **(Photo 2)**

Install the Conduit, and Splice the Cable. Run a length of straight conduit (metal or Schedule 80 PVC) from the LB fitting down into your cable trench to the depth required by your local electrical code; then, using a compression connector and adjustable pliers, attach a conduit sweep bend to the end of the straight section of conduit (if metal). At the end of the sweep, install another compression connector with a plastic bushing to prevent the underground (UF) cable from scraping against any sharp edges on the conduit. Next, feed the end of the UF cable into the conduit sweep, through your LB fitting and conduit nipple, and then into your interior junction box. **(Photo 3)** Splice the UF and power cables together. **(Photo 4)**

1 Stake out a trench, running from the LB fitting to wherever your outdoor box or fixture will be located.

2 Carefully set aside the sod as you dig the cable trench so that it can be replaced when the work is done.

3 Extend a conduit sweep into the trench. Then feed cable through the sweep bend to the junction box.

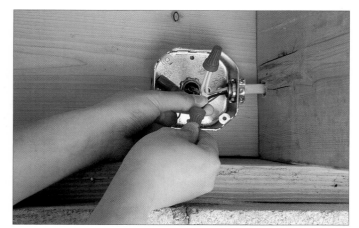

4 Splice the NM cable and exterior UF cable inside the interior junction box.

Lay the Cable, and Fill the Trench. Extend the UF cable along the bottom of your trench to the point where it will emerge; then pull it into the exit sweep. Secure the end of the cable in your exterior fixture, receptacle, or switch box. (If any pavement crosses the path of your trench layout, refer to the sidebar, "Trenching Under Sidewalks and Driveways," below.) Be sure to leave an expansion loop in your cable wherever it enters or leaves rigid conduit to prevent unnecessary stress on the cable. **(Photo 5)** Carefully shovel the excavated soil back into the cable trench; then replace the sod. Be cautious of any sharp stones. **(Photo 6)**

5 When laying cable in a trench, provide an expansion loop. This prevents unnecessary stress on the cable.

6 After refilling a trench, carefully replace the sod, and gently tamp it back in place.

CREATIVE
HOMEOWNER®

SMART TIP

Trenching Under Sidewalks and Driveways

If underground (UF) cable must be run beneath a sidewalk or a driveway, then the cable must be protected in rigid conduit. Run the trench for your direct-burial cable right up to the sidewalk or driveway; then continue it on the opposite side. To bridge the gap between the two trenches, cut a length of rigid metal conduit approximately 12 inches longer than the width to be spanned. You have a couple of ways to drive the rigid conduit under the slab. One way is to beat the end of the pipe into a point, and drive it beneath the slab using a sledgehammer. Another, preferred, way is to put a cap on the end of the pipe, and pound it through. (If the cap is left off, the pipe will go through a lot easier but will fill up with dirt that will be very hard to get out.) In either case, after the pipe emerges from the opposite side of the walkway or driveway, cut off the damaged end, and be sure to file away any sharp edges on the cut pipe. Wrap some tape around the cable sheath to protect it from abrasion where it enters the conduit.

Cap the end of a conduit pipe; then use a block of wood and a sledgehammer to drive it beneath a sidewalk or driveway slab to bridge between two trenches.

Outdoor Wiring Methods

Receptacles

Standard metal or plastic boxes are not acceptable outdoors because they aren't watertight. Watertight receptacle boxes are made of plastic, aluminum, bronze, or zinc-coated steel. If the cable is direct-burial type UF, it can be run directly in a trench at the code-specified depth. Wherever cable is exposed it must be protected in rigid conduit. Check your local code for variations.

HOW TO: *Install an Outdoor Receptacle*

Difficulty Level: 🦤

Tools and Materials

◆ Insulated screwdrivers	◆ Utility knife
◆ Multipurpose tool	◆ Adjustable pliers
◆ Long-nose pliers	◆ Rigid conduit
◆ UF direct-burial cable	◆ Conduit compression
◆ Receptacle (GFCI if	connectors (if metal)
needed)	◆ Mounting ears
◆ Weatherproof box	◆ Conduit sweep bend

Install the Receptacle Box. An outdoor receptacle box must be completely weatherproof, regardless of whether it will be mounted on a wall, post, or rigid metal conduit. **(Photo 1)** Attach special brackets, called mounting ears, to the back of the receptacle box if it will be attached to a wooden post; then screw the box securely in place. For a pipe mounting, first anchor a conduit sweep bend and a vertical section of rigid conduit at the end of your underground cable trench. (See the illustration on page 189.) Next, using a compression fitting, mount the receptacle box on top of the vertical section of conduit. **(Photo 2)** Be sure to center the box between 12 and 18 inches above the ground.

Pull the Cable and Strip the Wires. Attach a plastic bushing to the end of the conduit sweep; then fish the UF cable from the trench up through the pipe to the receptacle box. Pull the cable into the box; then secure it in place. **(Photo 3)** Using a utility knife and a pair of long-nose pliers, split and pull back about 10 inches of the thermoplastic cable sheathing to expose the inside wires. Cut away the peeled-back sheathing; then strip the wires, using a multipurpose tool. **(Photo 4)**

1 Mount an outdoor receptacle on a wall or freestanding post, or attach it to a deck.

2 Another way to mount an outdoor receptacle is on 2 or more lengths of rigid metal conduit in concrete.

3 To prevent cable from chafing on sharp edges of conduit, attach plastic bushings on the conduit ends.

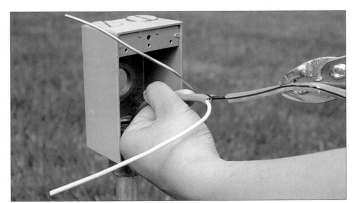

4 Because UF cable has a thermoplastic coating applied over the wires, the wires are difficult to strip.

Outdoor Wiring

Wire and Seal the Receptacle Box. Connect the black hot, white neutral, and grounding UF cable wires to the terminal screws on the receptacle. **(Photo 5)** Mount the receptacle securely in the box (using a GFCI receptacle if the circuit isn't GFCI-protected elsewhere on the circuit or at the service entrance panel); then place the foam gasket over the box to seal it. **(Photo 6)** Attach the waterproof box cover to complete the installation. Turn on the power to the circuit, and test it. If you used a GFCI receptacle, push the GFCI TEST button to test-trip the circuit; then push the RESET button to reset it.

5 *Join the hot and neutral wires to the receptacle terminal screws and grounding wire to the grounding screw.*

6 *Seal the outdoor receptacle box, using the waterproof foam gasket that comes with it.*

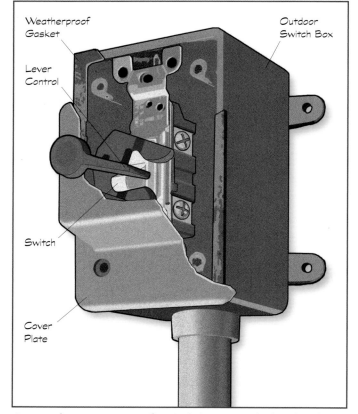

An outdoor waterproof switch box is sealed with a foam gasket. A lever on the cover controls a switch mounted on the cover plate's interior side.

Switches

Just like their receptacle counterparts, outdoor switch boxes are waterproof and sealed with foam gaskets. A control lever mounted on the surface of a switch box cover plate operates a conventional-style switch screwed to the inside face of the plate. UF cable is brought into a switch box through a rigid conduit into the box by means of a watertight compression fitting.

HOW TO: *Install an Outdoor Switch*

Difficulty Level: ➤

Tools and Materials

- Insulated screwdrivers
- Multipurpose tool
- Long-nose pliers
- Weatherproof switch box and cover
- Conduit compression fittings and connectors
- Knockout punch
- Utility knife
- Adjustable pliers
- UF direct-burial cable
- Standard switch
- Mounting ears
- Rigid conduit

Install the Switch Box. Attach mounting ears to the back of the switch box; then screw the box in place. Using a fitting, connect a vertical section of rigid conduit to the bottom of the switch box. Then couple a conduit sweep bend (if metal) beneath the vertical section of conduit running down into the end of your underground cable trench. Anchor the conduit in concrete. (See "Receptacles and Switches," page 188.)

Pull the Cable, and Strip the Wires. Attach a plastic bushing to the end of the conduit sweep (if you're using metal); then fish the UF cable from the trench up through the conduit to the switch box. **(Photo 1)** Pull the cable into the box; then secure it in place. **(Photo 2)** Using your utility knife, split open about 10 inches of the thermoplastic cable sheathing. To expose the inside wires, peel back and cut away the sheathing. Use your multipurpose tool to strip the inner wires. **(Photo 3)**

Wire and Seal the Switch Box. Connect the black hot and and switch-leg wires to the corresponding switch terminal screws; splice the neutral wires; and then pigtail the bare copper grounding wires to the switch and switch box (if metal) grounding screws. **(Photo 4)** Finally, push all the wiring neatly into the switch box; then screw the switch onto the box. Place the foam weatherproofing gasket over the switch box, and screw the cover plate in place on the box and over the switch. **(Photo 5)** After turning on the power, test the lever control on the cover plate to be sure that it operates the internal switch.

1 Mounting ears make a switch box easy to install. A cemented fitting connects conduit to the box.

2 Feed the UF cable from the trench and the cable from the fixture to the switch box.

3 Expose the wires in the cable, cut away the excess sheathing; then strip the inside wires.

4 Connect hot, fixture, and grounding wires; then splice the neutral wires.

5 Secure all the wiring neatly in the box, set the foam gasket in place, and screw on the cover.

Outdoor Wiring

Lights

Employ exterior lighting to provide required illumination and task lighting, or go further by providing decorative and accent lighting. Combined with motion sensors, you can even use exterior lighting as a part of your home security system. All outdoor lighting, whether practical or decorative, must be weatherproof. You can mount an exterior light on a porch ceiling, building wall, or freestanding post. Pipe-mounted fixtures are secured by a threaded compression fitting, while floodlights require special lamp-socket fittings having movable heads that can be adjusted in any direction. An additional movable head is often furnished for attaching a motion sensor. (See "Lamps and Yard Lights," page 190 and "Sensors and Timers," page 194.)

HOW TO: Install a Motion-Sensor Light

Difficulty Level: 🎣

Tools and Materials

- Insulated screwdrivers
- Knockout punch
- Saber saw
- Multipurpose tool

- Fish tape (nonmetallic)
- 14/2G NM cable
- Rectangular weatherproof light-fixture box
- Indoor switch box
- Wire connectors
- Outdoor light fixture with motion sensor

Install the Switch Box. Using a saber saw, make a wall cutout for an interior switch box; then fish cable to the opening from your power source. Pull the cable into the switch box, install the box, and secure the cable using the internal clamps. **(Photo 1)**

Install the Light-Fixture Box. Make a cable cutout in your exterior wall for the motion-sensor light; then fish a cable from the switch box to the light-fixture cutout. Pull the cable into the box; then install the box on the wall. Tighten the mounting screws until the flange around the box is sealed to the exterior siding. Secure the cable in the box. **(Photo 2)**

Wire the Switch. In the switch box, connect the black hot wires from both the branch-circuit and the fixture cable to the terminal screws on the switch. Then pigtail the bare copper grounding wires to the switch. Finish

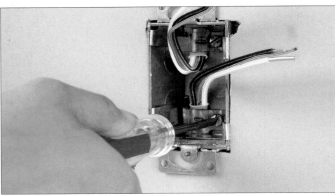

1 Cut an opening in an outer wall, and mount an interior switch box in the opening.

2 Cut a cable hole in the exterior wall for the fixture box. Fish cable from the switch box through the hole.

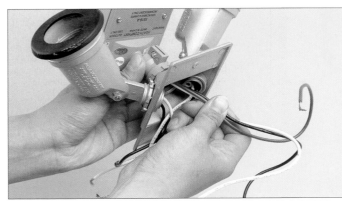

4 Assemble the motion-sensor light fixture according to the manufacturer's directions.

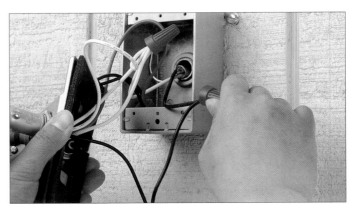

5 Pull the wires through the lamp mounting plate; then splice the wires and connect the ground.

wiring the switch by splicing together the white neutral wire from the branch-circuit cable and the white neutral wire from the fixture cable. **(Photo 3)**

Assemble and Wire the Light Fixture. Following the manufacturer's directions, attach the motion sensor to the weatherproof lamp socket **(Photo 4)**; then pull the lead wires for the sensor and lamp sockets through the mounting plate. Install the socket gaskets and washers to waterproof the fixture. Splice the red motion-sensor wire to the black lamp-socket wires. Next, connect the bare copper grounding wire from the switch box to the grounding clip in the light-fixture box. Place the wall gasket over the light-fixture box; then splice the white neutral wire from the switch box to the white neutral wire from the light fixture. Do the same with the black hot wire from the switch box and the black hot wire from the light fixture. **(Photo 5)**

Mount the Light Fixture. Push all the wires into the fixture box, mount the light fixture over the wall gasket, and screw the mounting plate to the box. Turn on the power and check the switch, lights, and sensor. **(Photo 6)**

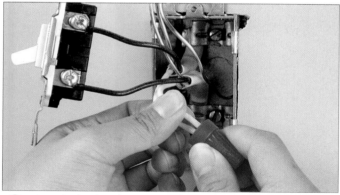

3 Attach the hot branch-circuit and fixture wires, pigtail the grounding wires, and splice the neutrals.

6 Tuck the wiring into the light-fixture box; then screw the mounting plate onto the box.

Outdoor Receptacle, Switch, and Fixture Circuit

A GFCI receptacle protects the circuit wires as well as the switch and fixture from shock damage in this outdoor circuit. Two-wire cable feeds power to the LINE screw terminal on the receptacle and proceeds to the switch and fixture from the LOAD terminal.

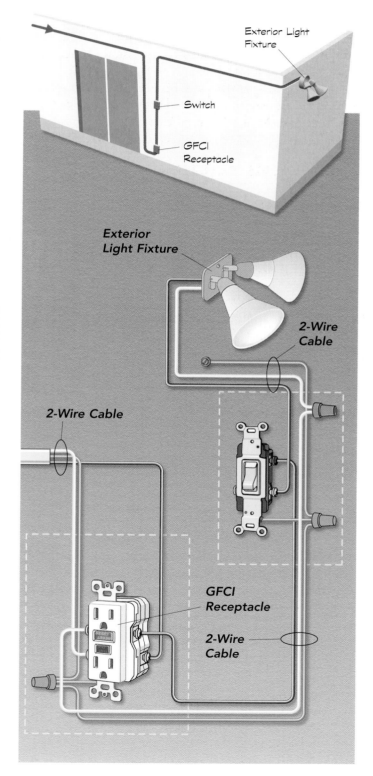

Exterior Light Fixture

Switch

GFCI Receptacle

Exterior Light Fixture

2-Wire Cable

2-Wire Cable

GFCI Receptacle

2-Wire Cable

Outdoor Wiring

Low-Voltage Lighting

Another type of outdoor lighting is low-voltage lighting. Because of the low voltage needed to power this type of lighting, it is much safer to use outdoors than lighting powered by a conventional 120-volt line. It is so low, in fact, that a short-circuit in low-voltage underwater lighting would not even be felt by a swimmer. For this reason, it is the ideal type of lighting for in-ground pools. More often, though, low-voltage lighting is employed to light a drive or pathway or to accent landscaping. Lamps for low-voltage lighting commonly range between 25 to 50 watts. You need only install a transformer to step down 120-volt power to 12 volts. Lighting controlled from a transformer can be strung together and connected to fixtures that can then be spiked into the ground along the length of the low-voltage wiring. Because there is little hazard associated with this kind of wiring, it doesn't need to be buried any deeper than 6 inches.

HOW TO: Install Low-Voltage Outdoor Lighting

Difficulty Level: 🐿

Tools and Materials

- Insulated screwdrivers
- Electrician's hammer
- Multipurpose tool
- 14/2G NM cable
- UF direct-burial cable
- Plastic or metal retrofit receptacle box
- GFCI receptacle
- Adjustable pliers
- Saber saw
- Knockout punch
- Fish tape (nonmetallic)
- 14/2 cable staples
- Wire connectors
- Watertight low-voltage transformer
- Low-voltage lighting fixtures with spikes

Install the Receptacle Box. Using a saber saw, make a cutout in an exterior wall for a retrofit receptacle box in a location near where you wish to install your low-voltage lighting system. Fish the 14/2G gauge cable to the opening from your power source (service entrance panel or nearby receptacle box). Pull the cable through the receptacle box; then mount the box. **(Photo 1)**

Install the GFCI Receptacle. In the receptacle box, attach the white neutral wire from the NM cable to the GFCI receptacle. Connect the black hot wire from the house branch-circuit cable to the terminal screw on the GFCI receptacle. Then, pigtail the grounding wire from the house branch-circuit cable to the grounding screw on the GFCI receptacle and the box (if necessary). **(Photo 2)** Secure the GFCI receptacle in

▶ *Hanging Solar Light*

▼ *Low-Profile Flare Light*

▶ *Copper Coachlight*

▼ *Low-Profile Well Light*

the box. Install the weatherproof GFCI receptacle cover plate and gasket, drawing the mounting screws tight for a good seal.

Install the Low-Voltage Lighting. Using the attached ground spikes, install your low-voltage lighting system by driving the spikes into the ground. Low-voltage lights can be positioned along a wall, drive, or patio. They may also be used to accent your garden or some other landscaping feature. **(Photo 3)** Lay the low-voltage cable that connects the lights in a trench at least 6 inches deep. Clip the wire leads from each light fixture to the underground cable. **(Photo 4)**

Wire the Low-Voltage Lighting. Leaving an expansion loop in the trench, run the low-voltage cable to the transformer box. Connect the low-voltage wiring to the 12-volt step-down transformer, following the manufacturer's installation guidelines. **(Photo 5)** Then mount the transformer below or alongside the GFCI receptacle box you installed previously. Plug the transformer into the GFCI receptacle, turn on the power, and test the system. **(Photo 6)** Once everything is in working order, refill the trench.

1 Make a cutout in an exterior wall for a retrofit switch/GFCI receptacle box.

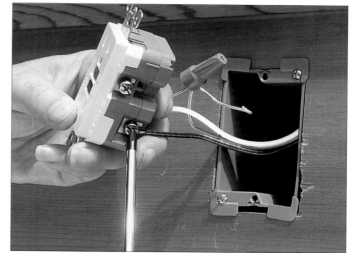

2 Attach hot and neutral wires in the GFCI receptacle box. Pigtail the ground wires to the grounding screw.

3 Position your low-voltage lighting system along a walk, drive, or other landscaping feature.

4 Lay the cable in a trench at least 6 in. deep and clip the wire fixture leads to the cable.

Outdoor Wiring

5 Following the manufacturer's directions, connnect the low-voltage wires to the 12-volt step-down transformer.

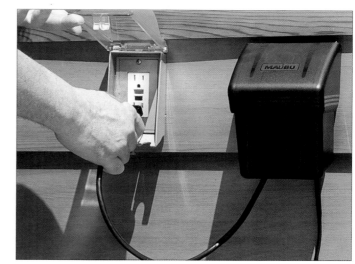

6 Plug the transformer into the GFCI receptacle, turn on the power, and test the lights.

Underwater Pool Lighting

Install underwater pool lighting in conformance with code requirements. Use wiring suitable for wet locations, and make all splice connections above water. All electrical components below water must be watertight. In addition, the entire lighting system must be grounded.

Underwater lighting can be standard 120-volt or low-voltage lighting (12 volts). A transformer is used to step down voltage for low-voltage lights. Low-voltage systems are highly recommended because even if a short in the wiring occurs, the current is so low that it will not be perceived by or endanger a swimmer.

CREATIVE
HOMEOWNER®

SMART TIP

Respecting Electricity and Water

Electricity and water can be a deadly combination. Always follow all safety procedures completely. An electrified pool can be the direct result of a job done carelessly.

◎ *If a fixture, gasket, or lens looks old or worn, replace it.*

◎ *Always use a replacement lens, bulb, or gasket made specifically for the fixture. Use the same manufacturer or a generic brand designed for the specific make and model. Forcing a different part to fit invites tragedy.*

◎ *Each fixture is designed to take a specific bulb. If the writing on the bulb is not readable, never replace the bulb with one that is higher than 400 watts. Heat can melt the resin that makes the fixture waterproof.*

Underwater Lighting Circuits

For safety, electrical wiring in and around swimming pools must be on a separate circuit. The wiring must also be suitable for wet locations. There are specific NEC requirements regarding underwater light fixtures (Section 680-20) and the transformers and ground-fault circuit interrupters (Section 680-5) that power them. Although 120-volt lighting systems are available, a 12-volt low-voltage system is advantageous. This type of system uses a weatherproof step-down transformer specifically designed to supply underwater systems. The voltage supplied is so low that a short circuit in the lighting system would be imperceptible to a swimmer and GFCI protection is not required. Low-voltage underwater lights are installed in either wet or dry niches on the interior sides of a pool. A wet niche is a waterproof, standard-size lamp housing connected by conduit to a junction box located above the water and away from the pool. A dry niche isn't waterproof.

▼ **Underwater pool lights** *can be installed in either wet- or dry-niche lamp housings. Unlike a dry niche, however, a wet niche is waterproof. This way you can replace a lamp without having to first lower the level of the water.*

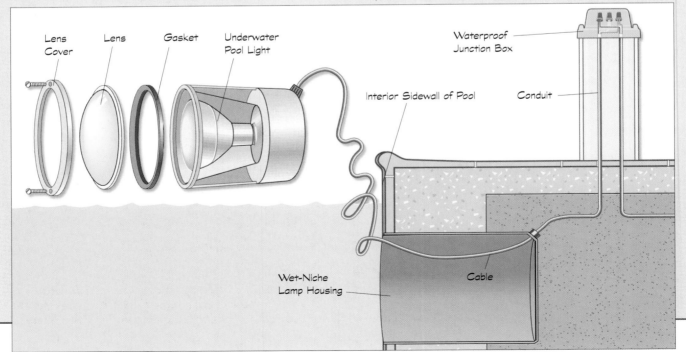

Lens Cover

Lens

Gasket

Underwater Pool Light

Waterproof Junction Box

Interior Sidewall of Pool

Conduit

Wet-Niche Lamp Housing

Cable

HOW TO: *Replace an Underwater Bulb*

Difficulty Level: 🔧

Tools and Materials

* Bulb and gasket replacements
* Insulated screwdriver

Remove and Disassemble the Fixture. Turn off the power at the circuit breaker. In the pool, unscrew the face-rim lock screw from the faceplate that holds the fixture in the niche. **(Photo 1)** Lift out the bottom, which is hooked into the niche. Uncoil the extra cord, and remove the fixture from the pool. Loosen the screws that hold the lens cap in place, and gently pry the lens from the fixture. **(Photo 2)**

Replace the Bulb, and Reassemble the Fixture.

Unscrew the old bulb, and screw in the new one. **(Photo 3)** Before reassembling the fixture, restore the power, and then briefly turn on the light to be sure it works. Turn off the power again, and reassemble the fixture. Because exposure to chemicals, heat, and compression can quickly wear down a gasket, remember to replace the old gasket with a new one. Place the new gasket around the lens as if it were a rubber band stretched around a drinking glass. If the faceplate screws into place, tighten the screws on opposite sides to apply even pressure on the gasket and avoid gaps that can cause leaks. Place the fixture under water for a few minutes, and check for air bubbles, an indication of a leak. **(Photo 4)** If you find a leak, disassemble the fixture and reseal the gasket. Once you are sure there are no leaks, replace the fixture in the niche.

1 Lean into the pool and unscrew the face-rim lock screw holding the fixture.

2 Loosen the lens-cap screws, and carefully pry the lens from the fixture.

3 Remove the burned-out bulb, and screw in the replacement bulb. Restore power, and test the unit.

4 Reassemble the fixture, and hold it underwater to check for air bubbles to be sure there are no leaks.

Outdoor Wiring

Pool Lighting

Pool lighting may be as varied as the lighting inside a house. Accent lights can be used to highlight fountains, landscapes, gardens, and other design elements in and around a pool. Task lighting can illuminate pathways to and around a pool, while underwater lighting may provide both beauty and safety for after-dark swimming and outdoor entertaining.

▶ **Internal pool lighting** dramatically focuses attention on, and accentuates, the drop-off in this hillside pool.

▼ **Exterior fixtures** provide ambient as well as accent lighting for this house and poolside patio.

▲ **Underwater lighting** emphasizes the vertical spray of this fountain and the downward flow of water over the wall.

▲ **Decorative pendants** light this poolside entertainment area, while hidden lighting illuminates the water.

◄ **Task, accent, and ambient lighting** are used effectively to unify this pool and landscape design.

CHAPTER 8

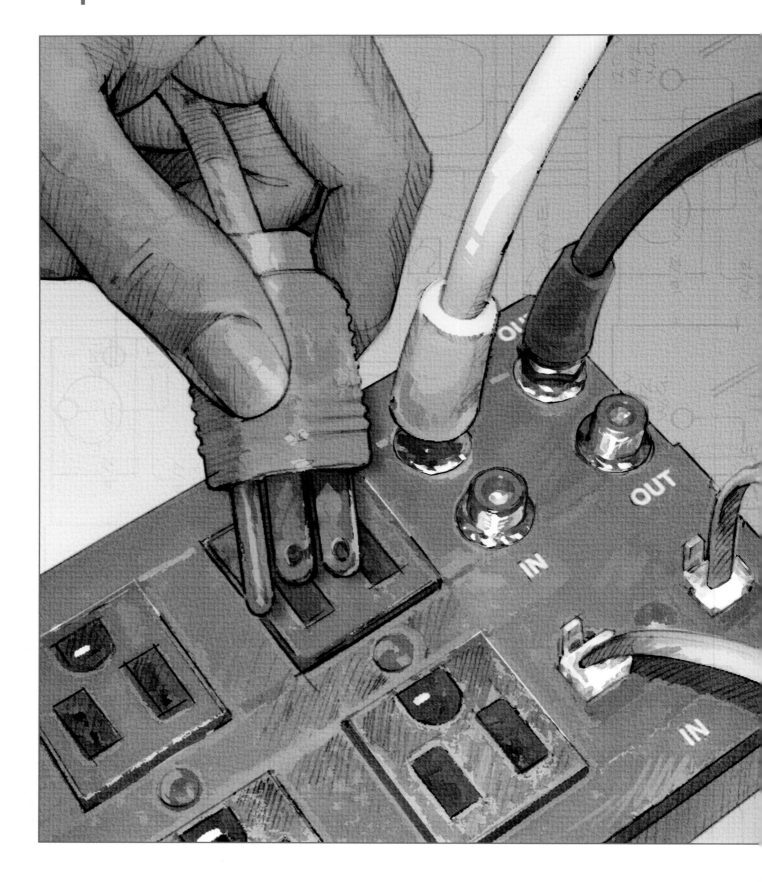

Emergency Power Equipment

Today's home needs some kind of protection against the possibility of property damage caused by lightning strikes and power surges, not to mention the threat of injury to you and your family and the inconvenience of power outages. A single lightning strike, for example, can contain 30,000 amps of electrical current—2,000 times more than a typical 15-amp residential circuit.

Electronic equipment is sensitive to lightning, which can destroy your expensive computer system and digital big-screen television. Anything with micro-circuits is at risk, including security systems and portable phones. Lightning traveling through phone lines can melt your modem. To make matters worse, a single

flash of lightning can consist of several discharges, increasing the odds for damage.

A well-designed lightning protection system will carry a lightning charge through lightning rods and cables on your home down to the ground and safely dissipate it.

A single strike of lightning can easily damage your home unless you have an effective system in place to carry the current safely to ground.

An effective system should even extend to nearby trees, outbuildings, and other structures that might attract a lightning strike. Another concern, however, is the possibility of damage caused by a power surge through your utility lines. A power surge from a lightning strike miles away can still damage your electronic equipment and telephone system.

To protect against a power surge, it is necessary to stop the surge from entering the house wiring at the main panel. This can be accomplished by installing a whole-house surge arrestor at the main panel and using individual surge arrestors, or suppressors, at points of use that protect each device or appliance at its outlet. To work properly, a surge protection system must also be well grounded because excess current is diverted back through your home's grounding system and into the earth. (See "Grounding Systems," page 21.) A good lightning and surge suppression system will offer little comfort, though, if you're hit by a major power outage lasting for days. For this, it is wise to have an optional standby generator as a backup source of emergency power. (See "Optional Standby Generators," page 220.)

Lightning Protection
Understanding Lightning

A lightning strike occurs after a buildup of negative charges of electrical energy in a cloud and positive charges of electrical energy in the earth. As the dry air between the cloud and the ground becomes moist, negative charges move downward to meet positive charges moving upward, creating a lightning bolt.

Lightning Rods

Lightning descends to earth in 150-foot steps. When a negatively charged strike is within 150 feet of a lightning rods, the positive charges in the earth surge upward through the lightning protection system to meet and neutralize the strike. An effective lightning protection system creates a cone of protection around a house. The positive charges flow safely from the ground through the cable to the lightning rod, then jump to the negatively charged lightning strike from the rod, not the surface of the house. Lightning rods are usually from 10 to 12 inches long, and contrary to myth, don't attract lightning to your home because they're not much higher than the roofline.

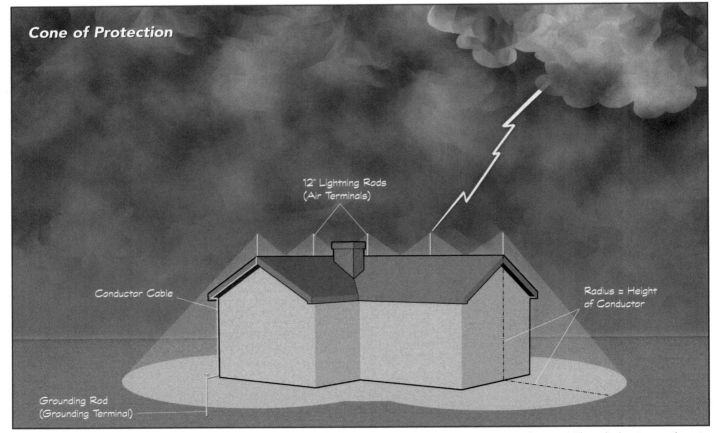

Cone of Protection

12" Lightning Rods
(Air Terminals)

Conductor Cable

Radius = Height
of Conductor

Grounding Rod
(Grounding Terminal)

An effective system *of lightning and grounding rods will form a protective cone over your home. When lightning strikes, it will hit the lightning rods instead of your house.*

Lightning Protection System Components

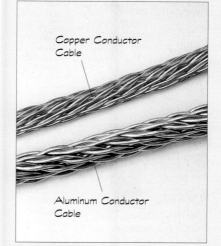

Low-resistance conductor cables carry the lightning current from the rods on your home and other structures safely down to the grounding rods.

Lightning rods, or air terminals, are vital components of any lightning protection system, detouring current away from your home into grounded conductor cables and, further, to grounding terminals.

Grounding rods, or grounding terminals, take the lightning current from the conductor cables and safely dissipate it into the ground.

Lightning Protection Systems

A lightning protection system provides a clear path for lightning to travel directly to the ground without causing injury or destruction to life or property. It consists of three major components: (1) lightning rods, or air terminals; (2) grounding rods, or grounding terminals; and (3) copper or aluminum low-resistance conductor cable to connect the terminals. Copper and aluminum components are used not only because they are excellent conductors of electricity but also because they are highly resistant to corrosion. Copper is preferred because it conducts electricity better than aluminum and less is needed to carry the same amount of current. However, aluminum is necessary on an aluminum or steel roof because copper coming into contact with aluminum or steel can cause corrosion. Nevertheless, even where aluminum is used, the grounding system must be copper. Aluminum cannot be used underground and must be spliced into the grounding wire at least 18 inches above the ground [NEC Section 250-64(a)].

Before beginning any work, check your local and regional building codes to see whether you must satisfy any special requirements. Also, be certain that all of the lightning protection components you install are listed by Underwriters Laboratories.

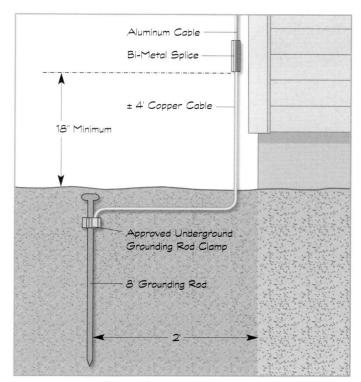

Copper grounding is always necessary in a lightning protection system, even when you use aluminum cable. Aluminum isn't permitted underground because it is vulnerable to corrosion from alkali in the soil. Connect copper and aluminum cables at least 18 in. above ground level.

Emergency Power Equipment

▶ *Various clips, clamps, and splicers* are used to secure cable, mount lightning rods, clamp cable to lightning and grounding rods, and connect cable runs and tie-ins.

When designing a lightning protection system, always include a minimum of two grounding rods as widely separated as possible. To calculate the total number of grounding rods, first measure the perimeter of your home, totaling the length of each exterior wall. If the perimeter is 250 linear feet or less, use two grounding rods; between 250 and 350 linear feet, use three grounding rods; and between 350 and 450 linear feet, use four grounding rods, and so on. Keep all conductor cable running horizontally or angled downward, and avoid sharp turns and U-turns.

To calculate the number of required lightning rods, measure the cumulative length of all roof ridges, including the garage roof and dormers. Antennas, chimneys, weather vanes, cupolas, gables, and other roof projections must all be connected to the main cable using bonding lugs or cable connectors. Other types of fittings are used for mounting, splicing, and clamping cables and rods. Be sure that you use the correct type of fitting for each purpose. Most importantly, make certain that the entire lightning protection system is well grounded. If only part of a system is grounded, lightning may flash sideways between grounded metal components on the roof or within the building, setting fire to flammable materials.

Lightning Protection Standards

Various standards for product specifications and installation methods are published regarding lightning protection systems. The National Fire Protection Association (NFPA) publishes "NFPA 780: Standard for Installation of Lightning Protection Systems" (1997). This 45-page document provides requirements for the protection of people, buildings, and property against lightning damage. The Lightning Protection Institute (LPI) publishes "Standard of Practice LPI-175," which establishes requirements for design, materials, workmanship, and inspection of professionally installed lightning protection systems. Underwriters Laboratories (UL) sets guidelines for the certification of systems materials and components in its publication, "Standard UL96A."

Mounting Saddles with Clamps

Cable Connectors

Grounding Rod Clamp

Flue Tile Mount

Multipurpose Clamp

Cable Clips

Cable Splicers

HOW TO: *Install a Lightning Protection System*

Difficulty Level: 🐾🐾🐾

Tools and Materials:

- Measuring tape
- Graph paper
- Sledgehammer
- Safety glasses
- ⅝"x12" copper lightning rods with mounting saddles
- ½"x8' copper-clad grounding rods
- ⅜"dia. 20-GA one-nail copper clips (loop type)
- 2½"x2¾" copper flue-tile mount with ⅜"x18" chimney rod

- Extension ladder
- Pencil and drafting tools
- Curved-claw hammer
- Shovel
- Work gloves
- ½" dia. bronze grounding rod clamps
- 15⁄32" dia. smooth-twist 32-strand 17-GA copper conductor cable
- Bonding lugs and connectors
- Crimp straight and tee cable connectors

Measure and Sketch the Roof System. Once you have determined whether your system will be copper or aluminum (these instructions are for copper only—do not use copper with aluminum), measure the length and width of the roof on your home **(Photo 1)**; then sketch the roof plan to scale on graph paper. Indicate the location and size of all elements on your roof, including chimneys, vents, exhaust fans, antennas, and other equipment. Also note on your plan the height of roof ridges and eaves. This information will be used to lay out the components of your lightning protection system.

Plan the Layout. Plan and sketch the location of each lightning and grounding rod, cable run, chimney rod, bonding lug, splicer, and connector. **(Photo 2)** Locate a lightning rod within 18 inches of each ridge end and spaced no more than 20 feet apart along the remainder of each ridge. On a flat or low-sloped roof, place lightning rods within 18 inches of the corners, at 20-foot intervals along the roof edges, and at 50-foot intervals across the flat or low-sloped area of the roof. Bond all antennas, vents, flues, stacks, and metal objects on the roof to the main ridge cable. Avoid unnecessary turns and bends when laying out your cable runs. Remember that every system requires at least two widely separated grounding rods. One should be located as close as possible and bonded (connected) to your service entrance grounding rod using a bonding jumper cable. The other should be located diagonally across at the opposite side of the house or as far from the first as otherwise possible. However, the distance between them should not exceed 100 feet along the perimeter of the house. If it does, add a third grounding rod somewhere between the first two. Use your finished layout to make a list of materials needed; then purchase them. Allow extra conductor cable for turns, branch runs, and terminal connections.

1 Before designing a lightning protection system, take measurements to sketch an accurate plan of your roof.

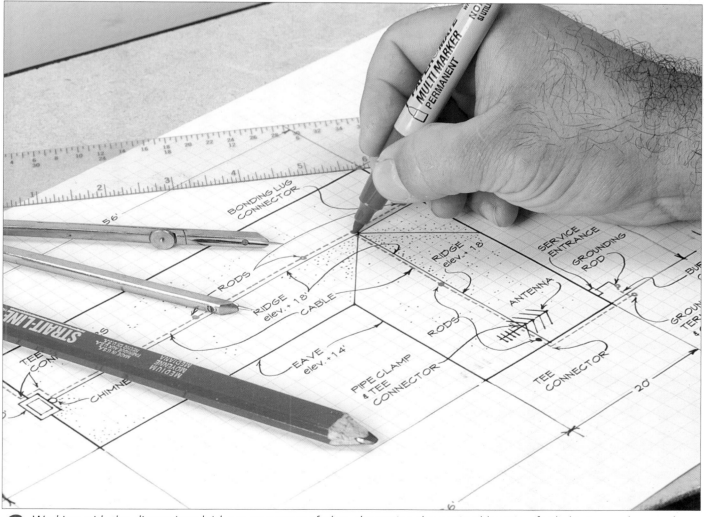

2 Working with the dimensions laid out on your roof plan, determine the optimal location for lightning and grounding rods, cable runs, and connectors. Using this information, compile a list of materials needed for your system.

Emergency Power Equipment

Install the Lightning Rods. Attach the lightning rods and mounting saddles on the roof using the planned layout. Adhere to the manufacturer's guidelines as well as to local code requirements when securing mounting saddles to a structure. **(Photo 3)** Using appropriate connectors, connect all objects on the roof to their own lightning rods and conductor cable or, if they contain metal ³⁄₁₆ inch thick or thicker, connect them directly to the main conductor cable using a bonding lug.

Install the Conductor Cable. Run conductor cable between the lightning rods and from each end lightning rod to a grounding rod. There must be at least two paths leading from the lightning rods to grounding rod connections. Make cable runs horizontal or downward, avoiding sharp turns and bends. Do not make a bending radius less than 8 inches or 90 degrees. Secure the cable, using loop-type clips spaced no more than 3 feet apart. Using crimp connectors, bonding lugs, and clamps, tie all chimneys, flues, antennas, and other roof equipment to the main conductor cable. Conductor cables running

down to grounding rods may be concealed under eaves or in exterior structural walls but must not be spaced more than 100 feet apart around the perimeter of the building. **(Photo 4)** At least two grounding rods are required for any lightning protection system.

Install the Grounding Rods. An 8-foot grounding rod must terminate each cable coming down from the roof. **(Photo 5)** Connect these cables to a grounding rods using grounding rod clamps. Make 1½ inches of lengthwise contact between the rod and cable, or heat-weld them. Locate grounding rods 2 feet away from the foundation, installing one as close as possible to the service entrance. Because they must extend at least 10 feet underground, bury the rods at least 2 feet deep.

Connect the Service Entrance Ground. Run a length of copper jumper cable in a trench between the grounding rod closest to the service entrance and the service entrance grounding rod. Using bronze grounding rod clamps, link the two grounding rods together. **(Photo 6)**

3 Follow code requirements and the manufacturer's recommendations when installing the lightning rods.

4 Conductor cable running to ground can be concealed behind roof ridges and under eaves.

5 Install a minimum of two 8-ft.-long grounding rods at remote locations, buried 10 ft. below the surface.

6 Place a grounding rod near the service entrance (SE). Run a jumper cable from it to the SE grounding rod.

Surge Protection

Electrical Surges

The major drawback to a lightning protection system is that lightning rods cannot stop electrical surges from coming into a house through utility lines, which is the most common way that lightning damages homes. Transient electrical currents from telephone, cable, and telecommunications lines can cause undesirable surges in voltage. The magnetic field created by a lightning bolt can cause voltage to flow through any conducting material such as the wiring or metal piping in your home. Therefore, an effective surge protection system is a necessity in every home—if it is to be safeguarded against these kinds of potential disruptions.

Whole-House Protection

Many people install low-cost surge arresters, or suppressors, that plug directly into an outlet, believing they are providing themselves with whole-house protection. Unfortunately, this is not the case. Surge suppression must be accomplished on two levels. First is at the main panel, where the surge can be prevented from entering the house wiring, and the second is at the point-of-use, where any surge remaining on a line can be removed just before it enters an appliance or other electrical device. Clearly, it makes sense to use a surge arrester to eliminate heavy surges before they enter your home, rather than after. A surge arrester will divert heavy electrical surges into your grounding system, permitting your point-of-use devices to serve as sensitive electronic filters, shutting down noise on the line, as well as stopping any remaining line surges. If your home has a sub-panel located 20 feet or more from the main panel, you should install a second device to protect it, too. In addition, some lightning protection systems may have a box devoted solely to the system that can be mounted adjacent to the main panel. This type of box contains modular electronics that are replaceable should they be destroyed by a lightning surge passing through the box. In effect, the box is sacrificed to protect your home.

Surge arresters may be directly wired to the main panel and mounted either on the inside or outside of the panel box. The type that mounts inside the panel box is usually preferred because it will keep the arrester safely contained should it explode, preventing a fire. A better system for containing lightning surges, and the easiest to install, is a whole-house protection system in which the surge arrester replaces a circuit breaker in the main panel. Because you have to have a circuit breaker anyway, it makes sense to build the protection directly into it. This type of breaker has a red light that indicates whether or not the surge arrester is functional. Once you install the device, whatever it is wired to will be automatically protected. Though the protection system is contained within the device for a particular circuit, the entire house will be protected—not just that circuit.

Point-of-Use Protection

Providing surge protection directly at an electrical outlet is common practice because it is easy to do—you simply purchase the device and plug it in. No wiring needs to be done. This is called point-of-use protection. These types of surge protectors perform several layers of filtering to eliminate the noise on house wiring and prevent damage to highly sensitive circuitry. They are often used to protect personal computers and home audio-video equip-

*A **surge arrester** is an essential part of any whole-house protection system, diverting power surges away from your house wiring and into the ground.*

***Point-of-use surge** protectors prevent damage to sensitive equipment like computer circuits and filter out noise on house wiring.*

ment. Some point-of-use surge protectors electrically isolate their connected plug-ins so that the noise generated by a printer, for example, will not cross over to the computer. Be sure to buy a surge protector that has receptacles arranged in such a way that a plugged-in transformer will not block any of the unused outlets. Also look for one that provides telephone or modem protection.

Grounding

Regardless of the quality of your surge protector, it cannot be effective unless it is connected to a good grounding system. An ideal grounding system will typically consist of one or more approved grounding rods and clamps. As a rule, the more grounding rods you have, the better the system. Be certain that the grounding wires are buried deeply enough not to be cut by your lawn mower or otherwise disconnected from the grounding system. Check local code for grounding wire depths.

A lightning strike produces a tremendous amount of power in the form of magnetic flux—lines of force moving through the atmosphere. These lines of force combine to induce a massive voltage and current pulse (fluctuation) in the utility lines. This pulse rides the line until it reaches and enters the electrical system within your home.

A main-panel surge arrester takes the space of a conventional circuit breaker. Though connected through one circuit, the device protects the entire house.

Mounted in your main panel, a whole-house surge arrester acts to remove lightning pulses from the line, diverting them to the house grounding system (grounding rods), transforming large pulses into smaller, easily managed pulses. Point-of-use protection devices then carry off the smaller pulses and any others generated within a house that might be able to damage sensitive electronic equipment.

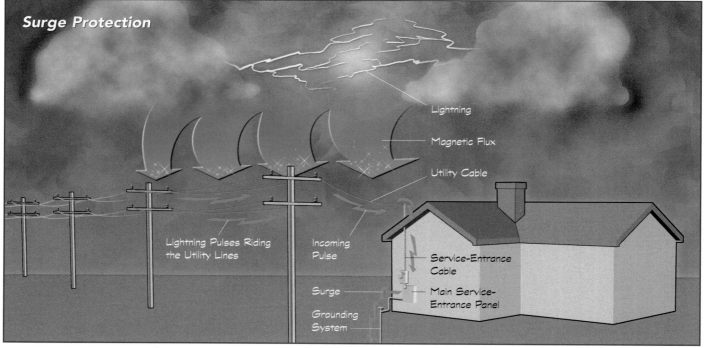

Surge Protection

Lightning
Magnetic Flux
Utility Cable
Lightning Pulses Riding the Utility Lines
Incoming Pulse
Service-Entrance Cable
Surge
Main Service-Entrance Panel
Grounding System

Lightning strikes produce a massive amount of power in the form of magnetic fluctuations traveling through the atmosphere. These forces cut into metal wire in power and telephone utility lines, generating a surge or fluctuation in voltage. Incoming surges from a lightning strike are diverted to a grounding system by a whole-house surge arrester. A point-of-use device plugged into an outlet prevents damage to sensitive microcircuits in computers and other equipment. Individual surge arresters give additional protection to phone lines, keeping your modem from meltdown, for instance.

HOW TO: *Install a Whole-House Surge Arrester*

Difficulty Level:

Tools and Materials:

- Whole-house surge arrester
- Long-nose pliers
- Insulated screwdrivers
- Multipurpose tool

Turn Off the Power. To install a whole-house surge arrester in a main panel, first turn off the main breaker in the panel. **(Photo 1)** This will cut power to the hot bus bars into which the circuit breakers are plugged. Remember that the power will remain in the panel at the point where it connects to the main breaker. Remove the panel cover and set it aside, taking care not to let the cover drop as you take out the last screw. **(Photo 2)**

Wire and Install the Surge Arrestor. Wire the surge arrester **(Photo 3)**; then push the it into the bus-bar

tabs, snapping it in place just as you would a standard circuit breaker. To wire the arrester, connect the hot red and black wires from the circuit you wish to protect to it. (The entire house circuitry will be protected even though the arrester is connected to just one circuit.) Next, connect the white pigtail wire at the back of the surge arrester to the neutral bus bar. Finally, attach the circuit's neutral wire to the service-entrance panel's neutral/grounding bus. (If the panel is a subpanel, the white and grounding wires will be separated. Attach the white wire to the neutral bus and the grounding wire to the grounding bus.)

Replace the Panel, and Restore Power. Replace the panel cover, and refasten the screws to complete the installation of the surge arrester. Throw the main breaker to restore power to the main panel **(Photo 4)**; then check the system. Depending on arrester model, a glowing red or green light will indicate that the circuit is receiving power and that the surge protection system is functioning properly.

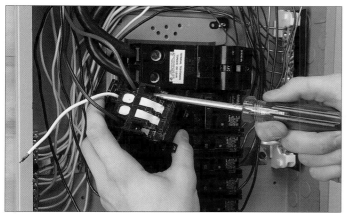

1 Turn off power at the main panel, and test the circuits before installing a whole-house surge arrester.

2 Remove the panel's cover. Here, the surge arrester will take the space of a double-pole circuit breaker.

3 Wire the surge arrester with the circuit you wish to protect. Also wire the ground/neutral bus.

4 Replace panel cover, and throw main breaker switch to test system. A glowing light indicates power flow.

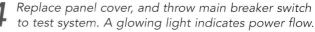

Emergency Power Equipment

Optional Standby Generators

What They Are and How They Work

In many areas of the country, both winter and summer storms can frequently cause power outages that may last for several days. Homeowners in isolated areas must not only be aware of, but must be prepared for the possibility that ice storms may bring down power lines. It takes just one extended power outage to convince a homeowner of the benefits of owning an optional standby generator. This differs from a required system and is termed optional because it is intended for use where one's life doesn't depend on the system (NEC Section 702-2). An optional system, for instance, is ideal for a private residence but not for a hospital.

The safest way to provide temporary power for your home during a power outage is by using a properly connected optional standby generator.

An important concern for the homeowner interested in installing a generator is hooking it up in accordance with legal requirements. Check your local code before starting work. You cannot, for example, connect a generator to your house unless it has a particular type of switch called a double-pole, double-throw switch. This switch has an OFF position that lies between two ON positions. One of the ON positions controls the utility power, and the other controls the standby generator power. Some switches made for this purpose may be labeled LINE (utility power), OFF, and GEN (generator power). Hooking a standby generator into a home using any other type of switch will place at risk anyone who works on the power lines.

Temporary Relief. An optional standby generator is basically a small gasoline-powered motor that generates a limited amount of electrical power. The main advantage of owning a generator is to provide temporary power to your home for essential appliances such as a freezer or refrigerator to keep food from spoiling, to power a few lights, to run a well pump, or to keep your house warm. It would not be practical to provide power to an entire house because of the expense and limitations of operating such a system. Gasoline is usually used to operate standby generators because, in most parts of the country, it is not cost-effective to install diesel, propane, or natural-gas generators in a private home.

Standby generators are heavy and noisy and require air to "breathe." Because of its great weight, you will need a dolly to move one if it doesn't have wheels. The generated noise and exhaust require a location outside the house or in a vented garage. Another possibility is to put the generator in a small shed or lean-to built just for it.

In any case, ventilation must be provided for the generator. Some generators come with a silencer for the exhaust system, as well as a kit for directing the exhaust safely outdoors.

Operation Schedule. How long your generator will run depends on the amount of time you need to draw power from it and the size of its fuel tank. If you have plenty of spare gasoline, you may choose to run the generator all day and then turn it off at night, weather permitting. Or, if you must conserve gasoline, you can run the generator for just one hour out of every four to keep your refrigerator and/or freezer cool or only when you need water or lights. If you choose to use it intermittently, run the generator for at least two to three hours just before you go to bed and again when you get up in the morning. Be sure to read the manufacturer's manual to determine whether you must add oil to the generator motor before starting it.

As an alternative to using a standby generator, homeowners sometimes consider powering a house with batteries. This isn't logical, unless you use solar-powered batteries. Also, batteries provide direct current (DC), while your house uses alternating current (AC). Running a house on batteries during a power outage would require a large investment in a power converter to transform one type electric power into the other.

Selection

Several factors will determine your selection of a home generator. You must consider the wattage, the type of generator motor, whether it is electric or pull-start, and its plug configuration (pattern).

Wattage. A generator has both surge and run wattage. Surge wattage is the power needed to start a device, such as a sump pump, while run wattage is the power needed to keep it running. Because surge wattage lasts for only a few seconds, you will need enough run wattage to satisfy the total wattage of the circuits you want to power. One or two lighting and power circuits, a refrigerator, and hot water and heating controls, for example, require at least a 4,500-watt generator. Preferably, a standby generator should be 6,300 watts or more. The larger the run wattage, the more circuits can be powered at once. Lower-wattage generators may not supply enough wattage to start several appliances at once. They can be used effectively, however, by operating only one or two appliances at the same time.

Type of Motor. The type, manufacturer, and quality of the generator motor you purchase will largely determine whether or not the engine will start without difficulty when the time comes to use it. Standby generators are often taken for granted until there is a power outage. Many low- to mid-range generators have engines that pull-start like lawn mower engines, and they are just as difficult to start. High-end generator engines are typically easier to start, even when they are not maintained for up to a year. The best engines usually have a key-operated ignition. Generators can be purchased at home centers.

Electric or Pull-Start. Because starting an engine by simply turning a key is a lot easier than pull-starting it, electric-start generators are widely preferred over the pull-start variety. Electric-start engines are also more reliable. Nevertheless, for best performance, it is a good idea to start your generator motor at least once or twice a year to verify that the battery works.

Plug Configuration. Low-power generators have a standard 120-volt ground-fault receptacle on their housings, into which you can plug appliances or extension cords. Mid-power generators characteristically have an additional 240-volt receptacle that looks like a standard receptacle with two horizontal rather than vertical slots. Also commonly used is a three-slot twist-lock receptacle that supplies 120 volts. If your generator must supply an entire house with power, though, it must have a female round twist-lock receptacle with four slots. This type of receptacle supplies both 120- and 240-volt power—exactly what is required to power a home. Two of the receptacle slots supply 240-volts, the third is neutral, and the fourth is the ground. A four-conductor, twist-lock extension cord (male on one end and female on the other), using a four-conductor cable, is needed to run power to the house.

The wattage should be prominently labeled on an optional standby generator. Be sure not to confuse the run wattage with short-lived surge wattage.

A high-end generator motor should be easier to start and more reliable than a low- to mid-range engine. It should also be able to go as long as a year without maintenance.

An electric-start motor is usually superior to a manual pull-start engine. This type of motor starts with a simple turn of a key, just like an automobile. The pull-cord is a backup.

Standby generators may have a variety of female receptacles, but only one that's labeled GFCI is ground-fault circuit protected. Only a four-slotted twist-lock receptacle labeled 120V/240V can be used to power an entire house.

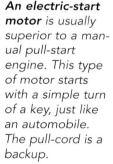

Emergency Power Equipment

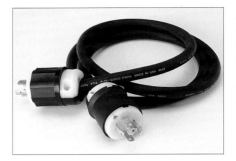

A twist-lock extension cord using a four-conductor cable is required to connect power from a generator to a house.

Placement and Hookup

An optional standby generator should be located as close as possible to the main panel. The longer the extension cord, the more voltage-drop will occur across the distance, reducing power available to your home. For ease of hookup, you can run an extension cord through a window or other opening, through a wall, or into wall-mounted male and female receptacles.

It is not permitted by code to connect an optional standby generator directly to your house wiring by plugging it into a dryer or range receptacle. When a generator is hooked directly to a house circuit, it can send electricity back to the utility—a process called back-feeding. Not only a code violation, it is extremely dangerous to utility workers because it can cause electrocution, not to mention the possibility of burning down your house. If a generator is installed improperly, it may back-feed to the utility, causing a brownout when power is restored. Power surging up and down the lines can even burn up the source generator. The standby generator must be installed using a transfer switch suitable for the intended use, and designed and installed so as to prevent the inadvertent interconnection of normal and alternate sources of supply in any operation of the transfer equipment.

CREATIVE HOMEOWNER® SMART TIP

Built-In Backup Power

Though readily available at home improvement centers, portable generators can be hard to find during a power outage. An alternative, emerging on the home improvement market, is the stationary emergency power generator. This type of generator is built into a home in much the same way as central air conditioning. Like a portable generator, the system automatically kicks in moments after an initial loss of power. Connected to a natural-gas line or propane tank, it eliminates the need for gasoline.

Whether your house is already built or under construction, a good optional standby generator system should be relatively simple and convenient to install, and it should not require coordination with your utility company or municipal government.

HOW TO: Install an Optional Standby Generator

Difficulty Level:

Tools and Materials:

- Knockout punch
- Cable ripper
- Long-nose pliers
- Electrical tape
- Optional standby generator
- Transfer-switch panel box with manual transfer switch
- ¾" dia. conduit nipple
- Wood or masonry screws
- 10/4G rubber, water-resistant cord with stranded wires
- 4-Prong twist-lock receptacle
- Caulking compound
- Insulated screwdrivers
- Wire cutter or multipurpose tool
- Wire connectors
- Panel grounding bus
- 30-amp, 240v breaker
- Power drill with 1⅟₁₆" spade bit
- 1" dia. conduit or threaded nipple
- 10/3G NM cable
- Cable clamps
- ¾" cable staples
- Outdoor receptacle box and weatherproof cover
- 240v 4-wire twist-lock extension cord

Mount the Transfer-Switch Panel. Turn off the disconnect switch on your main panel, and remove the cover. Remember that the line-side connections at the main disconnect switch will remain hot even when the panel is switched off. Punch a knockout from one side of the panel box, and attach a 1-inch-diameter conduit or threaded nipple to the panel. **(Photo 1)** Connect the transfer-switch panel box to the other end of the nipple, and securely screw the box to the wall. **(Photo 2)** Install the panel grounding bus at a convenient location inside the transfer-switch panel. **(Photo 3)**

Disconnect the Circuits. Using an insulated screwdriver, disconnect each hot black wire from the circuits you want powered by the standby generator. **(Photo 4)** Pull the assigned breakers from the hot bus in the panel box. **(Photo 5)** Carefully label the white neutral and bare copper grounding wire for each of the circuits, loosen their terminal screws on the neutral/grounding bus, and separate the wires from the bus. **(Photo 6)** Then tape together the hot, neutral, and grounding wires from each of the removed circuits for later reference. **(Photo 7)**

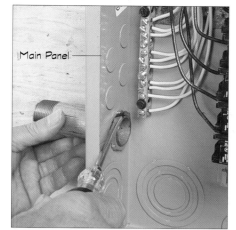

1 Turn off power, punch a knock-out, and install a conduit nipple.

2 Affix the transfer-switch panel to the nipple. Mount the panel.

3 Install the grounding bus in the new transfer-switch panel box.

4 Loosen the terminal screws on each selected breaker, and remove the black wires from the circuit.

5 After disconnecting hot wires, pull the selected circuit breakers from the hot bus in the main panel.

6 For the circuits selected, loosen the screws holding the neutral and grounding wires, and release the wires.

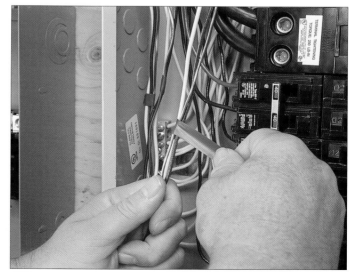

7 Set apart hot, neutral, and grounding wires for each circuit. Tape them together for ease of identification.

Wire the Main Panel. Pull a length of 10/3G gauge NM cable through the conduit nipple connecting the main panel to the transfer-switch panel. **(Photo 8)** Using a cable clamp, clamp the cable in the panel box, and rip back the cable sheathing, exposing the wires. Be sure you have enough wire to reach the appropriate terminals and bus bars. Using a wire stripper or multipurpose tool, strip the wires. Connect the white neutral and bare grounding wires to the main panel neutral/grounding bus. **(Photo 9)** Connect the hot black and red wires to a 30-amp, double pole 240-volt circuit breaker, and snap the breaker into the main panel hot bus. **(Photos 10–11)** Take care to relocate any breakers left stranded. They should be moved up directly beneath the new breaker.

Wire the Switch Panel. Connect the bare copper grounding wire from the 10/3G gauge NM cable to the switch panel grounding bus bar. **(Photo 12)** Next, attach the hot black and red wires to one of the 240-volt circuit breakers in the switch panel and the white neutral wire to the neutral bus bar. Using wire connectors, splice black, white, and bare extension wires to the disconnected circuits in the main panel **(Photo 13)**; then draw the extensions into the new switch panel by threading them through the conduit nipple. Connect the bare grounding wires to the grounding bus and the white neutral wires to the neutral bus. **(Photo 14)** Connect the hot black wire from each circuit to a breaker in the switch panel. **(Photo 15)**

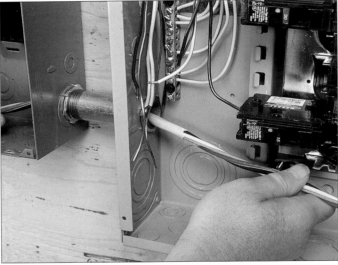

8 Pull No.10/3G NM cable through the conduit nipple into the main panel and new transfer-switch panel.

9 Attach the white neutral and bare copper grounding wires to the main panel neutral/grounding bus bar.

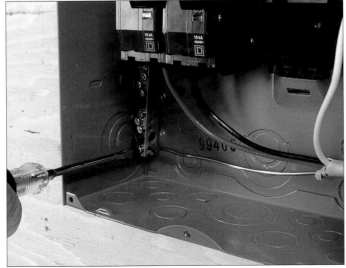

12 Connect the copper grounding wire from the NM cable to the grounding bus in the switch panel.

13 Splice insulated extensions to disconnected circuit wires in the main panel using wire connectors.

SMART TIP

Generator Safety

- Because they are powered by gasoline, standby generators emit carbon-monoxide fumes. For this reason, locate your generator outdoors in a well-ventilated area or in a vented garage or shed.

- If no electricity is generated after a long period of storage, follow the manufacturer's directions for resetting the generator polarity (positive or negative state).

- Ground the generator to the proper connection provided for this purpose on the motor base.

- If it must be stored, leave oil in the generator but do not store it with gasolne in the lines.

- Do not make modifications of any kind to a generator. Use a standby generator only in accordance with the manufacturer's instructions.

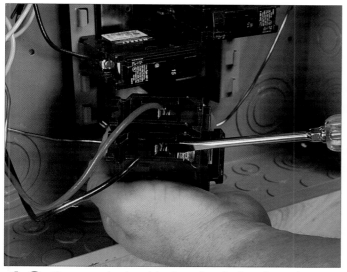

10 Connect the hot black and red wires from the cable to the new 30-amp, 240-volt circuit breaker.

11 Snap the new 240-volt breaker into the appropriate bus slots on the main panel hot bus.

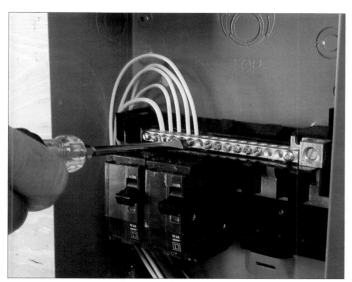

14 Attach extended neutral and grounding wires to the appropriate bus bars in the new switch panel.

15 Connect each extended hot black wire to one of the 120-volt circuit breakers in the switch panel.

Emergency Power Equipment

Install the Outdoor Receptacle. Using a power drill with a 1⅟₁₆ inch spade bit, drill a 1⅟₁₆ inch hole through an exterior rim joist. A ¾-inch-galvanized conduit nipple must be inserted through the hole to attach an outdoor weatherproof receptacle. (See Chapter 7, pages 199–200, "Outdoor Wiring.") Mount the receptacle in a location that will be convenient to your generator. Connect the outdoor receptacle box to the galvanized conduit nipple, and insert the nipple through the hole in the rim joist. **(Photo 16)** Screw the box to the exterior wall, and carefully caulk around it. Next, pull one end of a 10/3G gauge NM cable into the receptacle box, remove 10 inches of the cable sheathing, and clamp the cable in place. Using a wire stripper or multipurpose tool, strip and cut the cable wires, and then connect them to a four-prong, 240-volt, twist-lock receptacle that matches the one on the optional standby generator. **(Photo 17)** The hot red and black wires connect to the brass screw terminals on the receptacle, the white neutral wire connects to the silver screw terminal, and the bare grounding wire connects to the green screw terminal. Secure the receptacle in the electrical box, and install the weatherproof cover. Run the opposite end of the cable to the transfer-switch panel, using ¾-inch cable staples to secure it in place as you proceed. Using a knockout punch, remove a knockout, and pull the cable into the panel. Then clamp the cable in place with a cable clamp. Rip back the cable sheathing, and cut away the excess. Strip the insulation from the ends of the inside wires, and connect them to the remaining 240-volt circuit breaker. **(Photo 18)**

Connect and Test the Generator. Before you can connect the standby generator, you must first construct a custom-made extension cord. Cut a length of 10/3G

16 *Mount a weatherproof box for your standby generator.*

17 *Wire the receptacle into the box and ground it.*

18 *Wire the receptacle cable to the transfer switch panel.*

19 *Wire a 4-prong twist-lock plug to each end of a cord.*

20 *Switch panel to generator supply and plug in the cord.*

21 *Plug other end of cord into generator. Start the engine.*

gauge water-resistant rubber cord long enough to reach from the outdoor receptacle to the generator, allowing some extra length for slack. Remove 1½ inches of sheathing from the cord, and strip the insulated wires. Next, attach the wires on each end of the cord to a four-prong, 240-volt, twist-lock plug. **(Photo 19)** The plugs must mate perfectly with the generator and outdoor receptacles. As before, connect the hot red and black wires to the brass screw terminals, the neutral white wires to the sil-

ver, and the bare (or green) grounding wires to the green. Flip the transfer switch to the GENERATOR SUPPLY position, and plug one end of the heavy-duty extension cord into the outdoor receptacle. **(Photo 20)** Once the generator is secured in its final position, plug the opposite end of the extension cord into the designated generator receptacle. **(Photo 21)** Finally, test-start the generator. For safety, be certain to shut off the generator motor before disconnecting either end of the extension cord.

Transfer-Switch Panels

Some transfer switches come prewired and self-contained in their own panel box. The panel box has an already attached flexible conduit lead. You simply need to turn off the power, attach the conduit lead to the main panel box, pull the lead extension wires from the switch panel into the main box, disconnect the black wires going to the breakers you want powered by the generator, and splice them into the black lead wires from the switch panel. Connect the red wires to the breakers and the white wire to the neutral bus of the main panel. If there is a green wire, attach it to the grounding bus in the main panel. On many panels, the grounding and neutral bus will be combined into one grounding/neutral bus. Connect the generator power to the transfer-switch panel by inserting a female, four-prong, 240-volt, twist-lock plug into the receptacle on the face of the prewired switch panel.

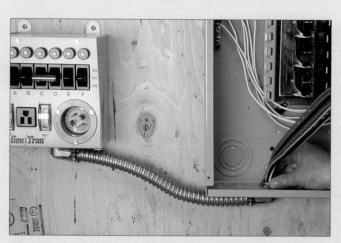

1 Some transfer-switch systems are prewired out-of-the-box, simplifying their connection to the main panel. Attach the conduit lead from the switch panel to the main panel; then pull the lead wires into the main panel.

2 Splice the hot black wires to the breakers, attach the hot red wires to the empty slots, and connect the neutral and ground to the grounding/neutral bus.

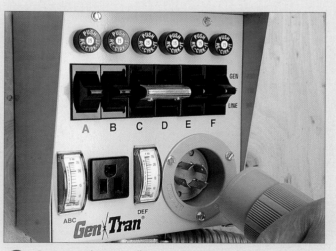
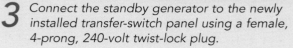

3 Connect the standby generator to the newly installed transfer-switch panel using a female, 4-prong, 240-volt twist-lock plug.

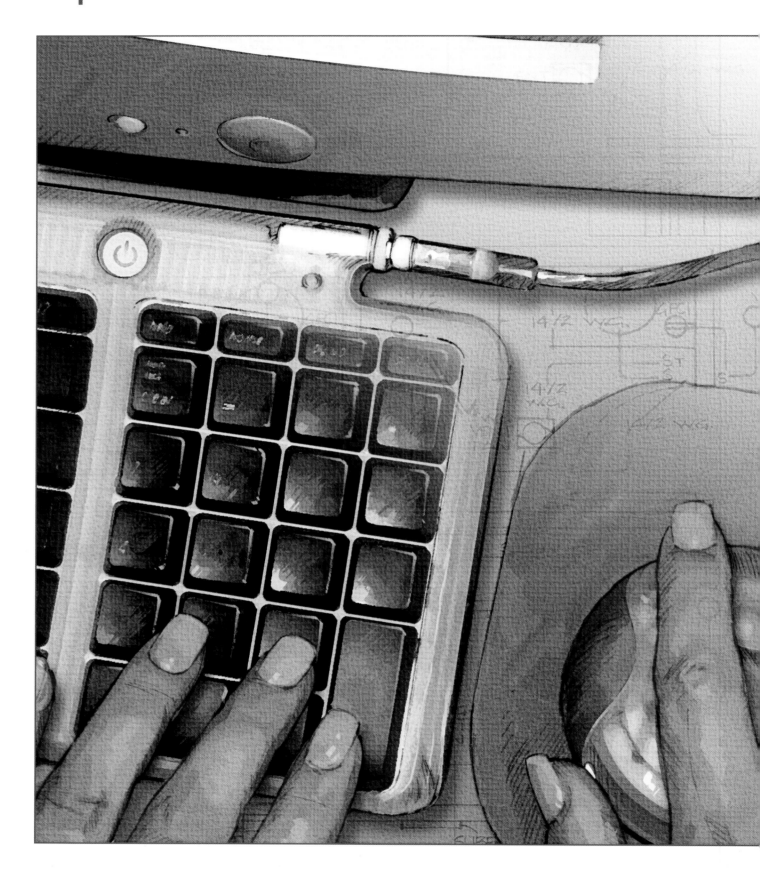

CHAPTER 9

Home Automation

Home automation has been growing steadily in the building industry since its inception during the 1970s. In the past, low-quality cable and poor connections resulted in noise and interference on communication lines. Today, structured wiring systems eliminate this problem. A structured wiring system is one that uses a wider bandwidth, allowing more information to pass through the wire. Structured wiring, such as Category 5 (CAT 5) wiring, is critical for phone, fax, and high-speed digital computer transmissions. It is being installed in many new homes; and new buzzwords like power-line carrier controls, design protocols, home networking, and smart house are rapidly entering our vocabulary. Originally, individual appliances were automated for the sake of cutting down on energy use, creating built-in security and providing simple convenience. Today's systems go much further—integrating all functions in a house and controlling them directly and remotely. All the electricity, heating, cooling, plumbing, lighting, and even communications, computer, security, and audio-video equipment are united by a single control system. Appliances merge with this system and can monitor themselves to schedule repairs and maintenance or simply let you know that you are short on milk and eggs. Through various Internet connections they will soon be able to download their own software upgrades or purchase the milk and eggs for you. Such systems may be controlled from a master console located in your home, programmed and run by your personal computer, or even controlled remotely from an outside location. Currently emerging systems even act as a residential gateway, or central entry point, through which outside data and services may enter your home and be distributed.

Smart Home Basics

Power-Line Carrier Control

Depending on the type, home-automation systems may be hardwired using special structured cable or conventional residential cable. Alternatively, they may be remotely controlled by radio-frequency signals. Running wires to connect light switches, thermostats, home theaters, and other devices to a microprocessor is extremely difficult to do in an existing home and is usually reserved for new construction. Surface wiring is an alternative, if you are determined to have a hardwired system. Some homeowners may choose this method because hardwired systems are extremely reliable. However, a hardwired home-automation system under retrofit conditions will cost thousands of dollars—an amount that will double for in-wall wiring. It is simpler and more cost-effective to install a system that transmits commands to your electronic devices through existing house wiring and/or radio waves.

A power-line carrier (PLC) is any automation controller that permits one-way command signals to be transmitted over a standard electrical system without needing to run additional wires. Coded digital pulses sent over wires control designated electrical circuits. The transmitter can be a simple wall-mounted keypad or a keychain remote. With a remote wireless transmitter, you can sit in your favorite armchair, lounge out in your yard, or even pull into your driveway and still be able to turn any device in the house on or off. If you want to turn off your upstairs lights while you're watching television downstairs, you can do it with a single push of a

Types of Signal Controllers

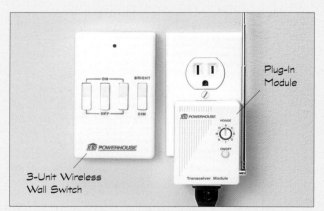

You can use a wall-mounted keypad to control any function from a single location inside your house, while a key-chain remote extends this control outdoors.

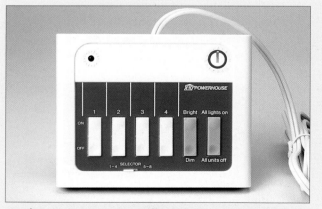

A remote switch transmits control signals to any number of plug-in receivers or control units (modules) within a house.

A plug-in master controller transmits signals onto a conventional alternating current (AC) line to control X-10 plug-in modules from any location you choose.

button. You can mount PLC transmitters and receivers in a wall like a standard receptacle or switch, or plug them into a standard electrical outlet. Use a master-control console to operate everything from one location. Today, you can control virtually any electrical device using keypads, touch panels, handheld remotes, or even your voice.

Timer Control

In the past, one mechanical timer could control only one device. Today, standard home-automation timer controls can independently or in combination perform multiple tasks throughout your house. Advanced timer controls operate directly or remotely and can even turn security switching on and off randomly. If power is interrupted, they have a battery backup.

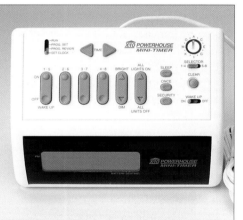

A remote timer control can command multiple modules to turn on or off at different times and even set intensity levels or work in conjunction with an alarm.

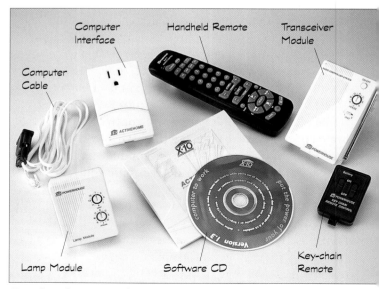

For the ultimate in home automation, install a computer software control system that operates everything from lights and appliances to home theater.

Computer Control

Current automation standards, or protocols, provide for interaction between computers and home-automation devices. Such systems allow the homeowner to download automation schedules into their personal computers. Currently, you can use available software to control devices at specific times and locations with the simple click of a mouse. You can even dial-up your computer by telephone and control any device in your house. Call home from the office, and your whirlpool can be running, the outside security lights turned on, and your food cooked by the time you get home.

Wireless Remote Control

Remote-control devices rely on radio-frequency transmissions to operate lights and appliances from a remote location within a limited distance of your home, such as from your yard, driveway, or garage. As mentioned earlier, these controls take the form of key chains, wall switches, or handheld remotes like the one you use to operate your television set. The transceiver, whether mounted on the wall or plugged into a receptacle, receives and transmits radio signals through your existing house wiring to control a specified appliance, fixture, or other device.

Home Networking

Home networking is entering the marketplace fast on the heels of home automation. Virtually every appliance used in the home today is available with some type of independently operated electronic processor. Home networking is a system of connecting circuitry to share information electronically. Such networking enables all of your appliances to work together under one brain or control system. There are three basic types of networks: computer, entertainment, and control. A computer network links personal computers (PCs) and peripheral devices, such as printers, scanners, and fax machines. An entertainment network connects equipment like TVs, VCRs, stereos, and DVD players. A control network (the brains of the system) joins lighting, switching, security, sprinkler, heating, ventilating, air-conditioning, plumbing, and other mechanical and electronic equipment to one command center.

Surge Control

Some home-automation systems use power lines to transmit their signals. Unfortunately, many appliances, like TVs and computer printers, can create noise on a wiring network, reducing the clarity of signals. When an automation system unintentionally turns itself on and off or occasionally doesn't work at all, this may be the

reason. If you suspect it is, unplug the appliance to see whether the system will then work properly. If an appliance is causing a problem, you must plug it into a high-end surge suppressor to filter out the noise. This type of suppressor is similar to the multiple-outlet adapter that you plug your computer into to protect it from power surges—but it must be premium quality and labeled "filter" on the box.

High-powered surges (lightning pulses) must be stopped before they enter the house wiring—not after. You cannot depend solely upon the multiple outlet suppressor to protect your system. Electronic devices are extremely sensitive, and home automation products are no exception. Systems can turn on and off by themselves if a surge, or spike, from a thunderstorm or other cause, travels down the power line. A power reduction, or

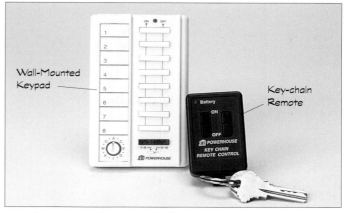

Wireless controls use radio frequencies, in-home or away from home, to remotely operate anything connected to your home-automation system.

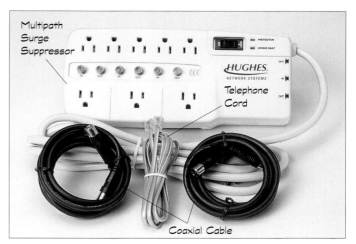

A multipath surge suppressor can eliminate noise on wiring that may interfere with home-automation signal transmission.

brownout, made by a utility company can also affect electronic devices. However, major surges can be minimized by installing a special type of surge arrester (suppressor) in the main service panel. The unit takes the space of a standard circuit breaker. You simply protect your home-automation control circuit through the surge-protection device. One device will protect an entire residential electrical system.

Data-Transmission Standards

Design Protocols

Every home-automation system consists of transmitters, receivers, and the signals transmitted between them. As one might think, any company can develop its own system of design standards, or protocols, and use them to receive and send signals along the wiring in your home to control their own automation products. The best known and most popular protocols are X-10, CEBus, and LonWorks.

X-10

X-10 technology controls circuits by sending signals from one point to another, eliminating the need to run wires. This makes X-10 especially suitable for existing homes. Not having to cut drywall and fish wires saves on labor and materials, reducing the installation cost of a complete home-automation system.

In an X-10 system, signals are transmitted by modulating radio-frequency (RF) bursts of 120-kilohertz (kHz) power. These RF bursts consist of a start code and a house code, along with function and unit codes. These are superimposed over the voltage on your house wiring. Simply put, a burst of power is equivalent to a digital one (1), and a lack of a burst is equivalent to a digital zero (0). A combination of ones and zeros (binary system) represents a particular command. X-10 systems provide 32 codes, known as address groups. There are 16 house codes and 16 unit codes that, in combination, provide up to 256 unique addresses to assign to individual devices. Each receiver in the system will respond to only one of up to six commands given for a set address: ON, OFF, DIM, BRIGHT, ALL LIGHTS ON, or ALL LIGHTS OFF. For example, an appliance module may receive a signal to turn on, while a wall switch is commanded to dim a light, and a wall receptacle is directed to cut power to whatever device is plugged into it. Modules are available for light switches and dimmers, occupancy sensors, timers, etc. Place a master controller by your bedside or armchair. For ultimate control, your computer can take charge.

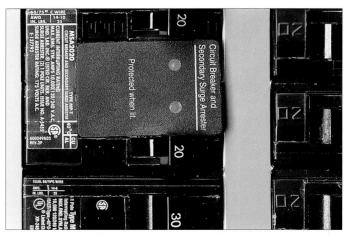

A surge-suppression device installed in your main panel will protect your entire house circuit against a massive electrical surge or brownout.

A lamp or appliance module can be programmed to any one of 16 house codes in combination with any one of 16 unit codes. The codes can control up to 256 devices.

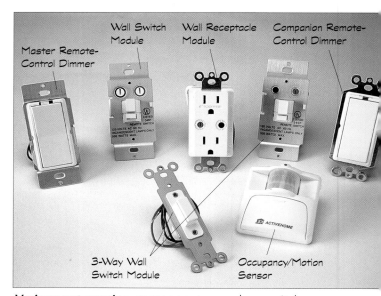

Master Remote-Control Dimmer

Wall Switch Module

Wall Receptacle Module

Companion Remote-Control Dimmer

3-Way Wall Switch Module

Occupancy/Motion Sensor

Various automation components—such as switches, receptacles, dimmers, and sensors—can be activated from a single master controller.

CEBus

Consumer Electronic Bus (CEBus) is a communications protocol for home-automation networks developed by the Electronics Industry Association (EIA) and the Consumer Electronics Manufacturers Association (CEMA). CEBus signals can be transmitted across AC power lines, low-voltage wires, category 5 cable, coaxial cable, radio and infrared frequencies, and fiber optics. CEBus standards were designed to augment the remote control and monitoring of mechanical, electrical, home entertainment, security, and other systems. CEBus devices communicate using an electronic command language, called Common Application Language (CAL), which includes device-specific commands like fast forward, rewind, volume up, temperature down, etc. This differs from the X-10 system in that it uses variable signals to change the intensity of each radio-frequency burst. The length of the burst determines whether the digital number created is a one or a zero. CEBus standards also make communications more reliable because they require that a system be able to recover from signaling errors.

LonWorks

LonWorks is a leading standard for home networking that provides a vehicle for communication between control products and systems. The protocol proposes design guidelines for LonWorks compatible products and systems and certifies and promotes them. The latest LonWorks-based standard, known as EIA-709, was developed by CEMA. It is now a widely supported industry standard, considered by some to be the best choice for automating lighting, heating, ventilation, air-conditioning, and other systems because of its compatibility with other formats. In addition to home automation, its systems are used commercially in transportation, energy management in major buildings, and industrial equipment control.

Smart House

Smart House is a limited partnership formed by the National Association of Home Builders (NAHB) that invites competing home-automation manufacturers to develop products and applications for Smart House technology to be used for control of security, utility, home entertainment, lighting, and other residential systems. The intention is to unify the wiring of such systems to simplify installation and reduce costs.

Smart House wiring consists of branch cabling for conventional power and digital data transmission; applications cable to transmit digital data and direct current (DC) voltage to operate control sensors; and communications cable for video and telecommunications wiring. These cables control appliances, monitor their status, and transmit information. The drawback to the Smart House system is that it is privately owned and requires custom wiring and service.

Regardless of which data transmission standard you use—X-10, CEBus, LonWorks, or Smart House—remember that power-line communications are seldom enough. To control the multitude of electronic devices and equipment commonly found in today's homes, other types of communication methods must also be supported, including wireless systems like infrared (IR) and radio frequency (RF) transmission.

Methods of Signal Transmission

Transmission Standard	Transmission Method	Relative Cost
X-10	Power line	Low
CEBus	Power line, twisted pair, coaxial cable, radio frequency, infrared, fiber optics	Low to moderate
LonWorks	Power line, twisted pair, radio frequency, additional types supported by third-party transceivers	Low to moderate
Smart House	Custom wiring only	Moderate to high

The standards listed above provide for data transmission using a variety of signaling methods, each with its own cost relative to the others.

Uses for Home Automation

Lighting Systems and Appliances

Uses for home automation are as varied as the users. You may, for example, wish to operate outside house lights using a key-chain remote. This comes in handy when you need to carry in groceries after dark or fumble with keys to unlock the door. If you're tired of reminding children to turn off the bathroom lights, zap them off using your chair-side remote. If you wish to turn lights on or off or dim them from your bedroom, hit your bedside remote. You can control a single device, like dimming a bedroom light, or an entire lighting system. Lighting is commonly automated. Initially, automation wiring let people turn lights on in different rooms at varied times for security. Automation has evolved to include outside security and walkway lights, among other things. Every member of a household can possess their own key-chain transmitter—providing complete home control, including activation of emergency systems. If someone with a health problem is in the garden, unable to get to the house for assistance, help can be summoned using a key-chain transmitter. A button sounds an alarm or transmits a call to the police or emergency medical service. You can control all of the lights and appliances in your home by connecting each to its own transceiver, plugging modules into standard receptacles, or replacing switches and receptacles with ones that are automated. Such equipment can be controlled by a computer or timing device; or activated by a heat, motion, passive infrared (light), or ultrasonic (sound) sensor.

Heating, Ventilating, and Air Conditioning

Energy management has become a major element in home automation. Heating, ventilating, and air-conditioning (HVAC) systems are easily programmed into a household computer system. With a click of a mouse, you can independently control the temperature in each room or zone in your house, resulting in significant energy and cost savings. You can program different temperatures for night and day and even have a temperature setting for when you go on vacation. Zone controls allow a homeowner to compensate for variable conditions in spaces exposed to different degrees of heat gain or loss. For example, conditions in a south-facing room with lots of glass will be significantly different from those in a north-facing room having a fireplace. If computers aren't your thing, you may decide to use another type of system, such as direct-wired X-10 signals or thermostats that work by sensing changes in outdoor temperatures. Such communicating thermostats may

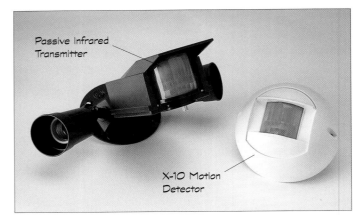

Outdoor transmitters, *like passive infrared and photocell controllers, can command both indoor and outdoor devices to switch on or off at a preset time.*

Communicating thermostats *can control and monitor the heating, ventilating, and air-conditioning systems in your home, either independently or by zone.*

have multiple indoor, outdoor, and wet-location sensors. Ports, known as contact closures, allow you to remotely select temperature and time settings. Other HVAC systems that lend themselves to automated controls include air-circulation devices like ventilating and exhaust fans, duct dampers, and motorized drapes, shades, doors, windows, and skylights. The possibilities are limitless.

Plumbing

Both water and natural-gas plumbing systems can be automated for user convenience and safety. Gas shutoff valves can now be electronically controlled to turn off when a fire is detected or at predetermined times. Likewise, water pipes can be turned off in an emergency or sprinkler systems set to start using a remote controller. Photoelectric sensors can even be used to automatically turn your water faucets on and off or to flush your toilet as you step away. Other possibilities include water softeners, pools, spas, clothes washers, clothes dryers, and water heaters—all of which can be tied into sensors, timers, and/or security systems. These systems usually have manual overrides or battery backup in case of power outages or malfunctions.

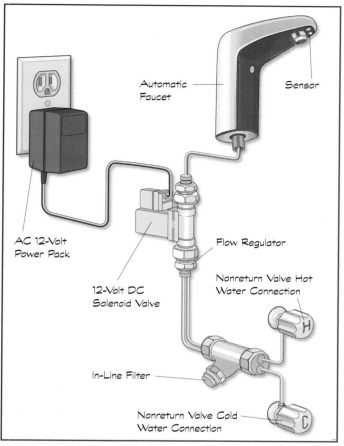

No-touch automatic faucet controls *use a wall-mounted sensor to initiate or stop the flow of water. Simply passing your hand in front of the sensor activates the faucet control.*

Home Security

Probably the most important aspect of home automation is its impact on home security—the enhanced ability to deter and prevent, or detect and apprehend intruders; to warn of smoke, fire, and carbon monoxide gases; to signal for emergency assistance. Home automation systems take self-contained components and tie them into a single, centrally controlled network for comprehensive protection. Such a network may consist of perimeter alarms, lights, detection sensors, communications devices, and system controllers. Good perimeter lighting, for example, is a known deterrent to prowlers. Motion detectors can warn of someone's presence on your property before an reaching your home. Gateways can be remotely controlled and monitored by closed-circuit television. Windows and doors may be fitted with alarms that detect the sound of broken glass. You can install magnetic switches that sense the opening of a window or door, or screens that sound an alarm when being cut. In the home, many types of detectors can be used to warn of smoke, fire, heat, or gas. These devices may all be circuited to sound an alarm in the home while simultaneously signaling an emergency service miles away. Your entire home-security system can be connected by an automatic telephone-dialing system that sends a prerecorded message directly to security monitoring stations, police and fire departments, emergency medical services, or to anyone you wish.

Use an automatic faucet *to turn water on or off without having to touch a faucet handle, enhancing personal hygiene in your bathroom or kitchen.*

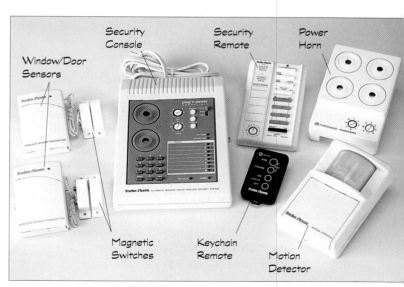

A voice-dial security system *can emit a siren alarm, flash all your lights to attract attention, and dial preprogrammed numbers to transmit a recorded message. Wireless systems can monitor multiple security zones, be programmed remotely, indicate alarm status, and trigger a silent alarm.*

Entertainment Systems

Another popular use for indoor automation is control of a home theater or entertainment center. Technological advances constantly bring new products onto the market, such as high-fidelity videocassette recorders (VCRs), laserdisc players, digital versatile disc (DVD) players, digital satellite systems (DSS), and interactive television. Add these to conventional devices like television sets, telephones, stereo receivers, videotape recorders, video game players, and countless other electronic gadgets and you have a recipe for a tangled web of wiring in your home. These systems must be carefully planned even when installed independently. They can be integrated into one system, however, using home automation. Controllers can be programmed to command sound, vibration, power switches, and communications between devices. You can, for example, install a device to remotely control a home entertainment center. You can program a system to turn on or off when you dial your telephone by letting it ring a set number of times. Or you may set the volume to automatically lower when the phone rings and resume when it is hung up. Automation controls can be programmed to operate everything from lighting levels to curtain closers, channel switching to equipment selection—all at the push of a button. Such custom programs are called macros.

Telecommunications and Networking

Science and technology have expanded telecommunications way beyond the simple exchange of voices over telephone wire. Today, telecommunications includes fax transmission, teleconferencing, multiple-line phone systems, on-line data transmission, message recording and retrieval, and even video exchange. As we have illustrated throughout this chapter, the telephone is itself an important part in many home-automation systems, serving as the vehicle for remote signaling and automatic security dialing.

One of the most important aspects of telecommunications today is the ability to network (connect) computer systems, including peripheral equipment and communications devices. This is especially valuable in a world where more and more people are working at home. Being connected to a network allows you to share computer files and equipment with anyone else who also happens to be connected to the same network. These local-area networks, or LANs, may be limited to one building or an entire neighborhood. Wide-area networks (WANs) may extend over greater distances. Clearly, an automated control system con-

Types of Automated Controls

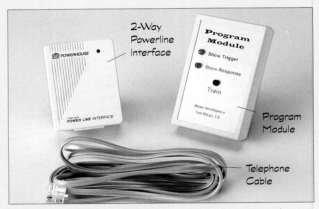

Use a transceiver, lamp module, and universal remote to set up a home theater system to control your A/V equipment and switches, and even dim your lights.

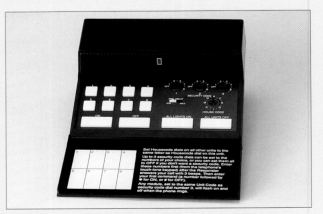

Dial in control commands to X-10 devices with telephone controllers. They also work with answering machines and voice mail. Security codes deter unauthorized access.

Macro controllers allow you to develop and automatically transmit complex sequences of commands for multiple devices.

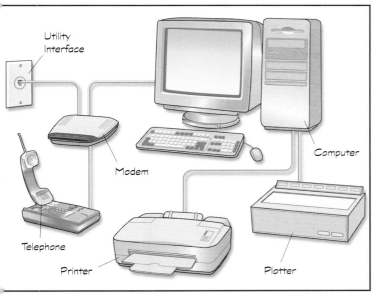

*A **computer** serves as a central control to operate a network of peripheral devices and equipment extending within and outside your home.*

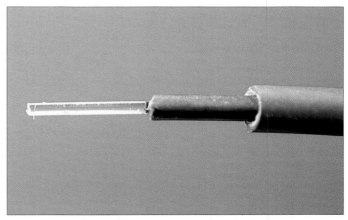

In the near future fiber-optic cables will play a central role in transmitting telecommunications signals to and from every home and place of business.

nected to a network could easily be shared over multiple locations.

With the advent of fiber optics, which uses laser-generated light to transmit signals through glass fibers, the scope of telecommunications promises to become even greater. In the near future, fiber-optic signals will carry vocal, musical, and computer-generated sounds; graphic, photographic, and video images; and data transmissions to every household.

Outdoor Systems

Aside from lighting and home security, you can automate your home to meet different outdoor needs. Lawn and garden watering are most commonly automated. A sprinkler system, whether above or in ground, can easily be tied to a timer set to turn the water on or off at a preset time. A controller can be programmed to set, change, or cancel watering times and even to actuate multiple spray zones at different times. Many lesser-known uses exist for outdoor automation. A hot tub or pool, for example, can be wired to fill automatically or sense when it is occupied. An occupancy sensor can be connected to an alarm that lets you know if someone, like a playing child, has fallen into the pool. Another use might be a de-icing system on your roof or under your driveway that can be activated remotely or by a temperature sensor. With rapid changes in technology, the choices available to homeowners in the future will be limited only by the bounds of their imagination.

*An **aboveground or underground watering system** is an ideal candidate for automation, providing a homeowner with convenience and reliability. You can program automatic sprinkler controls to operate multiple valve zones and to independently set or alter watering times for each zone.*

*A **sprinkler valve** connected to an irrigation controller will automatically activate your sprinkler system.*

X-10 Projects

Lighting Controls

Though home-automation projects can vary consider-ably in cost and difficulty of installation, lighting is an area that is relatively inexpensive and easy to master. It's a great way to get your feet wet before installing home-automation devices throughout your entire home. Handheld remote- and computer-controlled lighting systems are described in the following how-to sequences.

HOW TO: Install a Remote-Controlled Light

Difficulty Level: 🐾

Tools and Materials

- X-10 transceiver appliance module
- X-10 plug-in lamp module
- X-10 universal remote
- X-10 wall switch or dimming module (optional)

Install the Lamp Module. Plug the lamp module into the receptacle adjacent to the light you want to control. **(Photo 1)** For example, use a living-room table lamp visible from outside your house. Then plug the light into the lamp module.

Install the Transceiver. Plug the transceiver appliance module into a standard electrical receptacle near where you want to control the light. **(Photo 2)** For example, place the module near your favorite armchair or by your bed-side. Extend the antenna on the module. (As an alternative to installing a transceiver, you can install an X-10 wall switch or dimming module at an appropriate location in your house, either newly wired for this purpose or in place of an existing switch.)

Set the Codes, and Test the Remote. Following the manufacturer's recommendations, set the unit codes so that they will not interfere with each other. Adjust the dial on the transmitter and receiver module to the same house code. For example, set the dials to house code A and unit code 1. If you have additional X-10 units con-trolling other devices, set them to the same house code but different unit numbers. Any receiver that has the same house and unit number will be controlled by a transmitter sending that house and unit code. Once you have set the codes, point the universal remote at the transceiver, and press the appropriate control button to test the system. **(Photo 3)**

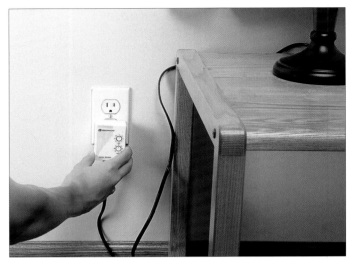

1 Install a lamp module to connect any plug-in light fix-ture to a remote-controlled home automation system.

2 A transceiver appliance module relays commands from a universal remote control to the lamp module.

3 Combinations of house and unit codes allow you to operate up to 256 separate devices remotely.

HOW TO: *Install a Computer-Controlled Light*

Difficulty Level: 🦇🦇

Tools and Materials

- X-10 transceiver appliance module
- X-10 plug-in lamp module
- Computer interface module
- X-10 universal remote
- X-10 wall switch or dimming module (optional)
- Serial cable
- Automation software

Install the Computer Interface. Install the remote-controlled system just as described previously. Next, plug the computer interface module into a receptacle adjacent to your computer. **(Photo 1)** Then plug the serial cable from the computer interface module into the serial-bus interface bus on your computer. **(Photo 2)**

SMART TIP

Safety Lighting

To make your home a safer place to navigate at night, install illuminated switches or consider placing occupancy-sensor lighting in hallways, stairways, landings, and other critical areas. If feasible, also provide emergency lighting with a battery back-up system.

Install the Software, and Program the System. Install the control software, and program the system settings, following the manufacturer's instructions. **(Photo 3)** Once done, you will be able to control the system using your preset computer program, by clicking your mouse on an icon, or simply by pressing a button on your keyboard. **(Photo 4)**

1 Plug a computer interface module into a surge-protected receptacle near your computer.

2 Using serial cable, connect the module to your computer's serial-bus interface.

3 Install the computer software, and enter your command-program settings.

4 Manually override or test the system. Click the mouse on an icon, or type a command on the keyboard.

Sprinkler System

An automated sprinkler system is a great convenience. You can control one or several sprinkler zones at preset times and adjust water-pressure levels for each zone, according to terrain and microclimate characteristics— all without the worry of remembering to turn the system off before going to bed. A moisture sensor can even be included to override the system settings on rainy days. Such a system can also be tied into weather monitoring instruments to automatically adjust for wind, humidity, and other weather conditions.

HOW TO: Install a Sprinkler Controller

Difficulty Level: 🐾🐾🐾   *(For standard 24-volt automatic sprinkler valves)*

Tools and Materials

- ✦ Automatic irrigation (sprinkler) controller
- ✦ 9-volt alkaline battery
- ✦ Insulated screwdrivers
- ✦ Multipurpose tool
- ✦ Long-nose pliers
- ✦ Watertight wire connectors

- ✦ No. 10x1¼" screws or masonry screws
- ✦ 18-GA, color-coded, multistrand, direct burial cable (14 GA for runs over 800')
- ✦ Pigtail connectors

Locate and Mount the Controller. Locate your sprinkler control indoors adjacent to a standard 120-volt AC receptacle. **(Photo 1)** (If yours is a 50-hertz unit, it will require a 240-volt receptacle.) The area should be fully shielded against intense sunlight, dampness, and temperatures less than 32 degrees or greater than 120 degrees Fahrenheit. Do not install the unit on a receptacle serving any high-voltage equipment or appliances such as garage door openers and clothes dryers. Also, do not use a receptacle controlled by an on-off switch. Most controllers can be mounted vertically or horizontally. Mount the timer using two No. 10×1¼-inch screws or masonry screws. Leave the screws extended from the wall ⅛ to ¼ inch, and place the keyholes on the back of the unit over the screws, and tighten them. **(Photo 2)** Do not plug in the transformer before you wire the unit.

Install the Battery Backup. Connect a nonrechargeable nine-volt alkaline battery to the battery terminal in the controller unit, and snap it into position. The battery will back up memory and preserve your schedule settings for up to six hours if there is a power outage. **(Photo 3)** The sprinkler system will not activate, however, until full power is resumed. If the battery fails, you will lose your programming, but most systems will

automatically default to a daily watering pattern of ten minutes per valve station, within hours of power resumption, while awaiting reprogramming. Replace the battery backup at least once a year, but be careful not to disconnect the transformer when doing so or you will lose your program settings.

Prepare the Wire. To wire sprinkler valves, use 18-gauge color-coded, multistrand direct-burial cable for runs under 800 feet in length and 14 gauge for runs exceeding 800 feet. **(Photo 4)** In either case, be certain that the cable you use has one more strand than the number of valves to be wired. (The extra strand is a common wire.) For example, if you are wiring eight valves, use nine-strand cable. If there are extra wires, you can tape these off for possible future use. Remember that all wiring below ground must have watertight connections and be approved for direct burial. Be sure to check local code requirements before doing any wiring.

Wire the Sprinkler Valves. Open the access panel on the sprinkler controller. Depending on the model, you will see four, six, or eight numbered station terminals for valve wires and one COM terminal for a common wire. If your model can accommodate a master valve, another terminal is marked MV. The common wire is usually the white neutral strand in the multistrand cable. The other strands are hot and are used to wire the sprinkler valves. Connect each hot valve wire to a station terminals in the controller panel—valve 1 to terminal 1, valve 2 to terminal 2, and so on. **(Photo 5)** Be sure that you wire only one valve to each terminal and that all contacts are secure. To prevent corrosion, use watertight wire connectors. Next, splice together the common valve wires, and pigtail them to the COM terminal in the controller panel. **(Photo 6)** For sprinkler controllers that must accommodate a master valve or pump starter, connect the color-coded wire from the valve or pump to the terminal marked MV and pigtail the common wire to the COM terminal along with the other common wires. To prevent pump damage, use a jumper wire to connect an unused terminal to one that is active.

CRE·TIVE HOMEOWNER®

SMART TIP

Sprinkler Wiring

As an alternative to using one multistrand wire, use two. Connect one to the front yard sprinkler zone and the other to the backyard sprinkler zone.

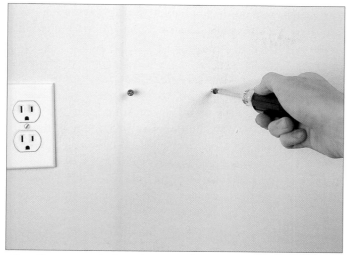

1 Choose an indoor location for your automatic sprinkler controller that is dry and out of direct sunlight.

2 Install No. 10x1¼-in. or masonry screws on the wall, mount the controller over the screws, and tighten.

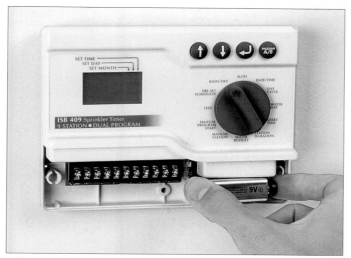

3 A 9-volt alkaline battery operates memory backup and enables you to program the timer.

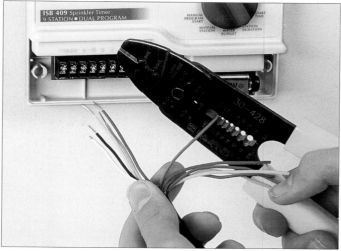

4 Use color-coded, multistrand direct-burial cable for the valves—one strand for each, plus one common wire.

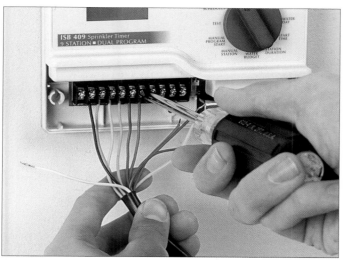

5 Connect a color-coded wire from each sprinkler valve to a station terminal in the controller panel.

6 Pigtail the common wires from each of the valves to the COM terminal.

Connect the Transformer. Turn the controller dial to the RAIN/OFF position. This position allows the system to be turned off without losing the programmed schedule settings. Do **not** plug in the transformer yet. Attach the pigtail connector at the end of the transformer wire to the 24-volt AC terminal in the controller panel. The display window should read OFF. If not, recheck the battery. Check all the wiring connections, and plug the transformer into the receptacle located near the box. **(Photo 7)** Then turn the dial to the AUTO/RUN position. **(Photo 8)** (If you install a system having more than one controller, each must be connected to its own transformer.) Replace the panel cover on the controller box. Following the manufacturer's instructions, select a preset watering schedule or program one of your own.

Optional Power-Line Interface. You may opt to add a two-way power line interface to your system to convert X-10 signals from the sprinkler controller onto the power line or relay X-10 transmissions on the line to the device. If there is one provided for this purpose, this device plugs into a jack in the automatic-sprinkler controller panel, using a standard RJ11 telephone connector and cable. This allows you to operate the system remotely.

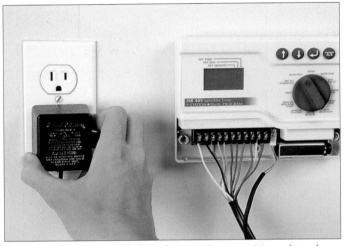

7 Set the control dial to the RAIN/OFF position. Attach the transformer pigtail connector to the controller.

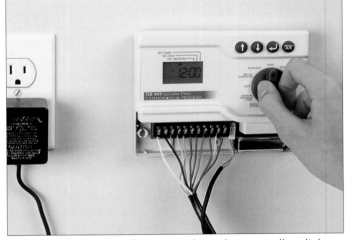

8 Plug in the transformer, and set the controller dial to the AUTO/RUN position.

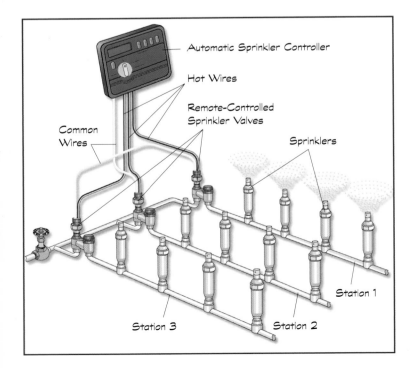

▶ **A two-way power-line interface** can be added to your automated sprinkler system to transmit messages between the system and your remote control.

◀ **Each sprinkler station** must be connected to its own station terminal in the automatic sprinkler controller. A valve opens when it receives a signal from the controller, turning the sprinkler on. After duration setting is reached, the controller closes the valve and opens the next one in the sequence.

Voice-Dial Home Security System

A simple voice-dial home security system will automatically dial up to four preprogrammed emergency numbers and transmit a digital recording over the connected lines when it is triggered by a connected device like a motion sensor or magnetic door switch. Once activated, it will send commands to flash lights on and off and sound power horns (sirens).

HOW TO: *Install a Voice-Dial Home Security System*

Difficulty Level: 🦇🦇🦇

Tools and Materials

- Master control panel console
- Master remote
- Lamp modules
- Insulated screwdrivers
- Plastic anchors
- Multipurpose tool
- RJ11 telephone connector
- Magnetic switch sensors
- Motion sensors
- Key-chain remote
- Power horns (sirens)
- Mounting bracket and screws
- Cat 5 low-voltage wire
- Alkaline batteries, as required

Mount the Master Control. Your master security control console should be mounted in a central location in your house near a modular phone jack and a standard AC receptacle. **(Photo 1)** The console may sit freely on a flat surface or be mounted on a wall. To mount the console on a wall, use the mounting screws and bracket provided by the manufacturer. If necessary, use plastic anchors to secure the screws to the drywall. Leave the screws extended from the wall ⅛ to ¼ inch, place the keyholes on the back of the unit over the screws, and tighten the screws. Remove the cover on the battery compartment, install a nine-volt battery, and replace the cover. Plug the cord on the console into the receptacle and the RJ11 telephone connector into the phone jack. Connect the system to its own phone line for added security.

Set the Master and Key-Chain Remote. Turn the code dial on the master security remote control to the same house code as the master console. **(Photo 2)** Install the batteries in the battery compartment, and switch the console to the INSTALL setting. Press the ARM button to activate the master remote; then switch the console to the RUN setting. If the master remote does not register at the master console, press the code button to set a new random code, and rearm the system. Install batteries in the key-chain remote, and arm it as you did for the master remote. Test both remotes. **(Photo 3)**

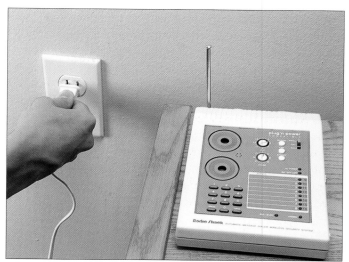

1 Centrally locate the control console where few obstructions will block transmission signals.

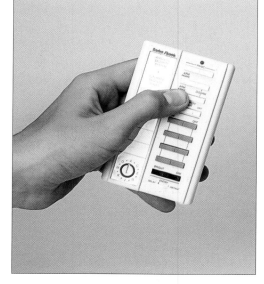

2 Set the dial on the master security remote control to the same house code as the master console.

3 Press the ARM buttons on your master and key-chain remotes to ensure that they are working.

Mount the Door and Window Sensors. Locate magnetic switch sensors so that radio frequency (RF) signals will not be blocked by large metal objects or appliances. The signals should pass through as few walls as possible. Using the mounting screws provided, place sensors as near as possible to the top of the door or window. **(Photo 4)** Where possible, mask the sensors behind curtains or drapes. Be sure the arrows on each half of a magnetic switch point to each other and release cleanly when the door or window is in operation. Most systems have settings that allow the alarms to trigger immediately for windows or after a preset entry delay period for doors. **(Photo 5)** Place the required batteries in the battery compartment of each sensor, and adjust the delays. Following the manufacturer's instructions, program (register) the devices at the console and test the system.

Mount the Motion Sensors. Mount your motion sensors between 5 and 6 feet above the finished floor, using the mounting brackets and screws provided by the manufacturer. **(Photo 6)** Motion sensors are designed to automatically look downward and need not be pointed at a downward angle. As with the door and window sensors, install the required batteries, set the triggering delays, program the console, and test the detectors.

Install the Lamp Modules. To control a security light, turn the house and unit code dials on a lamp module to match the settings you programmed into the master console. **(Photo 7)** This ensures that you will be able to operate the light using your remote controls. Plug the lamp module into a receptacle near the lamp you wish to control; then plug the lamp into the module. Be sure that the receptacle you use is not switch-operated so it cannot be inadvertently switched off. To install modules for other lamps, set the house code dial on each to the same setting as your master console, but set the unit code dials to any unused code that can be controlled by the remote. Plug the lamps into their corresponding modules. Again, be sure to use unswitched receptacles.

Install the Power Horns (Sirens). Set the house code dial on each power horn to the same code setting as the master console. **(Photo 8)** Set each unit dial to an unused code. Then plug the power horns into unswitched receptacles. To test a horn, press the ON button—on the master console or remote—that matches the house and unit code on the horn. The siren should sound for a preset period of time or until it is disarmed. To manually sound the siren, press the panic button.

Set Up the Dialer. Following the manufacturer's suggestions, program the master console to dial a friend, neighbor, or relative who can help in an emergency. **(Photo 9)** This person can then dial an emergency service if one is needed. To minimize false alarms, it is not recommended that you program your system to direct-dial an emergency service. (You can upgrade your security system, if you want, to one that is remotely tracked by a monitoring service.) Record a brief message in your master console, and play it back to hear what it will sound like to someone listening over a telephone line.

Once you have mastered installing a few X-10 projects like those above, you will have the confidence and skills required to set up an entire automated home-living system. Simply add components in any configuration you desire to custom-design the system of your dreams.

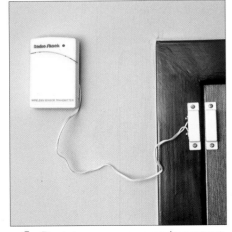

4 Remote sensors are an important part of any security system. Install them on doors and windows.

5 A magnetic switch is separated whenever a door or window is opened, activating an alarm.

6 Motion sensors should be set in areas within a home to detect the presence of an intruder.

7 At least one light should be set to operate from a security-light button located on your remote.

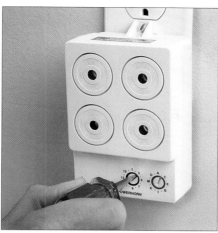

8 An effective deterrent to an intruder is noise. Include power-horns in your security system.

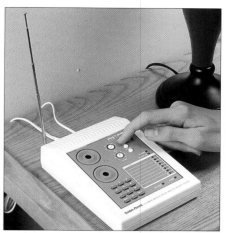

9 Program your master console to transmit an emergency message to preset phone numbers.

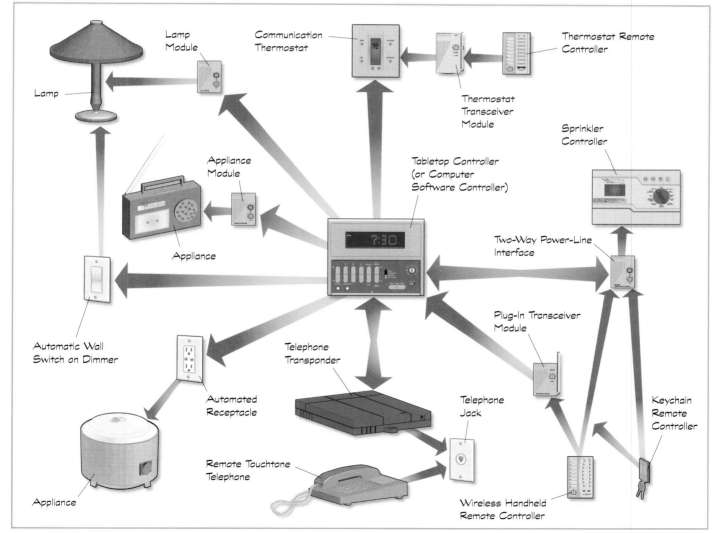

A typical home-automation system would most likely include a combination of devices such as wall switches, dimmers, lamp modules, timer controls, transceivers, remote controls, motion detectors, magnetic switch sensors, thermostat controls, and other devices. These are just a few of the many possible applications for an automated home-living system.

Glossary

A/V Audio/video.

AWG American Wire Gauge; a system of sizing electrical wire.

Accent lighting Spot lighting that focuses on decorative or architectural features.

Alternating current (AC) An electrical current that regularly reverses its direction, usually at 60 cycles per second.

Ambient lighting Indirect, background lighting.

Ampere, amp Measure of electric current flow required to move one volt of electricity across one ohm of resistance.

Ampacity Current-carrying capacity of an electrical wire, in amps.

Applications cable Electrical or fiber optic voice, video and data communications cable.

Armored cable Cable sheathed in flexible metal.

Backfeed Electricity fed back into a utility system while a standby generator is running. A double-pole, double-throw transfer switch is required to prevent this from happening, protecting the generator, wiring, and appliances from damage when service is restored.

Ballast Device that controls current in a fluorescent tube.

Bar hanger Bracket placed between joists or rafters to support a fixture box.

Bare wire Uninsulated grounding conductor in a cable.

Base pin Contact on the end of a fluorescent tube.

Bell wire Thin wire used for making doorbell connections.

Bipin Fluorescent tube having two base pins on each end.

Bonding Connecting metal parts to make an electrically conductive path.

Bonding jumper A connection that ensures continuous conductivity between metal parts required to be electrically connected.

Box extension Device attached to an electrical box to increase its capacity.

Branch circuit Wiring from a final fuse or circuit breaker to the outlets.

Breaker See *Circuit breaker*.

Brownout Partial loss of electric power.

Bus bar Common electric conductor for multiple circuits.

CFM Cubic feet per minute; usually a measure of air-volume movement.

CO/ALR Label designating approval for use with aluminum wire.

COM Common terminal.

CU/AL Label designating approval for use with copper, aluminum, or copper-clad aluminum wires.

Cable One or more wires enclosed in protective metal or plastic sheathing.

Cable sheathing Metal or plastic casing around wires in cable.

Category 5 (CAT 5) wire Four twisted pairs of high quality copper wire enclosed in sheathing; used for phone, fax, modem, and high-speed digital computer transmissions. Has high immunity to interference.

Choke ballast A ballast that lacks a transformer and which is used only in small fluorescent fixtures.

Circuit breaker Protective device that opens a circuit if an overcurrent occurs.

Circuit capacity Maximum current a circuit can safely carry.

Coaxial cable A primary conductor wire enclosed in concentric plastic foam insulation. It is covered by braided wire that acts as a secondary conductor and a shield against interference.

Common Applications Language (CAL) Language that allows diverse household systems to be integrated under one system of control.

Communicating thermostat An interactive thermostat that can be remotely controlled.

Communications cable Voice, video, and data communications.

Community antenna television (CATV) Source for cable television signals transmitted to multiple receivers.

Conductor A wire or material that offers minimal resistance to the flow of electricity.

Conductor cable Nonmetallic sheathing encasing two or more conductors.

Conduit Metal or plastic protective tubing that encloses electrical wires.

Conduit nipple Short section of conduit used to connect an interior junction box to an outdoor receptacle box, an LB connector, or two enclosers.

Connecting block Central-distribution junction hardware for telephone circuit.

Consumer Electronic Bus (CEBus) Design protocol established by the Electronics Industry Association.

Continuity tester Device used when power is turned off, to detect an electrical path between two points.

Continuous load A load where the maximum current continues for 3 hours or more.

Controller A device that, in a predetermined way, controls the electric power delivered to another device to which it is directly or remotely connected.

Cord Flexible wiring used for household plug-in appliances; not intended to be used as permanent circuit wiring.

Crimping ferrule Compression sleeve used to connect bare grounding wires.

Current Flow of electrons through a conductor.

Cut-in box Electrical box designed to install easily in existing construction.

Design protocol Control standard for home automation devices.

Detector Device that senses changes in ambient conditions due to temperature, motion, smoke, gas, flames, etc.

Digital satellite system (DSS) System that distributes video signals via satellite to an antenna dish receiver.

Digital versatile disc (DVD) Formerly digital videodisc; digital movie disc format having multiple layers.

Dimmer switch Variable intensity light switch.

Direct current (DC) An electrical current that flows in one direction only.

Double-pole switch A switch having two blades and contacts to alternately open or close power to a load from two sources.

Dry niche Pool light housing that is not waterproof; water level must be lowered to change a lamp.

Duplex receptacle Two 120-volt receptacles that are internally connected and housed in one receptacle box.

Electrical box Metallic or nonmetallic enclosure used for housing wire splices.

Electrical metallic tubing (EMT) Thin-walled steel tubing (conduit); not threaded.

Electrical nonmetallic tubing Polyvinyl chloride (PVC) conduit that must be concealed behind finished surfaces.

End-of-run Receptacle or switch box at the end position in a circuit.

Energy efficiency rating (EER) Measure of relative energy consumption.

Equipment grounding conductor Conductor that connects noncurrent-carrying metal parts of equipment to a grounding conductor and/or grounding electrode conductor.

Escutcheon plate   Protective plastic or metal plate.

Expansion loop   Slack left in any cable to allow for expansion and contraction.

Extension ring   Device added to an existing electrical box to increase its wire capacity. See *Box extension*.

Federal Communications Commission   Regulatory agency for broadcast communications in the United States.

Feeder cable   Circuit conductors between the service equipment and the final branch-circuit overcurrent device.

Feedhorn   Device at the focal point of a satellite dish that receives signals reflected from the dish.

Fish tape   Flexible metal or nonmetal strip used to pull cables through walls and conduit.

Fixed-temperature detector   A heat detector that uses the low melting point of solder or metals that expand when exposed to heat to detect fire.

Flame detector   Infrared (IR) or ultraviolet (UV) detector that senses and responses to the IR or UV emitted by flames.

Fluorescent tube   A glass tube having an internal phosphor coating that, when exposed to an electric discharge, transforms ultraviolet light into visible light.

Four-way switch   Switch used with two 3-way switches that allows a circuit to be turned on or off from three places.

Fuse   Safety device that melts to break a circuit, protecting the conductors from burning.

GFCI (ground-fault circuit interrupter)   A safety device that breaks a circuit when it senses a difference in flow between line and ground current.

GFCI circuit breaker   A combination circuit breaker and GFCI installed in the service panel in place of a regular circuit breaker. It monitors current flow in both hot and neutral wires. When the breaker detects unequal current in the wires it immediately shuts off power and protects the entire circuit.

Ganging   Joining two or more device boxes together.

Generator   A device that converts mechanical energy to electrical energy.

Glow switch   See *Starter switch*.

Ground   Connection between an electrical circuit or electrical equipment and the earth.

Grounding rod   See *Grounding electrode*.

Grounding conductor   Wire that grounds a

circuit or equipment but doesn't normally carry current.

Ground terminal   See *Grounding rod*.

Grounding bus bar   An electrical bus to which equipment grounds are connected and which is itself grounded.

Grounding electrode conductor   Grounding wire that carries current safely to earth when there's a short circuit.

Grounded neutral   The grounded wire that completes a circuit and returns current to the power source.

Grounding rod   A metal conductor entrenched in earth that maintains ground potential on other conductors connected to it.

Grounding screw   Terminal screw to which a bare or green grounding wire is connected.

HSTV   Home satellite television.

Hanger bracket   Adjustable bracket from which a ceiling box/fixture is suspended between ceiling joists.

Hardwired   Directly connected by electrical wires or cables.

Hertz   A unit of frequency measuring one cycle per second.

Hickey   Threaded fitting used to connect a light fixture to a ceiling box.

Home automation   System for remotely controlling the operation of electrical devices in a home.

Home networking   Complete home connectivity. Sharing of Internet access, printers, and files by all computers in a home.

Hot bus   Metal bar in an electrical panel that serves as the common connection between the circuit breakers and the hot line conductors.

Hot conductor   Ungrounded wire carrying electrical current.

House code   One of 16 address groups used in X-10 automation control.

IR   Infrared.

Impedance   Opposition to current flow in an alternating current circuit.

Infrared detector   Device that senses and responds to flickering infrared radiant energy, such as that emitted by flames.

Infrared transmission   Signal transmission along a beam of infrared (IR)light.

Instant-start starter   Applies high voltage to initiate a flow of electrons through a fluorescent lamp without preheating the electrodes.

Insulation-contact   Recessed light fixture housing approved for direct contact with insulation; also insulated ceiling.

Insulation displacement connector (IDC)   Telephone circuit junction wiring block

having a gas-tight seal that prevents bimetal corrosion.

Insulator   A nonconductor of electricity.

Integral transformer   Low-voltage transformer built into a device such as a light fixture.

Interactive television (ITV)   Television that permits user interaction, such as in game playing and voting, and can give immediate feedback.

Intermediate metallic conduit (IMC)   Threaded rigid metal conduit, but with thinner walls.

Ionization detector   A sensor that ionizes the air between electrodes, causing a current to flow. Smoke particles interfering with this flow set off an alarm.

Isolated-ground receptacle   A bright orange receptacle that is wired to a separate grounding system and protects computer equipment from power surges.

Jumper wire   Short length of single conductor wire used to complete a circuit connection.

Junction   Where wire splices, cable or raceway joints occur.

Junction box   Box in which all standard wiring splices and connections must be made.

Kilowatt   1,000 watts.

Kilowatt-hour (kWh)   Amount of energy expended in one hour by one kilowatt (1,000 watts) of electricity.

LB connector or fitting   A 90-degree connector used to bring cable through an exterior wall.

Lamp   A device that generates light.

Laser disc (LD)   High-resolution disc on which programs can be recorded for playback on a television set.

Lightning rod   A grounded metal rod placed on a structure to prevent damage by conducting lightning to the ground.

Line cord   Flat, four-conductor cord used to connect a telephone or other accessory to a phone jack.

Load   A device or equipment to which power is delivered.

Local-area network (LAN)   A system that links electronic equipment, such as computers and fax machines, to forms a shared network within a limited area.

LonWorks   A networking technology for automation controls.

Low-voltage   Voltage stepped down from 120 volts to 30 volts or less.

Low-voltage transformer   An electrical device with two or more coupled windings that step standard 120-volt power down to 30 volts or less.

Lumen   Flow rate of light per unit of time,

defining quantity of visible light.

Luminaire Lighting fixture.

Luminosity Relative brightness.

Macro A single customized programming instruction that results in a series of actions or responses.

Magnetic flux The total number of magnetic lines of force passing through a bounded area in a magnetic field.

Main breaker Circuit breaker through which utility power enters the main panel and connects to the hot bus.

Metal-clad (MC) cable Copper-type THHN/THWN cable with two or more conductors and an insulated ground. The conductors are wrapped in binder tape and the assembly is then clad in aluminum or steel armor.

Meter Device designed to measure the flow of an electric current.

Middle-of-run Receptacle or switch box lying between the power source and another box.

Motion/sensor detector Passive infrared (PIR) detector that senses movement across a detection field.

Nailing spur Nailing bracket attached to an electrical box.

National Electrical Code (NEC) Regulations governing the minimum safe installation of electrical systems and components.

Network Connection between computers, peripheral equipment, and communications devices that permits the sharing of files, programs, and equipment.

Network interface device Telephone utility device that connects house wiring to a telephone network.

Neutral bus bar Bus bar connecting the utility neutral wire to the house neutral.

Neutral conductor Gray or white grounded conductor used to complete a circuit and return current to its source.

Noninsulation-contact fixture Recessed light fixture housing not approved for direct contact with insulation; requires minimum of 3 inches clearance; also noninsulated ceiling.

Nonmetallic cable Two or more electrical wires enclosed in moisture-resistant, fire-retardant, nonmetallic (plastic) sheathing.

Non-polarized Having two positions or poles that are not exclusively positive or negative.

Ohm Unit of electrical resistance in a conductor.

Ohm's Law Current in a circuit is directly proportional to voltage and inversely proportional to resistance.

Occupancy detector A device that reacts to variables such as heat and motion to detect the presence of people.

Overcurrent Current that exceeds the rated current of equipment or the ampacity of a conductor.

Overload An excessive demand for power made upon an electrical circuit.

PIR detector See *Passive infrared detector*.

Pancake box Low-profile round electrical box that can be concealed behind or within a light fixture.

Parabolic aluminized reflector (PAR) lamp Bulb having an internal reflector of aluminum.

Passive infrared (PIR) detector Device that emits no signals but senses the body heat of anyone moving nearby.

Photocell A device having an electrical output that varies in response to invisible light; an electric eye.

Photoelectric detector Sensor that responds to changes in light levels caused, for example, by smoke particles.

Pigtail Flexible conductor that connects an electrical device or component to an electrical circuit.

Plug A fitting, with metal prongs for insertion into a fixed socket, used to connect an appliance to a power supply.

Plug configuration Number and pattern of prongs on a plug.

Point of demarcation Interface between telephone utility wiring and telephone wiring in a home.

Point-of-use protection Surge-suppression device used to filter line noise at the point where an appliance is plugged into it.

Polarized Having two contrasting positions, such as a positive and a negative pole.

Polyvinyl chloride (PVC) A thermoplastic resin used to manufacture nonmetallic conduit, boxes, and other electrical components.

Power horn Security alarm; siren.

Power line carrier control (PLC) Home-automation control system that uses the existing AC wiring in a home to transmit signals to receivers used to remotely switch lights and appliances.

Preheat starter Device that preheats the electrodes of a fluorescent lamp to arc start.

Primary winding The transformer coils wound on the input side of the transformer.

Programmable switch A switch that can turn lights on or off according to a preset schedule.

Pulse Brief, sudden change in a normally constant current.

Punch-down tool Special tool used for punching down IDC blocks.

Quad-shielded cable Coaxial cable having two layers of foil shielding, each covered by a layer of braided shielding.

RF See *Radio frequency*.

RG-6 quad-shielded cable Coaxial cable with insulated center wire and four layers of shielding; supports hundreds of channels and digital data. Used for cable TV, digital satellite systems, cable modems, and high-speed interactive video servers. Highly immune to interference.

Rain-tight Able to prevent the entry of water in a driving rain.

Rapid-start starter A device that uses a low-voltage winding to preheat fluorescent lamp electrodes to start an arc.

Rated power Electrical output a generator can provide continuously.

Rate-of-temperature detector Device that detects and responds to a rapid change in air temperature such as that produced by fire.

Receptacle Contact point at an electrical outlet for the connection of a plug.

Reflector lamp An incandescent lamp with a reflector built into the bulb.

Register To transmit and record remote coding information from a controlled device to a central controller.

Residential gateway A device that allows multiple PCs to share a high-speed Internet connection and peripherals, such as printers; enables homes to have their own network without extra wiring.

Remote transformer The use of remote transformers eliminates electrical interference caused by dimmers and provides simpler wire installation.

Resistance Opposition to current flow in a conductor, device, or load measured in ohms.

Ribbon wire Zip cord consisting of low-voltage conductors each with a different color plastic sheathing.

Ringer equivalency number (REN) A number, usually 1.0 or less, that represents the amount of power needed to ring a telephone.

Run wattage Power it takes to keep an appliance running after the initial startup surge.

Secondary winding The transformer coils wound on the output side of the transformer.

Service drop Overhead utility lines that bring electric service to a home.

Service entrance panel (SEP) Point where utility power enters the house wiring.

Short circuit Undesirable contact between a hot or ungrounded wire and a grounded or grounding wire.

Single-pole switch Electrical switch having one movable and one fixed contact.

66 block Connection block for a telephone circuit. Also called M block.

Smart House A control standard for home automation applications, such as entertainment, lighting, security, and temperature control.

Smoke detector An ionization or photo electric device that sounds an alarm when is senses products of combustion; it does not sense the presence of heat, flames, or gas.

Snap switch See *Toggle switch*.

Socket Metal shell into which a light bulb or plug fuse is inserted.

Spike Sudden and pronounced increase or surge in power.

Splice Mechanical connection between wires.

Splice box Square or octagonal junction box for splicing wires; accessible, plate-covered box that can be concealed in a wall or ceiling.

Spread spectrum modulation Power-line transmission that starts at one frequency and is changed to another during its cycle.

Standby generator Portable residential electric generator designed to power selected appliances or lamps temporarily during a power outage.

Starter switch A switch that works with a ballast to start a fluorescent tube only when sufficient power is available.

Start-of-run Receptacle or switch box at the beginning position in a circuit.

Step-down transformer A transformer that reduces electrical power at a primary winding to a lower voltage at a secondary winding.

Stranded wire Wires spun together to form a single conductor.

Structured wiring Wiring system composed of a central hub, high-performance cabling, and high-quality outlets; services can be redirected as needs change.

Surface raceway System for installing wiring, switches, receptacles, and fixtures without the need for demolition work.

Surge arrester or suppressor Device that diverts heavy electrical surges to a grounding system.

Surge wattage Power it takes to start an appliance. When it first kicks on, the appliance requires an initial surge. A generator must be able to accommodate the surge wattage. If it doesn't have enough power, the generator and connected appliance motors can burn out.

Switch Electrical control for turning power to a device on or off.

Switch box Electrical box used to contain a switch or receptacle.

Switch loop Installation in which power bypasses through a switch box and then loops directly back to the fixture.

TVRO Television Receive Only.

Task lighting Point-of-use directional lighting.

Telephone cable Four- or eight-wire cable use to connect telephone outlets. Also called station wire.

Telephone jack Device having a female connecting socket into which a telephone circuit wire may be plugged.

Terminal A position in a circuit or device at which a connection is normally established or broken.

Terminal screw A screw on a device where a wire connection is made.

Thermal-protected ballast Ballast protected against overheating resulting from an overload or a failure to start.

Thermoplastic Becoming soft when heated and hard when cooled.

Thermostat A device that automatically responds to temperature changes and activates switches controlling HVAC equipment.

Three-way switch An electrical switch used to control lights from two locations when used with others switches.

Time-delay fuse A plug fuse that can, for a limited time, withstand a heavy electrical load without blowing.

Toggle switch Snap ON/OFF switch activated by a lever.

Transfer switch Device that switches a load from its main source to a standby power source.

Transformer An electrical device that steps power up or down.

Transponder A control device that receives a remote signal and then sends out a signal of its own to another device.

Traveler wire A wire that transfers electricity from one three-way switch to another.

Tubing Thin-walled electrical conduit.

Twisted pair Two single, insulated wires twisted together to reduce interference with other pairs of wire.

Twistlock Receptacle or plug that can be locked in place, preventing accidental removal.

Type S fuse A plug fuse that can only fit into a fuse holder or adapter having the same amperage rating.

UL label Underwriters Laboratories' mark of evaluation and listing.

Ultrasonic sensor (US) Device that emits high frequency sound and then llistens for changes in the echo.

Ultraviolet (UV) light Range of invisible light just beyond violet in the spectrum.

Underground feeder (UF) cable Outdoor cable approved for direct burial.

Underwriters' knot A knot that ensures electrical wiring connections in a fixture will withstand the strain if the cord is jerked.

Underwriters Laboratories Organization that sets standards of manufacture, testing and evaluation of electrical products.

Unit code One of 16 individual addresses used for X-10 automation control.

Utility line Power supply cable provided and owned by a utility company.

Video cassette recorder Device for recording and playing back videotapes.

Volt Unit of electromotive force; pressure required to move one amp through a resistance of one ohm.

Voltage Potential difference between any two points in an electric current.

Watertight Designed for temporary immersion in or exposure to water; sealed with waterproof gaskets.

Watt Unit of electrical power usage.

Weatherproof Constructed to function without interference from weather.

Wet niche Waterproof pool light housing connected by waterproof wiring to a poolside junction box.

Whole-house protection Comprehensive surge protection involving both main panel and point-of-use surge arrestors, or suppressors.

Wide-area network (WAN) Computer or data communications network connecting devices over a greater distance than a local-area network (LAN).

Windings The wire coils of a generator, motor, or transformer.

Wire A flexible metal strand of various lengths and diameters, often electrically insulated, used to conduct electricity.

Wire connector Device for twisting two or more wires together.

Wire shield Metal guard nailed to a framing member to protector wiring behind from nail or screw penetration.

X-10 technology System that allows remote control of lights and appliances using the existing wiring in a home.

Zero voltage The level of voltage of any ground connected to the earth.

Zip cord Two-wire cord designed to split when pulled down the middle.

Index

Metric Equivalents

All measurements in this book are given in U.S. Customary units. If you wish to find metric equivalents, use the following tables and conversion factors.

Inches to Millimeters and Centimeters

1 in = 25.4 mm = 2.54 cm

in	mm	cm
1/16	1.5875	0.1588
1/8	3.1750	0.3175
1/4	6.3500	0.6350
3/8	9.5250	0.9525
1/2	12.7000	1.2700
5/8	15.8750	1.5875
3/4	19.0500	1.9050
7/8	22.2250	2.2225
1	25.4000	2.5400

Inches to Centimeters and Meters

1 in = 2.54 cm = 0.0254 m

in	cm	m
1	2.54	0.0254
2	5.08	0.0508
3	7.62	0.0762
4	10.16	0.1016
5	12.70	0.1270
6	15.24	0.1524
7	17.78	0.1778
8	20.32	0.2032
9	22.86	0.2286
10	25.40	0.2540
11	27.94	0.2794
12	30.48	0.3048

Feet to Meters

1 ft = 0.3048 m

ft	m
1	0.3048
5	1.5240
10	3.0480
25	7.6200
50	15.2400
100	30.4800

Square Feet to Square Meters

1 ft² = 0.092 903 04 m²

Acres to Square Meters

1 acre = 4046.85642 m²

Cubic Yards to Cubic Meters

1 yd³ = 0.764 555 m³

Ounces and Pounds (Avoirdupois) to Grams

1 oz = 28.349 523 g
1 lb = 453.5924 g

Pounds to Kilograms

1 lb = 0.453 592 37 kg

Ounces and Quarts to Liters

1 oz = 0.029 573 53 L
1 qt = 0.9463 L

Gallons to Liters

1 gal = 3.785 411 784 L

Fahrenheit to Celsius (Centigrade)

$°C = °F - 32 \times \frac{5}{9}$

°F	°C
-30	-34.45
-20	-28.89
-10	-23.34
-5	-20.56
0	-17.78
10	-12.22
20	-6.67
30	-1.11
32 (freezing)	0.00
40	4.44
50	10.00
60	15.56
70	21.11
80	26.67
90	32.22
100	37.78
212 (boiling)	100

Index/Conversion Table

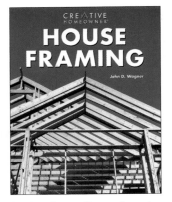
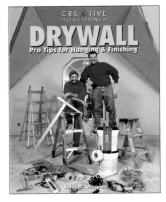
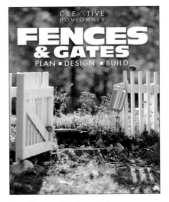

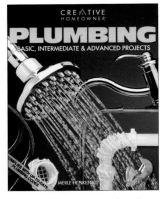
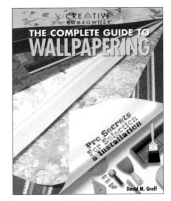

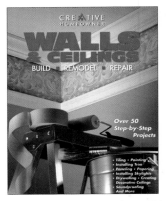